Gay and Lesbian Americans and Political Participation

Political Participation in America

Raymond A. Smith, Series Editor

FORTHCOMING

African Americans and Political Participation,
Minion K.C. Morrison, Editor

Disabled Americans and Political Participation,
Richard K. Scotch and Kay Schriner

East Asian Americans and Political Participation,
Tsung Chi

Jewish Americans and Political Participation,
Rafael Medoff

Native Americans and Political Participation,
Jerry D. Stubben and Gary A. Sokolow

Gay and Lesbian Americans and Political Participation

A Reference Handbook

Raymond A. Smith and
Donald P. Haider-Markel

Foreword by U.S. Representative Tammy Baldwin

A B C ☰ C L I O

Santa Barbara, California • Denver, Colorado • Oxford, England

Library of Congress Cataloging-in-Publication Data

Smith, Raymond A., 1967–
   Gay and lesbian Americans and political participation : a reference handbook / Raymond A. Smith and Donald P. Haider-Markel.
      p. cm.
Includes bibliographical references and index.
   ISBN 1-57607-256-8; 1-57607-731-4 (e-book)
    1. Gays—United States—Political activity—Handbooks, manuals, etc.
I. Haider-Markel, Donald P. II. Title.
   HQ76.3.U5 S59 2002
   305.9'0664'0973—dc21

                                         2002003519

07   06   05   04   03   02   10 9 8 7 6 5 4 3 2 1

ABC-CLIO, Inc.
130 Cremona Drive, P.O. Box 1911
Santa Barbara, California 93116-1911

This book is printed on acid-free paper.
Manufactured in the United States of America

*To the memory of Robert W. Bailey (1951–2001),
of Columbia and Rutgers Universities,
a pioneer in the study of lesbian, gay,
bisexual, and transgender politics as well as
a friend and mentor to us both*

Contents

Foreword

We stand at an interesting point in history for the lesbian and gay movement in America. The movement for social acceptance and legal protection has achieved some stunning results in a relatively short period of time, but many lesbian and gay Americans still face discrimination, violence, and social rejection because of their sexual orientation. Moreover, organized efforts to block further gains and overturn past victories continue into the new millennium, with no clear end in sight. The lesbian and gay movement continues to face these challenges, including some from within, such as the full inclusion of bisexual and transgendered people within the movement, with the eventual goal of achieving a society where LGBT identity is not a basis for discrimination or fear.

LGBT political participation, at one time limited to relatively secretive and anonymous homophile groups, now includes every type of activity in the U.S. system, from voting, to interest group lobbying and litigation, to the appointment and election of openly LGBT officials. LGBT participants in the movement and political system are also more diverse now than they were in the past, with greater numbers of women, ethnic and racial minorities, and persons from middle- and working-class backgrounds. The newer diversity within the LGBT movement has led to an increasing diversity of voices with new issues to be addressed, including same-sex marriage, adoption, parenting, conflicts over liberal versus conservative beliefs within the movement, acceptance of religious faiths, and gender and racial discrimination within the movement.

The increasing numbers of LGBT people participating in the movement and the broader political system has led to a long list of policy victories at the national, state, and local level. To list a few, twelve states have passed statutes to ban discrimination based on sexual orientation in public employment, more than two hundred local governments ban at least one type of sexual orientation discrimination, twenty-seven localities and three states ban discrimination based on gender identity, eight states and eighty-three localities offer some type of domestic partner benefits for public employees, forty-one localities and California have some type of domestic partner registry for domestic partners, and twenty-seven states have at least one type of law that records or punishes hate crimes based on sexual orientation. At the national level, significant legislation has passed to provide funding for AIDS/HIV programs, protections have been provided for persons with AIDS/HIV, numerous anti-LGBT bills and amendments were blocked in Congress over the past fifteen years, and President Clinton became the first president to openly court the LGBT vote as well as sign an executive order banning sexual orientation discrimination for civilian federal government employees.

Socially and culturally the LGBT movement has seen great gains as well. Public support for antidiscrimination laws covering sexual orientation has increased considerably in the past 20 years, support for openly LGBT candidates is on the rise, and tolerance of homosexuality and same-sex sexual relations is at an all-time high. At the same time media representations of LGBT people have become more diverse and positive, with several movies and television shows that have had LGBT characters in lead roles.

Although the importance of these changes cannot be overstated, one must also recognize that LGBT people still face considerable challenges. Since the 1980s numerous conservative groups have opposed public and private policies protecting LGBT civil rights, successfully banned the recognition of same-sex marriage in more than thirty states and by the federal government, fought against programs to protect LGBT youth from harassment, and passed federal and state laws that prohibit a variety of organizations from "promoting positive representations" of LGBT people.

Much still needs to be done to ensure that all voices are heard in our democracy. It is my hope that this book can contribute to our understanding of sexual identity and the role of LGBT Americans in the political process.

U.S. Representative Tammy Baldwin (D-WI)

Series Foreword

Participation in the political process is a cornerstone of both the theory and the practice of democracy; indeed, the word "democracy" itself means rule by the people. Since the formation of the New Deal coalition in 1932, the study of U.S. politics has largely been organized around the concept that there exist distinct "blocs" of citizens, such as African Americans, women, Catholics, and Latinos. This trend was reinforced during the 1960s when the expansion of the media and the decline of traditional sources of authority promoted direct citizen mobilization. And more recently, the emphasis on "identity politics" has reinforced the notion of distinct groups organized along lines of shared personal characteristics rather than common economic interests.

Although political participation is a mainstream, even canonical, subject in the study of U.S. politics, there are few midrange reference materials available on this subject. Indeed, the available reference materials do not include works that provide both a systematic empirical base *and* explanatory and contextualizing material. Likewise, because of the fragmentation of the reference materials on this subject, it is difficult for readers to draw comparisons across groups, even though this is one of the most meaningful ways of understanding the phenomenon of political participation.

The Political Participation in America series is designed to fill this gap in the reference literature on this subject by providing key points of background (e.g., demographics, political history, major contemporary issues) and then systematically addressing different types of political participation, providing both substance and context for readers. In addition, each chapter includes case studies that either illuminate larger issues or highlight some particular subpopulation within the larger group.

Each volume of the ABC-CLIO Political Participation in America series focuses on one of the major subgroups that make up the electorate in the United States. Each volume includes the following components:

- *Introduction to the group,* comprising a demographic, historical, and political portrait of the group, including political opinions and issues of key importance to members of the group
- *Participation in protest politics,* including marches, rallies, demonstrations, and direct actions
- *Participation in social movements and interest groups,* including involvement of members of the group in and through a wide variety of organizations and associations
- *Participation in electoral politics,* including a profile of involvement with political parties and voting patterns
- *Participation in political office-holding,* including elected, appointed, and "unofficial" offices from the local to national levels

The end of each book also includes an A-Z glossary featuring brief entries on important individuals and events; a chronology of political events salient to the group; a resource guide of organizations, newsletters, websites, and other important contact information, all briefly annotated; an annotated bibliography of key primary and secondary documents, including books and journal articles; excerpts from major primary documents, with introductions; and a comprehensive index to the volume.

Raymond A. Smith
Series Editor

Preface

It has often been noted that in the Western tradition homosexuality was first called the sin of sodomy, then regarded as the crime of buggery, next was considered the disease of psychological inversion, but now has become like an ethnicity. And where sinners are condemned, criminals are imprisoned, and psychological inverts are hospitalized, members of ethnic groups participate in politics.

Of course, lesbian, gay, bisexual, and transgender (LGBT) people have long participated in the political process as individuals. Unlike women, African Americans, and some other groups, for instance, they were never denied—on the grounds of their sexual orientation—the voting franchise or the right to hold political office. Indeed, LGBT historiography is replete with examples of holders of high political office, stretching back to Alexander the Great and the Roman Emperor Hadrian and up to FBI Director J. Edgar Hoover and U.S. Congresswoman Barbara Jordan, who are believed to have been LGBT.

Yet the political participation of LGBT people *as LGBT people* is a startlingly new phenomenon, scarcely three decades old. Before the Stonewall Riots of 1969, which are considered the foundational event of the modern LGBT movement, there were a few clandestine groups of activists who worked to improve the lot of LGBT people but no mass movement and certainly not even the hint of political power.

By most measures then, the explosive growth of LGBT political participation in the 1970s, 1980s, and 1990s is an extraordinary phenomenon, a truly remarkable development in American political history. Nonetheless, LGBT political participation has rarely been studied. This lack of previous examination is perhaps unsurprising, given that LGBT issues in general have rarely been addressed by mainstream American political science. The reasons for the paucity of research into LGBT politics are multiple, including the traditionally stigmatized status of homosexuality, the relative scarcity of empirical

data on the subject, and unresolved problems with operationalization of variables. In addition, a report by the American
Political Science Association documents that a number of LGB
political scientists indicate that they had been discouraged from
researching LGB topics and/or "had avoided pursuing research on
these topics for fear that it would not be taken as 'serious political
science.'" (American Political Science Association, Committee on the
Status of Lesbians and Gays in the Profession, 1995).

The minimal book-length social science literature that does exist
on LGB politics has been rooted mostly in postmodern political
theory, queer theory, or social movement theory focusing on identity
politics (e.g., Blasius 1994; Phelan 1989, 1994). There have, of course,
been some exceptions to this rule, such as behaviorist analyses of
LGB voting patterns (Hertzog 1996, Bailey 1998b), the impact of LGB
people on urban politics (Bailey 1998b), and the role of LGB people
in legislative politics (Rayside 1998). Each of these studies is
examined at length in this volume. Nonetheless, as noted by Robert
Bailey:

> The political study of gay men and lesbians did not start in
> mainstream political science but at the political peripheries of
> psychoanalysis, sociology, and historiography. . . . More
> recently, sexual identity and the gay rights movement have
> been housed in the "new social movements" literature or as an
> expression of the "values shift" evident in postindustrial
> (postmaterial?) societies. . . . Common as interest-group analysis
> is to American political science . . . its application to the study
> of sexual identity is limited. (Bailey 1998b, 195)

It is within this context that the present volume was
conceptualized as a reference work encapsulating and extending the
existing literature on LGBT political participation. Working within
the framework of the ABC-CLIO Political Participation in America
series, *Gay and Lesbian Americans and Political Participation* provides
an overview and analysis of LGBT political participation in four
crucial spheres of protest, social movement, electoral politics, and
public office.

Chapter One reviews the overall role of LGBT Americans and the
political process, including debates over the definition of
homosexuality and the variable estimates on the size of the LGBT
population, followed by a sociodemographic profile of the group.
Chapter One also includes a brief history of LGBT politics in the

United States, the place of the LGBT people in the U.S. political system, and pressing public policy issues. Chapter Two focuses specifically on protest politics by LGBT Americans, particularly the Stonewall Riots of 1969, which launched the modern movement for LGBT rights, the annual "pride marches" that commemorate Stonewall, and periodic small demonstrations and direct actions as well as three large marches on Washington, D.C. The chapter also provides more detailed analysis, based on original data, about individual participation in the signature form of LGBT protest politics.

The Introduction as well as Chapters One and Two were primarily authored by Raymond Smith, who is also general editor of the ABC-CLIO series *Political Participation in America,* of which this is one volume. He wishes to thank all of those who helped with the writing of his doctoral dissertation (upon which these chapters are in part based), in particular his academic advisor and dissertation sponsor, Bob Shapiro, as well as Bob Bailey and Nolan McCarty, who provided many insights along the way as part of his dissertation committee at Columbia University. He also wishes to thank the family members, particularly his parents Raymond and Dorothy Smith, and friends, who were so supportive during the writing of the dissertation. He is also grateful to the nearly 1,000 individuals who completed the dissertation survey, the results of which are reported in Chapters One and Two.

Chapter Three addresses LGBT social movement organizations, with a particular focus on the evolution of LGBT interest groups and the current activities of these groups at the local, state, and national level. Detailed descriptions of national LGBT groups are provided. Chapter Four explores LGBT participation in the electoral process, with attention to LGB voting behavior, LGBT involvement in party politics, and descriptions of how U.S. political parties address LGBT issues. Chapter Five provides a first-ever detailed look at openly LGBT elected and nonelected government officials, as well as important public figures in the LGBT movement. Chapters Three, Four, and Five were primarily authored by Donald Haider-Markel. He wishes to thank his wife, Michele Haider-Markel, as well as Ken Meier and Ken Sherrill for their assistance and patience.

Finally, the reference chapters of the volume include several key primary documents with introductions, a chronology of major events; an A-Z glossary, an annotated bibliography, and a resource guide. Collectively, the text and reference materials represent the first attempt to synthesize the full range of political participation by

LGBT Americans into a single volume. The authors hope that the end result will help to foster understanding of the ways in which LGBT people have developed a unique niche in the U.S. political system but at the same time can be understood as just one more group in the social fabric of the contemporary United States.

References

American Political Science Association, Committee on the Status of Lesbians and Gays in the Profession. 1995. "Report on the Status of Lesbians and Gays in the Political Science Profession." *Political Science and Politics* (September): 561–574.

Bailey, Robert W. 1998a. *Gay Politics, Urban Politics: Identity and Economics in the Urban Setting.* New York: Columbia University Press.

———. 1998b. *Out and Voting: The Gay, Lesbian, and Bisexual Vote in Congressional House Elections, 1990–1996.* Washington, DC: National Gay and Lesbian Task Force Policy Institute.

Blasius, Mark. 1994. *Gay and Lesbian Politics: Sexuality and the Emergence of a New Ethic.* Philadelphia: Temple University Press.

Hertzog, Mark. 1996. *The Lavender Vote: Lesbians, Gay Men, and Bisexuals in American Electoral Politics.* New York: New York University Press.

Phelan, Shane. 1989. *Identity Politics: Lesbian-Feminism and the Limits of Community.* Philadelphia: Temple University Press.

———. 1994. *Getting Specific: Postmodern Lesbian Politics.* Minneapolis: University of Minnesota Press.

Rayside, David Morton. 1998. *On the Fringe: Gays and Lesbians in Politics.* Ithaca, NY: Cornell University Press.

1

Overview

This chapter provides a general overview of lesbian, gay, bisexual, and transgender (LGBT) Americans and the political process, including a definition of the LGBT population and a review of its place in the political system. The chapter opens with a review of the basic demographics of LGBT Americans, beginning with a discussion of debates concerning the definition of LGBT. This includes whether "homosexuality" and "bisexuality" should be defined in terms of sexual attraction, sexual behavior, political self-identification, or some combination of these factors. Building upon these basic definitions, the next section examines the "numbers debate," reviewing the variable estimates on the size of the LGBT population, followed by a demographic profile from existing data sources and a discussion of the various subpopulations within the larger LGBT community. The appendix to this chapter provides a more in-depth analysis of previously unpublished data showing a demographic portrait specifically of the participants in LGBT politics who are the focus of this volume.

Having provided a broad definition of the LGBT population, the second section of this chapter discusses the relationship of this population to the U.S. political system. This section is intended to set the context for understanding the subsequent chapters on political participation. The chapter begins with a brief history of LGBT politics, including the "homophile" period before the Stonewall Riots of 1969, the period of "gay liberation" and lesbian feminism following

1

Stonewall, the impact of AIDS in the 1980s, and the movement of LGBT people toward the political mainstream in the 1990s. This section then moves to the place of the LGBT people in the U.S. political system and then on to a review of the internal politics of the LGBT community, in particular the conflict between the two approaches known as "liberationism" and "assimilationism." It then develops a framework for understanding views on LGBT issues and a brief discussion of the major areas of political contention at the start of the twenty-first century.

At the outset of a discussion of LGBT politics, it is perhaps essential to employ a relatively broad definition of the "political," such as that offered by Mark Blasius. Arguing that LGBT politics should go beyond the "narrow sense of concern with the formal structures of power in our society," Blasius writes that "besides the work of the explicitly political organizations, most of lesbian and gay culture is at the same time 'cultural politics,' the activity of calling into question and transforming the power relations that condition how sexuality is conceptualized, represented, and expressed behaviorally at the present time" (Blasius 1994, 4). Blasius cites LGBT scholarship, visual arts, sports, spirituality, and literature as vehicles for reordering power relations that achieve political ends without engaging the formal political process. Thus, the very act of "coming out" contests societal norms in which all individuals are presumptively regarded as being heterosexual until proven otherwise. The presence of committed same-sex couples, often with their children, challenges narrow legal definitions of "family." Some LGBT people, by their sheer ordinariness, reinforce the growing understanding that LGBT people are not per se threatening or unusual. Others by their nonconformity push the envelope of social acceptance. It is within this broader definition of "politics" that it is possible to begin the discussion.

Basic Definitions

The abbreviation "LGBT" has come into common use as a way to avoid the need to use the cumbersome phrase "lesbian, gay, bisexual, and transgender" repeatedly, while also not subsuming the four separate constituents of the LGBT community into a generic "gay" community (which employs the masculine form) or into a "queer" community (which has specific connotations toward political radicalism). It should be noted here that most of the general statements in this volume refer primarily to the situation of lesbians and gay men (i.e., "homosexuals"), and are less specific to the situation of bisexuals. Perhaps the most distinct set of issues pertains to individuals who are "transgender," (i.e., those who in some sense "cross over" from one gender to another, or "transgress" against gender norms).

The terms "lesbian" and "gay" refer to the same sexual orientation—homosexuality—in different genders. This sexual orientation is one in which individuals are predominantly attracted, sexually and affectionally, toward members of the same sex. Although the phrase "lesbians and homosexuals" is sometimes used, this is an erroneous usage in that it suggests that the term "homosexual" refers exclusively to men. Some female homosexuals, however, prefer to use the term "gay" for themselves rather than "lesbian," which is considered by some to have a more radical political connotation. The term "lesbian" (sometimes capitalized) is derived from the Greek Isle of Lesbos, home of the ancient Greek woman poet Sappho, who was believed to be a female homosexual. The term "gay" is of more modern provenance, emerging in the early twentieth century as a code word for male homosexuals in some urban communities.

The word "bisexual" refers to a complex category and has been used in a variety of different manners. Some individuals are considered "behaviorally bisexual" in that they have had sex with members of both sexes, either voluntarily, due to situational factors (e.g., incarceration), or through sex work (e.g., prostitution). Such behavioral bisexuals may or may not be bisexual in terms of sexual orientation, however, in that they may not experience a consistent and strong sexual attraction to members of both sexes. Self-identification as bisexual may also be used as a "half-way point" by individuals who are uncertain, or in denial, about being homosexual. For some, particularly youth, the label "bisexual" can be used to acknowledge same-sex attractions without renouncing opposite-sex attractions. Other individuals, of course, simply are bisexual in that they have experienced a significant degree of attraction to members of both sexes.

The final main category of sexual orientation, "heterosexual," or "straight," is widely recognized to refer to those who are predominantly or exclusively attracted to the opposite sex. Surveys of the general public have suggested that more people recognize and understand the term "homosexual" than "heterosexual," with the latter simply being regarded as "normal." Indeed, some heterosexuals believe that they do not have a sexual orientation, misconstruing the meaning of the category itself.

In some cases, the category "asexual" is also employed for those who have no sexual feelings or thoughts, but this term is rarely employed and nonstandard, as are other terms such as "polysexual" and "pansexual" to describe those with wide-ranging erotic expression. Some also employ the term "sexual orientation" or "sexual prefer- ence" to refer to an attraction to certain types of sexual behaviors (e.g., sadomasochism). However this is, again, a nonstandard usage, as these terms are most widely used to describe strictly the more lim- ited phenomenon of whether an individual is predominantly at- tracted, sexually and affectionally, to members of his or her own sex, of the opposite sex, or of both sexes.

The term "transgender" refers not to sexual orientation but to gen- der identity; a transgender person may be heterosexual, homosexual, or bisexual. The key in this case is not the gender of those to whom the person is sexually attracted, but the individual's own gender. Those who are "transgender" have in some way "crossed over" from one sex to the other by adopting the dress and demeanor of members of the opposite sex, or in some cases by actually having sex reassign- ment surgery ("sex-change operations"). In recent years, many LGBT organizations have officially altered their names to include "trans- gender," in part due to recognition that many LGBT people express themselves in ways that are regarded as "gender atypical," or more like those of the opposite sex. "Many G/L/B organizations . . . have opened their ranks to transpeople by signifying inclusiveness in their names. . . . More and more gay men, lesbians, and bisexuals are com- ing to realize that transpeople are not strange 'others,' but just hu- man beings struggling to live with dignity" (AEGIS n.d., 1).

In all, "transgender" remains a broad and somewhat fluid term, but the American Educational Gender Information Service (AEGIS) offers the following definition: "'Transgender' is a term used to de- scribe anyone who bends or challenges 'traditional' gender roles: gay cross-dressers, straight cross-dressers, transsexuals, drag queens and kings, transgenderists, androgynes, and gender benders of all sorts. As gay men and lesbians transgress heterosexual norms by loving members of the same sex, transgender people transgress norms by wearing clothing not generally associated with their own sex and in some cases by modifying their bodies to be more like those of the 'other' sex" (AEGIS n.d., 1).

A debate continues over the nature of sexual orientation, typified by two positions: the essentialist and the social constructionist. Es- sentialists by and large argue that sexual orientation is an innate characteristic that is stable over time. Thus, while they concede that the expression of sexuality is always shaped by the culture of any spe- cific time and place, there is a core "essence" that is always present.

Thus, from an essentialist perspective it is possible to speak of Alexander the Great as being "gay." Social constructionists, on the other hand, employ more postmodern approaches, which argue that sexuality, as with all culture, is fundamentally fluid, and that categories apply only to one particular time and place (if at all). Social constructionists note that the term "homosexual" was not even coined as an identity category until the nineteenth century, and that the concept of sexual orientation is not meaningful in many contexts. The essentialist versus social constructionist debate is echoed in many issue areas throughout the realm of LGBT politics.

Demographics

One of the more unique characteristics of LGBT individuals as a group—regardless of where one stands in the debate between essentialism and social constructionism—is the near impossibility of generating highly accurate estimates of the overall numbers of LGBT people. Indeed, LGBT people have traditionally had the attribute of relative "invisibility." LGBT people are born into the general population, and thus cannot be marked by virtue of birth into a particular social group or category. Some LGBT people do not even themselves recognize their sexual orientation until puberty or later. Further, most LGBT people can, at least to some degree, "pass" as heterosexual. This ability to pass has served to shield many LGBT people from individual discrimination, but also was among the reasons that an LGBT movement took so long to coalesce. It also means that even today, the LGBT population remains among the most hidden of all minority groups. Indeed, while ethnic and racial minorities (defined in various ways) have been counted and analyzed with great statistical precision, there is no consensus whatsoever about the number of LGBT people.

Although the methodological problems with acquiring a reliable estimate of the absolute number of LGBT people are complex, it may for present purposes be sufficient to state that the "numbers game" hinges on two key problems. The first problem is how the terms "lesbian," "gay," and "bisexual" are to be defined: In terms of sexual feelings and thoughts? Sexual behaviors? Active self-identification? Each of these definitions would produce different numerical estimates and have significantly different meanings for political action.

Insofar as one's sexual orientation may be said to exist prior to and regardless of any actual sexual activity, the broadest possible definition would be in terms of sexual thoughts, feelings, or fantasies toward members of the same sex. But this is also the most abstract definition, and the hardest to quantify accurately. The most common and forthright definition of bisexuality and homosexuality is simply in terms of actual sexual contact with members of the same sex. However, some people whose sexual orientation is homosexual or bisexual may not have same-sex contact because they believe it is morally wrong, because they are deeply "closeted," or because they simply do not have the opportunity to do so. Likewise, some people who are heterosexually oriented may have same-sex sexual contact because they may be, for example, incarcerated in single-sex environments or may be sex workers. Yet another definition might be to look at respondents' self-identification as lesbian, gay, or bisexual. For the purpose of analyzing LGBT politics, this is probably the most relevant designation. However, it must be recognized that many of those who may be bisexual or homosexual by some objective criteria may not subjectively consider themselves "gay," "lesbian," or "bisexual."

The second problem is that many people are to some degree or another "closeted," which is to say they have compelling reasons not to identify themselves as being LGBT to others, especially not in formal surveys conducted by strangers, thus distorting poll numbers. These reasons may be psychological and related to the process of "coming out" (i.e., acknowledging one's sexual orientation to oneself or to others) or they may be pragmatic and related to the multiple social, economic, and political disadvantages that accrue to those who are openly identified as being LGBT.

Thus, to a very great extent, the answer to the question of what percentage of the population is LGBT is in large part a function of *how* the question is asked, which in turn is shaped by *why* the question is asked. To take some practical examples, those interested in the use of homoerotic imagery in advertising might want to know how many people experience attraction to or arousal from images of desirable members of the same sex. Alternatively, researchers in AIDS prevention are generally interested primarily in behavior, because only actual sexual behavior can transmit HIV. Sexual thoughts and feelings, as well as self-identification, are thus secondary considerations for such researchers. From the point of view of the pollster for a big city mayor in a tight election, however, the crucial factor would be what percentage of the population has a political self-identification as LGBT, and thus might vote as part of a perceived "political bloc." For such pollsters, individuals who have homosexual thoughts, feelings, or behaviors, but who do not vote with homosexuality in mind would be of little interest.

It is within this context of conceptual fuzziness and methodological limitations that any review of the literature on the numbers of LGBT people must be understood. The "foundational" and most widely cited number in this entire debate is the statistic that 10 percent of the male population is exclusively or predominantly homosexual. This hotly contested 10 percent figure derives from the groundbreaking study *Sexual Behavior in the Human Male* published by sex researcher Alfred Kinsey of Indiana University in 1948 (cited in Hogan and Hudson 1998, 328–329). Although the famous Kinsey reports (including a subsequent report in 1953 on female behavior) were extremely wide ranging, perhaps their greatest impact was in moving the popular perception of the numbers of gay men from that of an occasional aberration to a sizable percentage of the population.

In a nutshell, the reports indicated that 37 percent of men had had at least one same-sex experience to the point of orgasm; of these 6 percent were predominantly but not exclusively homosexual and 4 percent were exclusively homosexual throughout their lives. (The equivalent figures for women were 12 percent, 6 percent, and 2 percent [Hogan and Hudson 1998, 328–329].) It is the summing only of the male numbers of 6 percent and 4 percent, however, from which the 10 percent statistic was derived. Kinsey's statistics were noteworthy also in that they reflected percentages that were stable across the five generations he studied.

As might be expected, Kinsey's methodology, particularly the selection of his sample, has been highly contested. Nonetheless, the statistic has remained cemented in popular consciousness, and has become part of LGBT culture with, for example, a consumer catalog for gay men called "10 Percent Productions" and a book on gay and lesbian youth called *One Teenager in Ten* (its sequel was *Two Teenagers in Twenty*). However, most subsequent studies—and there have been many—have registered figures below the 10 percent statistic. One of the most notable and controversial was a report released by the Alan Guttmacher Institute in 1993 indicating that only 1 percent of American men aged twenty to thirty-nine were homosexual. Predictably, detractors of the Kinsey statistic embraced the Guttmacher figure, while advocates of LGBT rights rejected the finding, arguing that many people will not disclose their homosexuality and that the study was flawed because it was not specifically designed to identify homosexuality. Various other studies have indicated single-digit statistics between the 1 and 10 percent marks, although some sampling limited to large cities has exceeded the 10 percent statistic.

In all, then, the question of the number of LGBT people remains unanswerable. From the standpoint of political participation, however, the absolute number of LGBT people is significant in an overall sense, but not decisive in terms of political impact. Thus, while the debate over numbers may provide a sense of the cap of LGBT influence, LGBT people will, for instance, constitute a majority in an electoral district only under the most extraordinary of circumstances. Nonetheless, it may not be essential to pinpoint what percentage of the population is LGBT (by whatever criteria applied).

For present purposes it may be sufficient to state that LGBT people have a strong political incentive to be perceived as being as numerous as possible. At the most basic level, this creates the appearance that LGBT people constitute a noteworthy portion of the population and therefore control such political resources as votes and money. At a deeper level, the appearance that a not-insignificant portion of the population is LGBT might help to make homosexuality seem less aberrant or deviant to the heterosexual majority. In these regards, LGBT people are not fundamentally different from other groupings in society that have not been meticulously counted or for whom advocates or opponents cannot determine an exact number (e.g., people with disabilities, undocumented aliens, the homeless, etc.).

If it is difficult to capture an overall picture of LGBT numbers, it becomes even more difficult to examine sociodemographic characteristics and subpopulations. Perhaps the most relevant observation when discussing the sociodemographic characteristics of the LGBT population is that they appear to be scattered more or less randomly and evenly throughout the population as a whole. The 1970s gay rights slogan "We Are Everywhere" (also the title of an anthology of documents in LGBT politics) appears to have some basis in fact.

Nonetheless, there are a few clear trends throughout most surveys in which people in more socially privileged categories tend to self-identify at higher levels than those in less socially privileged categories. Thus, most surveys indicate that more men self-identify as gay than women self-identify as lesbian and indicate that whites self-identify as gay or lesbian at higher rates than do members of ethnic minorities. Similarly, those with college educations and higher incomes tend to self-identify at higher rates. However, it is unclear to what extent these trends capture some objective sociodemographic data about LGBT people or whether they are artifacts of survey methods and/or of social conditions in the United States.

One line of argument, for instance, states that the modern categories of "gay" or "lesbian" have been constructed and perpetuated by more privileged strata of society—those with economic security, social influence, and political standing. To the extent that this is true, then it is simply a closed circle to find that larger numbers of people in these privileged categories tend to self-identify as LGBT. Another line of argument, which reinforces the previous argument, is that those who enjoy more security in their material circumstances are better situated to take the economic and psychological risks involved with self-identifying as LGBT. Thus, it would be expected that poll results would be slanted in the direction of higher numbers of people from groups with higher social standings.

Another broad trend in survey results is for urban dwellers to self-identify at higher rates than those living in suburban or rural areas. This finding appears to mirror empirical reality, reflecting not birth patterns but rather the tendency of many adult LGBT individuals to migrate to the more tolerant environment of cities, where their self-identification as LGBT may be heightened by interaction with an organized LGBT community. Another trend is for members of younger generations, who have been raised in a society more tolerant of homosexuality, to self-identify as LGBT at higher rates than older individuals who were raised in less tolerant times. The exception to this pattern is the youngest individuals, who may not yet have recognized or accepted their sexual orientation.

These broad trends appear to be replicated among those who participate in LGBT activism. A detailed overview of the findings of one study of LGBT political participation (see appendix) indicates that while the entire sociodemographic field is represented, it is once again skewed toward more privileged categories: male (53 percent); white (69 percent); in their prime earning years, twenty-one to fifty (83.5 percent); holders of at least a college degree (63.7 percent); and earners of annual household incomes over $35,000 (59 percent).

History of the LGBT Movement

If sociodemographic portraits of LGBT individuals in general and political participants in particular have tended in recent years to be skewed toward privileged categories, that has not always been the case. Indeed, in sharp contrast, the early years of the movement by LGBT people for equal rights and liberation is often grouped together with the other great political causes of oppressed groups in the 1960s, notably those for the movements for the civil rights of African Americans and for the liberation of women. Yet by the 1960s, each of these other movements had been active and visible in the United States for at least a century. In particular, the status of African Americans had been a point of fierce contention, from the founding of the Republic through the Civil War and beyond. During that period, blacks founded a wide range of institutions from the Tuskeegee Institute to the NAACP to the Southern Christian Leadership Conference, and developed a distinct social movement for equality. Similarly, women had been struggling against gender discrimination at least since the Seneca Falls Convention of 1848. During the Progressive Era at the turn of the twentieth century, advocates for women achieved a number of breakthroughs, culminating in 1920 with the acquisition of the voting franchise through passage of the Seventeenth Amendment.

By contrast, as late as the 1960s the LGBT movement—then in a precursor state commonly known as the homophile movement—was all but invisible, limited largely to the closed-door meetings of such small pioneering groups as the Mattachine Society, for gay men, and the Daughters of Bilitis, for lesbians. Both of these organizations had themselves been founded only in the 1950s, and although many of their roots were in radical-left politics, they quickly became cautious and nonconfrontational. The closest these groups came to mass political action were small picket lines at the White House and at Independence Hall in Philadelphia, which, while courageous moves for the time, were a far cry from the mass demonstrations of the next generation of LGBT activists.

The question of why a large-scale LGBT political movement took so long to develop has been a central concern of LGBT historiography. In his 1983 book *Sexual Politics, Sexual Communities: The Making of a Homosexual Minority in the United States, 1940–1970,* historian John D'Emilio examines the delayed emergence of large-scale LGBT political activism. In D'Emilio's analysis, the LGBT movement

constitutes a phase, albeit a decisive one, of a much longer historical process through which a group of men and women came into existence as a self-conscious, cohesive minority. Before a movement could take shape, that process had to be far enough along so that at least some gay women and men could perceive themselves as members of an oppressed minority, sharing an identity that subjected them to systematic injustice. But before the movement could become a significant social force, the consciousness and the conditions of daily life of large numbers of lesbians and homosexuals had to change so that they could take up the banner carried by a pioneering few. Thus activists had not only to mobilize a constituency; first they had to create one. (D'Emilio 1983, 4–5)

In the language of social science, sociologist Stephen O. Murray (1996) has coined the term "de-assimilation" to describe the process discussed by D'Emilio. Murray argues that most other marginalized groups, such as blacks or women, began with a clearly separate status within society and made political progress insofar as they could assimilate into the structures of the dominant society. Examples include the drives for residential racial integration and for gender wage parity. By contrast, LGBT people appear to be born spontaneously into every generation and distributed, more or less evenly, into all social classes and categories. Beginning from a position of such absolute assimilation, LGBT people—unlike blacks, women, or many other readily identifiable groups—have had to "de-assimilate" in order to achieve group identity. This de-assimilation took the form of creating separate LGBT neighborhoods in places like New York's Greenwich Village and San Francisco's Castro district, which were full of gay-specific institutions including community centers, bars, churches, bookstores, newspapers, athletic leagues, and so on. A subset of these institutions was designed for subpopulations within the larger LGBT community, such as women-only spaces for lesbians, and bars in neighborhoods such as Harlem, which were expressly for gay African American men. The need for the "extra step" of *creating* group identity, before group mobilization could occur, in part explains the delayed development of an LGBT political movement.

This delayed development was thus shaped (and also facilitated) by the particular circumstances of the radical culture of the 1960s in the United States. This culture emphasized resistance to authority, sometimes spontaneous and violent, explaining in part why the foundational event of the LGBT movement was a three-day riot in June 1969 that ensued after New York City police raided a Greenwich Village gay bar known as the Stonewall Inn. The riots at Stonewall proved to be a catalyst for a wave of national LGBT organizing, most of it in keeping with the left-wing politics of the day. The subsequent history of LGBT political participation has moved through several distinct phases, which are discussed at length at various points throughout the subsequent chapters of this volume and in the chronology in the back matter. In short, however, a fairly standard method for describing the post-Stonewall period regards the 1970s as dominated by a radical movement for "gay liberation" (including a large component of lesbian feminism), the 1980s as dominated by shock at the outbreak of AIDS at the start of the decade and angry protest in the late 1980s, and the 1990s as characterized by a sharp move toward the mainstream by LGBT individuals.

Positioning LGBT People in U.S. Politics

In his analysis "The Political Power of Lesbians, Gays, and Bisexuals," Kenneth Sherrill notes that "[t]he relative political powerlessness of gay people stands in contradistinction to their depiction by advocates of 'traditional values' as a powerful movement advancing a 'gay agenda' in American politics. . . . Gay people are saddled with the burdens of cumulative inequalities [such] that, as a consequence, the national majoritarian political process—particularly as manifested in the electoral system—is far more likely to deprive LGBT people of our rights than to protect our rights" (Sherrill 1996, 469). Sherrill highlights five specific dimensions of the relative powerlessness of LGBT people: numbers, public perception, safety, wealth, and cohesion and collective identity.

First is the question of "numbers." Although no one knows exactly how many LGBT people there are, it is safe to state that LGBT people are a small minority among an overwhelmingly heterosexual majority. Further, aside from a few urban enclaves, LGBT people are not geographically concentrated but scattered throughout the country, thus further diminishing their ability to assert significant numbers and minimizing their electoral impact.

Next, Sherrill raises the topic of "affection," or the public perception of gay people, forthrightly stating, "in addition to being outnumbered, gay people are despised" (Sherrill 1996, 470). In numerous polls of "affection" toward various groups, respondents direct their lowest ratings toward LGBT people (along with illegal aliens); indeed "no other group of Americans is the object of such sustained, extreme, and intense distaste . . . such hostility does not face any other group in the electorate" (470). This antipathy is translated into government policy, Sherrill argues, when politicians "advocate policies that deny gay people equal protection and opportunity in American politics. Gay Americans, almost uniquely, are placed in a defensive position by ballot initiatives and by legislation designed to deny protections against discrimination and to limit full participation on the basis of sexual orientation" (471).

Sherrill's third point concerns safety: "There is a substantial body of evidence to support the proposition that lesbians, gay men, and bisexuals are disproportionately the targets of bias-motivated violence . . . The lack of safety for gay people is both a source of and a consequence of gay people's powerlessness" (472).

Sherrill next raises the question of wealth. There is a widely held notion that LGBT people earn more than their heterosexual counterparts, a perception that works against the argument that they are disadvantaged. However, as Sherrill notes, "there are excellent reasons for believing that lesbians and gay men might earn less than others. People who are low in deference, respect, and safety may well be forced to accept jobs at low wages or, at the very least, trade off cash income for job security and freedom from harassment" (473).

Sherrill's final point concerns cohesion and collective identity, or what he terms the cost of being "born into a diaspora," meaning that LGBT people are "probably randomly distributed about the population at birth." Because LGBT people are only rarely raised by openly LGBT parents, they are by and large socialized to heterosexual norms in childhood. Thus, "large numbers—perhaps most—of gay people are never in the traditional social surroundings that enable them to develop the sort of gay identity that allows them to evaluate political objects in terms of 'is it good for the gay people,' as they might [for other group identities]" (474).

The political powerlessness described by Sherrill places a number of special political burdens on LGBT people. In his book on LGB voting behavior, *The Lavender Vote,* Mark Hertzog provides a listing of burdens on LGB people that affect their ability to participate in the political process and achieve political gains, including:

- Fear of personal rejection: Many "closeted" LGB people have reason to believe that parents, family or friends may end relationships if they reveal their sexual orientation.
- Fear of material or personal loss: In many jurisdictions, LGB people who reveal their sexual orientation are at risk of losing jobs and/or career opportunities, as well as custody of children.
- Fear of physical violence: LGB people are among the most common victims of bias crimes, including random, unprovoked "gay bashings" by strangers.
- Antisodomy laws: The Supreme Court ruled in 1986 that the Fourteenth Amendment right to privacy does not extend to

consensual same-sex sexual relations among adults, which are still criminalized by many U.S. states.

- Mandatory exclusion from employment: LGB people are not allowed to openly serve in the armed forces and are also excluded from teaching and counseling jobs in many schools.
- Family law: Same-sex marriage is illegal in all fifty states, and the U.S. Congress has passed a "Defense of Marriage Act" to block recognition of any future same-sex marriages. LGB people also have restricted rights to adoption and child raising.
- Permissible discrimination: It is legal to openly discriminate on the basis of sexual orientation in employment, housing, credit, consumer service, and public accommodation in most jurisdictions.

Overall, both Sherrill and Hertzog argue that even in the 1990s, LGB people should be understood as a greatly politically disadvantaged group—"powerless" in Sherrill's term, an "oppressed minority" in Hertzog's term.

Despite the many obstacles to LGBT political participation and the multiple impediments to LGBT equality, it must also be noted that extraordinary progress has been made in securing the rights of LGBT people over the past thirty years. For instance, more than half the states have repealed antisodomy statutes or had them vacated by state courts. Although only ten states have passed laws prohibiting discrimination on the basis of sexual orientation, dozens of municipalities and other jurisdictions have comparable local ordinances, so that such laws shield a large percentage of the LGBT population, at least in theory. Similarly, several openly LGBT individuals have held high elective and appointed offices; a variety of groups actively lobby on LGBT issues in Washington and in state capitals; and LGBT people have come to be a recognized core constituency group in the Democratic Party and as a potential voting bloc in elections. Further, Alan Yang (1998) has demonstrated positive trends in public opinion toward LGBT people and issues in such diverse areas as equality in employment and housing, attitudes toward homosexual practices, family issues, and personal freedom. Overall, because of the extremely low baseline from which the LGBT movement began, it must be argued *both* that major strides have been made and that serious inequities persist for LGBT people in the political arena. As noted by Urvashi Vaid:

As the American gay and lesbian movement approaches its sixth decade of political activism, it finds itself at a contradictory juncture: what Dickens would call the best of times and the worst of times. On one level, our movement has been a staggering, if controversial, success; yet on another level, gay and lesbian people remain profoundly stigmatized, struggling against the same crises—in health, violence, discrimination, and social services—that have plagued us for decades. . . . The system has adapted to our existence, but it has still not been challenged in fundamental ways. We are freer than we were in the 1940s and 1960s, but we have failed to realize true equality or win full acceptance as moral human beings. (Vaid 1995, 1–2)

Internal Politics of the LGBT Community

Much of the discussion of internal LGBT politics has been conceptualized in terms of two polar ideal-typical perspectives: "assimilationism" and "liberationism." Indeed, this duality has been regarded as a central organizing principle of all LGBT politics. The assimilation-minded typically emphasize the similarities between LGBT and heterosexual people and argue for inclusion in such mainstream institutions as marriage, the military, and public office. By contrast, the liberationist impulse is toward a redefinition, if not eradication, of existing social structures, such as the traditional nuclear family, capitalism, or the conventional state. To assimilationists, the putative excesses of liberationists may seem an embarrassment, while liberationists often view assimilationists as "sell-outs" to the dominant culture.

In many ways, the central question in the liberationist-assimilationist debate is whether the movement's primary goal should be to join the mainstream or to challenge and subvert it. Assimilationists argue that in order to maintain itself, the LGBT movement requires a tight focus on sexual orientation and LGBT identity, lest it lose cohesion and disintegrate into multiple, warring camps. As one influential assimilationist political work stated:

Any and all fellow outcasts are embraced as political partners, and the gay community has filled its dance card with a "rainbow coalition" of society's underdogs and benevolent but offbeat causes. . . . [Yet] even though gays constitute a far larger and broader constituency than any of these, association with other marginal groups only reinforces the mainstream's suspicion that gays are another microfaction of the lunatic fringe.

What are straights to be expected to make of the following cobbled together chants, all shouted vigorously during the 1988 Gay Pride March in New York City? "Cruise men, not missiles"; "The people fight back from Stonewall to South Africa"; "End racism, sexism, and war /Money for AIDS/ We won't take no more"; "First dogs and monkeys too/ Next time they'll cut into you"; Because our movement must first grow stronger before it can help its still weaker friends, we recommend [that] . . . the movement should eagerly ally itself with large, mainstream groups that can actually advance our interests (e.g., the Democratic Party, the National Organization for Women, or the Presbyterian Church). (Kirk and Madsen 1989, 181–182)

By contrast, liberationists tend to view the assimilationist approach as simply replicating the privilege structures of the dominant society. As liberationist transgender writer Riki Ann Wilchins states:

[The problem] of a gay rights movement based solely on sexual orientation [is that] . . . in application, it functions like a sieve, filtering out any issue not purely focused on sexual orientation. Left untouched is any problem that is about "sexual orientation AND." So we're not going to deal with queers of color, because that's sexual orientation AND race. We're not going to deal with issues of working-class queers or queers on welfare, because that's about gay AND class. And we're not going to deal with the concerns of lesbians, because that's about gay AND gender. Pretty soon, the only people we represent are those fortunate enough to possess the luxury of simple and uncomplicated oppression. That is, their race, class, and gender are "normal" and so go unmarked and unoppressed. This is why the gay rights movement and feminist movements have done an exemplary job of representing the needs and concerns of white, eurocentric, middle-class Americans, but not much of anything else. It is turning out to be a pretty pale and bland liberation struggle we're waging. To those at "the bottom," on the lower rungs of the oppression ladder, the new boss looks an awful lot like the old one. People with the greatest needs remain unrepresented and unaddressed. (Wilchins 1997, 84)

Many of the most heated arguments in the liberationism versus assimilationism debate have focused on the issue of "inclusion," or what types of people and behaviors and issues should be "defined in" as part of the LGBT community and which should be "defined out" as marginal or beyond the pale of acceptability. The debate over inclusion has had its most fundamental manifestation in the tension (and occasional antagonism) between the two largest groups: gay men and lesbians. Lesbian (and bisexual) women have often perceived implicitly sexist attitudes on the part of gay (and bisexual) men who, despite their sexual orientation, retain "male privilege." Similarly, many people of color have seen a replication of societal racism throughout the LGBT community, which is perceived as being dominated by whites. Thus, in one symbolic move, the 1998 New York City LGBT pride march had listed as the first two marching contingents "Women Only" and "People of Color." In some ways, the emphasizing of inclusivity is a way of curbing impulses toward "separatism." (Separatism has at times been identified as a third modality in LGBT politics along with assimilationism and liberationism, or sometimes as a radical version of liberationism. It has been applied in particular by lesbians who seek separate institutions and spaces, in part in reaction to perceived sexism among gay men.)

Other internal political debates within the LGBT community have not been over identity categories but rather over the place of groups associated with marginal and controversial views of sexuality. Notable among these groups have been advocates of sadomasochistic sex (i.e., the "leather" or "S & M" subculture) and pedophile organizations (e.g., the North American Man-Boy Love Association [NAMBLA]) that agitate for repeal of age-of-consent laws and advocate what they term "intergenerational" sexual relationships. These groups have posed a classic dilemma akin to that of civil libertarians called upon to defend speech that they may deplore. A pure liberationist perspective would be hard-pressed to exclude any group with a radical agenda, however offensive they might (or might not) find their particular message. Assimilationists, by contrast, more easily draw boundaries that exclude certain marginal groups.

The participation of both the leather subculture and of pedophile groups in the LGBT community has been hotly contested over time, yet over time a certain broad consensus has set in that differentiates between the two types of sexual "outlaws." Although the specifics are complicated, by the start of the twenty-first century, the LGBT community appears to have found in pedophile groups the outer limit of their tolerance, making the assimilationist perspective ascendant and leaving pedophile groups largely marginalized on the grounds that underaged youths cannot consent to sexual activity. In contrast, the "leather" subculture—since it involves consensual, if by some measures extreme, sex between adults—is very much integrated into the mainstream LGBT community, marking a liberationist victory.

Another area of debate is over participation by transgender individuals, as evidenced by a highly assimilationist opinion piece published in June 1998 in the *New York Blade News*. In the article, a self-described lesbian mother of two, Beren DeMotier, decried "this merging of 'trans' with 'lesbian, gay, and bisexual.' I hate it with greater fervor every year. Now that pride month is happening all around us, I have tons of reminders everywhere I look that we are being linked—like it or not—ideologically and legally. . . . [J]ust call me an 'integrationist.' I don't want to be different, 'queer' or outside the norm. I don't want to fell the patriarchy, join a socialist revolution . . ., or abolish the need for two bathrooms in your local McDonald's" (DeMotier 1998).

The liberationist response to DeMotier was swift and acrimonious, paralleling many earlier debates. One letter to the editor decried DeMotier's article as "one of the most hateful pieces of bigotry I have read in 20 years of being 'out'" and noted that many heterosexual feminists have asserted similar claims against the inclusion of lesbians in feminist organizations, suggesting that they pose a "lavender menace" threatening the advance of women as a whole (Low 1998). Another correspondent noted that "the author doesn't realize that the comfort she feels within her middle-class family life is only possible because of years of painful struggle on the part of people she thinks don't really have a place in the movement she feels proud of" (Gemerek 1998).

If the question of "inclusion" is the most important axis of conflict between assimilationists and liberationists, a close second is the question of "propriety," or how LGBT people should conduct themselves at LGBT pride marches and, by extension, in any public venue. Assimilationists would prefer that LGBT pride marches convey the message that LGBT people "are just like everyone else," and would thus prefer a community that leans toward conventional-looking people asserting conventional-sounding civil rights rhetoric. At the very least, they would seek to minimize "flamboyant" behavior in public that they feel will stereotype or stigmatize all LGBT people, especially once run through the sensationalizing lens of the media. Liberationists counter that many LGBT people may not be "like everyone else," and should not be forced to try to present themselves as such. The LGBT community, in their view, should emphasize celebrations of difference and opportunities to emphasize the most unique, individual, and colorful elements of the LGBT community—including behavior that is gender transgressive and/or sexually explicit.

Typology of Political Views

To develop a more systematic view of public attitudes toward LGBT people and issues, it is useful to review a typology presented by political scientist and commentator Andrew Sullivan in his work *Virtually Normal: An Argument about Homosexuality* (1995). Seeking to encapsulate the spectrum of political views, Sullivan offers a quadripartite typology, from most to least traditionalist: the "prohibitionists," the "conservatives," the "liberals," and the "liberationists." He uses all of these titles, however, in specialized ways that are not necessarily congruent with their day-to-day meaning or with their meaning elsewhere in this work.

At the most traditionalist end are the prohibitionists, who tend to think of homosexuality as a behavior rather than as an identity. Although they may concede that certain people are predisposed to homosexual behavior, they believe that it should nonetheless be strictly prohibited—and punished. They believe that "homosexuality is an aberration and that homosexual acts are an abomination . . ., transgressions that require legal punishment and social deterrence. All human beings, in this view, are essentially heterosexual, and the attempt to undermine this fundamental identity is a crime against nature itself" (Sullivan 1995, 21). In the prohibitionist views of the religious far right, sexual expression outside of the strict boundaries of marriage is forbidden. In particular, homosexuality is regarded as sinful "sodomy" based upon the behaviors of the residents of the Biblical city of Sodom, which was destroyed by God for its wickedness. Hence, this view supports antisodomy laws that criminalize virtually all same-sex contact and impose strong social sanctions, and it believes that LGBT people can be "cured" via various so-called "ex-gay" ministries. In short, this is the view that predominated in Western society until recent decades. More recently, however, the prohibitionist view has lost much of its power as a majority of society has come to accept, or at least tolerate, other forms of sexual expression (e.g., masturbation, adultery, premarital sex, divorce, and contraception) that are equally prohibited within the strictly prohibitionist perspective.

At the other end of the spectrum from the prohibitionists are individuals Sullivan calls the "liberationists," although he uses the term somewhat differently than it is used in this volume. Ironically, liberationists—who often use the moniker "queer" rather than "LGBT"— share the prohibitionists' lack of belief in homosexuality as a fixed, immutable characteristic. But whereas this is because prohibitionists believe in strict black-and-white distinctions and clear-cut categories, liberationists reject labels and categories of all kinds, arguing that existence in general, and sexuality in particular, is a shifting, changing, fluid phenomenon. Thus "the second predominant politics of homosexuality springs naturally out of the first. Or rather, it is a kind of reverse image of the first, locked in doctrinal combat with its arguments and theses. . . . For the liberationists, homosexuality as a defining category does not properly exist because it is a construct of human thought, not an inherent or natural state of being. It is a 'construction,' generated in human consciousness by the powerful to control and define the powerless" (Sullivan 1995, 56–57). From this basis, liberationists seek for individuals "to be liberated from the condition of homosexuality into a fully chosen form of identity, which is a repository of individual acts of freedom" (57). Although this approach presents the most potential for revolutionary change from the status quo, its tendency to eschew engagement with mainstream, and potentially mundane, interests limits its impact. Liberationist politics may benefit a small elite in certain urban and/or academic settings, but "other homosexuals, whose lives are no better for queer revolt, remain the objects of a political system which the liberationists do not deign to engage" (92).

Between the two radical extremes of "prohibitionists" and "liberationists," Sullivan finds two heads of the same centrist coin: "conservatives" and "liberals." By "conservative" Sullivan says he means "someone who essentially shares the premises of the liberal state, its guarantee of liberty, of pluralism, of freedom of speech and action, but who still believes politics is an arena in which it is necessary to affirm certain cultural, social, and moral values over others" (Sullivan 1995, 95). Conservatives, then, are those who "want to strike a balance—and sometimes a very precarious one—between allowing individuals considerable freedom of moral action and protecting the fabric of society that makes such liberties possible in the first place" (95). With regard to homosexuality, conservatives by and large maintain the view that the state should discourage homosexuality on the grounds that it is an inferior condition that can damage the fabric of society but also that the state should do so without persecuting homosexuals as individuals or curtailing their rights. Although this is perhaps the most traditional, and still most widely held, view of homosexuality in the United States, Sullivan argues that the mounting evidence about the ability of LGBT people to be well-adjusted and productive members of society is rapidly undermining the viability of this view, and that conservatives—as conservatives—are adapting to a new status quo.

The final category, that of the "liberals" is the perspective from which most mainstream LGBT political participation is anchored. Liberals are those who "believe that society is merely a neutral ground between competing individuals, whose private moral and social choices have no relevance for the public sphere" (Sullivan 1995, 96). Thus, "unlike conservatives, whose first recourse is to ask how society's interests are affected by this phenomenon [homosexuality] . . . liberals ask first how the individual is affected" (136). In practice, however, the contemporary liberal stand on homosexuality can have some illiberal results, such as hate speech codes, which may protect minorities from verbal abuse but that also undeniably abridge the rights of others to full self-expression. To Sullivan, then, the liberal is "guilty of a categorical error, trying to use easy remedies for a problem that knows no easy remedies; using the language of rights in an area where it is impossible to avoid the language of goods" (167).

Thus, in all, Sullivan lays out a typology akin to a bell curve. At either end are views that are extreme and attract relatively few followers, yet that have a certain pristine consistency to their own internal logic. For the bulk of those in the body politic, however, with public policy questions relating to homosexuality one must deal either with the increasing imbalance of the conservative philosophy of defending society without persecuting individuals or the liberal paradox of using illiberal means to pursue liberal ends.

Appendix: New Data on LGBT Political Participation

Who Participates in LGBT Activism?

In June 1998, 743 participants in LGBT pride marches in New York City; Philadelphia; Brooklyn; Hartford, Connecticut; and Asbury Park, New Jersey were asked to complete a survey providing background sociodemographic information about themselves as well as about their previous involvement with LGBT political participation. Participants were recruited both from among the marchers who were lining up waiting for the event to begin and among spectators who were waiting along the march route. (Among participants, the cohort was fairly evenly split between spectators (46.7 percent) and marchers (52.4 percent); however this is purely an artifact of the sampling technique, as the average march had far more spectators than marchers.)

Although the geographic focus of the survey recruitment was limited, the survey nonetheless provides a portrait of who participates in LGBT activism. The data below are compared to comparable data collected as part of the General Social Survey (GSS) in 1996 among people from the MidAtlantic region (i.e., the states of New Jersey, New York, Pennsylvania, and Delaware). Although this geographic region is the one that most closely overlaps that of the survey, it is an inexact match, excluding Connecticut and including not only the state of Delaware but also remote regions of the geographically large states of Pennsylvania and New York. This dataset is referred to below as the "GSS MidAtlantic cohort" (N=415).

In order to develop a general sense of respondents' level of political involvement, they were asked if they had ever participated in a variety of different types of LGBT political activism. The question asked about standard categories of conventional and unconventional political activity. Two questions asked about previous participation in marches, either "an LGBT pride march similar to this one" or an LGB March on Washington, D.C., which are major events that have been held in 1979, 1987, and 1993 (see discussion of the Pride Marches and Marches on Washington in Chapter 2). The other questions ask about several standard categories of participation used in political science: contribution of money, involvement with a group, writing to government officials, and attending demonstrations.

Perhaps unsurprisingly among a cohort of attendees at an LGB pride march, the most commonly cited form of previous involvement in LGB political activism was attendance at a previous pride march: nearly two-thirds (63.3 percent) had gone to a pride march previously. (Only 28.8 percent had been to an LGB March on Washington, but that is actually fairly high when it is recalled that such marches had occurred on only three days in the preceding two decades. This fairly high number may have been related to the relative proximity of these sites to Washington, D.C.) The second highest category, at 55.1 percent, was the fairly passive activity of "checkbook activism," or making a monetary contribution. Approximately one-third of the participant cohort as a whole had previously been actively involved with an LGB political group, written to a government official on an LGB issue, or attended an LGB protest or demonstration. In all, then, this cohort may well be broadly representative of those who are involved with political participation on LGBT issues. Who, then, are they in terms of their sociodemographic profile? Following is a portrait of the cohort.

Sex/Gender. Among participants, 44.8 percent (321) were female; 53.0 percent (380) male, and 1.7 percent (12) transgender. Among GSS respondents in the MidAtlantic region, 57.8 percent (240) were female and 42.2 percent (175) were male (the category "transgender" was not offered.) Overall, the findings from the pride march survey are consistent with previous ones, which indicate that in most surveys that include sexual orientation, men "significantly outnumber women among self-identifiers" as LGB (Hertzog 1996, 211).

Sexual orientation: Among participants, 30.7 percent (223) were lesbians; 49.1 percent (357) were gay; 3.4 percent (25) were bisexual, 14.6 percent (106) were heterosexual; and 2.2 percent reported "other" responses such as "uncertain" or "questioning." Heterosexual respondents were more than twice as likely to be women (76) as men (37), while bisexuals were about equally likely to be male or female. (The traditional categories of sexual orientation are of less clear meaning for transgender individuals, who reported being lesbian, gay, bisexual, and heterosexual in roughly equal numbers.)

The GSS does not ask sexual orientation; therefore no direct comparisons can be made. The best proxy question taps respondents who reported any same-sex sexual partner in the past five years (the middle dataset available between "in the past year" and "since age 18"). This is a highly problematic operationalization, since sexual orientation and sexual identity are by no means entirely congruent with sexual behavior. This "GSS national LGB cohort" numbered 98, which is 3.4 percent of the national sample of 2,904. These small numbers are to be expected given the lack of a question on sexual orientation in the GSS, as well as other methodological problems with identifying LGB individuals in surveys not specifically designed to detect their presence. Among all GSS national LGB respondents, 14 percent were from the MidAtlantic Region.

Overall, the profile of the survey cohort in terms of sexual orientation is noteworthy in two regards. First is the small overall percentage of participants (3.4 percent) who identify as bisexual. Significant definitional problems inherent in the concept of "bisexuality" (e.g., attraction versus behavior versus identity) make it difficult to draw any sharp conclusions from this finding. However, given that LGB respondents were nearly 23 times more likely to report being homosexual (i.e., either "lesbian" or "gay") than bisexual, it seems clear at the least that bisexuals represent by far the smallest component of the LGB presence at pride marches.

Perhaps of greater salience is the relatively high proportion of heterosexuals (14.6 percent). It should not be surprising that a certain percentage of the cohort would be heterosexual. Many individuals undertake advocacy work on behalf of groups to which they do not personally belong. Anecdotally, it appeared that many of the heterosexuals were participating with contingents like PFLAG (Parents, Family, and Friends of Lesbians and Gays) or of liberal mainstream religious groups, such as the Episcopal Church and the Unitarian Universalist Association. Such individuals might have a variety of personal reasons for participation in the LGB pride march, not all of which are purely altruistic. For example, as the president of the Brooklyn chapter of PFLAG wrote: "[W]hy do the straight parents of PFLAG march? Who would pass up an opportunity to be a 'Walking Saint'? We stroll down the street to the adulation of the crowd. There are applause, whistles, and shouts of love. . ." (Wong 1998).

Outness. A further measure of sexual orientation was added to the survey, a question about how "out" the respondent is. The term "out" is a somewhat complicated one, and no definition was provided. The general meaning is to be "out of the closet" or not actively concealing one's homosexuality or bisexuality from other people. Since heterosexuals cannot meaningfully be "in the closet" in terms of their sexual orientation they also cannot be "out," thus only LGB people were asked to answer this question and responses provided by heterosexuals were excluded. It was believed that most LGB individuals in attendance at a pride march would understand the term "out," although exact definitions of the term might vary. Among the 606 participants responding to this question, the reported level of outness was 7.94 out of 10. (The GSS does not address the question of outness.) However, these findings are also suggestive of the population into which this survey was able to tap. There is no particular reason to expect that a fully representative sample of the LGB community would identify equally across a ten-point scale. Indeed, the process of "coming out" may occur in a series of leaps rather than in steady progress. Nonetheless, the finding that even spectators reported a mean level of "outness" of 7.66 suggests that the average LGB individual surpasses a significant threshold of "outness" before they are at the point of attending LGB pride events. Although the pool of those LGB individuals who would, on average, score their outness below 7.66 is of unknown (and unknowable) size, it was not reached by this survey.

Racial/Ethnic Self-Identification. Standard demographic categories for race and ethnicity were used in this question. Because of a growing recognition that many people are of bi/multiracial extraction and may identify with more than one category, respondents were asked to check all that applied, and to double-check their single most important identification if any. Those who checked more than one category were placed into the category of "bi/multiracial," the exception being those who double-checked any category. Since those who double-checked any category were signaling that one ethnic identity predominated for them, they were placed in that category rather than the bi/multiracial category.

Among 726 participants, 12.9 percent (94) were Latino/Hispanic; 7.2 percent (52) were African American; 2.4 percent (17) were Native American; 69.0 percent (501) were White/European-American; 3.2 percent (23) were bi- or multiracial; and 1.4 percent (10) were "other." Race/ethnicity is an interviewer-coded response in the GSS, with only three categories: white, black, and other. Among GSS respondents in the MidAtlantic region, 75.9 percent (315) were white, 15.7 percent (65) were black, and 8.4 percent were "other."

Among GSS national LGB respondents, 79.6 percent (78) were white, 11.2 percent (11) were black, and 8.2 percent (8) were "other." However, since some Latino respondents probably identified their race as "white" or "black," it is not possible to draw direct comparisons between the GSS data and the survey data other than to note that there were notably fewer blacks among the participants (although not the nonparticipants) than among the GSS cohorts.

Overall, participants reflect the broad range of racial/ethnic identifications that one might expect to find in the urban Northeast. For this area, numbers of Native Americans, at 2.4 percent, are unexpectedly large. However, this finding may have resulted in part from the failure of the survey to include the term "American Indian" along with Native American, a term that it is possible that some participants may have thought refers to being "native born" (i.e., nonimmigrant).

Age. Rather than ask respondents to report specific age, which might prompt a higher nonresponse rate, they were asked simply to identify their age bracket. Among the 729 participants responding, the modal category was "age 21–35" (48.0 percent; n=350), with the second most common category being "age 36–50" (35.5 percent; n=259); together the 21–50-age range accounted for more than four-fifths (83.5 percent) of the cohort. The mean among participants on this five-category scale was 2.55 (SD=.78) or midway between the categories of "age 21–35" and "age 36–50 years old." Those "age 51–70" were 11.0 percent and those "over age 70" were only 0.7 percent.

In the GSS, age is calculated from reported date of birth. In the GSS dataset, age is an interval-level variable, but when it is recalculated to match the age categories used in the survey, the sample is roughly comparable to the GSS MidAtlantic and national LGB cohorts in terms of age of respondents, suggesting that the survey samples are broadly representative of the population at large.

Overall, it is not surprising to find a general skew toward the younger age brackets, because surveys have consistently indicated that younger people self-identify as LGB at higher rates than do older people (e.g., Hertzog 1996). The relatively small number of those under 21 (4.8 percent) can be interpreted by understanding that some LGB people under 21 have either not recognized their sexual orientation or have not yet "come out." In addition, many have fewer resources and less ability to travel to events such as pride marches.

Level of education and annual household income. Standard educational categories were used for this question, which is part of establishing the socioeconomic status of respondents. In cases in which individuals checked more than one category (e.g., high school diploma and college degree), they were listed only in the highest category checked. The participant cohort is relatively well educated, with the modal category (35.0 percent) being the roughly one-third at the college-degree level. Including those at the graduate and professional degree level (28.7 percent) and those who have had at least some college (21.3 percent), the large majority of participants (85.0 percent) were educated beyond the high school level. The mean among participants on this five-category scale was 3.7 (SD=1.1) or somewhat below the college degree level. The GSS assesses educational level by number of years of education completed, making direct comparisons impossible; however, taking 12 years of school to mean high school graduation, participants are more likely to have been educated beyond the high school level than members of either GSS cohort. The implications of education are considered below in tandem with the discussion of annual household income.

Annual household income. At the level of household income, the participant cohort is a relatively middle-class cohort. Although the modal category for annual household income was "$20,001–$35,000" (25.4 percent), 59 percent of the cohort had a household income above the mode. However, 15.3 percent reported household incomes below $20,000. The mean on this six-category scale was 3.1 (SD=1.6), or roughly at the "$35,001–50,000" category.

Overall, this research cohort is both well educated and comparatively affluent. This finding was to be expected, given that the literature on collective action in interest groups has long recognized that "our pressure group system appears to be heavily populated by the middle class . . . Group membership is positively associated with higher income groups, higher levels of education, and higher levels of living." This is the case, in part, because relatively to the lower classes, "the upper classes can afford to belong to more organizations because they have more resources. Some of these resources are economic in nature, including greater disposable income and more free time; others are largely psychological" (Hrebenar 1997, 33–34).

Although participation in LGB pride marches is not entirely congruous with membership in a pressure group, the same general pattern appears to apply. In this regard, then, this LGB cohort is comparable to political activists among the general population.

In sum, insofar as LGB people can be found in every sociodemographic class and category, and insofar as LGB pride marches attempt to bring together all portions of the community, it would be expected that the participant cohort would reflect a very broad range of sociodemographic categories. Broadly speaking, though, as would be anticipated from previous findings, participants tend toward sociodemographic categories that are more, rather than less, privileged in that they are:

male (53 percent);
white (69 percent);
in their prime earning years, 21–50 (83.5 percent);
holders of at least a college degree (63.7 percent); and
earners of annual household incomes over $35,000 (59 percent).

The obvious exception to the general profile of membership in more privileged categories is in terms of sexual orientation, since the LGB orientations are clearly less socially privileged than the heterosexual orientation. However, even within the LGB orientations, this would appear to be a more privileged group in terms of "outness," which is rated on the upper end of the scale for all categories.

Why Do People Participate in LGBT Pride Marches?

Attendees at the five 1998 LGBT pride marches in the northeastern United States highlighted above (Manhattan; Brooklyn; Philadelphia; Hartford, Connecticut; and Asbury Park, New Jersey) were asked to rank the reasons they participated. (This quantitative data is derived from the same research cohort whose sociodemographic characteristics are described in Chapter 1. Qualitative comments were derived from subsequent open-ended questionnaires distributed at LGBT community centers in New York City and Philadelphia.)

The choices of reasons offered fell into the nomenclature of incentives for political activity introduced in James Q. Wilson's 1973 book *Political Organizations:* material ("tangible rewards: money, or things and services priced in monetary terms"); solidary ("intangible rewards arising out of the act of associating," such as feelings of support or camaraderie); and purposive incentives ("intangible rewards that derive from the sense of satisfaction of having contributed to a worthwhile cause"). Participants were asked to rank six reasons for participation, two of each type.

These results reveal that among the participant cohort as a whole, material incentives were comparatively unimportant. By a wide margin, the lowest-ranked item (with a mean ranking of an extremely low 5.67 out of 6) was "I am working or have other moneymaking opportunities at the march." This was not an unanticipated response, given the voluntary nature of these events and that most LGBT organizations do not have paid staff. The other type of material incentive, "I wanted to see the entertainment" was a modest but by no means insignificant motivator (with a mean ranking of 3.95 out of 6). Among those who provided a score for this item, 13.0 percent scored it as the first or second more important reason. This question was meant to get at the degree to which the colorful, parade-like elements of the march were an attraction. Given that outrageous sights are a signature characteristic of LGB pride marches, it is to be expected

Table 1.1

Personal Reasons for Participating	Incentive Type	Number of Responses	Mean Ranking
I wanted to show my support for the LGB community.	Purposive	616	1.76***
I wanted to have fun and a good time.	Solidarity	606	2.41***
I wanted to be out among so many other LGB people.	Solidarity	565	3.13***
I wanted to make a political statement.	Purposive	563	3.44***
I was interested in the entertainment, such as the parade floats.	Material	540	3.95***
I am working or have moneymaking opportunities at the march.	Material	350	5.67

Significance level of paired t-test between each item and the item that follows it (*p<.05, **p<.01, ***p<.001)

that this element would be an attraction to many participants, and that many would find the march "entertaining." Nonetheless, the ranking of this item fifth out of six suggests that simple entertainment was not *per se* a major motivator of attendance.

By contrast with material incentives, a mix of purposive and solidary incentives were ranked high. By a substantial margin, the predominantly purposive incentive of wanting to show support for the LGB community was the highest ranked (with a mean ranking of 1.76 out of 6). Of those who provided a score for this item, 79.5 percent scored it as the first or second most important reason for attending. Although "support" is undefined, this statement can be taken at face value as reflecting respondents' desire to express their concern about a broad range of issues relating to the LGB community, from its fundamental right to exist to the details of specific policy areas. One participant commented on feeling "a sense of unity with all the varied, colorful, diverse aspects of our community." Another reported "getting the satisfaction that the biggest ovations at the parade were for the gay cops, firefighters, and teachers—average Joes and Janes like me."

The next highest ranked item (with a mean ranking of 2.41 out of 6) was the solidary incentive of wanting to have fun and a good time. Among those who provided a score for this item, 57 percent scored it as their first or second most important reason for attending. This is a solidary incentive that would clearly be denied to anyone who did not attend and which (unlike many types of entertainment) cannot be purchased or priced in monetary terms. One participant said the march offered "a sense of happiness, [I was] kind of a giddy, joyful spectator." Another said "I get to be with my friends and share in an activity with people who share similar experiences with me, if not the same views that I do." Another simply felt the "joy of watching, marching, and celebrating life."

Next was the solidary incentive of being "out with so many other LGB people" (with a mean ranking of 3.13 out of 6). Among those who provided a score for this item, 30.3 percent scored it as their first or second more important reason for attending. Even for minorities that have their "own" neighborhoods and institutions, the scale and public nature of an event like a march can provide a special type of solidary incentive. This is especially true for LGB people who, unlike racial or ethnic minorities, generally grow up in isolation from other LGB people. Indeed, anecdotally many LGB people remark that they clearly remember their first pride march for the simple reason that, having once felt "alone in the world," they are part of a massive, if transient, majority.

Similarly, the "invisible" quality of the lives of many LGB people (first "in the closet" and later in closed, private settings) may make the public nature of the event particularly meaningful. One New York participant commented on enjoying "seeing my people out in numbers." Another cited "a sense of belonging and acceptance." A third said "I attend the march with the same mindset I would have attending a 4th of July or Veteran's Day parade. The benefits have to do with camaraderie." Others noted that "you feel you are not alone in being gay," and "I saw others like myself; I know I'm not 'the only one.'"

Interestingly, the lowest-ranked of the purposive and solidary incentives was wanting "to make a political statement" (with a mean ranking of 3.44 out of 6). Among those who provided a score for this item, 30.4 percent score it as their first or second most important reason for attending. Although this item does not indicate the nature of the political statement, or whether it is intended for within the LGBT community or for the larger society, the purposive quality of this item is unmistakable. For instance, one participant noted "It's nice to be able to walk down the street and have bystanders know you're gay—raising public awareness of the 'gays' around us." Another said "My hope is that our behavior exposed will help dispel fear and discrimination toward our life and community." Given that the highest-ranked of all the reasons was the purposive desire to show support for the LGBT community, the ranking of this item can be interpreted to mean that the showing of support has a political component but is not limited to politics.

Estimations of the Political Salience of Pride Marches

When asked about how politically important pride marches are, a striking 88.7 percent of participants felt that marches are either "very important" (54.5 percent) or "somewhat important" (34.2 percent) in advancing the overall interests of LGB people. Fewer than 1 percent of participants regarded them as "not important." On this four-point scale, the mean for all participants was 3.4 (SD=.71) or half way between the two highest categories, "very important" and "somewhat important."

As might be expected, most gave a low ranking to the idea that marches harm LGB people by perpetuating stereotypes; presumably most of those who feel that such media perpetuation of stereotypes is highly significant politically do not choose to attend. It should be noted that this finding does not assess the degree to which respondents believed this to be true, simply that they did not score it high on the reasons that marches may have political significance. With a mean ranking of 5.65 out of 6, this lowest-ranked item is a true outlier. Only 4.1 percent of those who assigned a score to this item scored it as their first or second more important reason.

The highest-ranked item (with a mean ranking of 2.14 out of 6) is the ability of marches to build community among LGB people. Of those who provided a score for this item, 67.4 percent cited it as the first or second most important reason. Since the question asked about political significance, it can be inferred that while community building may have many cultural, psychological, or other types of benefits, respondents were recognizing the political salience of group solidarity. Indeed, by scoring it most highly, there seems to be an im-

Table 1.2

Reasons for Political Significance	Number of Responses	Mean
Marches help to build community among LGB people.	605	2.14***
Marches show society that there are a lot of LGB people.	590	2.44*
Marches show politicians that LGB people are politically mobilized.	585	3.08***
Marches help to involve people in the LGB community.	567	3.46***
Marches help promote an LGB political agenda to the larger society.	548	3.83***
Marches harm LGB people by perpetuating stereotypes in the media.	385	5.65

Significance level of paired t-test between each item and the item that follows it (*p<.05, **p<.01, ***p<.001)

plicit recognition that community-level action is the *sine qua non* of LGB political progress, and therefore the most important political goal of LGB pride marches. As one Philadelphia participant put it, marches "help to show the solidarity among gays and lesbians that is needed to stimulate political change."

Not far behind the first-ranked choice was the ability of marches to show society that there are a lot of LGB people (with a mean ranking of 2.44 out of 6). Among those who provided a score for this item, 57.1 percent cited it as the first or second most important reason. It is important to note that insofar as this item is political, it is nonspecific as to what it seeks to achieve politically and it is directed at society rather than at the political system *per se*. From this item, it is unclear what exactly would be accomplished by having society at large know the number of LGB people. Indeed, the population size of many ethnic minorities has been meticulously calculated, yet these groups remain politically disadvantaged. Therefore, the endorsement of this item may simply be taking the next step from the preceding item: first the community must be built, then it must be recognized by the larger society. As one Philadelphia participant wrote, marches can simply show that "there are more GLTB people than the straight world perceives." A more sophisticated interpretation would be that respondents see political advantage in a recognition by the society at large that LGB people are a nonnegligible portion of the population and thus more "normal" than popular conceptions may have led the heterosexual majority to believe. Another participant in Philadelphia commented that marches can "say to everyone that 'No, we are not all monsters, but people as well.'"

The next item was that marches demonstrate to politicians that LGB people are politically mobilized (with a mean ranking of 3.08 out of 6). Among those who provided a score for this item, 36.6 percent scored it as the first or second most important item. This is the highest-ranked item to be directly specifically at the political system, with a focus on the narrow band of individuals who make up the class "politician" and to the relatively narrow focus of "political mobilization." Neither of these two terms are specifically defined here, but the statement might reasonably be interpreted to mean that marches demonstrate that there are many LGB people who can lobby and demonstrate about issues and can contribute money and votes to office seekers. This item is in keeping with the sequence that has already emerged, in that it would follow that once community has been built, and the reality that there are nonnegligible numbers of LGBs has been established, the next step would be for that community to use those demonstrated numbers to exert influence on those with political power. Indeed, one participant in Philadelphia explicitly connected the two issues, noting that "there is strength in numbers and we are seen as active voters." Another summarized that "they make us more visible. They result in (generally) positive publicity. They help serve as a counterweight to the religious right's events/marches."

The fourth item (with a mean ranking of 3.46 out of 6) was the idea that marches help to involve people in the LGB community. Among those who provided a score for this item, 29.6 percent scored it as the first or second most important item. This item turns away from the larger society to a concern about the internal dynamics of the LGB community. It may be interpreted as an acknowledgment that marches are the most high-profile event held each year by LGB communities, and that for many LGB people (including some who are still closeted), marches represent a major first point of contact with the community. Insofar as community-building was ranked as the most important political dimension of marches, it would be expected that attracting new people into the community would be a high priority. The relatively low ranking of the importance of involving new members in the community may reflect a recognition that, although new members are important, the community already exists and current members form its base. This relatively low ranking may also reflect an acknowledgment that marches are one-time annual events rather than ongoing activities (except for the small number of people who help to maintain the sponsoring organizations year-round). Thus the opportunities for marches to serve as a point of entry to the community for new members is very time limited; one cannot "join" a march for more than a few hours. Still, one Philadelphia participant said that marches "allowed me to bring newly out friends to something that would make them feel like part of a larger community."

It is perhaps somewhat surprising that the fifth-ranked item (rated at 3.83 out of 6) is that marches help to promote an LGB political agenda to the larger society. Among those who provided a score for this item, only 15.3 percent scored this as the first or second ranked item. As very conspicuously public events, marches make claims to a place in the larger society, yet respondents did not see them as highly useful "soapboxes." This comparatively low score can be understood partly in light of the possible order effect discussed above, as well as in several other different ways.

One possibility is that respondents did not understand the idea of a political "agenda" or perhaps even the word "agenda" itself. Similarly, they may not perceive a unified "LGB political agenda," thus obviating the possibility that such an agenda could be promoted. Although it is certainly the case that any hypothesized "LGB political agenda" would be extremely heterogeneous, it also seems reasonable that the broad contours of a political agenda of liberation and equality could be discerned. Further, it has already been seen that the vast majority of respondents endorsed the idea that marches are of some importance in promoting "the overall political interests of LGB people." Thus, the lack of a clearcut "LGB political agenda" does not seem likely as the main source of the low score for this item.

Another possibility, however, is that even if there could be said to be an "LGB political agenda," it is not substantively presented by marches. It could certainly be argued that marches are more about style than substance, more about form than content and thus marches of this sort (as opposed to targeted, smaller-scale demonstrations) are unable to send any single, clear message. Respondents seem to believe that they can build community and demonstrate overall numbers and political mobilization, but not articulate a specific LGB agenda.

One other possibility, by no means mutually exclusive with the previous possibility, is that respondents believe that the larger society simply is not listening. The vast majority of the "larger society," even in the very cities in which the pride marches were occurring, were not physically present at the march and therefore could not directly perceive any political agenda. Although LGB marches do garner a certain degree of media attention, such attention is usually limited and often sensationalized. In any case, media attention cannot be counted upon to accurately reflect an LGB political agenda.

1998 LGB Pride March Sites—United States

Albany, NY	Claremont, CA	Huntsville, AL
Albuquerque, NM	Cleveland, OH	Hyannis, MA
Allendale, MI	Columbus, OH	Indianapolis, IN
Anchorage, AK	Dallas, TX	Iowa City, IO
Asbury Park, NJ	David, CA	Jacksonville, FL
Atlanta, GA	Dayton, OH	Kansas City, MO
Augusta, ME	Denver, CO	Kapa'a Kaua'i, HI
Baltimore, MD	Detroit, MI	Knoxville, TN
Bangor, ME	Disney World, FL	Lansing, MI
Berkeley/East Bay,	Elmira, NY	Lawrence, MA
CA	El Paso, TX	Las Vegas, NV
Boise, ID	Eureka/Arcata, CA	Long Beach, CA
Boston, MA	Fairbanks, AK	Los Angeles, CA
Boulder, CO	Flagstaff, AZ	Louisville, KY
Brooklyn, NY	Ft. Lauderdale, FL	Macon, GA
Bronx, NY	Ft. Smith, AR	Manchester, NH
Buffalo, NY	Fresno, CA	Marin County, CA
Burlington, VT	Grand Rapids, CO	Miami, FL
Cape Cod, MA	Greenville, NC	Milwaukee, WI
Cedar Rapids, IO	Hartford, CT	Minneapolis, MN
Charleston, WV	Hollywood, CA	Missoula, MT
Cheyenne, WY	Honolulu, HI	Monterey, CA
Chicago, IL	Houston, TX	Myrtle Beach, SC
Chico, CA	Huntington, NY	Nashville, TN

New Orleans, LA
Northampton, MA
New York/
    Manhattan, NY
Oakland, CA
Oklahoma City,
    OK
Orlando, FL
Palm Springs, CA
Pensacola, FL
Philadelphia, PA
Phoenix, AZ
Portland, ME
Portland, OR
Providence, RI
Queens, NY
Riverside/San
    Bernardino,CA
Rochester, NY
Sacramento, CA
Salem, OR
Salt Lake City, UT
San Antonio,TX
San Diego, CA
San Francisco, CA
San Jose, CA
San Juan, PR
San Luis Obispo,
    CA
Santa Barbara, CA
Santa Cruz, CA
Santa Fe, NM
Santa Rosa, CA
Sarasota, FL
Seattle, WA
Simi Valley, CA
St. Louis, MI
Syracuse, NY
Tacoma, WA
Tallahassee, FL
Tampa Bay, FL
Toledo, OH

Tucson, AZ
University Park, PA
Visalia, CA
Washington, DC
West Palm Beach,
    FL
Wichita, KS
Wilmington, DE
Worcester, MA

Source: "World-Wide
    Pride" (1998) *The
    Jersey Gaze*, p. 32.

Canada:
Barrie, Ontario
Calgary, Alberta
Edmonton,
    Alberta
Halifax, Nova
    Scotia
Kelowna, B.C.
Kitchener, Ontario
London, Ontario
Ottawa, Ontario
Prince George,
    B.C.
Sudbury, Ontario
Toronto, Ontario
Vancouver, B.C.
Victoria, B.C.
Windsor, Ontario
Winnipeg,
    Manitoba

Europe:
Amsterdam,
    Netherlands
Belfast, Northern
    Ireland
Berlin, Germany
Beilefeld,
    Germany

Birmingham,
    England
Bordeaux, France
Brighton, England
Brno, Czech
    Republic
Brussels, Belgium
Budapest,
    Hungary
Cannes, France
Cologne,
    Germany
Copenhagen,
    Denmark
Derry, Ireland
Dresden,
    Germany
Dressau, Germany
Dublin, Ireland
Frankfurt/Oder,
    Germany
Frankfurt,
    Germany
Freidrichshafen,
    Germany
Stockholm,
    Sweden
Glasgow, Scotland
Hamburg,
    Germany
Helsinki, Finland
Lausanne,
    Switzerland
Leeds, England
Lille, France
Lisbon, Portugal
London, England
Lyon, France
Madrid, Spain
Manchester,
    England
Marseilles, France

Montpellier,
France
Munich, Germany
Nantes, France
Neubrandenburg,
Germany
Newcastle,
England
Oldenburg,
Germany
Paris, France
Rennes, France
Rome, Italy
Strasbourg, France
Toulouse, France
Valletta, Malta
Vienna, Austria
Zurich,
Switzerland

Latin America:
Asuncion,
Paraguay
Bogota, Colombia
Buenos Aires,
Argentina
Curatiba, Brazil
Lima, Peru
Mexicali, Mexico
Montevideo,
Uruguay
Rosario, Argentina
Santiago de Chile,
Argentina
Tijuana, Mexico

*Asia, Africa, and
Australia:*
Adelaide, Australia

Auckland, New
Zealand
Brisbane, Australia
Haifa, Israel
Harare, Zimbabwe
Jerusalem, Israel
Johannesburg, S.
Africa
Melbourne,
Australia
Perth, Australia
Sydney, Australia
Tel Aviv, Israel
Wellington, New
Zealand

Source: "World-Wide
Pride" (1998) *The
Jersey Gaze,* p. 32.

Groups Listed as Participants in Pride Marches in Asbury Park, New Jersey, and in Brooklyn, New York

*Asbury Park,
New Jersey*

ACLU-NJ
African American
Lesbians United
Bisexual Network
of New Jersey
Dignity New
Brunswick
Gay Circles
Gay Activist
Alliance in
Morris County
(GAAMC)
Gay and Lesbian
Community
Center of NJ

Gay and Lesbian
Youth in New
Jersey
Gay, Lesbian,
Bisexual Youth
Group
Gay Officers
Action League
(GOAL)
Green Party
Human Rights
Campaign
Integrity
Lambda Families
of New Jersey
Metropolitan
Community

Church of
Christ the
Liberator
Monmouth
Transgendered
Group
New Jersey
Lesbian and
Gay Coalition/
Personal
Liberty Fund
New Jersey's
Lesbian and
Gay Havurah
Prevention
Resource
Network

Pride Center of
New Jersey
Rainbow Place of
New Jersey
Same-Sex
Marriage Task
Force
Staten Island AIDS
Task Force
Trenton Gay and
Lesbian Civic
Association

Source: "World-Wide
Pride" (1998) *The
Jersey Gaze,* p. 32.

Brooklyn, New York

African Ancestral
Lesbians United
for Societal
Change
Asian and Pacific
Islander
Coalition on
HIV/AIDS
Asian Lesbians of
the East Coast
Audre Lorde
Project
Beyond Words
Book Group
Bronx Lavender
Community
Center
Bronx Lesbians
United in
Sisterhood
Bronx Pride
Brooklyn PFLAG

Center for Anti-
Violence
Education
Coalition of Latina
and Latino
Lesbians and
Gays
Colombian Gay
and Lesbian
Association
Dignity Brooklyn
Dignity New York
District Council
37-AFSCME
Empire State Pride
Agenda
Front Runners
Gay and Lesbian
Arab Society
Gay Asian and
Pacific Islander
Men of NY
Gay Men of
African Descent
Gay Men of the
Bronx
Gay Men's Health
Crisis
Gay Officer's
Action League
GRIOT Circle
Heritage of Pride
Jason, The Musical
Ignite
Entertainment
Kilawin Kolektibo
Las Buenas Amigas
Latino Gay Men of
New York
Latinos and
Latinas de
Ambiente, NY

Lavender Light
Gospel Choir
Lesbian and Gay
Big Apple Corps
LGB People of
Downstate
Men of All Colors
Together
Men of Color
AIDS
Prevention
Unit,
NYC Dept. of
Health
Metropolitan
Community
Church of NY
Minority Task
Force on AIDS
NYC Gay and
Lesbian Anti-
Violence
Project
Park Slope Safe
Homes Project
Passing Twice
People of Color
AIDS Service
Organization
People of Color in
Crisis
Personal Personals
Pride At Work
Puerto Rican
Initiative to
Develop
Empowerment
Queens Pride
Queer "N" Asian
Groups
Radical Faeries

Robert Boston
Performances
Shades of
Lavender
Sirens Motorcycle
Club
Sistahs in Search
of Truth,

Alliance, and
Harmony
South Asian
Lesbian and
Gay Association
Stonewall
Veterans
Association

Unity Fellowship
Church of
Christ/ NYC
WKTU Radio

Source: Brooklyn Pride, 1998

References and Further Reading

American Educational Gender Information Service (AEGIS). n.d. *Transgender: What Is It?* Decatur, GA: AEGIS.

Bailey, Robert W. 1998. *Out and Voting: The Gay, Lesbian, and Bisexual Vote in Congressional House Elections, 1990–1996.* New York: National Gay and Lesbian Task Force Policy Institute.

Blasius, Mark. 1994. *Gay and Lesbian Politics: Sexuality and the Emergence of a New Ethic.* Philadelphia: Temple University Press.

D'Emilio, John. 1983. *Sexual Politics, Sexual Communities: The Making of a Homosexual Minority in the United States, 1940–1970.* Chicago: University of Chicago Press.

DeMotier, Beren. 1998. "The 'T' in LGBT." [Letter to the editor.] *New York Blade News* (3 July).

Gemerek, Keith. 1998. "Writer's Comfort Came from Others' Struggle." [Letter to the editor.] *New York Blade News* (10 July): 17.

Golden, Howard. 1998. Proclamation: Second Annual Brooklyn Pride Parade Day. Proclamation by the Office of the Borough President, Borough of Brooklyn, City of New York. Reprinted in *Brooklyn Pride, 1998.*

Hertzog, Mark. 1996. *The Lavender Vote: Lesbians, Gay Men, and Bisexuals in American Electoral Politics.* New York: New York University Press.

Hogan, Steve, and Lee Hudson. 1998. *Completely Queer: The Gay and Lesbian Encyclopedia.* New York: Henry Holt.

Hrebenar, Ronald J. 1997. *Interest Groups Politics in America.* 3d ed. Armonk, NY: M. E. Sharpe.

Kirk, Marshall, and Kirk Madsen. 1989. *After the Ball: How America Will Conquer Its Fear and Hatred of Gays in the 90's.* New York: Plume.

"Let the Dykes March." 1998. *Philadelphia Gay News* (29 May–4 June): 10.

Low, Halley. 1998. "Transgender Column Was Hateful Bigotry." [Letter to the editor.] *New York Blade News* (10 July): 17.

Murray, Stephen O. 1996. *American Gay.* Chicago: University of Chicago Press.

Sherrill, Kenneth. 1996. "The Political Power of Lesbians, Gays, and Bisexuals. *Political Science and Politics* (September): 469–473.

Sullivan, Andrew. 1995. *Virtually Normal: An Argument about Homosexuality.* New York: Alfred A. Knopf.

Vaid, Urvashi. 1995. *Virtual Equality: The Mainstreaming of Gay and Lesbian Liberation.* New York: Anchor Books.

Wilchins, Riki Anne. 1997. *Read My Lips: Sexual Subversion and the End of Gender.* Ithaca, NY: Firebrand Books.

Wong, Alice. 1998. "Why Do Parents March?" *Brooklyn Pride:* 37.

Yang, Alan. 1998. *From Wrongs to Rights.* New York: National Gay and Lesbian Task Force Policy Institute.

2

Protest Politics

As with many marginalized populations, political participation among lesbian, gay, bisexual, and transgender (LGBT) people (as *openly* LGBT people) of necessity began outside the political system proper. Indeed, at least until the 1990s, LGBT politics was virtually synonymous with protest politics. The modern LGBT movement as a whole regards as its foundational event the now-legendary Stonewall Riots of June 27–29, 1969. Another signature form of LGBT protest was launched on the first anniversary of the riots. These are the sometimes raucous parades, called pride marches, that have been held in increasing numbers every year since. In a more self-consciously political mode, LGBT communities have also organized four mass marches on Washington, in 1979, 1987, 1993, and 2000, each stressing a different theme of the day. Finally, the smallest but most targeted protest activities of the LGBT movement have been demonstrations and direct actions, small-scale protests on a particular subject and focused on a particular narrow audience. The first part of this chapter reviews the history of these forms of protest; the second part then turns to a more in-depth examination of the signature form of LGBT protest politics, the annual pride march, reviewing how and why the phenomenon of pride marches expanded nationally and internationally, and presents new data on why individuals choose to participate in this form of protest politics.

A History of LGBT Protest Politics

This section offers a brief chronological history of LGBT protest politics as it has been conducted through the major periods of modern LGBT political history: the Stonewall period, the gay liberation era of the 1970s, the AIDS activism of the 1980s, and the turn to the mainstream of the 1990s. A case study of each of these three types of protest politics is offered, one drawn from each of the three post-Stonewall decades.

The Stonewall Riots and Their Aftermath

Although many of the historical details of the Stonewall Riots are disputed, the essential facts were captured in the *New York Times* of June 28, 1969: "Hundreds of young men went on a rampage in Greenwich Village shortly after 3 A.M. yesterday after a force of plain-clothesmen raided a bar that the police said was well known for its homosexual clientele. . . . The young men threw bricks, bottles, garbage, pennies and a parking meter at the policemen, who had a search warrant authorizing them to investigate reports that liquor was sold illegally at the bar, the Stonewall Inn, 53 Christopher Street just off Sheridan Square."

Although the *Times*'s version is factually accurate, it provides no sense of the historic import of the event. Ironically, the mocking coverage of the same day's *New York Daily News* actually captured the event more accurately: "Queen power reared its bleached-blonde head in revolt. New York City experienced its first homosexual riot. . . . The crowd began to get out of hand, eye witnesses said. Then, without warning, a gay atomic bomb. Queens, princesses, and ladies-in-waiting began hurling anything they could lay their polished, manicured fingernails on. . . . The war was on. The lilies of the valley had become carnivorous jungle plants."

As John D'Emilio (1983) and others have noted, gay bar patrons had previously resisted police, notably in Los Angeles, San Francisco, and Berkeley—all to little lasting effect. By contrast, the Stonewall Riots provoked three additional nights of clashes with police, and, most importantly, galvanized an LGBT population already radicalized by the black liberation, women's, antiwar, and New Left movements of the 1960s. Unlike any previous event in LGBT history, the riots led to a cascade of organized activities that quickly radiated out from the

New York epicenter, due in part to the concentration of the U.S. media in New York.

Thus, in the waning months of the 1960s, the movement for "gay liberation" was begun. In a precursor of future LGBT pride marches, a group of 500 demonstrators marched down Christopher Street on July 2 to protest the raid of the Stonewall. The radical Gay Liberation Front (GLF) was founded in New York, which rejected the conciliatory incrementalism of the old homophile groups. In November Gay Liberation Front activists joined hundreds of thousands of antiwar demonstrators in Washington, D.C. December brought the launching of a Gay Liberation Front chapter in Chicago, even as the new movement's first schism occurred when the Gay Activist Alliance (GAA) split off from GLF.

When New York police raided another gay bar, the Snake Pit, a mere nine months after Stonewall, some 500 GLF activists gathered almost immediately to protest. In April the GAA sponsored its first "zap" (i.e., disruption of a political event) by heckling New York Mayor John Lindsay, while the GLF protested the presentation of a paper at the American Psychiatric Association meeting on the use of electroshock aversion therapy to treat homosexuality. In May, at the Second Congress to Unite Women, lesbian feminists protested homophobia in the National Organization for Women, and a newly formed group called Radicalesbians issued a manifesto on "woman-identified women."

In all, less than a year had passed since the Stonewall Riots, but a decisive break with the closeted, clandestine past had occurred throughout the LGBT movement. Another major development occurred when, on the first anniversary of Stonewall, LGBT activists in New York, and to a lesser extent in Chicago, Los Angeles, and San Francisco, held commemorative street marches. Although generally referred to as "liberation" or "freedom" marches at the time, they evolved into the pride marches that have been held annually throughout the nation since 1970.

The 1970s: The Period of "Gay Liberation"

For the LGBT community, the 1970s was a heady period, and the pride marches of the day reflected the priorities and perspective of the times. At least in certain enclaves in the largest cities, a public LGBT community emerged that could wield a degree of both political and economic clout. Gay men, in particular, formed a new sexual culture built around bars and bathhouses that pushed the possibilities of the sexual revolution to its bacchanalian heights (or depths, depending upon one's perspective). Lesbians remained a cornerstone of a burgeoning feminist movement that it seemed might actually "level the patriarchy" and achieve the full emancipation of women.

Amidst such feelings of both confidence and celebration, LGBT protest politics took on an increasingly outrageous tone, pushing sexual and gender boundaries and violating taboos as an end in itself. The staid picket lines of the early homophile movement had required men to don business suits and women to wear long-hemmed dresses, but pride marches and other forms of protest politics encouraged the shocking, uninhibited, and exhibitionistic.

It is in this context that LGBT pride marches became entrenched as fixtures in the major cities of the United States. On the last weekend of each June marches have taken place in New York, Chicago, Los Angeles, San Francisco, and other large cities. For instance, from humble beginnings in 1970, the San Francisco "Gay Freedom Day" march grew to 50,000 in 1972, then to an estimated 200,000 in 1977, and 350,000 in 1978, by which time it was the largest LGBT march in the United States (Stryker and van Buskirk 1996). By the late 1970s LGBT communities in many smaller cities and states began a new tradition of separate, smaller marches on other weekends in June.

Of course, LGBT protest was not limited to one day a year. Throughout the decade, smaller demonstrations and direct actions were carried out that were often stunning in their boldness. Prior to Stonewall, perhaps the largest-scale forms of LGBT political protest had been the small, orderly picket lines held at Independence Hall in Philadelphia each July 4. But over the course of the 1970s, LGBT protest became increasingly bold. In March 1971 some 2,000 activists protested anti-LGBT New York State laws in a rally in Albany. The battle shifted to the New York City Council in 1974, which would remain the target of protests until 1985. These and dozens of other small protests had a powerful impact, as a series of anti-LGBT laws and policies were overturned throughout the decade, including the decriminalization of consensual same-sex acts in a dozen states; passage of the first laws prohibiting anti-LGBT discrimination; the election of the first openly LGBT political figures; and the launching of numerous new LGBT political groups, including the National Gay (and later, National Gay and Lesbian) Task Force.

Still, one of the most painful and best-documented protests occurred in the waning months of the decade, when Dan White, the murderer of openly gay San Francisco supervisor Harvey Milk, was convicted only of manslaughter rather than murder. White had clearly premeditated the murder of two of his political opponents, Mayor George Moscone and Milk, and deprived the LGBT community of perhaps its single most important leader. A massive spontaneous candlelight march was organized from the LGBT neighborhood, the Castro, to City Hall where rioting broke out and continued throughout the night, with windows smashed and fires set.

Following on the heels of the Milk murder and a vociferous anti-LGBT "Save Our Children" campaign headed by the singer Anita Bryant, there came in 1979 an entirely new type of LGBT protest drawing upon the archetype of the 1963 March on Washington for Jobs and Freedom. At that event, tens of thousands of African Americans and other supporters of the civil rights movement had gathered on the National Mall to hear speakers, including most notably the Reverend Martin Luther King Jr. Although protest marches and demonstrations had been a mainstay of the civil rights movement in cities throughout the segregated South, the March on Washington for Jobs and Freedom was an event of a distinct kind, designed expressly to mobilize massive numbers to converge simultaneously at one location.

The March on Washington for Jobs and Freedom was a galvanizing event in the struggle for civil rights and also a profound influence on other major movements of the decade. The 1960s would later see marches for women's liberation, which created momentum for the ultimately failed Equal Rights Amendment to the Constitution. Likewise, marches and rallies against the Vietnam War were integral components of the decade's larger New Left and youth empowerment movements, which resulted, for instance, in the lowering of the voting age to eighteen through the enactment of the Twenty-sixth Amendment in 1971.

Thus, it was perhaps inevitable that the model of LGBT pride marches as well as other civil rights marches would eventually be merged into an LGBT march on Washington. Organized by numerous and fractious grassroots committees, the 1979 march may well have been made possible by the galvanizing effect of the Milk assassination. In the end, that October over 100,000 protestors from every state and ten foreign countries descended upon Washington, D.C., to mark what was only the tenth anniversary of Stonewall. In retrospect, the 1979 march represented the high point of pre-AIDS LGBT political activism. The appearance of the AIDS epidemic as a classic "exogenous shock"—wholly unexpected and unanticipated—a mere twenty months later would radically reshape LGBT politics.

The 1980s: The Plague Years

In the first editorial of 1980 in the LGBT newsmagazine *The Advocate,* editor David Goodstein could write, "I foresee that the next ten years will be the best in the history of humankind" (Thompson 1994, 195). Such optimism would prove to be unfounded, particularly for the many gay men who by the summer of 1981 had begun to take sick and die of a previously unknown immune disorder. The disease, soon named acquired immunodeficiency syndrome (AIDS), was to make an indelible impact on the course of the LGBT movement, marked most of all by a quickly mounting death toll. As of mid-June 1982, 184 people had died of AIDS; by the end of 1984 the number was 7,699; by June 1987 the number had reached 20,849. The large majority of those dying were gay or bisexual men, many from the urban neighborhoods that were the mainstays of the gay movement. Although lesbians had not been infected with HIV in comparably large numbers, they shared a great deal of the stigma of AIDS, while seeing much of the earlier promise of the women's movement dashed by the "Reagan revolution" of the early 1980s.

At LGBT pride marches the confident and celebratory mood of the 1970s soon gave way to a siege mentality in which the LGBT community felt attacked not only by the AIDS virus but also by an increasingly homophobic general population. Inevitably, the epidemic added a somber new note to the annual pride events:

> AIDS service and volunteer organizations are featured prominently in the floats and walking contingents in most of these parades. Protest groups carry placards and banners with AIDS slogans, adding a militant dimension to the events. In many parades, it has been customary to include a moment of silence in memory of those who have died of AIDS, sometimes followed by a "moment of rage" designed as a cathartic release of anger and sorrow. (Smith 1998, 343)

Likewise, the second LGBT March on Washington, held on October 11, 1987, took as its theme the need for action around the AIDS epidemic and featured the largest mass civil disobedience event since the Vietnam War, as well as the first unfolding of the full AIDS Memorial Quilt on the National Mall. The occurrence of that march in October led to the designation of that month as Lesbian and Gay History Month at many colleges and universities and of October 11 as "National Coming Out Day." (Some cities, particularly in areas with hot summers, also choose to hold their pride events in October rather than

June.) Yet if pride marches were the preeminent form of LGBT protest expression in the 1970s, it was undoubtedly AIDS-targeted demonstrations and direct actions that best characterize the 1980s. Indeed, throughout the decade, LGBT protest was essentially synonymous with AIDS protest, which was itself was virtually synonymous with one group, the AIDS Coalition to Unleash Power or ACT UP.

Case Study: The Direct Action of ACT UP

Many speeches, protests, and meetings had come before it, but just as a single atom begets a nuclear explosion when it tips the balance of radioactive material into critical mass, something incredible happened in the history of the LGBT movement in March 1987.

Six years into the AIDS epidemic, the general population had finally begun to pay attention—but not in the ways that most activists had hoped. Public opinion polls revealed a skyrocketing of homophobic attitudes. Right-wing pundits clamored for mandatory testing and compulsory quarantine. The Supreme Court halted a decades-long trend of expanding personal freedoms by upholding the constitutionality of antisodomy laws.

Amidst this ferment, the playwright, novelist, and activist Larry Kramer, a controversial firebrand, gave a historic speech in early March 1987 at the Lesbian and Gay Community Services Center in New York's Greenwich Village. In his speech, Kramer caught the attention of the audience by declaring that most of them might be dead in five years, and then asked a simple, pointed question: "Do we want to start a new organization devoted solely to political action?" The answer would soon prove to be a resounding yes.

Kramer's speech in 1987 had a galvanizing effect similar to that of the Stonewall Riots among a population of sick, dying, frightened, and dispirited people. A few days later, some 300 activists attended the first meeting of the newly founded "AIDS Network," soon to be renamed the AIDS Coalition to Unleash Power, or more commonly by the descriptive acronym ACT UP. By month's end it had organized its first action.

The flyer for the first ACT UP action (which is reprinted in the appendices of this volume), began "NO MORE BUSINESS AS USUAL!— Come to Wall Street in front of Trinity Church at 7 AM Tuesday March 24 for a MASSIVE AIDS DEMONSTRATION" to demand "immediate release by the Federal Food & Drug Administration of drugs that might help save our lives," as well as the "immediate abolishment of cruel double-blind studies wherein some get the new drugs and some don't," and "immediate release of these drugs to everyone with AIDS." It also called for the immediate availability of the drugs at affordable prices; immediate massive public education to stop the spread of AIDS; an immediate policy to prohibit discrimination in treatment, insurance, employment, and housing of HIV-infected people; and the immediate establishment of a coordinated, comprehensive, and compassionate national policy on AIDS. It concluded: "President Reagan, nobody is in charge! AIDS IS THE BIGGEST KILLER IN NEW YORK CITY OF YOUNG MEN AND WOMEN. Tell your friends. Spread the word. Come protest together . . . AIDS IS EVERYBODY'S BUSINESS NOW." The sponsoring organization was identified as the AIDS Network, "an ad hoc and broad-based community of AIDS-related organizations and individuals."

This inaugural protest set up the confrontational tenor and tone that would become ACT UP's hallmark, as well as several important tactical and organizational precedents. "For example, no permit was sought or provided for the demonstration. Police responded by immediately barricading the picket and limiting its movement. By pre-arranged agreement, however, several volunteers swung into the traffic lanes in an attempt to block cars and trucks from entering Wall Street. The news media was thereby provided with images of 'homosexuals' being handcuffed and dragged into police custody" (Medley 1998, 172).

Subsequent ACT UP meetings in New York would draw as many as 800 people attracted to the organization's central goal of being a "diverse, non-partisan group united in anger and commitment to direct action to end the AIDS crisis." Just as in the case of Stonewall, news radiated out from New York, the nation's largest city and its media capital. Early in 1988, chapters were founded in Boston, Chicago, Los Angeles, and San Francisco. Within two years there would be over a hundred ACT UP chapters throughout the world, sponsoring demonstrations, media campaigns, and other forms of direct action on topics such as drug pricing and access, funding, research, and accurate media coverage. Even amidst an organization so decentralized, a number of major coordinated events stand out as the most important demonstrations, including:

- A "No to *Cosmo*" picketing of *Cosmopolitan* magazine by the ACT UP Women's Caucus for downplaying the risk of HIV to heterosexual women
- A one-day shutdown of the FDA involving more than 1,000 protestors and a takeover of the U.S. headquarters of the pharmaceutical company Burroughs-Wellcome

- A highly controversial "Stop the Church" protest of more than 4,500 at St. Patrick's Cathedral against Catholic opposition to condom distribution and safer-sex education, during which several demonstrators entered the cathedral itself
- Several "political funerals" of people who had died of AIDS, including an "Ashes Action" during which cremated remains were scattered on the lawn of the White House.

A combination of desperation, irreverence, and theatricality, ACT UP would go on to be perhaps the most important new social movement of the decade—controversial, innovative, media savvy, chaotic, and, ultimately, remarkably effective.

The 1990s: A New Assimilationism?

Into the 1990s AIDS remained a major theme at LGBT demonstrations and marches, but by 1993 ACT UP had peaked, as evidenced by the creation of a less militant splinter group called the Treatment Action Group (TAG). Likewise, dramatic advances in anti-HIV medications after 1996 led to declining death rates and a lifting of much of the sense of communal calamity among LGBT people. Although some subgroups, particularly gay men of color, remained disproportionately affected by HIV/AIDS, as the so-called early crisis phase of AIDS in the LGBT community appeared to pass, attention returned to more general issues. Other than important AIDS demonstrations held in the 1990s, for instance, one of the decade's most significant moments of LGBT political protest followed the murder in 1998 of Wyoming college student Matthew Shepherd. The young, frail Shepherd had been violently attacked, tied to a fence, and left to die at least in part because of his sexual orientation. There ensued a wave of candlelight vigils, memorial services, and even a raucous street demonstration calling for hate crimes legislation that snarled traffic in Lower Manhattan—protests held with an intensity unseen since the height of AIDS activism.

Similarly, most pride marches in the 1990s no longer carried on the outrageousness of the 1970s or the somberness of the 1980s. Writing in 1998 about pride marches, *Philadelphia Gay News* Associate Editor Kevin D. Melrose wrote that "[n]early three decades after the fight for civil rights became a full-fledged movement, gays and lesbians are still grappling with the significance of pride and, perhaps more importantly, how it should be expressed. In some respects, a need for visibility has been replaced by a desire for acceptance, and a demonstration of outrage by a celebration of culture" (Melrose 1998, 1). Gay cultural commentator Daniel Harris has complained that the events have lost touch with their protest roots, with the San Francisco march becoming "this sort of civic procession for all these city councilmen and the mayor, and all of these people who want to assure gay people how much they liked us" (1). Urvashi Vaid of the National Gay and Lesbian Task Force urges a reorientation of the events toward transformative politics: "I think there's a need for a political action that's focused around lesbian, gay, bisexual, and trans realities. The vision that we have for the society—those are the things I'd like to see at pride celebrations" (1). Yet in the 1990s pride marches often lacked any such coherent vision or purpose, and attempts to imbue them with one often failed, as was the case with a 1994 march for the twenty-fifth anniversary of Stonewall, in which the intended focus on international LGBT rights was lost in a wash of consumer items and the quadrennial Olympics-style "Gay Games."

In all, the topics of the highest-profile LGBT protests in the mid- to late-1990s involved attempts by LGBT individuals to gain access to some of the most conservative institutions in mainstream society. A Christian LGBT group called Soul Force exhorted the Reverend Jerry Falwell to moderate his homophobic rhetoric, while protestors within mainline Protestant denominations called for ordination of openly LGBT ministers and recognition of committed same-sex unions. Picketers visited offices of the Boy Scouts of America after that organization went all the way to the Supreme Court to successfully enforce a policy excluding openly gay scouts and scoutmasters. Perhaps most acrimonious of all were the debates over allowing lesbians and gay men to serve openly in the U.S. military and over opening the institution of marriage to same-sex couples. These questions of "gays in the military" and "gay marriage" were major focuses of the 1993 and 2000 Marches on Washington.

Case Studies: The 1993 and 2000 Marches on Washington

The 1993 March on Washington was held just six years after the 1987 march, but circumstances had changed markedly. Perhaps most importantly, twelve years of rule by the Republican Reagan and Bush administrations, which had been perceived as highly hostile to LGBT rights, had given way to the much friendlier Democratic administration of Bill Clinton. Further, much of the hysteria around AIDS had peaked in the late 1980s, and activists had succeeded to a striking degree in achieving their goals, including legal protection of people with HIV/AIDS from discrimination through the Americans with Disabilities Act and funding for HIV/AIDS treatment through the Ryan White CARE Act.

Nonetheless, there was frustration in some quarters that after more than a decade of rearguard actions, forward progress on LGBT issues could not be more quickly achieved. Clinton pleased many activists by including mention of LGBT people in his campaign, including even the speech accepting his nomination as president by the Democratic Party, and appointing a number of LGBT individuals to high positions in the federal government. However, Clinton's attempt to reverse the military policy that prohibited openly LGBT people from serving in the U.S. armed forces ignited a firestorm of protest from conservatives inside and outside the military. Congress, although controlled by Democrats, threatened to write the ban directly into federal law and there was no comparable groundswell of support from a left wing that was ambivalent in its feelings about the armed forces in general.

Thus the 1993 march turned out to be neither a celebration of advances nor a condemnation of Clinton, who was out of Washington that day. At the time of the march, the final "don't ask, don't tell" policy for the military had not yet been decided, and so the mood of the entire event was tentative. Of course, AIDS issues were addressed, and the march reportedly had an important galvanizing effect for many individuals and small LGBT organizations, especially those from outside the largest cities. But the focus fostered by the "Save Our Children" campaign and Harvey Milk assassination in 1979 and the AIDS epidemic in 1987 was not recaptured in 1993.

Far more contentious was the next LGBT march on Washington, dubbed the "Millennium March" of April 2000. Although never adopted formally as a theme, "Faith and Family" was widely circulated as the slogan for the event. Given that many LGBT people have felt rejected by and are estranged from both their faiths and their families, this initial emphasis inflicted damage on the Millennium March from which it would never recover. The damage was compounded when the two lead organizations, the Metropolitan Community Church (MCC), an LGBT Christian denomination, and the Human Rights Campaign (HRC) were perceived as imposing the agenda for the march from the "top down" in contrast to the more disorganized but genuinely grassroots organizing for the previous marches.

Early in the process, a number of other organizations, including some representing LGBT ethnic/racial minorities, were asked to sign on as cosponsors of the event but then felt that they had been added as "tokens" to demonstrate wide-ranging support. An overly assimilationist approach was seen in the decision to exclude even the words "lesbian, gay, bisexual, or transgender" from the official title of the march, which was at one point planned not as a march at all, but simply a mass rally on the National Mall. Perhaps the most serious blow came when the Human Rights Campaign, a Washington, D.C.–based national lobby, endorsed the Republican senator from New York, Alphonse D'Amato, for reelection despite strong opposition from within the New York LGBT community. An "Ad Hoc" Committee for an Open Process developed, at first to protest and later to call for an outright boycott of the Millennium March.

Deprived of the support of New York City, one of the most important bases for any LGBT action on the East Coast, the Millennium March suffered further by contrast, and to some extent in competition, with a 1999 event called "Equality Begins at Home." Held in March 1999 under the leadership of the more left-leaning and grassroots National Gay and Lesbian Task Force, the Equality Begins at Home events included lobbying, socializing, and educational and other activities chosen by local activists in the capital city and/or major city of every U.S. state.

The Millennium March did ultimately take place, and had a respectable attendance level, particularly among people from outside the largest cities. Nonetheless, the rifts between the national-level sponsors and many state and local organizations were not easily healed, and the situation was complicated by a money embezzlement scandal afterwards. One common critique after the event was that it might be the last national march of its type, that state- and local-level action might henceforth be more appropriate given the expansion and diversification of LGBT communities in the nation. Other lessons regarded the continuing need for broad and deep support for coordinated national-level action, as well as a compelling cause around which LGBT people might develop a consensus for action.

The Logic of Protest: LGBT Pride Marches

The survey above of the history of LGBT protest politics in the first part of this chapter was intended to provide a broad historical overview. Part two below provides a more analytical view focused on the signature form of LGBT protest, the pride march. This form of protest was chosen for study because, unlike demonstrations, the marches occur on a regular, structured basis and not simply sporadically in response to specific events. Also, unlike marches on Washington, these events occur frequently enough and in enough locations to allow for a diversity of examples. The first section below examines the remarkable expansion of pride marches and their scope in the late 1990s; the second section explores the ways in which pride marches are politically salient.

The Expansion of Pride Marches

Despite the AIDS epidemic and the gradual turn toward conservatism in society as a whole, pride marches have not only continued in the largest cities but also proliferated in smaller cities and even some suburban and rural areas in the United States and abroad. Indeed, by 1983 LGBT pride marches had spread far enough to warrant the creation of the International Association of Lesbian/Gay Pride Coordinators (IAL/GPC), a nonprofit organization of representatives of sixty cities worldwide that sponsor pride events. The group has sponsored an international conference each October to "conduct corporate business, discuss future plans, political concerns, merchandising, operations, logistics, for the planning of a variety of Gay Pride events that are held around the globe" (IAL/GPC website, www.interpride. com). The group also has chosen a theme each year, which in 1998 was "Unity through Diversity."

The IAL/GPC's official listings of pride events indicated that in 1998 such events were scheduled for 203 locations throughout the world (World-Wide Pride 1998). More than half of these events (116) were scheduled for sites in the United States. These events vary enormously in size, from large estimates of about half a million or more in the biggest cities to just a few hundred participants in the smallest locales. Most, although not all, of these events are scheduled during June and involve an actual march through the streets of the city. However, an unspecified number occur in other months and may involve rallies, festivals, and other activities without an actual processional-type march. Moreover, it is possible that additional events have been held that for some reason have not been included on the IAL/GPC list. Therefore, a complete listing of pride events might be larger than this list. Overall, the IAL/GPC estimated that, in 1996, some 10 to 12 million people worldwide participated in LGBT pride events.

In the United States the truly nationwide scope of LGBT pride marches can be seen by the fact that a total of forty-five states are represented on the listing—every state except three sparsely populated plains states (Nebraska, North Dakota, and South Dakota) and two Southern states (Virginia and Mississippi). Among the states, the largest number of events was scheduled for California (twenty-five), followed by New York (ten), Florida (nine), and Massachusetts (seven).

The list of U.S. locations includes many of the urban locales that might be expected. Indeed, pride events were scheduled for all but five of the largest forty cities in the United States—the exceptions being Tulsa, Oklahoma; Memphis, Tennessee; Austin, Texas; Virginia Beach, Virginia; and Ft. Worth, Texas. (Of these five cities, four were within same-day driving distance to pride events in other cities in the same state.) Also of note is that nearly half (twenty-three) of state capitals were the site of a pride march, including such small cities as Boise, Idaho; Augusta, Maine; Salem, Oregon; Charleston, West Virginia; and Cheyenne, Wyoming. In addition, events were listed for the nation's capital, Washington, D.C.; and San Juan, capital of the U.S. commonwealth of Puerto Rico.

Among U.S. metropolitan areas, as designated by the U.S. census, all twenty-one areas with a population over 2 million hosted a pride event. Of the twenty-two areas with between 1 and 2 million residents, seventeen (77 percent) sponsored a pride event. In addition, of the twenty-six metropolitan areas between 600,000 and 1 million in population, fifteen (58 percent) sponsored pride events. A number of metropolitan areas sponsored more than one pride event, including four separate marches in the New York City area (in the boroughs of Manhattan, Queens, Brooklyn, and Bronx); six in Greater Los Angeles (Claremont, Long Beach, Los Angeles/West Hollywood, Orange County, Riverside/San Bernardino, and Simi Valley); and four in the San Francisco Bay area (Berkeley, Marin County, Oakland, and San Francisco).

Less extensive, but still striking has been the spread of pride marches to other countries. Canada leads the rest of the world with pride marches in fifteen cities in five of the ten provinces, including five provincial capitals. Europe was led by Germany (eleven events), followed by France (ten), and the United Kingdom (eight). Overall, thirteen of the fifteen members of the European Union hold pride events (all except Luxembourg and Greece), with the capital city of each of the thirteen hosting an event. Four other European countries host pride events, as do five cities in Australia, three in Israel, three in

Argentina, two in New Zealand, and two in Mexico. In addition, pride events are held in five other countries in Latin America and two countries in sub-Saharan Africa.

Although the specifics vary, the typical march involves a line-up of different types of LGBT groups, each composing a separate contingent that may carry banners or placards. The larger marches also include parade-type floats, often featuring performers. The march usually sets off around noon, or another predetermined time, and generally proceeds either out of or toward an established LGBT neighborhood, passing spectators and sometimes a formal reviewing stand along the way. Most marches end near a festival, street fair, or other gathering where participants can spend the rest of the afternoon.

A wide variety of different groups participate, for example: community groups, including community centers that are designed to serve the entire LGBT population in a given area; constituency groups that serve only some subpopulation, particularly ethnic or racial groups; religious groups; health concerns groups, including those focused on HIV/AIDS; overtly political groups; social groups built around common recreational activities; and arts and entertainment groups. Although these groups do overlap considerably (e.g., many HIV/AIDS groups target specific ethnicities; many constituency groups are also partly social or political), these categories provide a sense of the makeup of the overall marches.

Much like an ethnic group that has come of age, LGBT people have begun to seek a "place at the table" of the political process. Pride marches may be communal cultural celebrations, but they are also incontrovertibly political events. At the most basic level, marches forcefully assert the community's fundamental right to a public presence. A community that has traditionally been rendered invisible is in full view on at least this one day; individuals who have historically been forced into isolation gather together in solidarity. In this regard, LGBT people are much like any other minority group seeking to make claims on the dominant culture, a slot on the agenda of the larger society. Indeed, Richard Herrell argues that the Chicago LGBT pride march should be understood precisely in the same terms as marches staged by ethnic groups: "The gay and lesbian parade in Chicago has adopted and transformed the parades of 'ethnic groups'—the city's Irish, Polish, Mexicans, Italians, and so forth. 'Ethnicity' has become a model for gays and lesbians who now think of their community as one like other communities in Chicago, like them in having a space and a special parade to claim that space symbolically one day each summer, to express their relative cultural autonomy in the city, and to speak as a community with interests to legislators and other policy makers, but critically different from them in their historical exclusion from normative society" (Herrell 1992, 226).

Contemporary Pride Marches: Five Examples

The tradition of the diffusion of pride marches is reflected in the sites beyond New York City from which new data are presented in Chapter 1 as well as below: the Connecticut state capital, Hartford; the Mid-Atlantic regional hub city of Philadelphia, Pennsylvania; the seaside town of Asbury Park, New Jersey; and the borough of Brooklyn, New York. Following are descriptions of the specific marches, based upon published materials as well as upon direct observations by the author, who attended each of the events in June 1998 and wrote up field notes for each.

Hartford, Connecticut.   Although they are within easy travelling distance of both New York City and Boston, LGB activists in Connecticut launched their own statewide pride event in 1981, meeting in back of the Old Statehouse. From the vantage point of 1998, one founder of the Connecticut pride march recalled, "It may seem hard to understand now, but it took a lot of courage to be there that day. Not just for me, but for a lot of people. In fact, there were people handing out masks for those who wanted to preserve their anonymity" (Downton 1998, 21).

The event is now coordinated by the LGBT group Connecticut PRIDE, which employs a special effort to make the event truly statewide by sponsoring a rally in New Haven the previous weekend and soliciting the involvement of LGBT groups throughout the state. As one organizer noted, "Connecticut might be a small state geographically, but it really is like a clutch of city states. That's one reason that it's somewhat difficult to get everyone together and working towards an event that is truly representative of all the different communities" (Downton 1998, 22).

The 1998 march was held in downtown Hartford rather than the city's LGB neighborhood. Marchers began to gather around 11 A.M. on Saturday, June 20. At noon, the lineup of some fifty marching contingents, including several floats, began to wind through the core of the business district, circling the Old Statehouse, and concluding with a festival in Bushnell Park.

Philadelphia. Begun in 1988, the Philadelphia march sponsored by a group called "Diversity in Pride" was celebrating its tenth anniversary in 1998, with a distinctive rainbow logo inside the figure of the Liberty Bell. Although the nation's first regular LGBT picket lines had once been held at Independence Hall on July 4, Philadelphia has long since been eclipsed as a major site of LGBT activism. Similarly, the city's march is neither a statewide gathering for the geographically dispersed state of Pennsylvania, nor a major East Coast event like the New York march, but focuses primarily on the LGBT population in the city itself and in immediately adjacent sections of New Jersey, Delaware, and Pennsylvania.

With clearing skies and encouraging weather forecasts after several days of rain, marchers began arriving around 10:30 A.M. on Sunday, June 14, with numbers increasing steadily until noon. The marchers lined up on closed-off streets in Center City, a largely LGB-populated area dubbed "The Gayborhood." The march, which included a number of parade floats and performing contingents, proceeded down Chestnut Street past Independence Hall, the Liberty Bell, and other parts of the city's historic district, ending in a festival at Penn's Landing. The parade took about one and a half hours to complete the route, ending around 1:30.

Subsequent press reports indicated that an estimated 35,000 to 45,000 people participated in the march and festival (Melrose 1998). This number is more than some cities attract, but fewer than one-tenth of the number who attended the pride march in 1998 in New York City. Given that the metropolitan population of New York City is only three times larger than Philadelphia's, the latter's march remains an event of modest proportions for the nation's seventh largest city.

Asbury Park, New Jersey. In 1992 members of the New Jersey Gay and Lesbian Coalition adopted the first weekend in June for their statewide event. In a state in which the most influential regional cities, New York and Philadelphia, lie outside state boundaries, the group decided: "We want a parade that is uniquely New Jersey. We want a parade in a venue that is not an impossible commute from the remote regions of the state. We want a parade in a town that has historically been and continues to be gay friendly" (Pople 1998b, 15).

Their choice has been the seaside town of Asbury Park, whose "boardwalks and scenic ocean vistas screamed New Jersey to us," which has a "thriving gay community and supportive city government," and is in a "central Jersey location" (Pople 1998a, 8).

On June 7, 1998, marchers in the Asbury Park event began to congregate about 11 A.M. in a park at the intersection of Main and Sunset Streets, in a neighborhood with a large LGB presence located several blocks away from the Asbury Park boardwalk along the Atlantic Ocean. Contingents began to form shortly before noon, and the march commenced at approximately 12:15. The march proceeded through a park along a lake, through a residential neighborhood, and onto the once-thriving but now largely abandoned boardwalk. The route proceeded down most of the length of the main boardwalk area, then into a park in which a festival was being held.

The 1998 New Jersey State Pride March and its accompanying festival drew some 8,000 participants, according to estimates by organizers, which they said was double the previous year's attendance. Press reports indicated that "[t]hose marching in the parade represented a cross-section of the state's gay community, organizers said. There were outrageously dressed drag queens and leather-clad lesbians on motorcycles along with clergymen and same-sex couples pushing baby carriages. Heterosexual friends and family members from Sussex County to Cape May also came out to support gay relatives" (Heyboer 1998, 19).

Brooklyn. By 1997 the diffusion of pride marches had reached within the major cities. For four years the New York City borough of Queens had been staging its own march, one of many steps taken to emphasize its character separate from the overwhelming influence of Manhattan. In 1997 the borough of Brooklyn made a similar move by launching its own march and multicultural festival, drawing an estimated 10,000 participants, including 68 marching groups and 15 "dignitaries" ("Pride Grows" 1998).

The second annual Brooklyn event in 1998 emphasized local interests, stating its intention to bring "the Borough to the realization that our Gay, Lesbian, Bisexual, and Transgender community is an integral and vibrant part of Brooklyn"("Pride Grows" 1998). One organizer wrote that "[w]hen we march proudly through the streets, your neighbors see that we are not strangers. They see that lesbians, gays, bisexuals, and transgender people are their friends, family members and neighbors. They can actually see us as human beings just like themselves. No longer are we divided into warring camps" (Montana 1998).

The Brooklyn march commenced at Grand Army Plaza in the Park Slope area of the borough, a neighborhood with a large lesbian community. There had been heavy rainfall the previous day and throughout the night. On the morning of Saturday, June 13, the rain had stopped but the skies remained overcast and weather forecasts called for further thunderstorms. Marchers began to arrive in significant numbers at approximately 11 A.M. along the area between the check-in booth and the lineup for the march route, which was along a closed-off road at the edge of the Plaza. By 11:45 A.M. marchers were beginning to assemble at the designated lineup areas. Within a few minutes, however, a full-fledged thunderstorm broke out, pelting the city with an inch and a half of rain—more than the city's usual rainfall for all of June. The Brooklyn event was expected to draw 15,000 to 20,000 participants, but even though the skies did eventually clear, the downpour suppressed turnout at the parade and festival to an estimated 5,000 (Szymanski 1998).

New York City.   Notwithstanding the ongoing diffusion of pride events, even within its own city limits, the New York City march remains among the nation's premier pride events. Shifting from an emphasis on liberation, the Christopher Street Liberation Day Committee disintegrated in 1984, to be replaced by Heritage of Pride (HOP), a nonprofit group that continues to organize the event. A volunteer organization, HOP not only participates in the LGBT event during June, but maintains a year-round presence in politics, community building, AIDS activism, and other areas. Although keeping the same basic structure, HOP has added various innovations, such as the 1986 introduction of the "Moment of Silence" in remembrance of those who have died of AIDS.

New York Pride marches generally attract about half a million participants, including approximately 300,000 spectators and 200,000 marchers. Marchers gather on or about 57th Street and proceed three miles down Fifth Avenue, which is painted with a lavender line down the center of the road, into Greenwich Village. The march moves past the Stonewall Inn before ending in a street festival. In 1998 the pride march was one of eighteen public events scheduled for Fifth Avenue. Of the eighteen, eleven were designated as "parades," including nine ethno-religious parades: Greek, Irish (St. Patrick's Day Parade), "captive nations," Jewish/Israeli (Salute to Israel Parade), Puerto Rican, German (Steuben Day Parade), Hispanic, Italian (Columbus Day Parade), Hare Krishna, and Polish (Pulaski Day Parade), as well as Labor Day, Veteran's Day, and Easter parades. The other events included a museum festival, a book festival, a mile run, and a Catholic mass. (There is demand for additional events on Fifth Avenue, but opposition from local residents has kept a moratorium on new parades down Fifth Avenue in place since 1971).

Even after nearly three decades, the pride march remains a focal point for much of the New York LGBT community. As HOP co-coordinator Michael Bath commented, the community "can fight all year long about this and that, but when it comes down to it, when it really counts, we come together. Even though Pride is a political statement—you know, taking the center of Manhattan and marching down the street, saying you're proud of who you are—it's also a huge celebration" (McGarry 1998, 12). The 1998 march was typical; as the *New York Times* described it: "The Gay and Lesbian Pride March captivated spectators with startling costumes, booming music and showy dancing, as it had done since 1969. Nearly 100 lesbian and gay motorcyclists roared down the avenue. Transvestites clattered behind in clingy evening gowns and stiletto heels. But the parade also brought out a quieter spirit [of more ordinary-looking people]" (Hu 1998).

The Political Impact of Pride Marches

LGBT people have a strong incentive to be perceived as being as numerous as possible. At the most basic level, this will create the appearance that they constitute a noteworthy portion of the population and therefore control such political resources as votes and money. At a deeper level, the appearance that a not-insignificant portion of the population is LGBT might help to make homosexuality seem less aberrant or deviant to the heterosexual majority.

Thus, LGBT people have an interest in simply having society understand that they *exist* in significant numbers. Media coverage of the spectacle of large-scale marches—particularly those that include hundreds of thousands of mostly LGBT participants—are one of the single most potent counterarguments that the LGBT community can make to the popular perception that they constitute only a tiny percentage of the population. Mass marches are, in short, one of the most compelling means of overcoming invisibility and, hence, achieving visibility. Concomitant with the display of numbers, of course, is a show of mobilization—a demonstration that the community has the internal cohesion and organization to carry out large-scale collective action, that is, it is not simply one of the countless possible "latent groups." Another part of mobilization is self-assertion: where they were once rendered invisible, then at best ghettoized to particular neighborhoods, LGBT communities can use pride marches so that at least on one day a year they may stake a symbolic claim to the very geographic center of their cities.

The visibility that accompanies LGBT pride marches is directed at three main audiences. First, there are the relatively small number of people who actually encounter the march firsthand, either intentionally or accidentally as part of other activities. Second, there are those who are specifically tuned into major public events, predominantly politicians and other public figures who seek out information about public activity. Third, and most important, is general media exposure, through television, radio, print, and other outlets. It is through the media that the majority of people ever find out that the event even happened and get some sense of its scale and content. In his analysis of the Chicago LGBT pride march, Richard Herrell (1992) argues that the success or failure of a march to achieve visibility is in large part a function of media coverage, which in turn focuses on numbers of participants, contingents, attending dignitaries, and spectators, as well as the length and duration of the march. (Given the outrageous dress and demeanor of many people at LGB pride marches, and the tendency of the media to seek out the sensational and titillating, it should be noted that some LGBT people feel that media coverage ends up harming the community as much as, or more than, helping it.)

Although "visibility" is perhaps the most commonly cited reason that LGB pride marches are politically important, this concept has come under some fire in recent years. As columnist Dan Savage noted in 1998, "When Pride parades began, the statement went something like this: 'We were invisible for too long! We're coming out!' . . . They spoke of people coming out of the shadows, coming out of dark bars. . . . We demanded the lies stop and the truth be told. And these were powerful statements, and we were moved by them . . . three decades ago" (Savage 1998, 48). Savage goes on to say, "Some argue that 'we are everywhere' parades still have meaning for gays and lesbians who've just come out" and that "I'm willing to concede that in some cities, the claiming visibility/liberation parade still has meaning. It still works in Missoula, Montana, for instance" (Savage 1998, 48). Savage's point is valid, insofar as LGB people in the largest cities do have other opportunities for visibility. Still, the size and breadth of pride marches remain uniquely capable of attracting attention and demonstrating numbers.

Indeed, beyond offering the opportunity for visibility in the larger society, LGBT pride marches and their accompanying activities also provide a venue for conducting a wide range of political activities within the broadest cross-section of the LGBT population, including many people who may be "closeted" or otherwise disconnected from the community throughout the rest of the year. Indeed, at one level, marches are conceived of as gigantic clearinghouses for information about issues of interest to the LGB community. The New York march's co-coordinator, Janice Thom, noted that the organizing body "doesn't have a message per se, [but] . . . sets up venues for all the organizations and all the folks who want to come and be whatever it is they feel they're being when they're being gay . . . We set up a platform and allow people to do whatever they want on that platform. I don't know that the organization has a message other than: We deserve our civil rights, our equal rights, and to be free" (McGarry 1998, 12). Among the political activities conducted at pride marches are petition signing and letter writing, solicitation of new members for political groups, voter and political party registration, campaigning, and symbolic shows of support by political figures.

Petition Signing and Letter Writing

At marches, LGBT political organizations sponsor petition-signing tables on topics like repeal of antisodomy laws, support for same-sex marriage, and passage of antidiscrimination laws. At the 1998 Asbury Park march, for instance, the New Jersey Lesbian and Gay Coalition distributed preprinted postcards to Governor Christine Todd Whitman and two state assemblymen asking them to oppose a state version of the federal Defense of Marriage Act, which would prevent New Jersey from recognizing same-sex marriages performed in other states. The Coalition also collected signatures and distributed information kits about a possible state domestic partnership law to provide legal recognition of gay and lesbian relationships and allow for a variety of spousal benefits.

Also available was the Coalition's newsletter, providing updates and sample letters on such topics as New Jersey's U.S. senators' positions on the then-pending ambassadorial nomination of James Hormel, an openly gay man, and on the Employment Non-Discrimination Act (ENDA), a federal statute offering job protections to LGBT people. Along the same lines, the Philadelphia Lesbian and Gay Task Force distributed an "Update Call to Action," asking people to make phone calls and write letters to city and state officials on such issues as implementation of educational reforms, revision of policies, and the addition of sexual orientation and gender identity as protected categories in the Pennsylvania Civil Rights Initiative.

Solicitation of New Members for Groups

LGBT political groups also commonly solicit new supporters at pride marches. For instance, representatives of the Human Rights Campaign (HRC), the nation's largest LGBT political organization, are ubiquitous at LGBT pride marches. The representatives at pride marches in 1998 distributed a flyer (with a convenient mail-in envelope for contributions) that outlined the HRC's work on political campaigns, education and outreach, action programs, and legislative lobbying. As the group's quarterly newsletter noted:

> Because gay people are anywhere and everywhere, organizing in the gay and lesbian community can pose a challenge. But the pride season presents a unique opportunity since it gives lesbian, gay, bisexual, and transgender people a reason to come together. . . . Every year, the Human Rights Campaign makes an all-out push to participate in gay prides across the country. From May through September (and often beyond), HRC deploys scores of staff, interns, members and friends to celebrations from Seattle to Tampa, from San Diego to Philadelphia. . . . "Our presence at pride festivals provides more than visibility for HRC. It is a chance to meet people where they live and get them talking to each other as we build HRC connections," [says Frank Butler, an HRC membership organizer and veteran of dozens of prides]. (Vecchiollo 1998, 14)

The HRC reported that in Atlanta the group "signed up 400 instant members, which is quite phenomenal—more than a 100 percent increase over last year. Another 1,000 people pledged to join"(14).

In addition to a national group like the HRC, pride marches provide a major opportunity for local and state political groups to make contact with potential members. In Asbury Park, the New Jersey Gay and Lesbian Coalition/Personal Liberty Fund sponsored a large booth distributing membership information. Further, solicitation is not limited to LGBT groups, but is also conducted by allied groups. In Asbury Park, for instance, the Lindcroft, New Jersey, branch of the National Organization for Women distributed pamphlets on which the cover read "Lesbian Rights Are Your Concern!" and featured a photo of NOW president Patricia Ireland at a rally protesting the ban on LGBT people in the military.

Voter and Political Party Registration

Pride events provide opportunities for LGBT people to be registered as voters and/or as members of a political party. The premier nationwide effort is "Promote the Vote," a voter registration, education, and mobilization program sponsored by seventy-one LGB community centers and thirty-three LGB health and human services organizations claiming to represent memberships of 359,087 individuals and estimated voters of more than 856,200. "By creating a visible, informed, and vocal voting constituency at the local, state, and national levels, Promote the Vote seeks to impact local, gubernatorial, judicial, state, federal, and presidential elections and enhance the advocacy and organizing capability of LGBT centers and service organizations" ("Promote the Vote," Pride '98).

The New York chapter of Promote the Vote deployed volunteers at 1998 pride events in Manhattan, Queens, Brooklyn, and the Bronx. Promote the Vote literature analyzed the importance of the 1998 race for U.S. senator from New York and reported that in its first two years the project "registered more than 30,662 people to vote and collected almost 7,000 pledges from people already registered. Also, in those two years, more than 35,733 voters were contacted by phone, a minimum of 250,250 by mailings, and 137,635 through canvassing, leafleting, and tabling" ("Promote the Vote," Pride '98). Although not all of these activities occurred at pride events (many of them took place during primary and general election campaigns), pride marches provide a key opportunity to reach LGBT voters who might otherwise be inaccessible.

Voting activities are not limited to LGBT-specific activities. In Asbury Park, the small Green Party of New Jersey sponsored a booth seeking to solicit LGBT supporters with materials on their progressive views on such issues as the environment, workers' rights, education, campaign finance reform, the economy, and peace. Notably, Green Party materials only mentioned sexual orientation issues in passing, clearly using the pride event not to tap into a group of LGBT people per se, but rather into a group of people they felt likely to be sympathetic to their overall left-leaning positions.

Campaigning

Mark Hertzog (1996) has demonstrated that the number of self-identified LGBT voters is larger than that of Asian American voters, comparable to Latino voters, and may before long match the number of Jewish voters. Robert Bailey (1998b) has shown that the LGBT vote is coherent and numerically large enough to be statistically significant, increasing from 1.3 percent in 1990 to 5.0 percent of the electorate in 1996. Bailey (1998a) also found that the LGBT vote can have an important impact in urban congressional districts; analyzing poll data from elections in 1990 and 1992, he finds rates of LGB self-identification as high as 8.3 percent in medium and large cities.

As such, it is not surprising that some aspiring office seekers make speeches and walk in the march in order to court LGBT voters. The 1998 New York City march, for instance, included Democratic senatorial candidates former U.S. Representative and 1984 Vice Presidential Candidate Geraldine Ferraro, U.S. Representative Charles Schumer, and New York City Public Advocate Mark Green. Ferraro's campaign literature subsequently distributed in LGB neighborhoods included a photo of the candidate at the pride march. In addition to being joined by contingents of supporters along the route of the march itself, the candidates lined up to address a rally, being joined by gubernatorial hopefuls such as New York City Speaker Peter Vallone and New York Lieutenant Governor Betsy McCaughey Ross, as well as politicians with secure seats who nonetheless sought to shore up their electoral base, such as U.S. Representative Jerrold Nadler who represents much of the Upper West Side of Manhattan. Gay and lesbian politicians are also offered a publicity boost; for instance the two New York grand marshals were newly elected council members Phil Reed, an HIV-positive gay man long involved with civil right issues, and Margarita Lopez, a lesbian with a history of grassroots organizing.

However, the New York march also included Mayor Rudolph Giuliani, who was unexpectedly met along the parade route by a group of protestors opposed to what they perceived as his lack of concern about antigay violence and his attacks on civil liberties. "Once [Giuliani] reached 41st Street, the 20 marshals pulled off their official T-shirts and in a matter of seconds used the chains they wore to join themselves together in a human barricade that stretched across 5th Avenue. Their shirts now read 'Rudy, get out of our parade.' All 20 protestors, part of an ad hoc group called Take Back the March, were arrested and charged with disorderly conduct. . . . The mayor appeared stunned at the protest" (Askowitz 1998, 1). Equally striking was the message advanced by Housing Works, an AIDS advocacy group angered by cuts in funding for people with AIDS, which sponsored a float with "posters of the mayor's face and bold letters screaming 'AIDS Criminal + Murderer'" (Askowitz 1998, 1). Thus, it is clear that simple participation in the march does not guarantee a positive reaction for politicians and may indeed provide a platform for their political adversaries. Although in the case of Giuliani, the criticism came from his political left, it is also clear that politicians stand to be attacked from their political right for participation in LGBT pride marches.

Symbolic Shows of Support

Pride marches provide an opportunity for politicians and other public figures to write letters and issue proclamations avowing support for the LGBT community, thus placing their views on record. Such symbolic shows of support entail little monetary cost to politicians and allow them to shore up support among various voting constituencies.

Perhaps most notably among the year's endorsements, President Clinton wrote a letter, offering "warm greetings to everyone taking part in the 1998 Gay and Lesbian Pride Celebration," that was widely reprinted in pride materials. Clinton's message marks an astounding change from the hostility of previous presidential administrations, from whom it would have been unthinkable to hear the message that "[e]vents like the Pride Celebration help us to recognize anew that working in a spirit of community is not a hope but a necessity, and that our individual dreams can only be realized by our shared efforts. . . . Our nation stands to lose if we let prejudice and discrimination stifle the hopes or deny the potential of a single American. I commend each of you for your dedication" ("Pride Grows in Brooklyn" 1998).

Proclamations declaring "Gay Pride Month" were issued by, among others, the Democratic mayors of New Haven and Hartford, Connecticut. The Hartford Proclamation goes so far as to adopt terminology used by LGB militants in referring to the Stonewall "Rebellion" and to include not only LGB people but also explicitly "people who do drag and transgender people" (Peters 1998, 19). The Hartford Proclamation also includes language that, while probably standard, goes so far as to "urge all residents of the City of Hartford to give assistance and support in every way possible to achieve the purpose" of the pride celebrations (Peters 1998, 19). In New Haven, the proclamation forthrightly states that "the gay community is a vital force in the economic, social, and cultural life of this City" and that "it is important to celebrate diversity and pride in one's identity as a means to fostering understanding and ending discrimination in all its forms" (Neslefano 1998, 22).

Perhaps more surprising than the endorsement of Democratic mayors was that of a Republican, New Jersey Governor Christine Todd Whitman, who is widely considered one of the last remaining moderate "Rockefeller Republicans." The New Jersey proclamation was scarcely more conservative than those of the Connecticut cities, using the term "Stonewall Rebellion" and casting the LGBT community as political players, stating that "the organized gay, lesbian, and bisexual community enjoys a close working relationship with various local, state, and federal government agencies in the areas of AIDS education, teenage suicide prevention, bias crimes reduction, and other issues that beset the community" (Whitman 1998, 4). In sharp contrast, however, a controversy ensued when the Republican governor of Connecticut, John Rowland, for the third consecutive year refused to issue such a proclamation. One Connecticut organizer asked, "I wonder, if he really doesn't consider us to be citizens of Connecticut worth recognizing as part of this state's cultural diversity, then what does he think we will do when it comes to deciding who to vote for come election day in November?" (Downton 1998, 23).

Conclusion

Political outsiders, particularly oppressed minorities, often first find their political voice in the form of protest politics. This has especially been the case for the LGBT minority, who trace the start of their emancipation to a three-day riot at the Stonewall Inn in the summer of 1969. Since then, protest politics remains a mainstay of the LGBT community, as it did especially during the height of the AIDS crisis. Although pride marches, the signature form of collective action in the LGBT community, have become largely ritualized and have gravitated away from overt protest, targeted demonstrations and direct actions and periodic marches on Washington remain as confrontational as ever. Like many other minorities, however, LGBT people have developed other outlets for political expression, including involvement in social movements and interest groups, engagement with political parties and voting as a bloc, and even to a limited degree political office holding. These will be the subjects of the forth-coming three chapters.

References and Further Reading

Askowitz, Andrea. 1998. "Pride and Protests. 20 Arrested at Parade during Demonstration." *New York Blade News* (3 July): 1.

Bailey, Robert W. 1998a. *Gay Politics, Urban Politics*. New York: Columbia University Press.

———. 1998b. *Out and Voting: The Gay, Lesbian, and Bisexual Vote in Congressional House Elections, 1990–1996*. Washington, DC: National Gay and Lesbian Task Force Policy Institute.

D'Emilio, John. 1983. *Sexual Politics, Sexual Communities: The Making of a Homosexual Minority in the United States, 1940–1970*. Chicago: University of Chicago Press.

Downton, Joseph. 1998. "Before the Parade Passes By: Planning the 1998 Connecticut Gay Pride Festival." *Metroline* (21 June): 21–23.

Herrell, Richard K. 1992. "The Symbolic Strategies of Chicago's Gay and Lesbian Pride Day Parade." In *Gay Culture in America,* edited by Gilbert Herdt. Boston: Beacon Press.

Hertzog, Mark. 1996. *The Lavender Vote: Lesbians, Gay Men, and Bisexuals in American Electoral Politics*. New York: New York University Press.

Heyboer, Kelly. 1998. "Thousands Converge by the Sea for March Celebrating Gay Pride." *Newark, New Jersey Star-Ledger* (8 June): 19.

Hogan, Steve, and Lee Hudson. 1998. *Completely Queer: The Gay and Lesbian Encyclopedia*. New York: Henry Holt.

Hu, Winnie. 1998. "Spirit and Spectacle in a Show of Pride: Gay Marchers Take to the Streets in High Heels and Harleys." *New York Times* (29 June): B4.

LeDuff, Charlie. 1998. "Whipping Rains Clog Traffic and Disrupt Subways. *New York Times* (14 June): 37.

"Let the Dykes March." 1998. *Philadelphia Gay News* (29 May–4 June): 10.

McGarry, Mark. 1998. "The Sun Always Rises on Pride." *Body Positive* (June): 11.

Medley, Ronald. 1998. "Demonstrations and Direct Actions." In *Encyclopedia of AIDS: A Social, Political, Cultural, and Scientific Record of the HIV Epidemic,* edited by Raymond A. Smith. Chicago: Fitzroy Dearborn Publishers.

Melrose, Kevin D. 1998. "Pride Divide? Events Show Movement's Evolution." *Philadelphia Gay News* (12–18 June): 1.

Montana, Rita. 1998. "Unity through Diversity." *Brooklyn Pride,* 16.

Neslefano, John Jr. 1998. "Proclamation Pridefest 1998," New Haven, Connecticut, 22.

Peters, Michael B. 1998. "Proclamation Pridefest 1998," Hartford, Connecticut, 19.

Pople, Laura. 1998a. "Debunking Parade Myths." *The Jersey Gaze,* 8.

———. 1998b. "Pride Marches On." *Pride Guide '98,* 14–16.

"Pride Grows in Brooklyn." 1998. *Brooklyn Pride,* 15.

"Promote the Vote," *New York Pride '98,* 21.

Ramirez, Anthony. 1998. "Let It Rain on Parades, Residents Say." *New York Times* (4 October): 6.

Savage, Dan. 1998. "Pride: A Dead Metaphor." *Out* (June): 48.

Smith, Raymond A. 1998. "Marches and Parades." In *Encyclopedia of AIDS: A Social, Political, Cultural, and Scientific Record of the HIV Epidemic,* edited by Raymond A. Smith. Chicago: Fitzroy Dearborn Publishers.

Stryker, Susan, and Jim van Buskirk. 1996. *Gay by the Bay: A History of Queer Culture in the San Francisco Bay Area.* San Francisco: Chronicle Books.

Szymanski, Katie. 1998. "Rain Doesn't Dampen Mood at Brooklyn Pride." *New York Blade News* (19 June): 11.

Thompson, Mark, ed. 1994. *Long Road to Freedom:* The Advocate *History of the Gay and Lesbian Movement.* New York: St. Martin's Press.

Vecchiollo, Dominic. 1998. "Pride Is Bustin' Out All Over." *HRC Quarterly* (Summer): 14.

Whitman, Christine Todd. 1998. "Proclamation Pridefest 1998." *The Jersey Gaze,* 4.

Wilson, James Q. 1973. *Political Organizations.* New York: Basic Books.

"World-wide Pride." 1998. *The Jersey Gaze,* 32.

3

Interest Group and Social Movement Participation

At the end of World War II, gays and lesbians began a struggle for equality in U.S. society. This struggle has taken many forms, from personal transformation and social movement activism to legal transformation and interest group politics. The attempts by individuals and groups to transform self and society are the efforts of what has come to be called the lesbian, gay, bisexual, and transgender (LGBT) movement. At the start of a new century the LGBT movement is still struggling to achieve social and political equality, but it looks very different from the early days of the 1950s and 1960s. The structure, organizations, tactics, and goals of the movement have evolved to the point where it is now a relatively familiar fixture in local, state, and national politics. The evolution of the gay movement is similar to the evolution of other social movements, such as the black civil rights movement, the women's movement, and the antiwar movement. Unlike these other social movements, however, the LGBT movement is still relatively young.

Similar to racial and ethnic minority groups, LGBT people face discrimination in various aspects of their lives, including harassment, violence, and the specter of rejection from friends and family. In the workplace, research suggests that gay men may earn between

11 to 27 percent less than their heterosexual counterparts (Badgett 1995), and public opinion polls consistently show a strong dislike of homosexuals (Yang 1998). As a numerical minority lesbians and gays often cannot protect themselves from the heterosexual bias of the majority.

Furthermore, unlike most other minority groups, lesbians and gays are not a clearly recognizable group, making it difficult for gays and lesbians to recognize one another and act collectively. To complicate matters, antigay opponents question whether lesbians and gays have a legitimate claim to being oppressed. They argue that homosexuality is not an innate characteristic like race or ethnicity, and suggest that discrimination based on acquired or chosen orientations is legitimate. Perhaps even more problematic, gays and lesbians are more "disliked" by the majority population than other oppressed groups (Wilson 1994).

Following the paths of other groups, such as blacks, women, Latinos, and Native Americans, gays and lesbians created a broad-based social movement to raise individual and societal consciousness. The LGBT movement encompasses gay leaders, politicians, interest groups, consciousness-raising groups, journalists, religious groups, publications, artists, activists, and heterosexual individuals and organizations. The movement is still evolving and has encompassed a variety of causes at one time or another, including the homophile movement, the gay liberation movement, lesbian feminism, AIDS activism, and "queer nationalism."

The Homophile Movement

The first gay rights group in the United States, the Chicago Society for Human Rights, was established in 1924 by an immigrant named Henry Gerber. But the police soon broke up Gerber's group by arresting him, ensuring that he would be fired from his post office job, and confiscating the group's property. During the 1950s and 1960s the LGBT movement was small but was housed within a network of groups and their local chapters. These early groups tended to refer to themselves as homophile organizations and mostly refrained from direct action tactics. However, gay and lesbian organizations were not able to sustain themselves until after World War II and the peak of the Red Scare, the notion that communists were infiltrating the government.

Although many social movements seem to arise out of spontaneous protests and even human tragedies, the original homophile movement did not appear to have a catalyst, except perhaps the mobilization of people for World War II and subsequent social upheaval during and following the war. Indeed, the first LGBT membership organization in the United States, the Veterans Benevolent Association, formed shortly after the war. Similarly, the formation of the Mattachine Society in 1951 appears to have been a response to government crackdowns on homosexuals and communists but not to a single event.

Founded by gay communists in Los Angeles, the Mattachine Society adopted a structure similar to that of the American Communist Party—a pyramid composed of five levels with the leaders at the top determining policies that would flow downward. To protect the identities of members, the Society was organized as a hierarchical collection of autonomous "secret cells." In 1953 the Mattachine Society began publishing *One* magazine, but *One*, Inc., quickly became its own organization. The Daughters of Bilitis (DOB) became the first lesbian homophile organization in 1955. In the early 1960s both the DOB and the Mattachine Society became national organizations and had chapters on both coasts.

The publication of *One* and DOB's *The Ladder,* along with organized conferences and the creation of regional associations, helped to create a loose network among the existing homophile organizations. The assimilationist strategies and tactics of the Mattachine Society and the DOB tended to drive this loose network of individuals, publications, and groups.

The organizations composing the gay and lesbian movement did not share a universal strategy of gay liberation during the early years. Each group, however, did adopt similar tactics for achieving their goals. The Veterans Benevolent Association formed a coalition with the NAACP and began a media and lobbying effort to end the military's arbitrary use of undesirable discharges that lasted until 1954. The Mattachine Society, however, focused both on individual consciousness raising and ending discrimination in the private and public spheres as the main goals of the movement. The Mattachine Society's statement of Missions and Purposes reads: "To unify those homosexuals isolated from their own kind. . . . to educate homosexuals and heterosexuals toward an ethical homosexual culture. . . . to lead the more . . . socially conscious homosexuals . . . [and] to assist our people who are victimized daily" (Adam 1995, 68).

The DOB was more assimilationist from the beginning, focusing largely on developing a positive homosexual identity that would not offend the general public. DOB's stated goals were: "Education of the variant . . . development of a library on the sex deviant theme . . . public discussions to be conducted by leading members of the legal, psychiatric, religious and other professions . . . [and] advocating a mode of behavior and dress acceptable to society" (Adam 1995, 69–70). However, during the 1960s, the DOB expanded its goals to include pursuing changes in law regarding homosexuals through legal and legislative challenges.

Throughout the 1950s and 1960s the existing homophile organizations staged protests against police harassment, began using the courts to defend their rights to mail publications and to congregate, and became involved in the Democratic Party—largely through mayoral races in New York and San Francisco. The first use of collective protest at the national level to call for an end to employment discrimination against homosexuals is thought to be a 1965 picketing of several federal departments and agencies, as well as the White House. It was not until the late 1960s, however, that such confrontational tactics began to supersede conventional and assimilationist forms of political behavior within the movement.

The early homophile movement created an internal structure composed of formal organizations, at least in part, because it was the best way to keep the identities of participants secret. But the structure had, for a time, helped to quell divisions within the movement. In the Mattachine Society there were tensions between the communist founders and more conservative members of the organization over the goals and tactics of the organization and the movement. At Mattachine's first convention in 1953, its founders ceded control of the organization to a number of gay conservatives called the Anti-Communist Coordinating Council. Mattachine's new leaders "adopted a low-profile, accommodationist stand that defined movement strategies for more than a decade" (Vaid 1995, 53).

The activities and tactics of New Left social movements helped reignite divisions within the LGBT movement over strategy as the 1960s progressed. By 1965 members of the Mattachine Society and the DOB were calling for more militant action, including street protests, on the part of homophile groups. These divisions and subsequent splinter groups paved the way for the rise of the gay and lesbian liberation movement of the early 1970s.

The Gay Liberation Movement and Lesbian Feminism

On the night of June 27, 1969, New York Police raided a gay bar in Greenwich Village called the Stonewall Inn. The raid, although not unusual, was distinct because of the violent rioting by patrons that followed and because LGBT people mobilized around the event. The riots gave rise to new organizations and also highlighted existing divisions within the older homophile groups.

The events of 1969 gave rise to a relatively new branch of the movement. The new branch can be distinguished by its focus on LGBT liberation, both as personal liberation and societal liberation and, to a lesser degree, civil rights for gays and lesbians through legal change rather than on accommodations to the norms of heterosexual society. Urvashi Vaid (1995) refers to this new branch of the movement as a cultural rather than political movement. This cultural movement focuses on creating a positive gay identity and relies more on confrontation and protest forms of collective action in pursuing civil rights.

The Stonewall riots spurred the creation of many new groups at the local, state, and national levels. This marked the beginning of the end, however, for the older homophile organizations and their focus on building local chapters across the nation. A new generation of activists was born in the wake of the riots to build the modern movement. But to the chagrin of some activists, the same organizations became increasingly national in focus throughout the 1970s. Local groups, meanwhile, began to specialize their goals, each creating issue niches to ensure survival. The San Francisco gay community followed this pattern. Throughout the 1970s, new gay groups became increasingly specialized; some focused on religion, others on parenting, and still others on race relations.

In the years immediately following Stonewall the basic unit of the movement became the consciousness-raising group. These were groups that gave individuals space to develop a positive self-identity as gay people. Keven Burke and Murray Edleman state that consciousness-raising groups were usually composed of eight to ten persons, and while they often had a leader in the beginning, the "intent is for [the group] to function without a leader" (Burke and Edleman 1972, 13). These groups were, in part, a counterresponse to the increasing levels of institutionalization within the movement. The new militants were "deeply suspicious of leaders, bureaucracies, and political parties" and directly challenged the movement structure that homophile organizations had created" (Adam 1995, 82–83).

It was during this period that stark contrasts between the East and West Coasts began to appear in the movement. West Coast groups from the 1960s, including the Society for Individual Rights (SIR), focused attention both on legal reform and community organizing. In contrast, East Coast chapters of the Mattachine Society and other groups did not cultivate the social networks that give social movements their power, instead most East Coast Mattachine chapters focused on litigation and lobbying efforts.

At the end of the 1960s and beginning of the 1970s both old and new formal movement organizations began to focus more on direct action protests, even while some continued to pursue the slow tactic of legal and legislative reform. Urvashi Vaid argues that the new liberation branch of the movement introduced four ideas to the movement:

(1) the notion that coming out and pursuing gay and lesbian visibility held the key to [gay] freedom; (2) that queer freedom would profoundly change gender roles, sexism, and heterosexual institutions like the family; (3) that gay, lesbian, and bisexual people were an integral part of the broad demand for social change and needed a political philosophy that made connections to race, gender, and economic issues; and (4) that the creation of a gay and lesbian counterculture was an essential part of establishing lesbian and gay identity. (Vaid 1995, 57)

The new politics and tactics of gay liberation allowed the movement to more closely align itself with other social movements, such as the black civil rights movement (especially the black power movement), and the women's, Chicano, radical hip, and antiwar movements. Furthermore, as Vaid (1995) points out, the lesson of Stonewall and the years following was that the movement could not survive without the centralizing force of large organizations, but also that the central organizations would not survive without the grassroots. Hybrid groups, such as the Gay Activists Alliance (GAA), were able to combine direct action protests with legislative lobbying and electoral involvement. For example, in its initial attempts to pass a New York City ordinance banning discrimination against homosexuals, the GAA both directly lobbied politicians and conducted "zaps" (organized protests) outside the homes and offices of politicians.

Although the aftermath of Stonewall led to the creation of new groups trying to capture the anger and energy raised, the pressure to institutionalize the movement was not visible until 1973 when the first nationally orientated gay rights group formed—the National Gay Task Force (later called the National Gay and Lesbian Task Force). The rise of the religious right and its antigay ballot initiative campaigns during the late 1970s also created pressures to institutionalize the movement. For example, after the first round of antigay ballot initiatives in 1977, activists met in Denver at the National Gay Leadership Conference, sponsored by Dignity International, the Gay Rights National Lobby, the National Gay Task Force, and the United Federation of Metropolitan Community Churches. The over 400 representatives from various LGBT groups determined that the movement had to focus on education, legislation, and organization. The formation of the Gay Rights National Lobby in 1978 marked the creation of the first national group that actively attempted to build relationships between local activists and national leaders in order to lobby Congress.

The rise of a new gay and lesbian liberation movement was in large part a rejection of the assimilationist strategy of the older homophile organizations, and was a direct result of the politics of institutionalization. The excitement fueled by Stonewall gave disgruntled activists a new base of gays and lesbians who could be mobilized to form new organizations. Mark Thompson describes the evolution of the movement during the 1970s: "The first post-Stonewall phase had emphasized "liberation"—consciousness-raising, coming out, grassroots protest—like the hippie, peace, and feminist movements out of which many gay and lesbian leaders arose (and which continued to spawn counterculturalists like the Radical Faeries, who first gathered in 1979). . . . many concluded that it was time to shift our battleground from the self and the streets to the corridors of power. Taking on political parties, media, and corporations would require large organizations, professional skills, and fund raising" (Thompson 1994, 177–178).

Groups such as the Gay Liberation Front (GLF) formed immediately following Stonewall and called for more radical forms of political action. Almost immediately, however, the GLF was split over tactics and the pursuit of issues not directly related to gays. Ideologically moderate gays and lesbians split from the GLF to form the Gay Activists Alliance (GAA), in part because they wanted to keep a lower profile while pursuing gay civil rights. Founders of the GAA were not only looking for less radical politics and tactics, but also wanted a more formal organizational structure and control at meetings.

The 1970s also highlighted gender divisions within the movement. The conflict over a cultural movement versus a political movement was not created by differences between lesbians and gay men, but while gay men increasingly attempted to institutionalize the movement within mainstream political organizations, lesbians increasingly turned to creating a counterculture. Lesbian counterculture, rooted in music festivals and other alternatives to the "bar scene," created a new generation of lesbian activists that questioned the dominance of gay men and male-orientated organizations within the movement.

Some lesbians formed new groups, such as Lesbian Feminist Liberation, which previously had been a subcommittee of the New York GAA. Lesbian activists tended to be opposed to strong leadership positions, hierarchical organizations, and assimilationist politics, which is often attributed to a shared feminist ideology.

AIDS Activism and Assimilation

After its emergence in 1981, the AIDS epidemic shed even greater light on the fault lines within the gay and lesbian movement. In the short term, the financial and community needs created by the AIDS epidemic made the pressures to institutionalize the movement stronger than they had ever been. In the long term, however, it was precisely the increased institutionalization spurred by AIDS that drove a new generation of gay and lesbian activists to focus on grassroots organizing and collective protest rather than legal reform and legislative lobbying. These activists were, at least in part, revitalizing the liberationist aspect of the movement.

AIDS mobilized gays and lesbians who had not participated in the movement or its formal organizations in the past. Newly mobilized activists were more likely to be middle class, white, male, and previously closeted. Their newfound activism highlighted the tensions within the movement that had existed since the 1950s—the conflict over centralized, bureaucratic organizations versus the power of grassroots activism and non-mainstream political participation. Further, the new activists' participation brought questions of gender, racial, and economic bias to the forefront of the movement once again.

The internal pressures helped lead to the creation of a separate AIDS movement with ties to the original gay and lesbian movement. Similar to the way in which the 1970s liberation movement grew out of discontent with older homophile groups, the AIDS movement was, in part, a reaction to the excesses of gay liberation in the 1970s.

The AIDS movement largely represented a return to institutionalized forms of politics and an effort to mainstream gay and lesbian culture.

During the 1980s, membership-based organizations grew in importance and national groups came to dominate the movement over local groups. By 1986 the National Gay and Lesbian Task Force (NGLTF; previously NGTF) moved its offices form New York to Washington, D.C., and the Lambda Legal Defense and Education Fund (LLDEF) increased its size and its aggressiveness in litigation. The Human Rights Campaign Fund (HRCF) absorbed the Gay Rights National Lobby and began to abandon a structure that had connected grassroots activists with national leaders.

New national groups and programs formed to deal with AIDS within government institutions, including the AIDS Action Council (1986), the creation of an ACLU gay and lesbian rights project and their hiring of an AIDS lobbyist, the National AIDS Network (1984), the National Minority AIDS Council (1987), the National Leadership Coalition on AIDS (1988), the Interfaith AIDS Network, and National Organizations Responding to AIDS (1986).

The national groups increasingly moved toward a strategy of institutional forms of politics, with some AIDS organizations literally becoming bureaucracies within the system. Urvashi Vaid argues that activists made four decisions on a strategy for dealing with AIDS: "degaying, desexualizing, decoupling AIDS-specific reform from systemic reform and direct action" (Vaid 1995, 74). The first three choices were a strategy of institutionalization, or as Vaid refers to it, a "mainstreaming" of the movement to make it less threatening to heterosexuals. Meanwhile, the direct action tactic was a polar opposite strategy, built on the belief that nothing would occur until LGBT people made their presence, and pain over AIDS, visible.

In the late 1980s some activists had grown weary of the slow legislative and legal process. Groups such as ACT UP and the Lesbian Avengers formed and returned to a grassroots form of direct action in an attempt to speed the distribution of funding for AIDS, speed the Food and Drug Administration's release of new drugs, and to protest discriminatory practices.

But throughout the 1980s many movement groups continued to focus on policy change through lobbying and litigation. With the support of the mayor, gays in Chicago pushed for the passage of an antidiscrimination law, which eventually passed in 1987. Led by the Northwest AIDS Foundation, gay activists were able to pressure the governor of Washington to create an AIDS task force that had gay representatives and to pressure the legislature to pass legislation funding AIDS programs and preventing discrimination against people with AIDS. In Buffalo, New York, gays formed a coalition with African Americans and the local Democratic Party to pass a law protecting gay and lesbian city employees from discrimination.

Urvashi Vaid sums up the impact of AIDS on the movement: "There is no question that AIDS forced the LGBT movement to institutionalize, nationalize, and aggressively pursue the mainstream" (Vaid 1995, 74). Existing national groups clearly felt the pressure to institutionalize the movement in order to force a governmental response to AIDS. Groups representing the new AIDS movement felt these pressures even more keenly and quickly moved to be become part of medical and service sector bureaucratic structures.

Growing opposition from the religious right also created pressures for institutionalization. As the religious right increased its presence in the Republican Party, ran candidates for local offices, and organized antigay ballot initiatives across the county, many in the LGBT movement turned to the Democratic Party and institutionalized forms of political behavior. In Chicago, for example, the Gay and Lesbian Democrats began endorsing mayoral candidates in 1983. Their political muscle led to mayoral appointments of gay men and lesbians.

What many in the LGBT movement failed to notice, however, was that the religious right was building its power from the ground up in a highly localized form of movement structure. The structure of the LGBT movement, meanwhile, was increasingly top down in nature, with national leaders and organizations developing goals and tactics.

Case Study: Radical Queer Activism

Although many gay and lesbian organizations worked together to respond to AIDS, some national organizations engaged in turf wars to gain leadership of the movement. Specifically, distrust between the NGLTF and HRCF grew as the NGLTF followed a strategy of making connections at the grassroots and the HRCF focused on raising money for elections and lobbying members of Congress.

Local groups were also experiencing division. In New York City, the Gay Men's Health Crisis (GMHC) resisted becoming involved in confrontational politics and was intent on remaining a low-key service organization. This drove activists calling for more radical action to split from the GMHC and form the direct-action group AIDS Coalition to Unleash Power (ACT UP) in 1987. Similar divisions occurred in other cities, including Seattle. ACT UP's first slogan was "Silence = Death," but later slogans included bumper stickers that read "The Catholic Church would rather see you die than wear a condom!" The group's efforts at influencing governmental policy have traditionally been indirect, involving demonstrations and rallies. Members took their first action in March 1987 when 250 activists blocked rush-hour traffic on Wall Street. ACT UP has staged some of the most famous direct action protests since the civil rights movement, including breaking into television news studios during live broadcasts, interrupting Catholic masses in New York City, and temporarily shutting down the New York Stock Exchange.

Some protests were more targeted. Direct action by ACT UP had an effect on the 1992 presidential campaign; the threat of protests by ACT UP in Little Rock, Arkansas, forced Democratic candidate Bill Clinton to condemn an Arkansas antisodomy law. Throughout the 1992 presidential campaign ACT UP chapters engaged in a coordinated effort to harass the candidates and brought more attention to AIDS. ACT UP members also launched significant protests outside the conventions of both major parties, with 1,500 protestors at the Republican National Convention (Thompson 1994, 391–392).

Moderate gay and lesbian activists routinely criticized the tactics of ACT UP and other protest groups. As AIDS organizations grew, women and minorities increasingly began to feel the tensions of sexism and racism within the movement. AIDS had brought many new activists into the movement, but many of these activists were middle- to upper-class white males. The organizations they created tended to reflect their concerns and status and not those of women and minorities. These tensions even occurred in organizations like ACT UP where frustrated lesbians broke away to form the Lesbian Avengers. Indeed, as early as 1991 some male ACT UP members also wanted the group to take more radical actions, but also to address broader LGBT issues.

ACT UP has always been composed of local chapters, there is no formal national coalition of chapters, but chapters have often coordinated activity with conference calls. The chapters thrived in over thirty cities in the late 1980s and early 1990s, but they had dropped off sharply by 1994. Although no accurate membership figures are available, the trend was apparently reflected in the Chicago chapter, which dropped to 10 members in 1996 from 100 in 1990 (Worsnop 1993, 205).

Some chapters of ACT UP still existed in 2001, including in New York City; Philadelphia; Boston; Washington, D.C.; and San Francisco. ACT UP/Golden Gate formed in 1990 after some members of the original ACT UP/San Francisco were unhappy with the group's move away from AIDS treatment issues to focus on public policy and political issues. ACT UP/San Francisco has also developed a reputation for violence and disruptive activity. However, the two groups were able to work together until 1994. The ACT UP/Golden Gate chapter changed its name to Survive AIDS in 2000 to avoid confusion with a group using the name ACT UP/San Francisco that espoused views with which most AIDS activists disagree.

In 1990 chapters of the radical new gay protest group, Queer Nation, sprang up around the country. Queer Nation and the radical offshoot of ACT UP in New York, Treatment Action Guerrillas (TAG), continued to practice direct action protest in the early 1990s, with Queer Nation holding kiss-ins and other events meant to garner media attention. In September 1991 activists from TAG covered the Arlington, Virginia, home of Senator Jesse Helms with a giant condom dropped from a helicopter.

Queer Nation was founded in New York City by four gay men who had belonged to ACT UP but wanted to attack homophobia and heterosexism and who were especially concerned about hate crimes against gays. Perhaps even more so than ACT UP, Queer Nation represented a brief return to the notion of homosexual liberation rather than assimilation. During 1991 Queer Nation chapters sprang up around the country in Philadelphia, Los Angeles, and Boston. But other new militant liberationist groups formed around the country as well: in New York, Art Positive; in San Francisco, Boys with Arms Akimbo; in Chicago, Helms' Angels; and in Los Angeles, Stiff Sheets.

However, beyond the 1993 March on Washington the tactic of direct action has largely fallen by the wayside—even the remaining chapters of ACT UP turned their attention to elections and legislative lobbying by 1995. Most ACT UP chapters collapsed in 1994 and 1995. In the course of interviewing the few existing chapters in 1995, Donald Haider-Markel (1997a) found that ACT UP chapters in the southwest had moved away from protest activities and begun to participate in electoral politics and legislative lobbying efforts. AIDS and the politics surrounding the disease were tamed as the epidemic entered its second decade. New drugs held the promise of controlling the disease, while gay-related organizations became an informal part of the medical bureaucracy in order to ensure funding for health care and research.

But at least one group of lesbians has continued to use direct action. In the same vein as ACT UP and Queer Nation, the Lesbian Avengers was formed in 1992 by six political activists in New York

City who wanted to do more in the way of building a grassroots lesbian movement. The women used the 1993 Gay Pride Day to distribute 8,000 fluorescent green club cards that said "Lesbians! Dykes! Gay Women! We want revenge and we want it now" (Schulman 1993, 8). The group's symbol is an exploding bomb. In the group's handbook, the group describes itself as "a direct action group using grassroots activism to fight for lesbian survival and visibility. Our purpose is to identify and promote lesbian issues and perspectives while empowering lesbians to become experienced organizers who can participate in political rebellion. Learning skills and strategizing together are at the core of our existence" (Schulman 1993, 3).

Although the group is composed solely of local chapters, the Lesbian Avengers have gained a reputation as a fearsome force to some anti-LGBT activists, such as the Reverend Fred Phelps. According to one account of a protest, Phelps and his family were protesting at the funeral of a gay man in San Francisco in 1997 with their usual "God Hates Fags" signs. A contingent of the Lesbian Avengers chased Phelps away from the funeral and forced them to jump into a moving van.

Lesbian Avenger groups currently operate in Atlanta; Boston; Chicago; Cincinnati; Corvallis, Oregon; Minneapolis; San Francisco; Washington, D.C.; and Wilmington, Delaware. There are as many as fifty chapters in the United States and several overseas. The San Francisco chapter formed in 1993 and has perhaps been more active than any other. In November 1994 the group sent Governor Pete Wilson a package on each of the five days leading up to election day. Each package contained a different gift—an enema, toilet paper, stool softener, and a small card reading: "To: Pete Wilson. Because you're full of shit. From: the Lesbian Avengers." The action was in response to Wilson's vetoes of several pro-LGBT bills (San Francisco Lesbian Avengers 2001a). In 1995 members of the group charged the San Rafael headquarters of Exodus International, an organization whose mission is to "cure" homosexuals, and unleashed 1,000 crickets. The panicked staff called 911, saying, "There are lesbians here with bugs" (San Francisco Lesbian Avengers 2001b).

In 1999 a chapter of the Lesbian Avengers was founded in Rochester, New York. The group mobilized for June Queer Pride activities by creating a 20 foot banner displaying Avengers logos and the slogan "Rochester Queer Pride" and hanging it across an interstate highway. In August 1999 the group held an action at the Rochester Jesus Rally. They marched with a 20 foot banner that read "Democracy and Theocracy are not compatible" and received favorable media coverage.

The 1990s and Beyond

During the early 1990s the LGBT movement achieved some of its greatest gains at the national level with the passage of the Ryan White CARE Act, the Hate Crimes Statistics Act, and the Americans with Disabilities Act. In 1992 the movement saw its political stature increase through the election of President Clinton, the victories of openly gay and lesbian candidates throughout the country, and the defeat of the religious right in several key elections. However, the old debate between the radical founders of the Mattachine Society and its conservative members continued to be reflected in the movement divisions of the 1990s. The LGBT conservatives of today are still largely concerned with being viewed as respectable by the mainstream and therefore believe that the movement should present a mainstream image.

Although local and state gay and lesbian organizations abound, the center of movement activity remains at the national level. The largest national groups, the HRCF (now HRC), NGLTF, and Lambda Legal Defense and Education Fund (LLDEF), have not established true local, state, or regional chapters to connect the grass roots to the leadership. The Parents, Families, and Friends of Lesbians and Gays (PFLAG) group is probably the greatest exception to this general rule. The PFLAG has established over 100 local chapters around the United States. It fosters grassroots input and works to coordinate the activities of local groups. As its name suggests, however, the PFLAG is largely composed of heterosexuals, which seems to limit the group's capacity to become a lead organization in the movement. The NGLTF, however, continues its efforts to coordinate the activities of state and local groups through its regional field directors and the HRC has taken similar actions. Involvement with the movement has increasingly come to mean writing a check rather than more direct forms of participation. The NGLTF has tried to establish networks between local and national groups, while the HRC has moved toward a donor-centered strategy of legislative lobbying and contributing to election campaigns as a political action committee (PAC).

Coordination among existing groups has increased at certain points (e.g., during the effort to include sexual orientation in the Hate Crimes Statistics Act of 1990), but distrust and the desire to be the main voice of the movement has often meant that each group works alone. As in the 1980s, therefore, the movement continues to be dominated by a top-down structure, where national groups operate on the assumption that access to politicians is the key to victory, while most groups disregard the importance of creating a groundswell at the grass roots. Urvashi Vaid (1995) argues that dependence on access to politicians without a formal grassroots mobilization network is part of the reason for the movement's failure to overturn the military's ban on homosexuals in 1993. The existence of a top-down structure may also have made it more difficult for the movement to block federal legislation against recognizing same-sex marriages for the purpose of federal benefits (called the Defense of Marriage Act) in 1996.

The continued institutionalization of the movement during the 1990s meant that the movement's main focus was on legislative lobbying, electoral campaigns, and litigation. The movement achieved many successes in these areas, but also accumulated many defeats. Some movement leaders were able to gain considerable access to President Clinton by mobilizing the gay community behind his candidacy in 1992. Key in the support of Clinton was a gay consultant from California, David Mixner. Estimates of the gay and lesbian vote for Clinton in 1992 vary around 75 percent (Bull and Gallagher 1996, 95).

More movement activists also became directly involved in Democratic Party politics—at the 1992 Democratic National Convention 133 delegates were gay or lesbian, compared to 98 at the 1988 convention and 77 at the 1980 convention (Bull and Gallagher 1996, 85). Electoral involvement often paid off. In Los Angeles, one of Mayor Riordan's first acts of patronage was to appoint an openly gay man as deputy mayor. Gay Republicans, while still being kept at arm's length by their party, began to play a larger lobbying role through their organization, the Log Cabin Republicans, by educating moderate Republican politicians on issues such as AIDS. For example, the Log Cabin Club had a role in the gubernatorial elections of Pete Wilson in California and William Weld in Massachusetts. Wilson balked on gay rights legislation but Weld became one of the most progay governors in the country. More openly LGBT people were elected to local, state, and national offices, while some incumbent politicians were reelected after coming out of the closet. LGBT political action committees, including the Gay and Lesbian Victory Fund, were formed at the local and national levels to support lesbians and gays running for public office.

Activists engaged in legislative lobbying were successful in passing antidiscrimination laws in several states, including Minnesota and California, while local ordinances were passed in over 100 cities and counties. A new legislative front was also opened with many groups successfully lobbying for domestic partner benefits and official registration in cities and counties throughout the country. Legislation concerning hate crimes based on sexual orientation was passed in at least half the states. Groups such as the LLDEF continued to fight through the courts and accumulate victories in gay and lesbian adoptions, same-sex marriage, AIDS discrimination, the repeal of anti-sodomy laws, and in cases against the military.

However, the 1990s also demonstrated that the religious right presented the greatest threat to the LGBT movement. After Pat Robertson's failed presidential bid in 1988, Robertson tapped Ralph Reed to lead his new organization, the Christian Coalition. The Coalition was formed to provide an outlet for the thousands of Christians that Robertson's campaign had brought into the political process, and like the conservative religious groups that preceded it, the Christian Coalition found one of its greatest rallying cries in the supposed threat posed to the nation by homosexuals.

Campaigns by the religious right to repeal and prevent gay rights laws by ballot initiatives were attempted throughout the country and actually reached the ballot in several states and localities, including St. Paul (Minnesota), Cincinnati, Colorado, Oregon, Idaho, and Maine. In nearly every ballot initiative, gay rights activists were forced to create formal organizations, some for the first time, but had difficulty coordinating their efforts with other state and national groups. This was especially true in states such as Idaho and Oregon, where the gay movement was largely cultural and commercial in nature, with little structure in the way of formal organizations. Even in Colorado, where formal organizations existed at the local level, activists floundered while attempting to create a statewide group to coordinate the efforts of existing groups in 1992.

The debate over gays in the military presents perhaps the greatest defeat in LGBT politics of the 1990s. National LGBT groups lacked coordination and a strong connection to grassroots activists. As more religious right-supported Republicans were elected to Congress, furthermore, the lack of unity and coordination within the gay movement became more apparent. When President-elect Clinton announced that he would end the ban on homosexuals in the military, the religious right began gearing up for a campaign to stop the effort. In contrast to the mobilization efforts of the LGBT movement, the religious right was able to coordinate its campaign against repealing the gay ban with sympathetic members of Congress and the military and was also able to effectively mobilize at the grassroots and apply constituency pressure on the White House and Congress. The end result of these internal politics was to contribute to the failure to lift the ban on gays in the military.

In the early 2000s, LGBT interest groups, especially those at the national level, continue to battle for supremacy in the movement, each believing that its values and tactics represent what movement activists want. Instead of presenting a united front to policy makers, national groups often lobby on their own behalf, usually without the benefit of coordination with other LGBT groups.

The pressure to institutionalize the LGBT movement in the 1990s also stemmed from the mainstream goals of the movement: the drive for legal protection through litigation and legislation. Litigation victories are achieved through the use of professional lawyers and often work best when coordinated with other political activities. Gaining civil rights through the legislative process, furthermore, requires someone to coordinate political strategy, while employing legislative lawyers, lobbyists, media coordinators, and mobilizing support from the grass roots.

But in the early 2000s, national LGBT groups had begun to make some changes that seemed to recognize the need to mobilize grassroots supporters, involving local activists directly in the movement, as well as maintaining professional national organizations. Further, a broader trend in American politics, the devolution of national government power to states and localities, has forced national groups to reconsider the notion that ultimate protection of LGBT rights can only be gained with federal laws.

In April 2000 LGBT activists met in Washington, D.C., for the Millennium March on Washington for Equality, billed as the largest LGBT march on the capital, including similar marches in 1993, 1987, and 1979. Estimates put the 2000 crowd at between 300,000 and 800,000, but unbiased estimates were not available. Regardless, the march was a show of strength as well as a show of weakness. A significant number of state and local LGBT leaders refused to participate in the march because they believed it was draining important resources from state and local groups, as well as pulling attention away from the states as a center for political action. The debate between national and local was not resolved by the march, nor will it be resolved in the near future.

Organized Local Groups

Although national LGBT groups are clearly important, many social scientists have long argued that the LGBT movement has historically really been a local movement, with most activity occurring in cities.

Literally thousands of local political LGBT groups have formed in the United States since 1924. However, many of these groups exist only for a short time. By 2001 an estimated 800 local political LGBT groups were in existence, but perhaps five times that number of social and cultural groups exist. Most of these groups are fairly small, with fewer than 50 members, and perhaps fewer than 200 have a significant operating budget or paid staffers. And many local groups are, in fact, chapters for national and international groups. Even so, local chapters are often as active as nonaffiliated local groups, and often have access to more resources. But it is these small local groups that provide many LGBT people with their first taste of LGBT activism, and some would argue that these groups comprise the backbone of the movement. In this section we briefly discuss the experience of LGBT groups organizing at the local level, with attention to their achievements as well as their difficulties.

Of the many local LGBT groups that have existed, some form rather spontaneously around particular events or for a particular purpose. Once the problem has been addressed, they often disband. However, sometimes the group may gain a broader purpose. For example, in 1996 the Charlotte, North Carolina, County Commission voted to cut funding for the arts because commissioners believed some of the money was funding gay-themed plays. In response, local LGBT activists energized the Mecklenburg Gay and Lesbian Political Action Committee, a local LGBT group that had officially formed in 1996 in the months just prior to the vote. Through campaigns, events, endorsements, and public education, the group was able to defeat a number of the commissioners in 1998 and have the funding decision reversed. Even after its victory, the group continued to operate, endorsing candidates for the Charlotte City Council in 1999 and again for the County Commission in 2000.

The oldest continuously active local LGBT group in the country is the Washington, D.C., Gay and Lesbian Activists Alliance (GLAA). It was formed in 1971, largely through openly gay Frank Kameny's run for Congress that same year. In 2001 the GLAA still had about 100 members and had become increasingly professionalized over time. Although the group established a website in 1996, an activist email list, and even created its own letterhead and business cards, its impact on the movement and District of Columbia politics was perhaps greatest in the 1970s and 1980s. The GLAA's leaders attribute much of the group's success to a diverse membership, several highly active core members, and a history of strong leaders.

The group was involved in local elections from the beginning, sending questionnaires to school board candidates in 1971 and rating the candidates based on their responses. The group has a long list of accomplishments that continues to grow. They include helping pass the nation's first ban on sexual orientation discrimination in public schools in 1972; successfully lobbying the D.C. Council to include sexual preference in the city's 1973 human rights ordinance; showing political muscle in the 1978 campaign and election of Mayor Marion Barry; successfully lobbying the D.C. Council to pass a hate crime policy in 1990 and a domestic partners benefit package for city employees in 1992; and after ten years of leading the charge, repealing the antisodomy law in 1993.

Because the group has been so successful, by the late 1990s the GLAA was largely acting as a watchdog on the D.C. government. Over the past several years the GLAA has monitored the Alcohol Beverage Control Board's nude dancing policy, proposals to use unique identifiers in HIV testing surveillance, the actions of the Office of Human Rights, and the activities of the police department by holding regular meetings with the D.C. police chief.

Of course, one key way LGBT activists can influence local politics is to become involved with local political parties or groups that are affiliated with parties. As highlighted in Chapter 4, some LGBT activists turned to electoral politics and especially the Democratic Party in reaction to the increased presence of the religious right in the Republican Party. In Chicago, for example, the Chicago Gay and Lesbian Democrats began endorsing mayoral candidates in 1983. Their political muscle led to mayoral appointments of gay men and lesbians. In Pennsylvania the largest lesbian and gay political membership organization in the state is the Liberty City Lesbian and Gay Democratic Club, located in Philadelphia. The group endorses only Democratic candidates based largely on their positions on LGBT issues.

In San Diego, California, the predominately gay and lesbian Democratic Club has sent delegates to every national Democratic Party convention since 1980. In 2000 twelve delegates from the local club were selected to attend the convention. In San Francisco two local Democratic clubs have long been involved in party politics and local government. During the 1999 mayoral runoff between incumbent Mayor Brown, a popular incumbent because of his work on lesbian and gay issues, and openly gay City Board Supervisor Tom Ammiano, the Alice B. Toklas Lesbian and Gay Democratic Club spent more than $173,000 in support of Mayor Brown's campaign (Wilson 2000). The largest Democratic club in San Francisco, the Harvey Milk LGBT Democratic Club, has been active in city politics since the late 1970s. In 1996 the club helped ensure the passage of the city's Equal Benefits Ordinance, which required companies that contract with the city of San Francisco to grant domestic partner benefits to their employees. In 2000 the group upset some LGBT activists by endorsing Democratic presidential candidate Bill Bradley over Al Gore.

But many local LGBT groups try to maintain a nonpartisan image, endorsing candidates who are LGBT supportive, regardless of party affiliation. The nonpartisan San Antonio Equal Rights Political Caucus (SAERPC) formed in 1991 and endorses candidates for elective office, sometimes more than one candidate per race, and reports the endorsements to its mailing list of 2,000 local voters. State and local candidates from both parties often attend forums held by the SAERPC, but not all of the group's members have been happy with its endorsements. In 1995 a group of Republican members broke from SAERPC to form a local chapter of the Log Cabin Republicans, and in 2000 some Democratic members split and formed a new local chapter of the Stonewall Democrats. The attempts by the group to remain nonpartisan seem to slowly be bringing about its demise.

The total number of local groups continues to grow and existing groups continue to expand their activities. As previously nonpolitically active LGBT people become involved across the country, the need for local groups has grown. So, too, has the need for local chapters of some national groups grown, such as Parents, Families, and Friends of Lesbians and Gays and the Log Cabin Republicans (described in greater detail below). Perhaps for the foreseeable future, most LGBT people who become politically active will have their first contact with local political, or perhaps social, LGBT groups.

Case Studies: The Passage of LGBT Policies

To better illustrate the role of LGBT organizations and activists in local politics, below we provide four case studies of the passage of policies banning discrimination on the basis of sexual orientation and instituting bias crimes. Although local LGBT groups do far more than lobby on civil rights and hate crime policies, the passage of these types of ordinances has often been the first policy goal of local groups.

Buffalo, New York. During the 1960s a chapter of the Mattachine Society was formed in Buffalo. By 1973 the group had begun publishing its own newspaper and operating an information hotline. During the 1970s another gay group, Gay Professionals (GP), formed, but the group focused on a largely nonpolitical agenda. Even with this long history of formal organizations, however, gays and lesbians in Buffalo had little political influence.

In 1984 Buffalo enacted an antidiscrimination ordinance protecting gay and lesbian city employees from discrimination. The passage of the ordinance does not appear to have been the result of an organized campaign by gay groups. Instead, a few closeted gay men working within the county Democratic Party convinced the mayoral challenger (the current city council president) that the ordinance would show him as a progressive politician. The insider politics strategy allowed the limited bill to pass the council with the support of sympathetic Democrats, but the conservative mayor hobbled the implementation of the law by refusing to assign an agency to handle discrimination cases.

Ithaca, New York. In front of more than fifty cheering supporters, the city council of Ithaca, New York, adopted the first law in the state that applied to transgendered persons, by offering them recourse in crimes motivated by bias, in June 2000. The mayor had previously agreed to sign the law, which increased penalties for municipal offenses motivated by hatred, including acts based on an individual's sexual orientation as well as "gender identity and presentation." Similar efforts in New York City had been unsuccessful.

Although there were no nonaffiliated local LGBT groups involved, two key statewide groups were. Roey Thorpe, the Ithaca field organizer for the Empire State Pride Agenda, played a key role in the law's passage, as she and other Pride Agenda staff helped draft the law and lobbied for its passage. Also playing a key role in lobbying for the law was the first statewide transgender political organization in New York, the New York Association for Gender Rights Advocacy. The group's point person in Ithaca, Pauline Park, described the law as "historic" and predicted it would help in the "passage of fully transgender-inclusive hate crimes laws and anti-discrimination laws elsewhere in the state" (ESPA 2000).

Also playing key roles on the city council committee that drafted the law were Ithaca's lesbian city prosecutor, Margaret McCarthy, who oversaw the committee's drafts, and Ithaca's openly lesbian councilperson Pat Pryor, who participated on the committee. At McCarthy's prompting, the law was drafted to create four new misdemeanors, each punishable by a fine of up to $1,000 and/or up to a year's jail time: Bias-Motivated Harassment; Bias-Motivated Intentional Criminal Mischief; Bias-Motivated Reckless Criminal Mischief; and Bias-Related Graffiti Making. The law was also worded to ensure that a conviction would stay on a criminal's state record and could be used as evidence in any later offense. The law would also make it more likely that police would receive training on identifying hate crimes and work more closely with the LGBT community.

Portland, Maine.   Gay groups in Portland began their push for an antidiscrimination policy early in 1991. In May 1991 an openly lesbian city council member introduced a motion that would revise the city's nondiscrimination policy for city employees and add the words "sexual orientation." This incremental change was approved by the council. In 1992, however, gay groups pushed for a comprehensive local human rights ordinance that resembled the Maine Human Rights Act, but would also include sexual orientation. This policy would prevent discrimination against gays and lesbians in public and private employment, public accommodations, education, and housing. Local groups convinced a straight council member to introduce the ordinance and sought assistance from state and national groups, including the Gay and Lesbian Advocates and Defenders.

The salience of the issue was increased when the council sought the city attorney's opinion on whether the state's home rule law allowed the city to pass such ordinances and whether the city could allow civil redress in cases of discrimination. Allowing for civil redress rather than creating an administrative arm to handle cases of discrimination was a compromise solution for members worried about the cost of creating a new agency. After the city attorney agreed that the council had the authority to pass the ordinance, the council adopted the ordinance by a vote of seven to one in May 1992. Although opposition to the ordinance had been minimal during its consideration, soon after the law passed a group of local citizens formed to gather signatures in an effort to repeal it. The referendum was placed on the November 1992 ballot, but the ordinance was upheld in a vote of 57 to 43 percent.

Rochester, New York. The Rochester city council enacted an antidiscrimination ordinance protecting gay and lesbian city employees from discrimination in 1983. An established lesbian and gay movement characterized Rochester with its own interest groups and publications. Gay and lesbian activists first became involved in institutionalized forms of political participation in 1973 when the newly formed Gay Political Caucus, an arm of the Gay Alliance of the Genesee Valley (GAGV), began circulating questionnaires to local political candidates. Under pressure from activists, the Rochester police commissioner appointed a liaison to the gay and lesbian community in the mid-1970s. GAGV speakers were also able to regularly address police during training programs. By the early 1980s, gays had become a major force in the local Democratic Party.

Efforts to pass the ordinance were assisted by the election of an openly gay man to the city council in 1983. Even with the election of sympathetic political elites, however, gay groups were not unopposed in their struggle to pass an ordinance. Local religious fundamentalists publicly protested the ordinance, but gay groups were able to overcome the visible opposition and pass the law on the first try in December. The fairly high level of issue salience may, in part, explain why the ordinance was limited to city employees. Finally, given the strong organizational infrastructure of the gay community in Rochester, it is not surprising that they were also able to pass a domestic partners ordinance and registry in 1994.

State-Level Organizations and the Difficulties of State Politics

Although LGBT groups have been active at the national level for twenty-five years and at the local level since at least the 1950s, few states saw statewide activity by gay groups before the 1980s. In fact, much of the organizing at the state level has only begun to occur since about 1988. Part of the reason gay activity in state government has been slower and often inconsistent is because the membership in gay groups varies by the education and income level of the general population, the relative size of the gay population, and public and elite support.

Another reason the strength of gay groups varies across the states is because the movement itself is divided over whether political efforts should focus on the states or on other levels of government. For example, the director of New York state's main gay lobbying group, Empire State Pride Agenda, said, "Our movement has been . . . back and forth about a really coordinated focus on the state houses . . . [despite the fact that] . . . many issues affecting our lives are . . . decided by state legislatures" (Freiberg 1998). The executive director of Montana's statewide gay group said in a discussion over the wisdom of a year 2000 march on Washington, D.C.: "The queer community in Montana needs to put pressure on Helena, not Washington, D.C. Montana laws affect Montanans, not a good deal of the federal legislation" (Freiberg 1998). Furthermore, increasing activity by religious right groups in state legislatures has provided a greater incentive for gays to countermobilize in the states.

Perhaps the increasing involvement of gay groups in state-level politics is best exemplified by the 1998 calls for a coordinated "50 State Action" in the spring of 1999. The State Action eventually included marches, rallies, and lobbying in state capitals, and was planned by the Federation of Statewide Lesbian, Gay, Bisexual and Transgender Political Organizations, which itself just formed in 1997. The action also helped to create several statewide groups in states where they did not previously exist.

Threats to the gay community in a state often provide the greatest incentive to form and maintain local and statewide organizations. For example, a 1978 California antigay initiative, Proposition 6, motivated gays to form a statewide group called NO on 6 that organized fund-raising campaigns, grassroots mobilization, and voter registration. The group raised $1.3 million and defeated the initiative. In the wake of the campaign, multitudes of LGBT groups formed throughout the state and a number of gay politicians were elected. Three antigay ballot initiatives in Oregon (1988, 1992, and 1994) led to the creation of statewide groups to fight the measures. These groups left an institutional legacy in two Oregon groups—Right to Pride and the Rural Organizing Project.

In New York the state's main statewide LGBT group is the Empire State Pride Agenda, a nonpartisan LGBT advocacy organization. The group's stated mission is to end discrimination and prejudice on the basis of sexual orientation. To this end the group has offices in Albany, Buffalo, New York City, and Rochester, and its activities include lobbying the state legislature, electing supportive candidates to office, organizing constituent pressure, and educating the public. Dwarfing many other statewide groups, Empire has a full-time staff of fourteen and a $2.2 million annual budget.

In Colorado gay politics has been dominated by a Denver-based organization called Equal Protection. This group had successfully lobbied the governor to sign an executive order banning discrimination against homosexual state employees in 1990. In 1992 Colorado LGBT activists faced antigay Amendment 2, a ballot initiative that would have repealed and banned laws protecting gay civil rights. The threat of Amendment 2 forced activists to attempt to create a formal statewide organization. Equal Protection, however, fought the creation of a new group and instead presented itself as the organization to lead the fight. This decision, while supported by some activists, alienated many others who believed that Equal Protection was too focused on the Denver area and would not represent their interests. Indeed, the choice of tactics and strategy for fighting Amendment 2 was complex. Equal Protection followed a "degaying" strategy, in which the issue was presented as one of discrimination rather than the morality of homosexuality. This strategy left Equal Protection unable to effectively counter statements made by the religious right about homosexuality, but more importantly, it alienated LGBT activists who saw the campaign as an opportunity to educate the public about LGBT people. Although Amendment 2 passed at the polls, with the help of national LGBT groups, Equal Protection sued the state of Colorado and the case went all the way to the Supreme Court, where the amendment was overturned in 1996 as a violation of the equal protection clause of the Fourteenth Amendment.

The 1994 antigay initiative in Idaho provides another example of gay mobilization to counter threats. Like Amendment 2, Proposition 1 would have banned local goverments from passing laws that prohibit discrimination based on sexual orientation. Prior to 1994 Idaho's gay community was fairly invisible outside of Boise, and no groups lobbied the state legislature or governor. To fight the ballot initiative, gays formed the No On One Coalition (NOC). NOC used the opportunity posed by the initiative to create the infrastructure of a movement in Idaho, in part providing the impetus to create Idaho for Human Dignity, the first statewide organization in Idaho for gays.

Although LGBT groups in the states are relatively new, they have already made a significant impact in state politics. Research suggests that these groups have had a significant influence on state adoption of antidiscrimination policies including sexual orientation, progressive AIDS legislation, hate crime laws including sexual orientation, and delaying or preventing consideration and adoption of bans on same-sex marriage. Even so, the ability of gay groups to influence policy in most states is often weakened by religious right groups with greater resources. For example, in Florida the Christian Coalition has more lobbying influence than any other single-issue or social-issue group, and in Michigan religious right groups play a major role in the state Republican Party and the policy-making process.

Additional examples of gay statewide groups include the Illinois Federation for Human Rights, the Louisiana Lesbian and Gay Political Action Caucus, Missouri's Privacy Rights Education Project, Montana's PRIDE!, Tennessee's Lesbian and Gay Coalition for Justice, and the Lesbian and Gay Rights Lobby of Texas. By 1998 thirty-six states had active gay groups involved in statewide politics. About 33 percent of these groups have only one paid staff member; another 33 percent have more than one paid staff member; and the reminder use all-volunteer staff. Most groups use their own staff or volunteers to lobby state governments, but some do hire professional lobbyists, a pattern similar to that used by other single-issue and social-issue groups in the states. By 2001 state LGBT groups had grown to thirty-eight, but most were still relatively weak.

Gay groups in the states tend to focus most of their efforts on lobbying the state legislature, but they also litigate, lobby the executive, and lobby bureaucratic officials, especially education and health officials. Gay groups have also increasingly become involved in electoral campaigns. For example, the Arizona Human Rights Fund, Oregon's Right To Pride, and Virginians for Justice endorse candidates for political office and contribute money to campaigns. In Texas the Log Cabin Republicans have fought state party officials to gain acceptance within the Republican Party and win recognition for gay assistance in the election of moderate Republicans.

In Wisconsin the local Log Cabin Republican group has done well for itself, but has sometimes run up against more progressive groups in the state. At the start of the 2000 legislative session, the state's only openly gay state legislator, Mark Pocan, publicly derided the group for public statements and letters that Pocan said undermined efforts to extend LGBT rights in the state. Pocan argued, "I wonder if they should be called the Uncle Tom Republicans" (Meunier 2000). Pocan also argued that the group had no real influence in Wisconsin politics. Interestingly, the liberal versus conservative LGBT divisions in Wisconsin have not prevented state LGBT groups from achieving a strong record of legislative success and grassroots mobilization.

In April 1998 California's only statewide LGBT and AIDS/HIV organization, the Lobby for Individual Freedom and Equality (LIFE), began making plans to shut down its operations. For a state that had been a focal point of LGBT activism since the 1950s the news was stunning. LIFE had been formed in 1986 by a coalition of local LGBT groups. It established The Institute, an affiliated think tank, in 1991. LGBT activists saw a need for a statewide group that could fight against antigay ballot initiatives, including those directed at persons with AIDS, and that could also lobby in the state legislature on LGBT and AIDS issues. The group was able to make effective use of grassroots organizations throughout the state, bringing pressure to bear in nearly all of the state's legislative districts.

LIFE helped provide many successes for the LGBT movement in California. The group helped ensure that sexual orientation was included in the state's 1987 hate crime law, secured legislative passage of a gay civil rights law in 1991 (later vetoed by the governor), helped pass the 1992 law banning employment discrimination based on sexual orientation, successfully lobbied for passage of the first statewide domestic partners bill in the nation (also vetoed), and successfully helped kill five bills that would have banned same-sex marriage in 1996 and 1997.

However, there were divisions within the organization, including the perception that the group was not always paying enough attention to AIDS issues. Further, leaders of the group were often divided, and the group's structure did not allow for a clean resolution of many issues. Perhaps most importantly the group was financially insecure from the start, and those problems were never solved.

Even as LIFE was collapsing, plans were laid to create a new LGBT civil rights lobby group and many existing AIDS/HIV organizations vowed to continue. It wasn't long before a new group formed called CAPE, the California Alliance for Pride and Equality, a nonprofit, nonpartisan, grassroots-based, statewide advocacy organization. CAPE's mission is similar to that of LIFE: the group is concerned with LGBT equality and safety and engages in lobbying elected state officials, educating the public, and forming alliances with other communities. By 2001 CAPE claimed 200,000 donors, volunteers, and supporters in California and was believed to be the largest and fastest growing statewide LGBT group in the country.

Conservative LGBT activists in California have also increased their presence and influence, largely through the California Log Cabin Republicans (LCR). In 2000 the local LCR was even able to obtain a private meeting with the Republican state party chairman. About sixty-five LCR members met with Chairman John McGraw, marking the first time in eight years that a chairman of the state Republican Party had agreed to meet with LGBT activists. McGraw said of the meeting, "They're Republican. We want to elect Republicans. Why shouldn't I treat them with the same respect as other Republicans? . . . Our party would be pretty boring if we didn't debate the issues" (Wisckol 2000). Chairman McGraw also appointed several LCR members to key positions in the state party. However, McGraw refused the group's request to rescind his support for Proposition 22, a state ballot initiative that banned same-sex marriage.

Even some conservative southern states are beginning to see significant LGBT political activity. LGBT activists in Louisiana have maintained a fairly strong lobbying effort in the state capital for more than eights years, and Alabama is seeing an increase in LGBT activism. In 2001 the third annual Southern Girls Convention was held in Auburn; the event is a political and musical rally for southern lesbians, including about sixty workshops. It was the first time the event was ever held in the Deep South. In Mississippi LGBT activists held their first statewide strategy meeting in July 2001. The meeting was to address hate crimes and discrimination, and was to be attended by representatives of the Mississippi Gay Lobby and University of Mississippi Gay, Lesbian and Bisexual Alliance, and held at the lesbian-owned Camp Sister Spirit in Ovett.

Transgender Groups

Although many lesbian and gay groups focus on transgender issues as well, some transgender activists have felt the need to form their own groups. Below we briefly describe some of these groups at the state and local levels.

In 1982 transgender activists in Washington, D.C., formed the Transgender Education Association of Greater Washington, Inc., to help educate and support transgendered individuals and their significant others, families, and friends. The group hosts many social activities as well as organizational meetings. At their 1999 Christmas event one speaker argued that transgendered people need to become more political: "If we learn anything from the feminist movement, it's that the personal is political. What you do, what you are, is political. But one of the problems is that because gender is so personal, we tend to think that if there's a problem about our gender then that must be personal, too. The gender system is an organized and systemic oppression. We can't change that system by passing better" (Napolitano 1999).

In addition, local chapters of It's Time America! have formed in several states, including Ohio and Maryland. In 1999 It's Time Maryland! faced a difficult year when a key activist from Baltimore, Tracy Ranta, was murdered in what many called a hate crime.

Transgender activists have been successful in having some local and state laws passed that ban discrimination against "gender variants" or "gender identity." About twenty-seven localities and the states of Minnesota, Connecticut, and Rhode Island have passed laws to protect gender identity. In most localities, such as Boulder, Colorado; Ann Arbor, Michigan; Atlanta, Georgia; and Louisville and Lexington, Kentucky, the laws were passed in the late 1990s. In addition, judges in New Jersey and Massachusetts have ruled that those states' civil rights laws protect cross-dressers and transsexuals, but those rulings may be challenged.

Rhode Island was able to pass its law in 2001. Gender identity had been included in the state's 1995 bill to ban discrimination based on sexual orientation, but the language was considered too controversial and was dropped. The Rhode Island Alliance for Lesbian and Gay Civil Rights fought for the bill, which was introduced by a Democrat, even though the group thought it was unlikely the bill would pass. On the last day of the legislative session the state senate passed the bill twenty-six to seventeen with almost no debate. The governor allowed the bill to become law a few days later without his signature.

Case Studies: The Passage of State Civil Rights Policy

Research on antidiscrimination policies for lesbians and gays suggests that state adoption of these policies is most likely when gay interest groups have significant resources, the salience of the issue is low, partisanship is avoided, conservative religious forces can be neutralized, the policy change can be framed as incremental in nature, and the gay community has the support of political elites. Below we examine attempts to pass antidiscrimination laws in Oregon and Wisconsin to clarify the role of LGBT groups in state politics.

Oregon. Gay activists in Oregon have attempted to pass a gay civil rights law nearly every legislative session since 1973. In an effort to reduce the salience of the issue, gays changed strategies and successfully lobbied the governor to sign an executive order in 1987 that banned sexual-orientation discrimination in state employment. Upon hearing of the governor's action, a new conservative group, called the Oregon Citizens' Alliance (OCA), mobilized to repeal the order at the ballot box. A group called Oregonians for Fairness formed to fight the 1988 initiative (Measure 8), but their campaign started late and was never able to shape the debate. In the wake of the ballot campaign, activists formed the first permanent statewide group, Right to Privacy (RTP), later Right to Pride.

In each legislative session following the 1988 defeat, RTP lobbied to pass gay civil rights legislation. They achieved limited success in 1991 when a pro–gay rights bill passed the state senate with the support of the governor, but the bill stalled in the house of representatives. Meanwhile, OCA continued to fight RTP in the legislature and at the ballot box. In 1992 and 1994 OCA placed measures before the voters to block the passage of local and state gay civil rights laws. Both initiatives were defeated, but by narrow margins.

Following the defeat of the 1994 initiative, RTP successfully lobbied to have another antidiscrimination bill introduced in the legislature. In a May 6, 1995, press release, David Casti of RTP described the situation: "After months of behind-the-scenes work, Right to Privacy has introduced a comprehensive civil rights bill in the Oregon Legislature, prohibiting discrimination on the basis of sexual orientation in employment, housing, public accommodations and real estate transactions." The bill (HB 3459), like many others before it, failed to receive a hearing.

In 1997 a limited gay civil rights bill came closer to becoming law than any gay civil rights bill in Oregon during the twenty-five years that they had been introduced. Many high-profile companies in the business community supported the bill. Openly gay and Republican Representative Chuck Carpenter was the chief sponsor of the bill (HB 2734), which covered only employment discrimination. When the Republican leadership failed to give the bill a hearing in committee, Carpenter used a rare procedural maneuver—a motion to have the bill go directly to the house floor. The Republican leadership, backed by the OCA, called a recess to avoid voting on the bill. Carpenter reached a compromise with the leadership, whereby HB 2734 was allowed to die in committee and a new bill was drafted and sent to a different committee. The new bill (HB 3719) was given "priority" status. Even with opposition lobbying by OCA, Carpenter and RTP were able to ensure that HB 3719 passed quickly from the House Commerce Committee by an eight-to-one vote and in the full house, forty votes to twenty.

In the state senate Representative Carpenter testified before committees and built bipartisan support, but the bill was again stalled in committee by the Republican leadership. Carpenter teamed up with Democrats in the senate, who threatened to block senate activity on any legislation until the gay civil rights bill was put to a floor vote. He was unable to replicate his house victory and the bill failed one vote short of a majority.

Wisconsin. Wisconsin became the first state to protect lesbians and gays from discrimination in 1982. David Clarenbach (D-Madison) was the main sponsor of the legislation; his cosponsors were four Democrats from safe legislative seats in Milwaukee. The bill simply added the category "sexual preference" to the existing state civil rights laws. Clarenbach introduced the legislation in every session from 1975 to 1981 but did not bring the issue to a vote, thinking that the process required some long-term "softening-up" of political elites on the issue. His strategy had four parts: (1) to present the bill as a civil rights measure consistent with Wisconsin's progressive tradition; (2) to defuse the morality issue by seeking support from mainline religious organizations; (3) to gather bipartisan support for the bill; and (4) to use gay and lesbian activists to do the groundwork in building political support. Clarenbach decided to push for passage of the bill in 1981 when his legislation to repeal Wisconsin's anti-sodomy law lost by one vote. Owing to the potential controversy the bill would generate, Clarenbach perceived that he had only one session to pass the bill; if he failed, opponents would have time to countermobilize.

The bill was framed as an incremental extension of protections that the state's two largest cities had already implemented. Using gay and lesbian activists to contact individuals for support resulted in endorsements by the Catholic archbishop of Milwaukee and by mainstream Protestant denominations. The effort was to isolate the Moral Majority as the sole religious group opposing the legislation. To avoid having the legislation designated as a "Democratic bill" that could be used as a campaign issue, several Republican legislators were persuaded to support it. Although the number of Republicans supporting passage was small, the Republicans were highly visible (one later was the Republican candidate for the U.S. Senate, another became lieutenant governor) and provided the margin of victory on several votes. The National Gay and Lesbian Task Force was instrumental in providing resources to gay activists in the state.

The strategy was successful though the margins were close. The legislation passed the lower house by a vote of forty-nine to forty-five. In a compromise for opponents, the Senate Committee on State and Local Affairs and Taxation offered an amendment that specified affirmative action was not necessary in regard to sexual preference. This compromise passed the senate in February 1982 by voice vote (the key vote was one of "nonconcurrence" with the assembly bill, which failed thirteen to nineteen). The assembly then accepted the senate language, and Republican Governor Lee Dreyfus signed the bill into law on February 25, 1982. Dreyfus reputedly signed the bill immediately to prevent any groundswell of pressure for a veto to materialize. As further illustration that the elite process remained relatively nonsalient, the final passage of the bill occurred in an election year, and it did not become a key issue in either the legislative or gubernatorial races that year.

Organized National LGBT Groups

This section describes the main national LGBT groups in greater detail, including general interest groups, more specialized groups, and the relationships between movement groups. Finally, we offer a brief case study of GenderPAC, a group concerned with gender rights founded by transgendered activists.

The universe of national groups has become increasingly diverse over time, with new, more specialized groups forming throughout the 1990s, while few of the older groups have died out. According to surveys of national groups conducted by the *Washington Blade* between 1995 and 1997 the number of individual contributors to the largest six LGBT groups increased from 203,000 to 370,000, an increase of 82 percent; and contributors increased 161 from 1993 (Chibbaro and Keen 1997). Of the largest eleven LGBT groups in 1997, nearly all saw increases in their budgets between 1995 and 1997 (overall a 29 percent increase), with a combined 1997 budget of $25.5 million. However, the numbers are small when compared to opposition groups such as Focus on the Family and the Christian Coalition. The combined budgets of the top six religious conservative groups opposed to LGBT civil rights amounted to almost $380 million in 1997 (Chibbaro and Keen 1997).

By 1999 the eleven largest national LGBT groups saw their budgets increase 43 percent over 1997 levels, to almost $40 million. However, the number of contributors to the six largest groups rose only 5 percent from 1997, to 393,000 (Chibbaro 1999). Based on previous *Washington Blade* surveys, the budget increases reflect a ten-year trend for the main national LGBT groups, but increases in the number of individual contributors to these groups had begun to level off by 1999, suggesting that even as the number of individual contributors has not increased much, the amount of money they are contributing has increased. The *Blade* surveys also suggest a growth in the total number of LGBT groups since 1987, with groups increasingly developing specialized issue niches (Chibbaro 1999), a phenomenon noted by Haider-Markel (1997b) that has consistently occurred in other issue areas. Furthermore, in 1999 the budgets of the top LGBT groups still remained small relative to the top six religious conservative groups opposed to LGBT civil rights, whose combined budget in 1999 was at least $404 million, ten times the budgets of the top sixteen LGBT groups (Chibbaro 1999).

Interestingly, Lou Chibbaro Jr. also suggests that if we estimate the LGBT population in the United States as 4.3 percent (a number similar to what voting exit polls suggest), or 9 million adults, the 415,168 people who contribute to the largest sixteen LGBT groups constitute only 4.6 percent of the LGBT population (Chibbaro 1999). Although these numbers are low, they are similar to the proportions of potential group members to actual group members for other interest groups in the United States.

In the early 2000s national LGBT groups continue to grow, as well as to begin to address issues previously downplayed, such as transgender issues. As for most Americans, participation with interest groups is an important way for LGBT people to become involved in politics. Indeed, only voting exceeds interest group membership as a means for political participation in America. As with all interest groups, however, we should be concerned about who joins and participates and subsequently, whom interest groups are representing. LGBT groups, like other interest groups, most often reflect upper-class white majority values, simply because these are the values of a group's members. These are the people who have the discretionary income to pay membership dues and contribute to political candidates. As such, the LGBT interest group universe may not always represent all of the views of LGBT Americans. But most national groups do acknowledge this problem and have strived to increase diversity. We begin our discussion with general interest groups.

General Interest Groups

Human Rights Campaign (HRC).   In 1978 LGBT activists formed the Gay Rights National Lobby with a goal of creating a network of grassroots activists to lobby Congress on lesbian and gay issues. The group could not maintain itself and in 1981 transformed itself as the Human Rights Campaign Fund (HRC); the HRC is currently the largest gay and lesbian interest group in the country.

In the late 1980s the HRC began to grow quickly and by 1991 had an annual budget of $4.5 million. In 1996 the HRC had over 150,000 members nationally, a budget exceeding $8 million, and a staff of fifty-two. By 2001 the group's annual budget had grown to $21 million and it had almost 400,000 members.

HRC activities include lobbying the federal government on gay, lesbian, and AIDS issues; educating the general public, participating in election campaigns, organizing volunteers, and providing expertise and training at the state and local levels. For example, in 1994 the HRC's Americans Against Discrimination project, cochaired by retired Arizona Senator Barry Goldwater and former Oregon Governor Barbara Roberts, worked with states and communities throughout the country targeted by antigay ballot initiatives and referenda. The program was instrumental in defeating antigay measures in Oregon and Idaho in 1994.

The HRC maintains the largest full-time lobbying team in the nation devoted to LGBT issues, with twelve full-time lobbyists. Two of the group's biggest accomplishments in the 1990s were helping to bring the Employment Non-discrimination Act within one vote of passing and orchestrating an address to the group by President Clinton, marking the first time a sitting president addressed an LGBT group. The HRC's political action committee makes financial and in-kind contributions to Republican, Democratic, and Independent candidates for federal office. In addition, they offer political expertise in outreach, organizing, and fundraising within the lesbian, gay, and bisexual community.

Perhaps more than any other gay organization, the HRC often attracts criticism for being elitist and catering to the concerns of upper-class gays and lesbians. Activists have been concerned that the HRC spends too much time raising money at glitzy $150-a-plate dinners and too little time on political activity. The HRC also seeks major donors through its Federal Club. The Federal Club is an annual giving program for those contributors who support the HRC at $1,200 a year or more.

At the highest contribution level, called the President's Cabinet, members are expected to contribute $250,000 or more. Those who contribute at these high levels have the ear of HRC board members. However, without such significant efforts to raise funds, the HRC would be unable to make contributions to so many congressional campaigns or to political parties. For fiscal year 2000, about 34 percent of the HRC's revenues came from membership dues; 33 percent from its Federal Club and Council Program for large donors; 21 percent from special events, such as dinners; 5 percent from corporate or foundation grants; and 7 percent from other revenue sources.

The HRC is a hierarchical organization, with no local chapters, and its board meetings are closed. In each region of the country, however, HRC field directors do attempt to coordinate the group's activities. The executive board makes all decisions for the organization and individual members do not have a formal means of communicating issues or concerns to HRC leaders. However, beginning in 1996, the HRC began holding a national convention, the first being OutVote '96. The convention drew over 200 activists for workshops and campaign training, but the convention did not include a formal means for participants to develop or direct HRC strategy or tactics.

In the mid-1990s the HRC began to focus more of its efforts on grassroots organizing by selecting coordinators in more than a dozen states and fifty congressional districts. The HRC has also increasingly reached out to local organizations to form partnerships. For example, the HRC formed a partnership with a local organization in Minneapolis—the two organizations combined funds to hire a full-time lobbyist for the 1996 Minnesota legislative session. In Georgia, the HRC worked with the Georgia Equality Project in an effort to fill Senator Nunn's seat with a gay-friendly politician, while in Illinois the HRC worked with Illinois Impact to register gay and lesbian voters, and in Maine HRC worked closely with local groups supporting the election of Dale McCormick, who would have been the first openly lesbian person to be elected to the U.S. House of Representatives. The HRC has also been providing organizing grants for state and local LGBT groups and their political activities. As part of this effort, the HRC began the Equality Fund grant program to provide financial support to statewide LGBT groups in 2000. For fiscal year 2001, the HRC distributed $114,000 to twenty-seven state lobby groups. The grants ranged between $2,900 and $5,000 for work on specific projects proposed by state groups, including hiring lobbyists, conducting state polls, and producing state legislature voting score cards.

Also in 2000 the HRC made its greatest effort yet to work with state organizations on state-level issues. The HRC provided staff support and technical assistance, mobilized HRC's grassroots network, developed legal analyses, and submitted written and oral testimony in twenty-four states. For example, the HRC helped Free State Justice, Maryland's main LGBT lobby group, to pass an employment bill prohibiting discrimination based on sexual orientation by providing funds to hire a lobbyist, assist in fundraising, and in developing strategy. The HRC also assisted the Vermont Freedom to Marry Coalition by raising funds to contribute to state legislators who had supported the passage of a civil unions bill, as well as to reelect Governor Howard Dean, who signed the bill. A grant to the Lesbian/Gay Rights Lobby of Texas helped to organize lobbying for passage of the Non-Discrimination in Education bill. The bill passed only one chamber, but it was the first time an LGBT nondiscrimination bill ever passed in a chamber of the Texas legislature. The HRC also played a key role in the passage of the Texas hate crime bill by mobilizing 2,200 HRC members to contact state legislators. In California the HRC supported California Alliance for Pride and Equality by providing a $5,000 Equality Fund grant to support their grassroots mobilization efforts, sending action alerts to HRC members to encourage people to lobby their state legislators, lobbied Governor Gray Davis's office for support of the gender nondiscrimination bill, and helped collect signatures in support of a domestic partner's bill. With the help of HRC grassroots mobilization and the submission of testimony and legal analysis, the Gay and Lesbian Alliance of Alabama was able to pass a hate crimes bill in the state house of representatives. The HRC also worked with the Arizona Human Rights Fund to organize constituent pressure on state legislators for a civil rights bill and repeal of the state's antisodomy law.

The HRC also sponsors the National Coming Out Project, an ongoing campaign to encourage gays and lesbians to let others know who they are. Other HRC programs include Speak Out Action Grams, a direct-mail effort that has generated more than a million messages to Congress, and the 5,000-member Field Action Network, which organizes and trains grassroots volunteers. The HRC describes the Field Action Network (FAN) as an organized national grassroots effort. FAN participants receive a monthly "action alert" and are trained to mobilize and respond to legislative situations and to work on political campaigns. Activities range from letter writing, to hosting house parties, to introducing friends and neighbors, to personal meetings with members of Congress, to getting out the vote on election day. HRC staff can also provide candidates with campaign advice. The HRC's political consultants, along with the Field Action Network, are responsible for organizing and coordinating HRC members to volunteer in local congressional campaigns targeted by the HRC. FAN participants also lobby congressional members at home, in their districts, educating them on issues affecting lesbians and gays.

The HRC's affiliated political action committee (PAC) has grown to become one of the fifty largest PACs in the country, and is the largest LGBT PAC. During the 1995–1996 election cycle, the HRC contributed more than $880,000 to gay-friendly candidates, political parties, and PACs. For the 1997–1998 election cycle, the HRC provided resources for almost 200 campaigns for congressional races. The HRC contributed $1.3 million to the 1999–2000 congressional and presidential races as well as providing other campaign resources, including educational advertisements (HRC Website).

Log Cabin Republicans (LCR). The Log Cabin Republicans (LCR) is the nation's largest gay and lesbian Republican organization, with a national office and more than fifty chapters in twenty-one states nationwide. In 2001 the LCR had seven full-time staff members and offices in Washington, D.C.; Boston; and Dallas. The group began lobbying in Washington, D.C., in 1993 and formed a political action committee that raises $100,000 per election cycle for Republican candidates. By 1996 LCR had six staff members and an annual budget of $700,000.

The first LCR group formed in 1978 to fight California's Proposition 6, a ballot initiative that would have banned homosexuals from teaching in the public schools, among other things. Indeed, the LCR was instrumental in enlisting the support of former California Governor Ronald Reagan to publicly oppose the measure. Prior to 1993 local chapters began coordinating through United Republicans for Equality and Privacy, but it wasn't until 1990 that all the local clubs joined together under the Log Cabin Federation. The Federation merged with the LCR in 1995.

The LCR views itself as fighting for the "mainstream" concerns of the gay and lesbian community, believing that most existing LGBT groups are too liberal and too affiliated with the Democratic Party. The LCR believes that the Republican Party better represents their views on crime, fiscal responsibility, foreign policy, individual rather than group rights, the size of government, and the role of free markets in society. As such, the LCR works with moderate factions of the Republican Party, hoping to direct the future of the party. In the broadest terms, the LCR's mission is to ensure equal protection of all citizens at all levels of government. The groups' members have input as to strategy through state and local LCR clubs.

According to the Federal Election Commission (FEC) website, the LCR PAC contributed $76,000 to local, state, and national candidates in the 1996 elections, but during the 1999–2000 election cycle, the LCR contributed only $15,000 directly to federal candidates, but spent almost $500,000 in targeted voter-turnout activities (FEC Website, 2001). Almost half of these funds were used for an LCR radio ad campaign in battleground states promoting George W. Bush's record, targeting independent swing voters, women, and suburbanites (LCR Website, 2000).

The LCR first gained national attention in 1996 when Republican presidential candidate Bob Dole refused a campaign contribution from the group. The LCR had endorsed Dole in 1996, but refused to endorse President Bush following the 1992 Republican convention. During the 2000 presidential race, Republican candidates accepted contributions from the group and met with LCR leaders during the primary season. Republican candidate George W. Bush refused to meet with the group until the primaries ended, but did eventually meet with dozens of LCR members. In an interview, the LCR's chief spokesperson, Kevin Ivers, described the meeting as historic and an important step (Alsdorf 2000).

The National Gay and Lesbian Task Force (NGLTF). The Task Force is the oldest surviving national gay and lesbian interest group in the United States. Formed in 1973, the group operates a lobbying arm and the nonprofit NGLTF Policy Institute, which is a national information center for educating and organizing around gay and lesbian issues. The Policy Institute's publications on LGBT civil rights, voting, and state legislative activity, among others, have been indispensable for activists and researchers. Both arms also work for gay and lesbian rights on the international scene. By 1995 NGLTF had a budget of $3.1 million and by 1996, 35,000 members and a staff of 21. By the late 1990s, the group began to face some criticism, as well as staff turnover and budget problems. Nevertheless, by 2000 NGLTF had grown to a full-time staff of 35 and a budget approaching $4.4 million (Smith 2001). In 2001 the group's budget dropped to $3.6 million and membership levels remained at about 35,000 as the NGLTF continued to face something of an identity crisis (NGLTF Website, 2001).

Although the Task Force is not structured as a federation of local chapters, the group's literature suggests that since 1996 it has been trying to build a grassroots movement with strong contacts with state and local groups. To accomplish this goal the Task Force holds an annual Creating Change Conference attended by thousands of activists. It started its Youth Leadership Training program in 1993 and has built partnerships with more than 120 groups through its Cooperating Organization program. The Task Force coordinates the activities of local and state groups through its "activist alert" network.

The Task Force sponsored the founding of the Federation of Statewide Lesbian, Gay, Bisexual and Transgendered Political Organizations in 1997 and has provided critical support to its success. The goal of the Federation is to build statewide organizations in all fifty states. In 1999 the NGLTF, through its Federation, launched a national campaign called Equality Begins at Home. The campaign organized 350 rallies, political and cultural events in all fifty state capitals plus the District of Columbia and Puerto Rico. To facilitate the campaign, the NGLTF awarded $5,000 grants to groups in every state and territory.

The Task Force addresses many issues, including antidiscrimination policies for gays and lesbians, antigay ballot initiatives and referenda, general homophobia, harassment and violence against gays and lesbians, sodomy laws, legal protections for gay and lesbian families, and funding of AIDS research and related health care. The NGLTF also tries to build connections with other civil rights groups focused on race and ethnicity, gender discrimination, abortion, and even the death penalty. Goals and strategy are decided in the national office—the structure of the group allows for limited input from local members, which lessens conflict within the organization. Although the Task Force often attempts to coordinate its activities with local and state groups, tensions between it and other national groups (especially the Human Rights Campaign) have restricted its cooperation with most national groups.

Even with its recent problems, the NGLTF has built an impressive record of accomplishments. In 1975 the group convinced the U.S. Civil Service Commission to make a ruling allowing homosexuals to serve in government employment. That same year the group helped convince U.S. Representative Bella Abzug (D-NY) to introduce the first gay rights bill in Congress. In 1978 the NGLTF released the first study ever to document sexual orientation discrimination in private companies. Between 1982 and 1984 the Task Force became the first national group to give significant attention to hate crime. It launched a national project on hate crime, established a crisis hotline, and began a series of reports on antigay hate crime. These actions culminated in the group's leadership of the national hate crimes coalition, which successfully lobbied for passage of the 1990 Hate Crimes Statistics Act in Congress. In 1991 the Task Force began a national boycott of the Cracker Barrel restaurant chain, which had fired some employees upon learning they were gay. It also began the Families Project with the National Center for Lesbian Rights, gave the first briefing on people of color and AIDS to the Congressional Black Caucus, and developed its Fight the Right Action Kit, which has been used by thousands of activists. The NGLTF started its Policy Institute with John D'Emilio as director in 1995, as well as hosted the first Youth Leadership Training Camp and held the first Progressive People of Color Grassroots Organizers Summit. And in 1996 the NGLTF coordinated simultaneous grassroots demonstrations and press actions in thirty-six communities across the country to raise awareness about the Supreme Court ruling on opposition to Colorado's Amendment 2. In the late 1990s the Task Force began publishing important first-ever reports on everything from LGBT voting to LGBT-related legislation in the states.

Parents, Families, and Friends of Lesbians and Gays (PFLAG). This is the largest organization in the world working for gay and lesbian rights comprised largely of heterosexuals. The first PFLAG group was founded in New York City in 1973, and other chapters formed around the country in the 1970s, but the national PFLAG organization was officially founded in 1981. The group was originally called the Federation of Parents and Friends of Lesbians and Gays. In 1996 the organization represented 27,000 households. By 2001 PFLAG had fourteen staff members in its national office, over 80,000 household memberships, and more than 450 affiliates worldwide. Indeed, until the mid-1990s PFLAG had the distinction of being the main LGBT group comprised largely of local chapters. However, in the 1990s a number of other groups began to create local chapters as PFLAG's national office faced criticism for not paying enough attention to the concerns of local chapters. During the 1980s the group largely focused on educational campaigns and as an information clearinghouse. Local chapters mobilized on LGBT issues in their areas.

The group professionalized in 1987 by establishing regional directors, hiring its first paid staff member, and establishing committees for specific issues. At that time the group's budget was only $16,000. By 1988 the group had 200 chapters and set up its head-quarters in Washington, D.C. In 1993 the group adopted the PFLAG name, restructured as a membership organization, began a formal affiliation process for chapters, and made board seats elected positions. From the mid-1990s forward, PFLAG has continued its efforts at mobilizing at the grass roots as well as lobbying the federal government.

As part of its seventeenth annual national conference in April 2000, PFLAG members baked apple pies for their first Apple Pie Lobby Day. PFLAG gave a pie to each member of Congress that met with them to discuss LGBT issues and legislation. During the conference banquet PFLAG also raised $90,000 for its Safe Schools campaign (O'Bryan 2000).

Specialized Groups

AIDS Action Council (AIDSAC). Founded in 1984, AIDSAC was the first national organization devoted solely to advocating at the federal level for more effective AIDS policy, legislation, and funding. The group also has a public education program. The Council represents more than 1,000 community-based AIDS service organizations throughout the United States. In 1998 the group spent $230,000 on lobbying Congress—up from $160,000 in 1997. By 2001 AIDS Action had a 20 person staff, a budget of over $2 million, and represented 3,200 community-based organizations. The group lobbies the federal government and keeps its member organizations informed of federal activity on AIDS/HIV. AIDS Action played key roles in the passage by Congress of the Ryan White CARE Act for AIDS programs, and led in the fight to reauthorize the Ryan White CARE Act in 2000 (AIDS Action Council Website 2001).

Family Pride Coalition (FPC). Formerly the Gay and Lesbian Parents Coalition International (GLPCI), the Family Pride Coalition (FPC) is a worldwide advocacy and support organization for gay and lesbian parents and their children. The Coalition provides information to gay and lesbian parents around the world, while trying to educate the public at large on issues concerning gay people. The group also lobbies local and state governments on occasion and participates in rallies with other groups.

The Coalition was founded as the Gay Fathers Coalition in 1979 and included "Lesbian" in its title in 1985. In 1980 the Coalition held its first national conference and in 1984 the group received tax-exempt status. In 1986 the Coalition adopted the GLPCI name. By 1996 the group's membership was divided equally between men and women, with over 6,300 member families and over 100 chapters in 9 countries. In 1989 the GLPCI started Children of Lesbians and Gays Everywhere—programs run by, for, and about the children of gays and lesbians. The GLPCI is less hierarchical than organizations such as the HRC and most of the organization's activities center around local chapters. Each year the group holds a Family Conference at which the main organization's board is elected and the group's policy positions are determined. The conference allows members more input into the composition and goals of the organization than any of the other groups examined in this analysis. The ability of the GLPCI to allow greater input from its members may be due, in part, to its high degree of specialization—the group's focus on the concerns of gay and lesbian parents.

The Coalition did not hire a full-time executive director until 1997 and officially changed its name to the Family Pride Coalition in 1998 by a majority vote of its members. In 2001 the Coalition had six staff members and a volunteer board and is positioned as a unique LGBT organization, whose membership differs from less specialized LGBT groups (Haider-Markel 1997a).

Gay and Lesbian Alliance Against Defamation (GLAAD). Founded as a national group in 1994, GLAAD formed as a New York City media watchdog group in 1985. The group is focused on fair representation of LGBT people in the media. The original group often protested *New York Post* stories on AIDS, but a Los Angeles group formed in 1988 focused its efforts on LGBT portrayals in movies and television. The Los Angeles chapter took the noted step of educating entertainment industry representatives about the frequently negative images of LGBT people the industry produced. The group is credited with the 1990s phenomenon of gay characters in television shows and support for the ABC sit-com *Ellen,* in which the main character comes out as a lesbian.

By 1998 GLAAD had ten chapters in different regions of the country, including the original two and those in Atlanta, Chicago, Dallas, Denver, Kansas City, San Diego, San Francisco, and Washington, D.C. GLAAD reported having 40,000 donors in 1997, but that number fell to 9,000 in 1999 (Chibbaro 1999). The group holds an annual event to award positive representations of LGBT people in the media. In the late 1990s GLAAD began to make more efforts on local media representations of LGBT people, in part to directly involve members with group activities.

Gay and Lesbian Victory Fund (GLVF). The Victory Fund is a political action committee (PAC) that supports gay and lesbian candidates for public office at all levels of government. The GLVF was founded in 1991 based on the success of EMILY's List, a PAC fund for female political candidates. The costs of joining this organization are quite high; an annual contribution of $100 dollars must be made with the promise of donating at least $100 annually to at least two candidates recommended by the GLVF. Members do not have the ability to select the candidates that the GLVF chooses to support, but once the Fund has endorsed a candidate, it informs members of that candidate's campaign. Members donate directly to the endorsed candidates, or send checks to the Fund, which bundles the contributions and forwards them to candidates.

In 1991 the group had only 181 members but saw that number jump to 3,500 by 1994 with total member contributions of more than $1.3 million by 1996. By 2001 the Victory Fund had more than 9,000 members and an office staff of 11, and had contributed over $2 million to LGBT candidates. Its board meetings are closed. During the 1996 election cycle, the group ranked as the fifteenth largest independent PAC in the country, giving more than $400,000 to candidates. The GLVF also provides staff and other resources to gay and lesbian political candidates (Rimmerman 1999).

Twenty-one of the Victory Fund's thirty-two openly gay candidates won their 1996 races (a 72 percent success rate; the previous highest win total was fourteen wins in 1994). Among the winners, Victory Fund candidate Ed Flanagan made history as the first openly gay person elected to a statewide office with his election as Vermont's auditor. The GLVF helped to add openly gay representatives to the state legislatures in Nevada, Connecticut, Montana, Rhode Island, Washington, and Illinois. Victory Fund candidate Sabrina Sojourner become the only openly lesbian African American in elective office by winning the U.S. Representative seat in the District of Columbia, and GLVF candidate Sebastian Patti garnered more than 1.1 million votes in his race for the Cook County (Illinois) Court—the highest vote total of any openly gay elected official in history.

GLVF activity and success has correlated with the total number of successful LGBT candidates. In 1991 the GLVF estimated that there were 52 openly LGBT officeholders around the country, but by 1998 that number rose to 146. Similarly, in the 1991–1992 election cycle, 40 LGBT candidates sought VF endorsement, but by 1995–1996, that number rose to 277 (Polman 1998). During the 1997 elections the VF had its highest percent of endorsed candidates win their races at 83 percent, with LGBT candidates winning office for the first time in states like Ohio and Virginia. By 2001 the Victory Fund had supported candidates in 32 states, with over 100 GLVF candidates ending victoriously (GLVF Website 2001).

Gay, Lesbian and Bisexual Veterans of America, Inc. (GLBVA). This is the only national, nonprofit chapter-based organization for gay, lesbian, and bisexual active duty, reserve, and veteran members of the U.S. armed forces, and their families, friends, and supporters. The group works to ensure all citizens the right to privacy, and the right to live free, open lives within American society, irrespective of race, creed, ethnic or cultural identity, national origin, age, economic or marital status, gender or gender identification, sexual orientation, or actual or perceived differences in physical or other ability. The GLBVA has eleven chapters around the country and holds an annual convention for its members.

Lambda Legal Defense and Education Fund (LLDEF). Founded in 1973, Lambda is the oldest and largest of several national gay groups that use litigation as a means for changing the status and treatment of LGBT people. The group's stated mission is to achieve full recognition of the civil rights of lesbians, gay men, and people with HIV/AIDS through impact litigation, education, and public policy work. Lambda has twelve full-time attorneys in its regional offices, which are located in New York, Los Angeles, Chicago, and Atlanta. Similar to the legal strategy of the National Association for the Advancement of Colored People (NAACP), Lambda litigates through test cases selected for the likelihood of their success in establishing positive legal precedents that will affect lesbians, gay men, and people with HIV/AIDS, usually by acting as counsel, cocounsel, or through filing amicus curiae briefs. Jon Davidson, supervising staff attorney in Lambda's Los Angeles office argues that Lambda's strategy "has been the history of the civil rights movement . . . courts have been an important engine for social change" (Boxall 1997). Lambda deals with a large variety of cases, including discrimination in employment and public accommodations; antigay initiatives; marriage rights; domestic partnership benefits; child custody; military service issues; immigration matters; antisodomy laws; inheritance rights; First Amendment free speech and associational challenges; and HIV/AIDS-related discrimination and public policy issues. At any given time the group is involved in about fifty cases seeking to realize equal protection under the law for LGBT individuals. For example, in 1996 Lambda served as cocouncil for opponents of the Colorado antigay rights ballot initiative, Amendment 2. In an historic decision (*Romer v. Evans*), the U.S. Supreme Court struck down the 1992 law. LLDEF also achieved another important victory in 1996 when a federal jury found a Wisconsin school district negligent for not protecting a gay high school student, Jamie Nabozny, from antigay harassment and abuse from other students in *Nabozny v. Podlesny*. The case helped prompt the U.S. Department of Education to issue federal guidelines addressing antigay harassment in schools. Other recent cases for which Lambda has served as council or cocounsel include the lawsuit over same-sex marriage in Hawaii (*Baehr v. Lewin*) and the successful effort by Colonel Margarethe Cammermeyer to stop the army from discharging her after she revealed that she is a lesbian (*Cammermeyer v. Aspin*). Lambda also maintains a national network of volunteer cooperating attorneys who work on cases as well as direct potential test cases to the group.

Jon Davidson, supervising staff attorney in Lambda's Los Angeles office explains: "The ultimate goal in this work has not been to change what [people] believe about homosexuality. . . . They can believe whatever they want to." Instead, he argues that the goal is to ensure that "the government treats everyone equally regardless of sexual orientation" (Boxall 1997).

Like most interest groups focused on litigation, Lambda is structured so that members have little say in what the group does. Decisions on what issues to address, in what cases Lambda should involve itself, and to what degree Lambda should work with other groups are all decided by an executive board composed of professional lawyers in closed meetings. In 1992 Lambda's budget was $1.6 million and by 1997 that had risen to $2.2 million. Lambda's budget increased to $5.5 million in 1999 with 25,000 contributors, but these figures do not reflect the considerable number of resources the group has through pro bono work by attorneys (Chibbaro 1999).

National Black Lesbian and Gay Leadership Forum (NBLGLF). The NBLGLF was founded in 1995 as a national group with a budget of $450,000. In 1988 Phil Wilson and Ruth Waters in Los Angeles founded the Black Lesbian and Gay Leadership Forum. The group's founders believed that existing LGBT groups were not addressing the concerns of black LGBT people. The group has its national office in Washington, D.C., and lobbies the federal government. The group also conducts educational campaigns for the public and works on AIDS prevention in the black community. The Forum holds a national conference, often exceeding 1,000 participants, to discuss issues and raise funds. By 1997 the group's budget was $850,000, over a quarter of which came from U.S. Centers for Disease Control grants. In 1999 the group apparently had few funds, but it did continue to operate (Chibbaro 1999). The group held its fourteenth annual conference in February 2001.

National Center for Lesbian Rights (NCLR).   Founded in 1977, the NCLR is a progressive, feminist, multicultural legal center that works toward advancing the rights and safety of lesbians and their families through litigation, government lobbying, public education, and by offering free legal advice. The NCLR has tackled some of the most difficult cases involving LGBT issues, including lesbian child custody, visitation, same-sex adoption, same-sex marriage, alternative insemination, domestic partnership, same-sex domestic violence, immigration and asylum, and youth. The NCLR has members in all fifty states and serves thousands of clients each year from around the country and overseas. The group has five paid staff members, but also has cooperating volunteer attorneys around the country.

National Latina/o Lesbian, Gay, Bisexual and Transgender Organization (LLEGO).   Founded in 1987 as National Latino(a) Lesbian and Gay Activists (NLLGA), LLEGO works for strengthening Latino/a communities at the local, national, and international levels; provides AIDS education and training programs for Latino gay men; defends the rights of immigrants; and acts as an information clearinghouse. Much of its work has been funded through a subcontract with the National Minority AIDS Council and through grants from the U.S. Centers for Disease Control and Prevention. For example, in 1997 the group received $600,000 in grants directly from the CDC, amounting to about 60 percent of the group's budget. The group has more than one hundred Latino/a gay, bisexual, or transgender chapters directly affiliated with it in forty-seven cities, eighteen states, and Puerto Rico. The group's national board meetings are open.

In the 1990s NLLGA hosted several major conferences to increase political organizing among LGBT Latinos. The conferences have attracted thousands of participants. In November 1998 the official name of the organization was changed to LLEGO, the National Latina/o Lesbian, Gay, Bisexual and Transgender Organization. Since its inception, LLEGO has provided technical assistance to more than 125 community-based organizations in the United States and Puerto Rico and disbursed more than $560,000 in seed funding to sociocultural and HIV/AIDS prevention education initiatives. LLEGO also hosted El Foro, the First National Symposium on the Dissemination of Innovative Latina/o LGBTQ Programs, which highlighted initiatives and interventions funded through LLEGO's Small Grants Initiative (LLEGO Website 2001).

National Stonewall Democratic Federation (NSDF). Formed in 1998, by 2001 the Federation had over 20,000 members belonging to sixty affiliated clubs in the states. The group played a significant role in the 2000 presidential election, with Democratic candidates catering to the group to gain its support. The NSDF formed in part to counter the efforts of gay Republican groups, and the group remains committed to educating voters about the difference between the parties on LGBT issues and educating Democratic politicians on LGBT issues. During the 2000 elections the NSDF contributed about $20,000 to Democratic candidates, according to the Federal Election Commission data (FEC Website 2001).

As part of its mission, the group trains local activists to help LGBT-positive Democratic candidates achieve elective office. The national group endorses candidates and provides campaign support where possible. In October 2000 the NSDF launched a $25,000 national print ad campaign to inform voters about George W. Bush's record on LGBT issues. The ads ran in major gay newspapers across the country, in states such as Washington, California, New York, Texas, Florida, Illinois, Ohio, Georgia, and throughout New England. The full-page ads asked "the number of times" George W. Bush has supported particular LGBT policies and showed that the sum of all George W. Bush's support was zero. The NSDF ran the ads in response to negative ads that the Log Cabin Republicans (LCR) ran about Democratic candidate Al Gore.

Service Members Legal Defense Network. Formed in 1993, the SLDN works toward ending discrimination and harassment of men and women in the military who are harmed by the 'don't ask, don't tell, don't pursue, don't harass,' and related policies, through direct legal assistance, watchdog activities, policy work, outreach and education, and litigation support. In 1995 the group's budget exceeded

$400,000 and by 2001 their budget had increased to $1.8 million with seventeen staff members. Although most of the SLDN's activities are focused on legal assistance, the group does lobby Congress, meeting with executive branch officials and military officials, and it conducts research on military actions and policies. The SLDN's lobbying prompted Secretary of Defense William Cohen to initiate a study of the use of the "don't ask, don't tell" policy. Also, in 1997 the head of the Pentagon's military personnel office issued a memorandum that acknowledged the existence of antigay harassment and directed commanders not to investigate a service member's sexual orientation outside of the guidelines set by the "don't ask, don't tell" policy. Since 1993 the group has provided legal assistance to more than 1,400 service members through a network of 200 attorneys across the nation. At any given time the group is addressing more than 100 cases (SLDN Website 2001).

National Interest Group Relationships

At the national level the gay and lesbian interest group system is increasingly diverse. Groups such as the National Gay and Lesbian Task Force and the Human Rights Campaign are large, established, and relatively well funded, while groups such as the Lambda Legal Defense and Education Fund, the Family Pride Coalition, the National Latina/o Lesbian, Gay, Bisexual and Transgender Organization, and the Gay and Lesbian Victory Fund are supported by relatively small membership rolls.

There is some interaction and resource sharing among gay and lesbian interest groups, especially concerning antigay local and state-level ballot initiatives. The ballot initiatives seem to be especially troubling to gay and lesbian interest groups and they have attempted to coordinate their efforts in this area with organizations such as the American Civil Liberties Union Lesbian and Gay Rights Project, the Institute for First Amendment Studies, the National Organization for Women, and the Unitarian Universalist Association. Most resource sharing, however, occurs between national and local groups and not between national groups. Groups battle for supremacy in the movement, each believing that its values and tactics represent movement activists. Instead of presenting a united front to policy makers, national groups have often lobbied on behalf of themselves, without the benefit of coordination with other LGBT groups. This self-interested behavior also occurs between groups that focus solely on litigation, as well as between groups that lobby and groups that litigate. Gay and lesbian litigation groups, however, are attempting to increase coordination and cooperation through the Roundtable, a meeting held twice a year between gay legal groups. At the 1994 Roundtable, legal groups were bitterly divided over same-sex marriage (some LGBT people object to emulating the heterosexual institution of marriage). The Roundtable decided not to become involved in the Hawaii same-sex marriage case for both ideological and strategic reasons.

The conflicts created by attempts to institutionalize the movement also came early in the movement's history. For example, the Gay Liberation Front (GLF), which formed immediately following the Stonewall Riots, was quickly split over tactics and the question of pursuing issues not directly related to gays. Ideologically moderate gays and lesbians split from the GLF to form the Gay Activists Alliance (GAA), in part because they wanted to keep a lower profile while pursuing gay civil rights. Founders of the GAA were not only looking for less radical politics and tactics, but also wanted a more formal organizational structure and control at meetings. Then in 1973 the GAA was split between participants who espoused a liberationist perspective, entailing participatory democracy within the organization, and those who believed that the GAA needed to be reorganized to lessen conflict. The plan of this second group was to establish a board of directors, a salaried staff, and to hold monthly meetings for members. Failing in the effort to tighten the GAA's structure, the second group resigned and formed Gay Action; a group soon renamed the National Gay Task Force and structured to reduce conflict. The GAA soon collapsed under the weight of the warring factions. Toby Marotta specifically attributes the split and collapse of the GAA to the fundamental tension between a liberationist social movement and the "imperatives of organization." In other words, the effort to create an interest group that could effectively lobby government created a conflict within the GAA that led to the birth of a more formally structured interest group and the death of the GAA.

The battle to end the ban on gays in the military presents a good example of the lack of unity and coordination between national movement groups. A lack of cooperation is cited as one of the main reasons gay groups were unable to overturn the gay ban. When President-elect Clinton announced that he would end the ban on homosexuals in the military, the religious right began gearing up for a campaign to stop the effort. In contrast to the weak mobilization efforts of the LGBT movement, the religious right was able to coordinate its campaign against repealing the gay ban with sympathetic members of Congress and the military and was also able to effectively mobilize at the grass roots and apply constituency pressure on the White House and Congress.

Caught off guard and realizing that a coordinated effort was necessary, a number of national groups created a last-minute coalition under a new organization called the Campaign for Military Service (CMS). It appears that the main reason a new organization was needed was because many groups mistrusted the two main national groups, the National Gay and Lesbian Task Force (NGLTF) and the Human Rights Campaign (HRC), and because neither the NGLTF or the HRC trusted each other enough to allow the other to coordinate the campaign. The coalition the NGLTF and HRC envisioned was to contain many groups that would pay for a staff with funds that would first go through either the HRC or NGLTF. Given the two groups' long history of competition for the lead spot in the movement, such a scenario was unlikely. The CMS suffered severely from the distrust and infighting among its member groups, making it difficult for it to coordinate the repeal of the gay ban. But the infighting was nothing new for the movement, organizational rivalries and ideological conflicts also thwarted the coordinating efforts of the North American Conference of Homophile Organizations (NACHO) during the late 1960s. Urvashi Vaid goes so far as to argue that the creation of the CMS was a "conscious strategy by some Los Angeles–based donors and activists, like [David] Mixner, to create a new national organization they could control" (Vaid 1995, 169). Although it is not clear if this was the purpose of the CMS, the desire to create one central organization is a result of the pressures to institutionalize the movement. Furthermore, existing groups' fears that such an organization might be created illustrates the distrust and problems that the politics of institutionalization creates within a movement. The end result of these internal politics was to contribute to the failure to lift the ban on gays in the military.

Although the evidence presented here is anecdotal, it does suggest that attempts to institutionalize the gay and lesbian movement create conflicts between groups and within groups. These conflicts will likely lead to the failure of some attempts at organization, but more importantly, they are also likely to lead to the creation of organizational structures that will lessen conflict and ensure organizational survival.

In the mid-1990s most national groups began to make more significant efforts to coordinate their activities and specialize their roles so as not to directly compete with one another for members and other resources. However, it remains to be seen if these renewed efforts will be lasting or if they will result in political victories.

Case Study: GenderPAC: Transgender Political Lobbying

GenderPAC is a national advocacy organization that focuses on eliminating gender stereotypes and ending discrimination and violence on the basis of how individuals look, act, or dress in terms of gender or sexual orientation (GenderPac Website 2001). To describe all gender-related issues, the group often uses the term "gender orientation." GenderPAC (PAC stands for Public Advocacy Coalition) describes gender as "how we look, act, or dress, and others' interpretation of our sex or sexual orientation," which includes transgender and sexual orientation. Like other national groups, such as the NGLTF, GenderPAC also focuses on the intersection of discrimination based on gender, race, ethnicity, class, and age. The group argues that gender identity should be protected as a civil right and works to this goal through general education programs targeted at the media and the public, congressional lobbying, and litigation.

Riki Wilchins formed GenderPAC in 1995 in response to the lack of inclusion of transgender and broader gender issues in the agendas of national lesbian and gay organizations. The group was formed as an association of existing national organizations and quickly established a presence in the nation's capital. In its first five years the group's annual budget grew to $250,000 (Krisberg 2000). In the late 1990s GenderPAC focused on several high-profile events, including the cases of Matt Stickney, a gay student in Vermont attacked for wearing feminine clothing to school; Darlene Jespersen, a feminist fired from Harrah's Casino for refusing to wear makeup; Peter Oiler, a truck driver terminated by Winn-Dixie for cross-dressing off the job; and JoAnn Brandon, who sued Richardson County, Nebraska, after her transgender son Brandon Teena, was killed for living openly as a man.

Starting in 1996 GenderPAC began an event known as the Annual National Gender Lobby Days. For several days each May the group coordinates meetings with members of Congress to educate them on discrimination and violence based on gender and gender perception. In 2000 the group mobilized 150 activists to attend its lobby days.

Activists were trained in lobbying techniques and began a Congressional EEO (Equal Employment Opportunity) Project to ask congressional representatives to sign a statement indicating that they would not discriminate in their congressional offices based on employees' gender orientation. The group's activities led thirty members of Congress to sign GenderPAC's Congressional EEO Project diversity statement. The group also held a reception honoring congressional representatives who signed the statement, including Representatives Janet Schakowsky (D-IL), Jerrold Nadler (D-NY), and Carolyn Maloney (R-NY). The activities of the Gender Lobby Days were supported by several organizations, including the NGLTF, the Gill Foundation, and the HRC. The activists were also able to raise over $35,000. Nevertheless, most of the group's revenue comes from member contributions and a few large donors.

In 2000 GenderPAC incorporated, formed a new board composed of individuals instead of groups, and filed for 501(c)(3) nonprofit status. The board does a great deal of fundraising and policy making for the organization and is composed of gays, lesbians, heterosexuals, cross-dressers, transgender, and trans-identified people.

In 2001 GenderPAC held the first National Conference on Gender in conjunction with its sixth annual National Gender Lobby Days in Washington, D.C., with over 450 participants attending from 35 states. Featured speakers included National Organization of Women (NOW) President Patricia Ireland and activist Angela Moreno from the Intersex Society of North America. GenderPAC activists were able to personally meet with representatives from 120 congressional offices during the three Gender Lobby Days. In June 2001 *Time Magazine* named GenderPAC's executive director, Riki Wilchins, one of 100 national innovators.

Although the group is focused on gender, confusion over cross-dressers, transsexuals, and trans-identified people has meant that many existing lesbian and gay groups have focused little attention on transgendered activists or general questions of gender. GenderPAC hopes to change that, helping all groups recognize that gender identity is a civil right.

Conclusion

This chapter examined the history and evolution of the LGBT movement in the United States, providing detailed information about a variety of LGBT groups at the local, state, and national levels. Although the LGBT movement has gone through many changes since the 1950s, some tensions and issues remain the same, especially those focused on gender and racial equity. Perhaps the most important changes in the movement stem from external events, such as the AIDS epidemic and the rise of religious conservatives in mainstream politics. These events have forced LGBT groups to reevaluate their goals as well as their internal structure and coordination with other LGBT groups and similar-minded non-LGBT groups.

However, it is clear that the modern movement is larger, more politically successful, and has mobilized more LGBT people than at any other point in the movement's history. Based on the growth and health of national, state, and local groups, the LGBT movement is still clearly in ascendancy and has not yet faced the declines other civil rights–oriented groups have faced in the past twenty years.

For better or worse, the movement has become more institutionalized in terms of creating formal organizations, hiring professional staff, and pursuing goals in the halls of government. As this mainstreaming has occurred, it has also created a pool of politically skilled LGBT leaders who have begun to seek positions in government, both elected and nonelected. Such a progression seems almost natural, with an increasing focus on government; LGBT activists should concern themselves with direct representation in government institutions and not depend solely on the "good will" of non-LGBT officials. Such a pattern of movement growth is consistent with the history of other minority groups and is discussed in greater detail in Chapter 5.

References and Further Reading

Adam, Barry D. 1995. *The Rise of a Gay and Lesbian Movement*. Rev. ed. New York: Twayne Publishers.

AIDS Action Council. 2001. "About AIDS Action." Web Site. http://www.aidsaction.org/

Alsdorf, Matt. 2000. "An Interview with Kevin Ivers of the Log Cabin Republicans." *PlanetOut News* (1 May).

Badgett, M. V. Lee. 1995. "The Wage Effects of Sexual Orientation Discrimination." *Industrial and Labor Relations Review* 48: 726–739.

Bailey, Robert W. 1995. "Identity Voting in Bi-racial Coalitions: The Lesbian and Gay Vote in Los Angeles, Chicago, and New York." Paper presented at the August meeting of the American Political Science Association, Chicago.

Boxall, Bettina. 1997. "Leading a Fight for Rights: The Lambda Legal Fund Has Been a Driving Force in Changing the Law's Treatment of Gays." *Los Angeles Times* (15 January).

Browne, William P. 1988. *Private Interests, Public Policy, and American Agriculture.* Lawrence: University Press of Kansas.

———. 1990. "Organized Interests and Their Issue Niches: A Search for Pluralism in a Policy Domain. *Journal of Politics* 52: 477–509.

Bull, Chris, and John Gallagher. 1996. *Perfect Enemies: The Religious Right, the Gay Movement, and the Politics of the 1990s.* New York: Crown Publishers.

Burke, Kevin J., and Murray S. Edleman. 1972. "Sensitivity Groups, Consciousness-raising Groups, and the Gay Liberation Movement." Paper presented at the August meeting of the American Political Science Association.

Button, James W., Barbara A. Rienzo, and Kenneth D. Wald. 1997. *Private Lives, Public Conflicts: Battles over Gay Rights in American Communities.* Washington, DC: CQ Press.

Chibbaro, Lou, Jr. 1997. "Gay Republican Lawmaker Forces Vote on Bill; Oregon Representative Bucks Party Line on Employment Bill." *Washington Blade* (9 May).

———. 1999. "Budgets Up, Donors Down; Biennial Survey Shows New Numbers at National Groups." *Washington Blade* (11 June).

Chibbaro, Lou, Jr., and Lisa Keen. 1997. "Untapped Majority Stirs: Information Technology May Help Explain Growth in Number of Donors to Gay Groups." *Washington Blade* (12 December).

Christensen, Jennifer. 2001a. "Lesbians, Allies Organize in AL." *Southern Voice* (12 July).

———. 2001b. "First State Gay Conference To Be Held in MS." *Southern Voice* (12 July).

Colby, David C., and David G. Baker. 1988. "State Policy Responses to the AIDS Epidemic." *Publius* 18: 113–130.

D'Emilio, John. 1983. *Sexual Politics, Sexual Communities: The Making of a Homosexual Minority in the United States, 1940–1970.* Chicago: University of Chicago Press.

Empire State Pride Agenda (ESPA). 2000. "Ithaca Adopts State's First Law to Include Protections for Transgender Persons." Press release (8 June).

Esteve, Harry. 1997. "House Republicans Bolted Monday from the State Capitol." *Register-Guard* (15 April).

Federal Election Commission. 2001. "Welcome to FEC.gov." Web Site. http://www.fec.gov/

Fox, Kara. 2001. "'We Have Been There Ever Since': Gay and Lesbian Activists Alliance Celebrates 30 Years of Hard Work." *Washington Blade* (20 April).

Freiberg, Peter. 1997. "Legal Knights of the Roundtable: Gay Groups Meet to Discuss Issues, Hammer Out Strategy." *Washington Blade* (10 January).

———. 1998. "50 State Capital Event Set for Spring of 1999; 'It's So Important to Focus on State Issues.'" *Washington Blade* (24 April).

———. 2000. "Name-dropping in San Francisco; ACT UP Chapter Changes Moniker to Distinguish from Other Group." *Washington Blade* (31 March).

Gamson, William A. 1968. *Power and Discontent*. Homewood, IL: Dorsey.

Gay and Lesbian Victory Fund. 1998. "Political Extremists Target Openly Gay Legislator." Press release (9 April).

Gay and Lesbian Victory Fund. 2001. "About the Victory Fund." Web Site. http://www.victoryfund.org/public/about/about.cfm

GenderPAC. 2001. "GPAC Home." Web Site. http://www.gpac.org/

Gray, Virginia, and David Lowery. 1996. *The Population Ecology of Interest Representation: Lobbying Communities in the American States*. Ann Arbor: University of Michigan Press.

Gutierrez-Mier, John. 2000. "S.A. Gay Groups' Political Influence Is Growing." *San Antonio Express-News* (27 February).

Haider-Markel, Donald P. 1997a. "From Bullhorns to PACs: Lesbian and Gay Politics, Interest Groups, and Policy." Ph.D. diss., University of Wisconsin-Milwaukee.

———. 1997b. "Interest Group Survival: Shared Interests versus Competition for Resources." *Journal of Politics* 59(3): 903–912.

———. 1998a. "The Politics of Social Regulatory Policy: State and Federal Hate Crime Policy and Implementation Effort." *Political Research Quarterly* 51(1): 69–88.

———. 1998b. "State and Local Government." In *Encyclopedia of AIDS: A Social, Political, Cultural, and Scientific Record of the Epidemic,* edited by Raymond A. Smith. New York: Garland Publishing.

———. 2001. "Lesbian and Gay Family Issues in the U.S. Congress." In *Queer Families, Queer Politics: Challenging Culture and the State,* edited by Mary Bernstein and Renate Reimann. New York: Columbia University Press.

Haider-Markel, Donald P., and Kenneth J. Meier. 1996. "The Politics of Gay and Lesbian Rights: Expanding the Scope of the Conflict." *Journal of Politics* 58(2): 332–349.

Hardin, Russell. 1982. *Collective Action*. Baltimore, MD: The John Hopkins University Press.

Human Rights Campaign. 2001. "What We Do." Web Site. http://www.hrc.org/about/whatwedo.asp

Jennings, M. Kent, and Ellen Ann Anderson. 1996. "Support for Confrontational Tactics among AIDS Activists: A Study of Intra-movement Divisions." *American Journal of Political Science* 40(2): 311–334.

Jeske, Timothy D. 1993. "Collective Action and the AIDS Epidemic: Seattle's Gay and Lesbian Community." Ph.D. diss., University of Washington.

Krisberg, Kim. 2000. "GenderPAC Builds a 'Natural Bridge'." *Washington Blade* (13 October).

Log Cabin Republicans. 2000. "The Gay Vote 2000." Web Site. http://www.lcr.org/press/20010122GayVoteAnalysis.htm

Log Cabin Republicans. 2001. "Log Cabin Republicans." Web Site. http://www.lcr.org/index.asp

Marotta, Toby. 1981. *The Politics of Homosexuality*. Boston: Houghton-Mifflin.

Meunier, Bill. 2000. "Pocan Blasts Wisconsin Log Cabin Club over DP, Mazomanie Beach Stances." *Wisconsin Light* (12–18 January).

Napolitano, Nick. 1999. "A Night for Celebrating, Sharing, Remembering; Local Transgender Group Holds Holiday Formal." *Washington Blade* (10 December).

National Gay and Lesbian Task Force. 2001. "About NGLTF." Web Site. http://www.ngltf.org/about/index.cfm

National Latina/o Lesbian, Gay, Bisexual and Transgender Organization. 2001. "Accomplishments." Web Site. http://www.llego.org/Accomplishments. htm

Nitkin, David. 1998. "Through Lobbying, Christian Conservatives Seek to Influence Florida Judiciary." *Orlando Sentinel* (20 April).

O'Bryan, Will. 2000. "Offering Their Voices for Equality; 17th Annual PFLAG Conference Draws Hundreds of Participants." *Washington Blade* (5 May).

Panem, Sandra. 1988. *The AIDS Bureaucracy.* Cambridge, MA: Harvard University Press.

Penning, Richard. 1998. "The Republican Party and the Religious Right in Michigan." Paper presented at the August meeting of the American Political Science Association, Chicago.

Perrow, Charles, and Mauro F. Guillen. 1990. *The AIDS Disaster: The Failure of Organizations in New York and the Nation.* New Haven, CT: Yale University Press.

Pilla, Jen. 2000. "Gay and Lesbian PAC Quizzes Candidates for Commissioner." *Charlotte Observer* (13 March).

Polman, Dick. 1998. "Openly Gay Candidates the Hot Topic in U.S. Politics; Seeing a More Tolerant America, They Want Straight Voters to Know They Share Concerns." *Philadelphia Inquirer* (3 May).

Rayside, David Morton. 1998. *On the Fringe: Gays and Lesbians in Politics.* Ithaca, NY: Cornell University Press.

Rimmerman, Craig A. 1999. "The Gay and Lesbian Victory Fund Comes of Age: Reflections on the 1996 Elections." In *After the Revolution: PACs, Lobbies, and the Republican Congress,* edited by Robert Biersack, Paul S. Herrnson, and Clyde Wilcox. Boston: Allyn & Bacon.

Rosenthal, Donald B. 1995. "Gay and Lesbian Participation in Urban Politics: Community Mobilization and the Structure of Regime Opportunities in Four New York Cities." Paper presented at the August meeting of the American Political Science Association, Chicago.

San Francisco Lesbian Avengers. 2001a. "1994 Actions." Web Site. http://www.lesbian.org/sfavengers/old/1994SFAvenge.html

San Francisco Lesbian Avengers. 2001b. "1995 Actions." Web Site. http://www.lesbian.org/sfavengers/old/1995SFAvenge.html

Schulman, Sarah. 1993. *Lesbian Avenger Handbook.* New York: The Lesbian Avengers.

Seelye, Katharine. 2000. "Gore Meets with Gay Leaders before Home Stretch in Iowa." *New York Times* (21 January).

Service Members Legal Defense Network. 2001. "About SLDN." Web Site. http://www.sldn.org/templates/about/index.html

Shilts, Randy. 1987. *And the Band Played On: Politics, People, and the AIDS Epidemic.* New York: St. Martin's Press.

Smith, Rhonda. 2001. "Task Force Grapples with Criticism: National Gay Oganization also Faces Personnel, Budget concerns." *Washington Blade* (5 January).

Sypert, Tracy, Marghe Covino, and Karen Ocamb. 1998. "Death of Life Lobby: What Happened? Money Woes, Control Issues Led to Dissolution." *Frontiers Newsmagazine* 17(1).

Thomas, Clive S., and Ronald J. Hrebenar. 1992. "Changing Patterns of Interest Group Activity." In *The Politics of Interest Groups: Interest Groups Transformed*, edited by Mark P. Petracca. Boulder, CO: Westview Press.

Thompson, Mark, ed. 1994. *The Long Road to Freedom*. New York: St. Martin's Press.

Vaid, Urvashi. 1995. *Virtual Equality: The Mainstreaming of Gay and Lesbian Liberation*. New York: Anchor Books.

Wald, Kenneth D., James W. Button, and Barbara A. Rienzo. 1996. "The Politics of Gay Rights in American Communities: Explaining Anti-discrimination Ordinances and Policies." *American Journal of Political Science* 40(4): 1152–1178.

Wilson, Thomas C. 1994. "Trends in Tolerance toward Rightist and Leftist Groups, 1976–1988." *Public Opinion Quarterly* 58: 539–556.

Wilson, Yumi. 2000. "Toklas PAC Got Money to Spend on Brown; Gay Group's Thousands Used against Ammiano. *San Francisco Chronicle* (1 February).

Wisckol, Martin. 2000. "McGraw Reconfirms Support of Prop. 22." *Orange County Register* (30 January).

Worsnop, Richard L. 1993. "Gay Rights: Are Gays and Lesbians Seeking Equal Rights or "Special" Rights?" *CQ Researcher* 3(9):193–216.

Yang, Alan S. 1998. *From Wrongs to Rights: Public Opinion on Gay and Lesbian Americans Moves toward Equality*. Washington, DC: National Gay and Lesbian Task Force.

4

Electoral and Political Party Participation

I n 1977 Harvey Milk was elected to the San Francisco Board of Supervisors. Milk was the first openly gay man to be elected to a public office in California. How did Milk achieve such a feat? Was it because of the high concentration of LGBT voters in San Francisco precincts? Bill Clinton was elected president in 1992 after a primary and general election during which his electoral viability was often in doubt. Did LGBT voters help Clinton get elected; did they help him get reelected in 1996? The 1998 race in New York for the U.S. Senate saw the unusual defeat of an incumbent U.S. senator, Republican Senator Alfonse D'Amato, and the election of Representative Charles Schumer (D-NY) to the seat. Although a variety of factors surely influenced Schumer's victory, how much of an influence did LGBT voters have in the contest?

In this chapter we examine these and related questions by analyzing LGBT participation in electoral and party politics. We begin with a discussion of LGBT voters, move to case studies of the antigay vote, then provide a more detailed examination of the LGBT vote in local, state, and national elections, before finally investigating LGBT participation with political parties in the United States.

Voting Behavior: The "Lavender Vote" Thesis

Any discussion of LGBT voting behavior must begin with a word of caution. Simply put, assessing the LGBT vote is frequently difficult simply because not all LGBT persons are willing to indicate their sexual orientation to pollsters. As such, available studies indicate the voting behavior only of openly LGBT persons, and the results cannot be generalized to the LGBT population as a whole. Furthermore, most polls only track the preferences and behavior of gay men, lesbians, and bisexuals. For this reason much of the following discussion refers only to "LGB" voters. Statistics preceded only by "LGB" indicate that data for transgender voters was not available. Few political polls have ever asked transgender persons to self-identify. Nonetheless, the available data can still provide important information about the political behavior of openly LGBT people, including answering the question of whether or not there is a "lavender vote."

The "lavender vote" thesis is really a series of specific hypotheses put forward by Mark Hertzog in his 1996 book *The Lavender Vote: Lesbians, Gay Men, and Bisexuals in American Electoral Politics*. Hertzog's nine hypotheses can be distilled into the following: (1) LGB (transgender voters were not included in the study) voters represent a significant subset of voters; (2) LGB voters have characteristics that distinguish them from other voters, such as a group consciousness; (3) sexual orientation has a distinct impact on voting behavior, even controlling of other factors, such as ideology; and (4) although LGB voters are not monolithic in their preferences, group consciousness or purposeful mobilization could ensure that LGB voters vote as a cohesive group. Although Hertzog found some evidence to support most of these hypotheses, some of the evidence was inconclusive.

In exit polls during elections, a small but significant portion of the voting population identifies as lesbian, gay, or bisexual. The size of the LGB voting population is comparable to many racial, ethnic, and religious groups, including Hispanics and Jews. During the November 1998 midterm elections, exit polls suggested that 4.2 percent of voters were lesbian, gay, or bisexual. The figure was 4 percent in 2000, 5 percent in 1996, only 2.2 percent in 1992, and only 1.2 percent in 1990. Of voters under 40 in 1998, 6.4 percent identified as LGB (Bailey 2000, 8). It should be noted that this increase is most likely due to higher rates of self-identification and better means for measuring the LGBT population rather than any increase in the absolute number of LGBT people.

As with the voting behavior of any citizen, the voting behavior of an LGBT person cannot be understood outside of the context of other personal attributes, such as occupation, gender, income level, education level, place of residence, party affiliation, and ideology. However, LGBT persons do appear to socialize to politics in a manner significantly different from heterosexuals. For most heterosexuals, family tends to play a very significant role in the development of party affiliation, ideology, issue positions, and eventual voting behavior. However, with LGBT individuals, the influence of friends and loose social networks often outweigh the influence of family and other factors. Most importantly, the groundbreaking research of Mark Hertzog and Robert Bailey finds that even controlling for all personal attributes that tend to influence voting behavior, including party identification and ideology, the sexual orientation of voters has a significant influence on voting behavior, as well as party affiliation, ideology, and issue positions.

Research suggests that the average self-identified LGB voter nationally is slightly different than the average heterosexual voter. The average LGB voter in 1990 tended to be slightly younger, better educated, less religious, more liberal, and more likely to live in a medium to large city, but he or she did not have a higher income. Indeed, LGB voters remain considerably more liberal than the average voter. In 1996, 47 percent of gay voters identified themselves as liberal, 37 percent identified themselves as moderate, and only 16 percent as conservative (Bailey 1998). By 1998 the average LGB voter had not changed much.

The most consistent pattern among LGB voters is that they tend to vote for Democratic candidates. LGB voters in 1998 were almost twice as likely to vote for Democrats over Republicans, even though LGB support for Republicans increased to 35 percent from 28 percent in 1996 (see Bailey 2000; NewsPlanet Staff 1998b). LGB voters supported Democratic congressional candidates by margins of 61 percent in 1990, 77 percent in 1992, 73 percent in 1994, 72 percent in 1996, and 85 percent in 1998 (Bailey 2000). LGB Democratic support was strong even in years when most voters went Republican, such as 1994. In addition, LGB voters in each of these elections did support Republican congressional candidates in sizable numbers, indicating that LGB voters can be a key constituency in close elections where moderate Republicans express support for gay civil rights, or even in races where the Republican is more pro-LGBT than the Democrat. The LGB vote went to GOP congressional candidates by a margin of

39 percent in 1990, 23 percent in 1992, 26 percent in 1994, and 28 percent in 1996 (Bailey 1998).

In addition, when both candidates in a race are pro-LGBT, LGB voters often rely on other factors, such as ideology, to make a choice. Most often this means that LGBT voters will select the more liberal candidate, such as Bill Bradley over Al Gore in the New York Democratic presidential primaries. This tendency posed a problem for Gore during the 2000 general election, as Green Party candidate Ralph Nader was able to draw some of the liberal LGB vote away from Gore.

In 1990 self-identified LGB voters were only 1.2 percent of the electorate, but these numbers likely undercount the number of LGB voters. To confound the influence of the LGB vote, LGB voters in 1990 were more divided in voting for House candidates than in any other elections; only 48 percent of LGB voters identified as Democrat, 23 percent as Republican, and 30 percent as Independent (Bailey 1998, 18). Not surprisingly then, 61 percent of LGB voters voted for Democratic House candidates and 39 percent voted for Republican candidates, the lowest percentage of Democratic support by LGB voters in the 1990s (Bailey 1998, 21).

With the 1992 presidential election, the numbers of LGB voters increased to 2.2 percent of the electorate. Bill Clinton received 72 percent of the LGB vote (versus 43 percent of the general population vote), reflecting the liberal Democratic leanings of many LGB voters. However, the 1992 election also saw the salience of LGBT issues increase, with candidate Clinton espousing many progay positions, and Republicans preaching an antigay agenda. In the elections for the U.S. House of Representatives, LGB support for Democratic candidates increased to 77 percent and decreased to 23 percent for Republican candidates (Bailey 1998, 21).

In 1994 LGB voters made up 1.6 percent of the electorate, but even as most voters voted decidedly Republican, LGB voters still voted largely Democratic. LGB voters cast 73 percent of their votes for Democratic House candidates and 26 percent for Republican House candidates (Bailey 1998, 21). LGB support for Democrats had decreased from 1992, but LGB voters appeared to play little role in the Republican takeover of Congress. LGB voters in 1994 were also considerably more optimistic than non-LGB voters about the direction of the country.

In 1996 gays and lesbians constituted 5 percent of the electorate, comparable to 5 percent for Latinos, and 3 percent for Jews. Lesbians and gays were also more likely to vote for Democrats, with 66 percent voting for Clinton, 23 percent voting for Dole, and 11 percent voting for other candidates, including H. Ross Perot (Hitt 2000). However, in urban areas, LGB voters were almost 9 percent of the electorate (Bailey 1998). Meanwhile, LGB support for Democratic House candidates remained about the same as 1994 (Bailey 1998, 21).

Interestingly, a *Washington Blade* survey of voting precincts in heavily gay neighborhoods throughout the country showed a decline in gay voter turnout in 1996, which is consistent for general population voting trends in 1996. For the 1984 and 1988 presidential elections, voter turnout in the "gay precincts" was about 67 percent, in 1992 turnout increased to 72 percent, but in 1996 average turnout dropped to 57 percent (Keen 1996). Furthermore, the *Blade* survey revealed that gay precincts averaged 71 percent support for Clinton, 16 percent for Dole, 4 percent for Perot, and 9 percent for others (Keen 1996).

In 1998 the number of LGB voters dropped from the 1996 high to 4.2 percent of the electorate (Bailey 1998). However, this pattern is probably the result of a general decline in voting during midterm elections, rather than a change in the LGB population. As Democrats increased their seats in the U.S. House of Representatives, LGB support for Democratic candidates actually declined from 1996, to 67 percent. However, LGB support for Republican candidates increased only to 33 percent (Bailey 1998, 21). LGB voters were still clearly handing most of their support to Democrats. LGB voters were clearly also more likely to believe that the country was on the right track compared to non-LGB voters and urban LGB voters voted strongly Democratic, with 85 percent voting for Democratic House candidates (Bailey 1998, 26).

Finally, during the 2000 election cycle, LGB voters again made their voice heard by influencing the presidential primaries and key congressional races as the Democrats attempted to gain a majority in Congress. During the 2000 primary season, of LGB voters in the California Democratic primary, 76 percent supported Gore and 24 percent picked Bradley. LGB voters were only slightly more likely to support Bradley than heterosexual voters by a few percentage points (NGLTF 2000). Analysis by Robert Bailey revealed that LGB voters in California were as racially diverse as the rest of the population, had slightly lower incomes, and were more likely to be under the age of forty-five (NGLTF 2000). In the general election LGB voters composed 4 percent of the electorate and largely supported Democrat Al Gore as well as Democratic congressional candidates. About 70 percent of LGB voters supported Gore, which may have ensured a Gore victory in key states such as Minnesota and Wisconsin, but Green Party candidate Nader received 4 percent of the LGB vote, which probably hurt Gore (Keen 2000c). Furthermore, a survey of 188 heavily gay precincts in seven cities by the *Washington Blade* found that 75 percent of voters who turned out in these precincts voted for Gore, 12 percent for Bush, 11 percent for Nader, and 2 percent for others. In 1996 these precincts had voted for the Democratic presidential candidate over the Republican by 71 percent to 16 percent. Turnout in these precincts was also up 10 percent over 1996 (Keen 2000). Based on exit polls nationally, the LGB vote in 2000 was 4 percent of the electorate, or over 4 million voters (Keen 2000).

Getting Out the Vote

LGBT groups have also been increasing efforts to turn out the LGBT vote. For example, in 1980 LGBT activists started Gay Vote 1980, a nationwide drive to pressure the major parties to adopt gay-rights planks in their platforms. The effort ensured that almost a dozen openly gay delegates were selected in the Iowa caucuses (Thompson 1994, 124). In 1992 LGBT voters formed a coalition of groups called VOICE '92 in order to register LGBT voters and get out the LGBT vote.

LGBT Vote 2000 was a "grassroots, nonpartisan campaign to encourage gay, lesbian, bisexual and transgendered people and their friends to register to vote" (Autman 2000). The group was formed nationally, but local chapters tried to encourage local LGBT persons to register, largely because significant numbers of LGBT people have limited their involvement in mainstream politics. Indeed, Mark Hertzog found that many LGB voters in 1992 were first-time voters.

Following the Democratic Convention in August 2000, LGBT activists mobilized to get out the vote and convince LGBT voters to support Vice President Al Gore. The National Stonewall Democratic Federation began campaigning at gay restaurants, festivals, neighborhoods, and bars to register voters and provide information on Gore's progay record. At the same time, the Human Rights Campaign (HRC) organized its annual National Coming Out Day with a particular focus on registering LGBT college students to vote. The turnout effort in 2000 was a result of the growing realization in the LGBT community, as well as among the political parties, that the LGBT vote could be the deciding factor in key states for the presidential race. Although a June 2000 Harris poll found that LGB voters planned to support Gore over George W. Bush, 83 to 16 percent, the poll was biased and did not reflect the potential for turning out to vote. Exit polls reflect the earlier bias showing that 70 percent of LGB voters went for Gore, 25 percent for Bush, and 4 percent for Nader.

Other factors came together in 2000 to cause more LGBT interest in elections and for LGBT groups to step up their voter mobilization efforts. These factors included a presidential race whose outcome might significantly change the composition of the Supreme Court and other federal courts, anti–same-sex-marriage ballot initiatives in Nevada and Nebraska, an Oregon ballot initiative that would essentially eliminate any discussion of homosexuality in public schools, control of the U.S. House of Representatives and possibly the Senate, and nearly 100 elections that involved LGBT candidates. The National Gay and Lesbian Task Force said their group "would use grassroots organizations in every state to register gay and lesbian voters and get them to the polls" and the executive director of the National Stonewall Democratic Foundation, said his group "would work with the Democratic National Committee and several unions to get out the gay vote, particularly in swing states such as Florida, Georgia, Ohio, Pennsylvania and Washington" (White 2000). Meanwhile, the largest LGBT group, the Human Rights Campaign, said it would "contribute $1 million to congressional candidates, run ads in gay media outlets, distribute voter guides and run a get-out-the-vote effort with particular emphasis on races in Pennsylvania and New Jersey" (White 2000).

However, attempts to mobilize LGBT people to participate in politics face countervailing trends in American society. As partisan identification has declined in recent decades and trust in government has decreased, Americans in general have decreased their participation in electoral politics. Furthermore, as a whole, eligible voters under thirty are less likely to vote, and self-identified LGBT persons are more likely to belong to this age cohort. Thus, LGBT groups focused on turning out the LGBT vote may need to increase their efforts as the new century begins.

Case Study: The Impact of the Antigay Vote

The antigay vote has made itself felt in a multitude of elections from those for local offices, to ballot initiative questions, to presidential contests. In this section we briefly examine the impact of the antigay vote in two elections, a race for a legislative seat in Oregon and a ballot initiative.

Oregon. In 1998 incumbent Representative Chuck Carpenter (R-7) lost his reelection bid in the Republican primary to a conservative backed by religious conservative groups. Carpenter had been the only openly LGBT legislator in the state assembly and his opponents had mobilized against him after he rallied the legislature to pass a bill banning discrimination based on sexual orientation. The Republican leadership had opposed the bill, and Carpenter took his political career into his own hands when he chose not only to support the bill, but to publicly try to convince other Republicans to support it as well.

Carpenter was first elected to the Oregon House of Representatives in 1994 as the first openly gay nonincumbent Republican state legislator in the country. He was reelected in 1996. As an incumbent his seat seemed safe. The events of 1997 changed all that. In 1997 the Oregon legislature began considering civil rights bills that included sexual orientation. Similar bills had been considered in the legislature almost every year since 1973. None of these bills had passed and the state had faced several anti-LGBT ballot initiatives since a 1988 initiative repealed an executive order issued by the governor that banned discrimination based on sexual orientation. Thus, anti-LGBT forces, especially the Oregon Citizen's Alliance, had significant experience in electoral campaigns.

In 1997 Carpenter took a series of steps that put his political career at risk. First, he introduced HB 2734, which would have banned discrimination based on sexual orientation in employment. The bill was assigned to the House Judiciary Committee, but the committee failed to take any action. Frustrated with the committee's inaction, Carpenter made a motion on the floor to have his bill pulled from committee and brought directly to the floor for debate and a floor vote. The move panicked the Republican leadership, who feared the bill might pass. Rather than provoke a direct confrontation, the leadership called for a recess and blocked Carpenter's motion. Although the leadership was very upset with Carpenter, and even asked him to resign from the party, they did reach a compromise the following day. Under the compromise, a new bill would be drafted and sent to a new committee and be given "priority" status. The new bill (HB 3719) eventually passed the house, forty votes to twenty, but languished in the senate. Carpenter had testified on behalf of the bill in the senate and worked with Democrats, but was unable to gain a majority. The bill died with the end of the session. The Republican leadership, still furious with Carpenter, demanded that he resign. When

Carpenter refused, conservatives began to look for someone to challenge him for his seat.

As the Republican primaries neared in 1998, conservative religious groups mobilized to defeat Carpenter. Conservatives within the state Republican Party had not forgotten Carpenter's effort to force a vote on the bill and recruited ultraconservative candidate Bill Witt to challenge Carpenter in the Republican primary. Witt was a founding member of the Oregon Christian Coalition and a major donor to the antigay Oregon Citizens' Alliance.

During the campaign Witt had the support of the Republican leadership and the conservative religious groups in the state. Although LGBT issues were not the only ones discussed, Witt was able to energize antigay sentiment in the electorate on the issues of same-sex marriage and "special rights" for LGBT persons. Outmaneuvered at the grass roots, Carpenter outspent Witt by a large margin, raising over $256,000, more than any state house candidate in Oregon history.

In the end, Carpenter lost by only fifty-four votes (Ivers 1998). Once Carpenter had conceded defeat, the executive director of the Log Cabin Republicans issued a statement saying, "This is a wake-up call for the whole gay and lesbian community across the country, despite their political affiliations. Log Cabin is fighting on the front lines against the religious right, and we need the gay community to recognize the crucial importance of that fight. You have to support the troops at the front" (Ivers 1998). Many attributed the loss to heavy grassroots campaigning by religious conservatives, and a lack of similar campaigning by Carpenter. Nevertheless, Carpenter clearly provided a lightning rod for antigay sentiment in Oregon, a fact that appears to have significantly contributed to his defeat at the ballot box.

Vermont. During the 2000 election cycle anti-LGBT sentiment manifested itself in several interesting ways across national, state, and local elections. However, one of the most interesting examples took place in the traditionally liberal state of Vermont. The story begins in 1997. A group of same-sex couples sued the state of Vermont for the right to marry, arguing that not allowing same-sex couples to marry constituted unlawful gender discrimination. In December 1999 the Vermont Supreme Court ruled that the state could not deny same-sex couples the protections, benefits, and responsibilities of their heterosexual counterparts. The court instructed the legislature to allow for same-sex marriages or create a similar system that would have the same benefits and responsibilities for the involved parties. During the 2000 legislative session, the Vermont legislature created civil unions, which provide same-sex couples with legal standing akin to marriage. Residents of Vermont were somewhat split on the issue, with a significant minority vocally opposing the civil union law. A multitude of town meetings were held on the issue before the legislature voted, with opponents often wearing white ribbons, and supporters of civil unions wearing pink ribbons on their sleeves. Many were angry. One opponent called the proposed civil union law a "radical experiment . . . . What is going to happen in the schools? Children are going to be taught that homosexual unions are normal. We're talking about something that strikes right at the heart of our culture" (Cobb 2000). Clearly opponents attempted to inflame antigay feelings.

Opponents to the civil unions law mobilized their forces for the September 2000 primaries, targeting those legislators who had supported the civil unions law or those candidates who stated support for the law, especially Republicans. The main group formed to oppose the law was the Vermont Defense of Marriage (VDM). The VDM campaigned heavily for the anti–civil unions candidates, and circulated "profamily" fliers. Many conservatives displayed signs during the campaign stating, "Take Back Vermont," apparently meaning that civil union supporters or homosexuals had taken over the state. The other main organization formed in opposition to civil unions was Take It to the People, a group formed to support traditional marriage.

At one summer meeting of opponents to the law, speakers argued that the "civil unions law was part of an agenda that also included teaching homosexuality in the schools" and that state-funded programs "teach the gay lifestyle" (Dillon 2000). And one legislator who supported the law, State Representative John Edwards, endured comments like "queer lover" following the law's passage (Puleo 2000a). One observer noted that those upset by the law "feel the state is being made into a gay theme park. That it's becoming the Disney Land of gay America" (Puleo 2000a). The Republican candidate for governor, Ruth Dwyer, echoed similar antigay concerns, arguing that LGBT activists want to turn Vermont into a gay mecca. Dwyer said of LGBT communities, "When you look at Provincetown and San Francisco, you have to ask is that what we want? Is that where you'd want to raise a family?" (Bandler 2000). During a radio interview, Dwyer also denounced the National Education Association for having what she called a "homosexual agenda" (Bandler 2000).

The results of the primary elections, and the effect of the antigay vote, were mixed as Vermonters turned out in record numbers to vote. Of the eight Vermont house Republican candidates targeted for defeat, four won and four lost. Among targeted Democrats running for legislative seats, one won and one lost. Of the two main Republican state senate candidates targeted, one lost and one won. And in the Republican primary for the gubernatorial nomination, the candidate (Ruth Dwyer) who took the strongest stance against civil unions won. At the same time, Vermonters voting in the Democratic primary nominated Ed Flanagan as the party's candidate for the U.S. Senate, making him the first openly LGBT candidate for Senate on a major party ticket in history.

As Vermont's Democratic Governor Howard Dean launched his general election campaign, he faced significant antigay rhetoric on the campaign trail for signing the civil unions law. Opponents held up signs saying "Dump Dean" and "Dean: Gone Homo." Indeed, polls on Dean's favorability rating fell twenty-two percentage points following his signing of the civil unions law. Although analysts suggested that voters were growing weary of Dean for a variety of reasons, his drop in the polls was largely attributed to his support of the civil unions law (Sneyd 2000a).

Finally, an August 2000 poll of registered voters in Vermont found that 54 percent opposed the civil unions law while 40 percent supported it and that the issue was rated the second most important to voters, ranking only behind education. Even more importantly, of opponents polled, 69 percent said that the issue would have a "major effect" on their vote, while only 29 percent of supporters said it would (Chibbaro and Keen 2000). In the last poll before the November election, likely voters named civil unions as the most important issue, over taxes, health care, and education (Keen 2000b).

During the general election campaign for state offices, the antigay rhetoric became even more extreme. In October, one anti–civil unions group began holding "education forums" on homosexuality. The group claimed it was trying to tell the "truth" about homosexuality and "that truth is going to shock you. I know that when I saw some of this information I didn't sleep afterwards, I was so concerned that the state of our affairs had gotten this far," argued Stephen Cable, the president of Who Would Have Thought Inc. (Schmaler 2000). Speakers at the forum argued that homosexuality is not a genetic condition, it can be cured, and that "the whole premise of the civil unions bill is based on a lie," because the issue is not about civil rights, nor can it be, because homosexuality is a behavioral disorder (Schmaler 2000). Cable also argued that Vermont Governor Dean's Department of Education was promoting homosexuality by sending the message that it is "normal, acceptable, healthy behavior" through its safe schools program (Schmaler 2000). And as incumbent Governor Dean campaigned throughout the state in October, he faced many angry voters hurling antigay assaults. At one stop a protestor asked the governor if he was bisexual while others held signs stating their opposition to the civil unions law. In another area, a roadside mural pictured Governor Dean dressed in drag with the words "Dean the Queen," while bumper stickers saying "I'm From Vermont and I'm Not Gay" were now common. As Dean's opponent, Ruth Dwyer, campaigned, she frequently encountered people like a sixty-one-year-old woman who said she wanted Dwyer to "go in there and fight for us. She should do something about the gay and lesbian thing. In the end, we're going to be as bad as Africa. We're getting 'em from all over the country and a lot of 'em are going to stay" (Puleo 2000b).

Upset with the antigay rhetoric of the campaign, Vermont's congressional delegation and former Senator Robert Stafford held a joint appearance to condemn the hate and scorn being spewed in the election campaign and called for "calm and respect" (Pagano 2000). The delegation was partly responding to flyers sent out by the Vermont Defense of Marriage Political Action Committee in October that stated, "Kick Howard Dean, Barbara Snelling and other pro–civil union politicians out of office . . . . Homosexuals from across the country are now planning special honeymoon trips to Vermont and, many experts predict, hundreds will stay to turn Vermont into a San Francisco-like rural homosexual haven" (Pagano 2000). One direct-mail flyer sent to voters showed a photo of two men kissing with a headline next to it saying, "Howard Dean & Doug Racine's Vision for Vermont?" The flyer also claimed that the civil unions law was passed because "a flood of money from the radical homosexual lobby" led the legislature to "cave in" (Keen 2000b). Perhaps because of the heated campaign, the number of antigay hate crimes increased over 1999 figures, with thirteen hate crimes reported in the first six months of 2000. The number of "hateful" incidents, including verbal abuse also increased dramatically (Keen 2000b).

The Vermont elections also attracted considerable national attention based on the civil unions issue. The attention led to record spending in the gubernatorial campaign, with most of the money coming from outside the state. About 91 percent of the incumbent governor's funds came from outside the state and 84 percent of his challenger's funds came from external sources (Paulson 2000). Interest groups that formed around the civil unions issue also gained considerable funding, about $250,000, and much of this money came from outside the state. Vermonters for Civil Unions reported 69 percent of donations coming from out of state, the Vermont Defense of Marriage political action committee reported 37 percent, and another group supporting civil unions, the Vermont Fund for Families, reported 99 percent of its money coming from out of state (Paulson 2000).

The results of the general election vote in Vermont were mixed, reflecting a significant antigay vote around the civil unions issue. Governor Dean was reelected and Democrats held control of the state senate, but several openly gay candidates for the state legislature and the U.S. Senate were rejected by wide margins. Republicans took control of the state house of representatives for the first time in fourteen years, but their margin did not appear large enough to overturn the civil unions law. Several Democratic state legislators who had supported civil unions lost their seats to Republican challengers who campaigned in opposition to the law, and exit polls suggested that voters angry with civil unions were more likely to support Republican candidates. Overall, at least sixteen civil union supporters were ousted in the election, eleven of whom were Democrats. Exit polls also suggested that the extreme tactics of some anti–civil unions candidates might have hurt them at the polls, especially in the race for governor.

Although the antigay vote or antigay sentiment is often difficult to capture empirically, the results from the 2000 elections in Vermont make clear that politicians may face penalties if they support LGBT rights. Even in a relatively liberal and tolerant state like Vermont, which has some of the strongest statutory protections for gay civil rights, antigay fears whipped up by inflammatory rhetoric may spell defeat for LGBT allies. This pattern is common in LGBT politics—whenever a new policy or issue is introduced, opponents tend to argue that if passed, the policy will lead down a slippery slope with more and more imposition of LGBT "values" on society. However, once the given policy is enacted, it becomes clear that opponents' fears were overblown, and passage of the policy becomes somewhat easier in the next state or locality.

The LGBT Vote at the Local Level

Because LGBT people tend to be more concentrated in urban areas, it is at the local level where the LGBT vote may have the greatest impact on the outcome of elections. In cities where LGBT people are concentrated in specific neighborhoods, including New York City, San Francisco, and Washington, D.C., the impact of the gay vote can be significant. However, as discussed at the start of this chapter, measuring the LGBT vote is often difficult. Previous research has made use of exit poll data as well as the voting patterns in districts or wards that have significant concentrations of LGBT voters.

Because LGBT persons are more concentrated in urban areas, LGBT issues are more salient in urban areas, LGBT and non-LGBT urban residents tend to have similar views, and because elected officials have been most responsive to LGBT concerns in urban areas, the LGBT vote is most likely to influence election outcomes in urban areas. Although the potential impact of the LGBT vote in local elections became a concern for some candidates early in the history of the gay movement, there is no guarantee that LGBT voters can influence election outcomes at the local level, and influence has often come only after years of coalition building by LGBT groups determined to make their issues more salient in local elections.

In San Francisco it is estimated that LGBT voters represent 17 to 20 percent of the 467,294 registered voters (Smith 1999). However, it wasn't until the 1970s that LGBT voters began to receive the attention of political candidates. Most dramatically, they were crucial in electing George Moscone as mayor in 1975 after Moscone had orchestrated the repeal of California's antisodomy law. With the help of Harvey Milk, Moscone was able to obtain almost unanimous support from LGBT voters and won his runoff election for mayor by only 4,400 votes. Without the support of the LGBT community, Moscone could not have won. Moscone clearly understood this and publicly thanked Milk and later appointed him to the city's Board of Permit Appeals, making Milk the first openly gay appointed official in the country.

During the 1999 runoff election for San Francisco mayor, openly gay candidate Tom Ammiano lost to incumbent Mayor Willie Brown Jr. by 40 to 60 percent of the vote. However, in predominantly LGBT neighborhoods Ammiano was able to capture most of the vote. In the Castro neighborhood 64 percent of voters supported Ammiano, with the central Castro precinct voting 76 percent for Ammiano (Smith 1999). Two other predominantly LGBT areas, the Mission and

Haight-Ashbury, voted for Ammiano 66 and 61 percent respectively (Smith 1999). Pollsters noted that while Ammiano did well with LGBT voters, he was unable to translate this into a broader electoral coalition. Interestingly, preelection polls also suggested that gay homeowners were less likely to support Ammiano than gay renters. Ammiano received LGBT support even though most local openly gay elected officials supported Brown, in large part because Brown was highly supportive of the LGBT community, even by San Francisco standards.

Although it is clear that LGBT voters developed a moderate amount of political muscle in San Francisco, other cities have seen similar patterns as LGBT people have become more important in local economies. In 1972 Los Angeles district attorney candidate Vincent Bugliosi campaigned at sixteen gay bars in his effort to shore up the gay vote. And by 1978 LGBT groups had formed in California to help finance candidates who supported gay civil rights. One of the first LGBT political action committees in the country, the Municipal Elections Committee of Los Angeles, was able to raise $40,000 for southern California candidates at one fundraiser in 1978 (Thompson 1994, 118).

LGBT activists continued to play a role in Los Angeles politics throughout the 1980s, including the 1989 mayoral election, but LGBT voter influence was part of a broader liberal and minority coalition that had supported Mayor Thomas Bradley. LGBT voters in 1989 were masked as part of the rainbow coalition Bradley had put together. However, 1992 riots over the acquittal of police officers accused of beating African American Rodney King splintered the old coalition, providing more of an opportunity for a clear and coherent LGBT vote. In 1993 Bradley announced he would not run for reelection and Michael Woo emerged as the candidate of choice for many LGBT voters. Woo had first been elected to the city council in 1985, representing the thirteenth district, which is the epicenter of the LGBT population in Los Angeles. The LGBT community had supported Woo on the council because he was supportive of LGBT issues. During the campaign, Woo also promised to appoint a gay or lesbian to the police commission. Woo's main opponent was Richard Riordan, who focused on the economy and courted conservative voters. Although Woo put together a multicultural coalition, the coalition was more unstable than that which had supported Bradley. In the primary, 5 percent of voters identified as lesbian or gay, and 40 percent of these voters supported Woo. Riordan received only 11 percent of the gay vote and a third candidate received 27 percent. However, in the runoff election between Woo and Riordan, Woo pulled 72 percent of the lesbian and gay vote (Bailey 1999, 150–156). Robert Bailey's 1999 analysis of the vote in 1993 suggests that voter sexual orientation played a significant role in vote choice, and in a multivariate model, the effect of sexual orientation on vote choice outweighed the influence of age, income, gender, and education.

Woo lost the race but Riordan did not ignore the bloc of LGBT voters or their importance for a reelection attempt. Riordan involved LGBT activists in his transition and one of his first appointments was an openly gay man as deputy mayor. Riordan tested his support in the LGBT community in the 1997 mayoral campaign where he faced a challenge from liberal state senator Tom Hayden. During the campaign, Hayden fought hard for the LGBT vote, even promising to enact a San Francisco-like domestic partner law requiring businesses on contract with the city to provide domestic partner benefits. Although Hayden pulled 54 percent of LGB voters, Riordan's efforts with the community paid off with 41 percent support. Interestingly, only LGB voters and African Americans gave over 50 percent of their votes to Hayden (Bailey 1999, 156).

East Coast cities have also felt the impact of the LGBT vote. In particular, LGBT activists in New York City have been a significant force in electoral politics since the mid-1970s. The city's economic and political situation began changing dramatically in the 1970s, which assisted in giving the LGBT community a stronger political voice. In the 1977 mayoral campaign's Democratic primary, LGBT support for Edward Koch over Mario Cuomo was presumed, in large part because Koch had represented heavily LGBT districts on the city council and in Congress. However, that support was never certain, even though he apparently won strong majorities in the city's LGBT neighborhoods. Indeed, part of Koch's support from the LGBT community may have resulted from speculation that he was a closeted gay man. The belief was reinforced by one campaign slogan, "Vote for Cuomo Not the Homo." Koch ran again in 1981, but the main LGBT Democratic groups endorsed Frank Barbaro. Barbaro was the first serious mayoral candidate in the city to make campaign appearances in gay bars, while Koch lost what LGBT support he had by failing to pass a LGBT civil rights bill and continuing his ties with antigay religious figures in the city. Support for Koch in the LGBT community also faltered as LGBT political tactics became more sophisticated and vocal, calling for real action rather than simply a lack of overt oppression. Koch was reelected, but by the 1985 election, his support in the LGBT community waned further as his actions on AIDS seemed inadequate at best. In the 1985 race, Koch faced opponents who more clearly recognized the import of the LGBT vote, and who actively campaigned in LGBT neighborhoods. Koch was again reelected, in part by pulling the Latino vote, but he overwhelmingly lost in LGBT neighborhoods.

By 1989 LGBT influence in New York City politics had become even more important. Exit polls in the 1989 New York City general election showed the LGB vote at 3.2 percent of the electorate, and that rose to 8 percent in 1993 (Bailey 1999, 107). During the 1989 campaign, David Dinkens tried to emulate Jesse Jackson's "rainbow coalition" by bringing together voters around identity issues, including race and sexual orientation. The strategy paid off for Dinkens. Indeed, following the 1989 election, New York City Mayor David Dinkens very publicly thanked his LGBT supporters for the key role they played in the mayoral election.

Similar patterns of LGBT politics have occurred in other East Coast cities, including Philadelphia, Boston, and Washington, D.C. For example, in 1999 LGBT activists played a key role in the election of Philadelphia Mayor John Street. Street repaid his LGBT supporters by hiring over a dozen to work on his transition team.

In the Midwest gays have made inroads in some medium-sized to large cities. In Ohio, LGBT voters helped to elect openly LGBT officials to city councils in Toledo and Dayton, and played a key role in the successful mayoral campaign of Michael Coleman in Columbus. LGBT activists have played a significant role in Chicago politics since the early 1980s. As with most areas, LGBT involvement in Chicago politics has largely occurred through the Democratic Party and LGBT interest groups. Robert Bailey conducted a study of the LGBT vote in Chicago by focusing on the voting patterns of wards where LGBT voters tend to be concentrated. These wards are located on Chicago's north side. During the 1983 mayoral primary, the main LGBT interest group at the time, the Chicago Gay and Lesbian Democrats, endorsed Jan Byrne over Harold Washington after Byrne promised support on LGBT issues. Even so, when Washington won the primary, many voters in the "gay wards" voted for Washington in the general election. Once Washington was elected, he began to pursue LGBT voters by appointing a number of openly gay and lesbian activists, denouncing homophobia, supporting an ordinance banning discrimination based on sexual orientation, and participating in gay pride events. LGBT voters repaid Washington by largely supporting him in his 1987 reelection.

The LGBT Vote at the State Level

Although LGBT voters may forever exert their greatest influence on local elections, the new century is likely to see a growing importance of the LGBT vote in elections for state offices and in state party politics. Indeed, LGBT activists are increasingly showing their strength in state-level LGBT interest groups. Gay issues may have increasingly appeared in state election campaigns because gay groups themselves have become more involved in electoral campaigns. For example, the Arizona Human Rights Fund, Oregon's Right To Pride, the Rhode Island Alliance for Lesbian and Gay Civil Rights, and Virginians for Justice endorse candidates for political office and contribute money to campaigns. In Texas the Log Cabin Republicans have fought state party officials, with mixed results, to gain acceptance within the Republican Party and win recognition for gay assistance in the election of moderate Republicans.

Of course, some states have longer histories of LGBT involvement in state-level politics. For example, in New York, candidates for state office were courting the gay vote in the early 1980s. In 1983 Governor Mario Cuomo made the first appearance ever by a New York governor before a gay group when he spoke at a dinner for the Fund for Human Dignity. And although the LGB vote nationally is typically 4 or 5 percent of the voting population, in several key states that percentage is a fair amount higher. For example, a 2000 *Washington Blade* poll found that 6 percent of likely voters in New Jersey were LGB, while almost 10 percent of primary election voters in California were LGB (Roundy 2000b).

States like California have a relatively long history of LGBT involvement in elections. During the 1998 California race for governor, LGBT Democrats quickly backed Gray Davis. However, all three Democratic candidates attended a debate held by the Stonewall Democrats, a California gay political group, suggesting the significant role played by the LGBT community in California politics. Although Davis struggled with the issue of gay marriages, he did promise to appoint more LGBT judges. During the 1998 elections LGB voters in California made up 5 percent of the electorate in general elections, higher than the national average of about 4 percent (Bailey 2000). LGBT voters appear to have provided key margins in Democratic congressional and state legislative victories in the state in addition to statewide offices, with 73 percent of LGB voters supporting Gray Davis. Only 58 percent of all voters supported Davis (Bailey 2000).

However, during the 2000 primaries, California LGB voters may have exercised their greatest political muscle. During the March primary a combination of a presidential contest and a antigay ballot initiative appear to have raised LGBT participation to its highest level in any state election, 6 percent of all primary voters and 11 percent of Democratic primary voters, according to exit polls (NGLTF 2000). In the Democratic primary the percentage of LGB voters matched the African American vote and was larger than the Asian American vote at 7 percent (NGLTF 2000). LGB voters composed only 2 percent of California Republican primary voters. In 1998 LGB voters made up only 5 percent of the California electorate (NGLTF 2000).

Although some states like New York and California have seen considerable LGBT involvement in state politics for twenty years or more, in the 1990s LGBT issues also began appearing in state elections with greater frequency, including the 1998 California, Minnesota, and Nebraska races for governor. During the 1998 Nebraska gubernatorial race debate, Republican candidate Jon Christensen said that he would not appoint gay people to leadership positions if he were elected governor. Even though LGBT groups have little influence on Nebraska state politics, LGBT groups received considerable public attention for criticizing Christensen's comments. The attention even led the state Republican Party to distance itself from Christensen's statements.

In another example, Ohio's 1998 gubernatorial race also saw significant LGBT activity on the campaign trail, but mostly for the unsuccessful Democrat Lee Fisher. During the 2000 gubernatorial campaign in North Carolina, the Democratic candidate, Mike Easley, became the first gubernatorial candidate in that state to actively seek campaign support from the gay community. Easley's strongest support came on hate crimes legislation.

Finally, LGBT issues even arise in the most unlikely state election contests. During a 1998 campaign for the South Carolina commissioner of agriculture, Republican Jim Gordon made gays an issue when he argued: "We can't have farming based on Bob and Bob being married and a new definition of marriage" (NewsPlanet Staff 1998a). State Democratic leaders, however, did call foul. The Democratic candidate for state attorney general said: "If he can tell the difference between broccoli or turnips or green beans grown by a homosexual, then I'd like to know about it" (NewsPlanet Staff 1998a).

The LGBT Vote at the National Level:
Congressional and Presidential Races

During the 2000 presidential campaign, LGBT issues came to play a significant role for both Democratic and Republican candidates. One key issue was a candidate's assessment of the military's "don't ask, don't tell" policy, which was instituted after the Clinton administration failed to achieve a policy that would integrate openly LGBT persons into the armed forces. By 2000 considerable evidence had established that the military policy was failing on several fronts. In response, both Democratic presidential candidates, Al Gore and Bill Bradley, promised that they would lift "don't ask, don't tell" and allow LGBT persons to serve openly. At one point Gore even indicated that he would use a candidate's position on the issue as a litmus test for appointment to the Joint Chiefs of Staff. The Republican National Committee reacted quickly to Gore's initial comments by producing a television advertisement saying that Generals Colin L. Powell and H. Norman Schwarzkopf would not have been able to pass "Al Gore's litmus test" (Myers 2000). All of the Republican candidates, meanwhile, were opposed to allowing LGBT persons to serve openly. Gore soon retracted his comments.

So why did the Democratic candidate come to feel so strongly about an issue that had largely been swept under the rug since 1993? Many analysts came to believe that Gore and Bradley were courting the gay vote, especially the gay vote in California, a state that had moved up its primary for the 2000 season. Moreover, LGB turnout for the March 2000 California primary was expected to be unusually heavy because of a ballot initiative asking voters to ban same-sex marriage. Gay activist David Mixner said that both Al Gore and Bill Bradley "realize the gay and lesbian vote will be extremely important in California. . . . It's a major reason you're seeing this issue emerge" (Green 2000). Gore was also appealing for LGBT funds. By December 1999 Gore had raised $3.1 million to Bradley's $3.3 million in California, and only $556,000 to Bradley's $1.3 million in the LGBT mecca of San Francisco (Underwood 2000). Although Gore had been supportive of LGBT concerns while vice president, Bradley made tremendous inroads in California by spending a considerable amount of time "on the ground" in the state. Bradley's work not only earned him more contributions, but also the endorsement of three San Francisco board supervisors, one of whom was openly gay.

Clearly the LGBT vote can be important, but the absolute size of the LGBT voting population is not the only relevant point. In many states, the percentage of LGBT voter turnout is similar to that of the Latino community (both about 5 percent) and higher than Jews (about 3 percent)(Hitt 2000), meaning that just like other groups, LGBT voters will have the most impact if they turn out to vote *and* vote as a bloc. If few LGBT voters turn out, their impact will be small even if they vote as a bloc. And as noted below, since 1992 Democrats have come to rely on an outpouring of donations from LGBT activists, helping party officials and candidates to understand the importance of addressing LGBT concerns.

Historical Involvement of LGBT Activists in Presidential Politics

LGBT activity in presidential campaigns obtained a "face" in 1972 when Madeline Davis and Jim Foster, two openly gay delegates, were allowed to address a television audience at the Democratic National Convention, even though the address was at 3 A.M. Foster stated, "We do not come to you pleading your understanding or begging your tolerance. We come to you affirming our pride in our lifestyle, affirming the validity to seek and maintain meaningful emotional relationships and affirming our right to participate in the life of this country on an equal basis with every citizen" (Shilts 1982, 64). Foster and others had worked on Democrat George McGovern's presidential campaign and helped ensure that gay voters supported him during the 1972 California primary, a state that proved key for the campaign. Indeed, Foster and others organized gays to collect one-third of the northern California voter signatures that McGovern needed to get on the ballot. In return McGovern had issued a seven-point gay civil rights plank that satisfied the demands of many gay activists at the time. During the same year San Francisco's Gay Activists Alliance disbanded and formed the Gay Voters' League, a group that subsequently endorsed the reelection of Richard Nixon. However, it was not until the 1976 presidential election that LGBT activists had much of an influence in presidential politics, and even Jimmy Carter backed off many of his LGBT-friendly statements later, during both the 1976 and 1980 campaigns. On the campaign trial President Gerald Ford was "zapped" by gay activists in Ann Arbor, Michigan; Ford was forced to admit that he was not aware that homosexuality was used as a basis for exclusion in immigration rulings.

In February 1976 Carter said he was opposed to discrimination on the basis of sexual orientation. But in June, Carter withdrew his support of a gay rights plank in the Democratic Party platform. The platform committee subsequently voted to remove the plank. By the time of the Democratic National Convention in July, all discussion of LGBT concerns was dropped, even though 600 LGBT activists held a protest.

Under guidance from President Carter, a policy barring gays from employment in the Foreign Service was lifted in 1977 and the Internal Revenue Service ended a draconian policy that had forced LGBT education and charity groups to publicly state that homosexuality is a "sickness, disturbance, or diseased pathology" before they could be granted tax-exempt status. In the same year fourteen gay and lesbian activists were invited to the White House for the first official visit ever. The activists met with Presidential Liaison to Minority Communities Midge Costanza. In 1979 President Carter appointed openly lesbian Jill Schropp to the National Advisory Council on Women in a White House ceremony. Even though President Carter thanked the LGBT community for their support in the past, in March 1980 President Carter issued a formal statement indicating that he would not issue an executive order banning antigay discrimination in the federal government. The statement also said Carter would not support a gay rights plank in the Democratic platform. However, other Democrats were showing more LGBT support during the campaign. Openly gay campaign staffers were visible for the first time. Senator Edward Kennedy's (D-MA) presidential campaign staff included LGBT activists, perhaps foreshadowing the campaign teams of future Democratic presidential candidates.

In 1983 Democratic presidential candidate Gary Hart took courting the LGBT vote one step further when he spoke to the main gay political action committee in Los Angeles. The event was the first time a presidential candidate from a major party addressed an LGBT interest group. However, during the 1984 portion of the campaign, Democratic candidate Jesse Jackson attended a meeting at the New York Lesbian and Gay Community Services Center. Some exit poll data from New York City and elsewhere suggested that Jackson was able to win strong majorities of the gay vote (Bailey 1999, 161).

In 1988 Democratic and Republican presidential candidates downplayed most LGBT issues, but did promise more funding for AIDS research. LGBT activists, including Julian Potter, played key roles in the campaigns of Democratic presidential candidates, including those of Richard Gephardt and Michael Dukakis. However, Jesse Jackson again put together a rainbow coalition of voters, which included a significant contingent of gays and lesbians. Indeed, Jackson appears to have pulled a majority of the lesbian and gay vote in urban areas (Bailey 1999, 161).

During the 1992 presidential election, LGBT voters had a more visible presence than in any previous election and at least some candidates responded. Most candidates and a significant portion of the media took notice of this new force in presidential politics. In October 1991 Democratic presidential candidate Bill Clinton said that if he were elected, he would drop the ban on gays in the military.

George H. W. Bush's 1992 reaction to LGBT voters was initially mixed but shifted quickly to the right. In a televised interview President Bush said that if he found out a grandchild was gay he would "love the child" but tell him that homosexuality is not normal and discourage him from working for gay rights (Thompson 1994, 391–392). Even with Bush's opposition to LGBT issues, the chairman of the Bush-Quayle campaign did meet with representatives of the National Gay and Lesbian Task Force in February 1992. Although the meeting accomplished little, Chairman Robert Mosbacher "seemed genuinely alarmed at [the] representation that gay and lesbian voters felt that President Bush was not doing enough on AIDS" (Vaid 1995, 123). Mosbacher made no promises on behalf of Bush, but the meeting raised the ire of some congressional Republicans and religious conservatives. Bush reacted by taking a stance against same-sex marriage and homosexuality in general and did little to tone down the rabid anti-LGBT rhetoric at the 1992 Republican National Convention. Urvashi Vaid argues that Bush's antigay rhetoric "motivated conservative gay Democrats and loyal gay Republicans, who had helped defeat Dukakis in 1988, to throw their support behind Clinton" (Vaid 1995, 124).

Perhaps because of Bush's treatment, but more likely because Democratic presidential candidate Bill Clinton was the most LGBT-friendly presidential candidate ever, LGBT enthusiasm for Clinton in 1992 was unprecedented. LGBT support for Clinton was evidenced through voting support, campaign volunteers and paid staff, and financial contributions. Indeed, LGBT voters were credited with playing an important role in the election of Bill Clinton as president in 1992. Estimates suggest that LGBT activists contributed at least $3.4 million to Clinton's victory. Gay activist David Mixner claimed he was able to raise $3.5 million in 1992 for Clinton and the Democratic Party (Bull and Gallagher 1996, 95). Candidate Clinton and subsequently President Clinton made LGBT people feel, for the first time, that they had real access to the levers of power at the national level.

In 1996 LGB voters represented 5 percent of the voting population and differed from the non-LGB population in their political views. Again LGB voters overwhelmingly supported Bill Clinton over Bob Dole, 63 percent to 23 percent, with the remaining 11 percent supporting Ross Perot or another third party candidate. However, it should be noted that more LGB voters selected the Republican presidential candidate in 1996 than they did in 1992 and decreased their support for Ross Perot (Bailey 2000, 19).

The 2000 presidential campaign was perhaps the most LGBT friendly ever. The main Republican candidates had considerably softened their antigay rhetoric. Senator McCain hired gay campaign staff and eventually met privately with the main LGBT Republican group, the Log Cabin Republicans. Senator McCain also was the first Republican presidential candidate to accept contributions from a LGBT group without hesitation. Governor George W. Bush met with the Log Cabin Republicans only after much consternation and delay. Candidate Bush had originally refused to meet with the group and only agreed to do so after some of his own campaign staff, including a lesbian, had resigned over the issue. All of the Republican candidates were opposed to key legislation supported by LGBT groups, such as hate crimes legislation. And in both 1996 and 2000 all of the Republican presidential candidates except Dole, McCain, and Bush signed a pledge to oppose LGBT "special rights" including same-sex marriage. The Democrats, meanwhile, were less outspoken on gay issues after the primaries and convention, but by then their pro-LGBT positions were clear.

Vice President Al Gore's 2000 presidential campaign had LGBT persons in key posts and gained the support of many national LGBT leaders. For example, Julian Potter, who was the White House liaison to gays and lesbians, campaigned for Gore in key primary states based on the Clinton administration's progay record. Openly gay Washington publicist Jeffrey Trammell served as Gore's chief adviser on LGBT issues and Donna Brazile, openly lesbian, served as Gore's campaign manager. As Gore faced the caucus and primary battles in early 2000, he met with twenty leaders of the National Stonewall Democratic Federation, a federation of local Democratic LGBT groups. Gore's Democratic opponent, Bill Bradley, also met with the group. Gore also became the first candidate for president of any major party to take direct questions from LGBT people when he fielded questions on a gay online network called Gay.com in January 2000, and he was the first candidate to argue that LGBT foreigners who are in a domestic partnership with U.S. citizens should have the same immigration rights as married heterosexuals.

LGB voters played a significant role in both the 2000 primaries and the general election. For example, during the California primary LGB voters constituted 6 percent of the total electorate, 11 percent of Democratic primary voters, and 2 percent of Republican primary voters (NGLTF 2000). Vice President Al Gore received 35 percent of all votes in the open primary, while Republican George W. Bush received 28 percent. However, LGB voters consistently backed Gore, at 51 percent, and only 8 percent supported Bush. LGB voters also supported Gore over Democrat Bill Bradley (76 to 24 percent), but were more likely to support Bradley than non-LGB voters. As such, LGB voters constituted a significant block for Gore's victory (NGLTF 2000).

Interestingly, LGB voters tended to give more support to Democrat Bill Bradley than non-LGB voters (18 percent to 9 percent), while Republican John McCain received less support from LGB voters (18 percent) than from non-LGB voters (25 percent). Further, LGB voters were more likely than non-LGB voters to support Green Party candidate Ralph Nader by five to one (NGLTF 2000).

During the 2000 general presidential election campaign, LGBT voters were an important block for both major party candidates, largely because the race was so tight. Indeed, even Green Party candidate Ralph Nader spent considerable time trying to mend fences with the LGBT community after Representative Barney Frank (D-MA) publicly criticized Nader for his "Johnny come lately" positions on LGBT rights. A poll of LGB likely voters in September 2000 found that over 80 percent said they would vote for Gore, 10 percent said they would vote for Green Party candidate Ralph Nader, and only 3 percent said they would vote for Bush, with only 7 percent undecided (Keen 2000c). Interestingly, LGB voters in California and New Mexico showed even more support for Nader, with 14 percent and 16 percent, respectively, indicating they would vote for the Green Party (Keen 2000c).

The Republican Party, led by George W. Bush put on its most "diverse" face for its summer convention in its effort to attract female and minority voters. The Republican convention even featured the first openly LGBT person to speak at a Republican convention, Congressmember Jim Kolbe (R-AZ). It was also clear that Bush and the party hoped to attract LGBT voters with economically conservative views. At minimum the Bush campaign tried not to alienate LGBT Republicans. Bush had originally refused to meet with representatives of the largest LGBT Republican group, the Log Cabin Republicans, but eventually he did meet privately with the members of the group as well as other gay Republican activists—a first for Republican presidential politics.

The LGB vote appeared to be even more important to the Democratic presidential candidate, Vice President Al Gore, even though a Harris poll in June 2000 showed gay and lesbian voters supported Gore over Bush, 83 percent to 16 percent. In all, LGBT activists saw 2000 as a key election year to mobilize with both the president and Congress at stake, as well as state legislatures, which would control redistricting, and the potential for appointments to several Supreme Court seats.

The LGB vote in the 2000 general election was a slightly smaller proportion of the overall electorate than in 1996, but represented more voters numerically. The LGB vote went from 5 percent in 1996 to 4 percent in 2000, with 70 percent of LGB voters supporting the Democratic candidate, Vice President Al Gore, and 25 percent supporting the Republican candidate, George W. Bush (Chibbaro 2000d). An additional 4 percent of LGB voters supported Green Party candidate Ralph Nader. By comparison, Gore had slightly more LGB support than President Clinton did in 1996, when he garnered 67 percent of the LGB vote. The LGB Republican vote also increased from 18 to 25 percent with the absence of Ross Perot on the ballot. Overall, the percentages can be roughly translated into 2,824,385 LGB votes for Gore, 1,008,709 votes for Bush, and 161,393 votes for Nader (Keen 2000c). In addition, given the LGB vote margins in some states, it appears the LGB vote helped ensure that Gore won thirty-three electoral votes from victories in Iowa, Minnesota, New Mexico, and Wisconsin, while the LGB vote for Bush helped ensure that he won four electoral votes in New Hampshire (Keen 2000c). Furthermore, based on Voter News Service figures of LGB voters, about 59,000 LGB people voted for Bush in Florida, while more than 166,000 LGB voters supported Gore (Chibbaro 2000d). Because most counts of Bush's victory in Florida would give Bush the state's electoral votes with less than a 3,000 popular vote margin, this means that all else being equal, LGB voters may have decided the outcome of the vote in Florida. Interestingly, a Log Cabin Republicans advertising campaign in Florida in the final days of the election may have switched enough LGB voters from Gore to Bush to decide the election.

LGBT Involvement in Congressional Elections

LGBT activists have been more active and have had more influence in U.S. House and Senate elections in the 1990s. As with presidential politics, LGBT activists had little involvement in congressional elections until the 1970s. Furthermore, it was not until the 1990s that pollsters began to systematically track the LGB vote.

When openly gay Frank Kameny ran for the U.S. House of Representatives delegate seat from Washington, D.C., in 1971, it marked the first recorded congressional campaign with LGBT involvement. Perhaps the first significant involvement of LGBT people in a congressional campaign occurred in 1972. New York representative Bella Abzug, a liberal activist, campaigned for the gay vote through multiple appearances in bathhouses. Representative Abzug went on to introduce the first gay civil rights bill in Congress in 1974.

In 1992 gays saw their political stature increase as several openly gay members of Congress retained their seats and gay political action committees contributed more than $760,000 to congressional candidates (Bull and Gallagher 1996, 95). During the 1994 congressional elections many gay-friendly members of Congress lost their seats at the same time that LGB voter turnout declined. By 1996 LGB voters were still giving most of their support to Democratic congressional candidates, but groups such as the Human Rights Campaign were contributing more money to moderate Republicans. With LGB support in 1996, Democrats were able to regain some seats in the House.

In 1998 LGB voters turned out in high numbers again, reversing the trend of recent years, but this occurred in a year of high turnout among African Americans and labor union voters as well. The voting bloc, which mostly voted Democratic, helped Democrats win back more seats in the House and Senate. For example, LGB voters helped to ensure a Democratic victory in the California Senate race, with 71 percent casting their ballots for U.S. Senator Barbara Boxer, compared with 54 percent of voters overall (Bailey 2000).

In the 1998 race for one of New York's U.S. Senate seats, LGB voters also helped to defeat incumbent Republican Senator Alfonse D'Amato and elect Representative Charles Schumer (D-NY), even after the largest national LGBT interest group, the Human Rights Campaign (HRC), endorsed D'Amato. During their tenures in Congress, D'Amato and Schumer had similar records on LGBT issues, a fact that contributed to the HRC's endorsement of D'Amato. Schumer defeated D'Amato 54 to 44 percent. Schumer mentioned LGBT people in his acceptance speech, indicating he would fight for unity in his new position. Schumer said, "There's no room for disunity, for discrimination based on race or sexual orientation or ideology" (Boerner 1998).

Gay groups did not originally support Schumer. During the Democratic primary Schumer lost endorsements from most gay groups in the state, with candidates such as Mark Green receiving the bulk of LGBT endorsements. During the general election, however, many local and state LGBT groups, elected officials, and voters threw their support to Schumer. A poll conducted prior to the election showed that 67 percent of LGB voters supported Schumer (Boerner 1998). Over 100 LGBT people also volunteered to work on Schumer's campaign. Based on election-day exit polls, 77 percent of LGB voters cast votes for Schumer. However, LGB voters constituted only 3 percent of the sample in the exit poll (Boerner 1998). According to gay activists, the Schumer victory was attributed to a coalition of LGBT, women, Latino, and black voters.

With partisan control of the House and Senate in play during the 2000 election, voting blocs, including LGBT voters, were especially important. LGBT groups representing Democrats and Republicans made special efforts to turn out the vote and focus on key districts where the LGBT presence was large. With the LGB vote constituting 6 to 9 percent of the electorate in key states such as California and New Jersey, the LGBT community was especially important in the election (Roundy 2000b). To capitalize on the LGBT vote, the National Stonewall Democrats (NSD) began a "Take Back the House" project, targeting swing districts where the LGBT vote was significant and where LGBT resources could influence the outcome. The NSD endorsed twenty House candidates, four of whom were gay or lesbian. In addition, the national Log Cabin Republican Federation endorsed thirty gay-friendly Republican candidates for the U.S. House. The LCR contributed campaign funds and ran its own radio ads that stressed the progay voting records of their endorsed congressional candidates in several states, including California, Vermont, Maryland, and New York. In Illinois, Mark Kirk, the Republican House candidate in District 10, had a long history of working with the local LCR chapter and campaigning in LGBT areas.

Antigay attacks were also prevalent during the 2000 congressional races. In Utah the National Republican Congressional Campaign Committee ran antigay television ads against Democratic U.S. House candidate Jim Matheson. The ads stated that Matheson had received campaign contributions from openly gay Representative Barney Frank (D-MA) and the Human Rights Campaign. A narrator on the ad asked "Will the Boy Scouts be forced to accept homosexual leaders?" (Chibbaro 2000d).

In the 2000 Virginia Senate race, LGBT activists made their voices heard throughout the campaign as they struggled to reelect Senator

Chuck Robb (D). Robb had one of the most progay voting records in the Senate, motivating many first-time LGBT activists to support him. LGBT activists, including the state's only openly gay elected official, held fundraisers for Robb throughout the state, raising $85,000 and bringing out hundreds of activists. Jay Fisette, an openly gay member of the Arlington County Board, said of the events, "I think this is really groundbreaking for the GLBT community in Virginia. It is clearly the first time that people throughout the state have really stepped forward and addressed the importance of politics and political leadership in the gay community" (Roundy 2000a). Local elected officials, who subsequently may have paid more attention to LGBT issues, also attended the campaign activities. One of the events was held in Roanoke by the Gay and Lesbian Voters League of Roanoke, and was the first such event in that city. LGBT activists also showed their support by setting up a website to describe Robb's record on LGBT issues. For Robb's campaign staff, LGBT activists also held a weekly gay and lesbian volunteer day when activists could make phone calls, send out flyers, and engage in other volunteer work.

In the same race, the gay Log Cabin Republican Club of Northern Virginia, voted to endorse Robb's opponent, George Allen, after Allen met with the group and pledged not to discriminate in his hiring practices while also expressing support for a gay-inclusive GOP and hate crimes legislation. In return, the LCR also contributed funds to Allen and volunteered for the campaign. Even so, Allen had accused Robb of wanting to "impose same-sex marriage on Virginia" (Roundy 2000a).

During the 2000 congressional elections, both liberals and conservatives in Florida courted the LGBT vote; with some political advisors arguing that the LGBT vote might be larger than the Hispanic vote in Florida. Both U.S. Representative Bill McCollum, an Orlando conservative running for the U.S. Senate, and state Representative Elaine Bloom, a Miami Beach liberal campaigning for the U.S. House, sought the LGBT vote, with Bloom even appearing at the Broward County Gay and Lesbian Center in Fort Lauderdale with her gay son and Candice Gingrich, a lesbian activist with the Human Rights Campaign and half-sister of former Speaker of the House Newt Gingrich. McCollum quickly found that courting the LGBT vote by pushing for hate crimes legislation and meeting with gay and lesbian groups might alienate his conservative base. After McCollum began his new, more moderate strategy, the conservative Traditional Values Coalition said in a mass mailing to churches, "Congressman McCollum is the new darling of the homosexual extremists. He has a tough race but he is looking for votes in all the wrong places" (Wasson 2000). Nevertheless, the example demonstrates that LGBT voters can increasingly play an important role in congressional elections, even when traditionally conservative candidates are running.

As with ascertaining the number of LGBT voters, determining the impact of the LGBT vote is often a tricky process. Recently political scientists have made some progress in this regard. Mark Hertzog (1996) found that the LGB vote was large enough and cohesive enough in supporting progay candidates (regardless of party) to be a decisive block in salient elections where the voting margins are within 5 to 10 percent.

Importantly, as in most of politics, the key is perceptions. If politicians believe that the LGBT vote is important to victory, the LGBT vote will be courted. Academic research is unlikely to influence these perceptions much. For example, during the 2000 congressional races in Florida, several politicians campaigned for the LGBT vote under the belief that LGBT voters represented 10 percent of the voting population (Nevins 2000). However, no statewide study of voters has ever found a self-identified LGB contingent of 10 percent and the numbers only begin to approach 10 percent in heavily urban areas (Hertzog 1996, 258–259).

Political Party Involvement

As many journalists and academics have begun to note, LGBT activists have increased their mainstream political participation in the last decade. One aspect of this "mainstreaming" has been an increased effort to work within existing political parties' systems. However, some LGBT activists have focused their party activity on third parties, such as the Libertarian Party, and some have even tried to start their own parties, such as the Cure AIDS Now Party and the Queer Party. Below we outline the ideologies and activities of the two largest political parties within the United States and examine their relations with the LGBT community. We also briefly examine a few smaller parties that have made special efforts to attract LGBT activists or taken positions on LGBT issues. (Although we cannot cover LGBT involvement with every party, interested readers should note that there was early involvement with third parties. For example, in 1971 Indiana gay activist Charles Avery was named executive secretary of the newly formed People's Party.)

Relations with the Democratic Party

Of the two major political parties and all the minor parties in the United States, LGBT people have clearly found the most acceptance and influence within the Democratic Party. This is true at the national level and within state parties. Democrats have traditionally been more supportive on civil rights issues. As Democrats came to define LGBT issues as civil rights issues in the 1970s and 1980s, LGBT support naturally followed. Public opinion polls support this notion and find that Democrats tend to be less opposed to homosexuality, LGBT civil rights, and have more positive feelings toward LGBT people (Moore 1993, 33; Adam 1995, 133; Layman and Carmines 1997; Yang 1998). Interestingly, Democratic elites seem to be more supportive of gay civil rights than are the masses, but clear majorities of the elites and masses support LGBT civil rights (Lindaman and Haider-Markel 2000). In this section we discuss LGBT relations with the Democratic Party at the national level as well as within state and local party systems.

LGBT activism within the Democratic Party began in the 1960s, but was not significantly visible until the 1970s. By October 1979 Americans for Democratic Action, a national party activist group was calling on the U.S. Senate to support a bill banning job discrimination on the basis of sexual orientation.

Starting in 1980 LGBT persons began to appear in significant numbers in the national party operations. A nationwide drive to secure a gay rights plank in national party platforms, "Gay Vote 1980," resulted in about a dozen gay delegates in the Iowa caucuses. Indeed, LGBT persons were well represented at the 1980 convention. An openly lesbian delegate to the Democratic National Convention, Virginia Appuzzo, used her position to coauthor the first LGBT civil rights party platform plank for a major political party in the United States. The plank opposed the U.S. ban on homosexual immigrants and discrimination based on sexual orientation. Appuzzo helped strengthen the language of the 1980 plank at the 1984 convention. The trend continued in 1982 during the Democratic Party's midterm convention in Philadelphia, where more than sixty-five lesbian and gay activists pressured the party to take a stronger stand on gay civil rights.

By 1992 LGBT representation in the Democratic Party seemed to have reached a peak. For some LGBT activists, however, the attention to LGBT issues was not enough. During the 1992 convention, 20,000 activists protested for more AIDS spending. At the same time, two people with AIDS, Elizabeth Glaser and openly gay Bob Hattoy, jointly addressed the convention delegates.

LGBT influence in the Democratic Party was also made clear when Vice President Gore became the first vice president ever to address a gay group in 1998 when he spoke to an HRC meeting. In his speech Gore argued: "The cause we celebrate tonight is not some narrow special interest. It is really the cause that has defined this nation since its founding: to deepen the meaning of fundamental fairness, . . . to build a good and just society on this bedrock principle: equal opportunity for all, special privilege for none" (Price 2000).

More importantly, Democratic President Clinton became the first president to address an LGBT group in November 1997 when he gave the keynote address at an HRC meeting. President Clinton mostly spoke of recent struggles with Congress on trade issues, but his speech before the HRC was just as historic as Harry Truman's address before a black civil rights group fifty years earlier. Without the coaxing skills of the president's advisor, Richard Socarides, the event might not have occurred.

LGBT activists have made their voices heard in the Democratic Party through fundraisers as well. During President Clinton's second term, LGBT activists raised record amounts for the Democratic Party through special dinners hosted by the president. In December 1999 LGBT activists raised a record-breaking $900,000 for the Democratic National Committee (DNC) at a luncheon hosted by President Clinton in Washington, D.C. The event was organized by openly gay DNC Treasurer Andrew Tobias and required contributors to pay $10,000 or more per person (Chibbaro 1999). The luncheon was the third LGBT fundraiser held by the DNC in three years, with the first event in 1997 raising $290,000. The second event in 1998 raised $401,000 for the DNC (Chibbaro 1999). Openly LGBT people also served on the DNC's site search committee of the 2000 national convention.

Even with the support LGBT people have given to and received from the Democratic Party, in 1999 the DNC had still not designated the DNC Gay and Lesbian Caucus as an official "operating caucus," which would give it a seat on the DNC executive committee. Other caucuses, such as the African American, Asian Pacific, Hispanic, and Women's caucuses, do have official status.

In response to this incomplete acceptance by the DNC, LGBT activists created the Stonewall Democrats in 1998. The organization is a federation of forty-five local clubs with a total of 10,000 members. Most of the local clubs were previously independent local Democratic Clubs, with some even sharing the Stonewall name (Cassels 1999).

In 1999 President Clinton nominated gay financial writer Andrew Tobias to be treasurer of the DNC. The nomination placed Tobias in the highest-ranking position ever attained by an openly LGBT person in a major U.S. party. Tobias had made himself known to Democrats by making over $236,000 in political contributions, including $183,000 to the DNC since 1993 (Rothaus 1999). The DNC voted in March 1999 to place Tobias in the post. Tobias had also cochaired LGBT fundraising dinners for the DNC in 1997 and 1998 (Chibarro 1999). In 2001 four other LGBT people were named to positions in the DNC. Mark Spengler was promoted to base vote director, Campbell Spencer was named national gay and lesbian base vote director; Clay Doherty became the executive director of the Gay and Lesbian Leadership Council of the DNC, and Christine Kenngott was tapped to be the deputy director of marketing.

The number of LGBT delegates participating in Democratic conventions is a clear way to measure LGBT participation in party politics. As mentioned, the number of delegates to the national convention held every four years has generally increased over time. For example, for the 2000 campaign, Ohio's Democratic Party adopted an affirmative action policy stating that five of its allotted 170 seats for the nominating convention would have to be filled by gay delegates. By comparison, the party reserves six slots for young Democrats, two for Asian Americans, three for Hispanics, and thirty-six for African Americans. The allotment demonstrates LGBT integration into Ohio Democratic politics. In 1996 the Ohio delegation only had one seat held by an openly LGBT person, and he dropped out. And in 1992 there was one lesbian delegate and one lesbian alternate. By comparison, twenty-six delegates and twenty-two alternate initial delegates from Iowa were openly gay or lesbian in 2000 (Chibarro 2000b). Although few of the initial delegates would go to the national convention, the state Democratic Party was required to send at least two openly gay delegates.

Although the numbers are difficult to track, LGBT people have also disproportionately contributed to the Democratic Party. The DNC estimates that it received $3 million in donations from LGBT contributors in 1996. Between December 1997 and February 1999, the Clintons attended three DNC gay and lesbian fund-raising events, which raised $1.2 million (Bumiller 1999). During October 1999 LGBT events raised about $2.5 million for the Democratic Party, including about $850,000 for the Democratic Congressional Campaign Committee. Hillary Clinton's New York Senate campaign took in $125,000 at a December 1999 LGBT event (Hitt 2000).

LGBT Democratic activists were also caught up in the controversial White House "coffees" and overnight stays at the White House, part of a broader scandal involving fundraising by the Democratic Party. Openly gay Fred P. Hochberg was named as a contributor who attended a White House coffee event. Hochberg was later nominated by President Clinton to be deputy administrator of the U.S. Small Business Administration. From 1993 to 1996 Hochberg contributed $75,750 to the DNC and helped raise additional funds for the Clinton-Gore reelection committee (Chibbaro 1997d).

Even though lesbians and gays have found a relatively tolerant home in the Democratic Party, transgendered persons have not received the same amount of acceptance or support for specific legislation. Much of the disparity arises through ignorance on the part of politicians. For example, during the 2000 presidential campaign, Democratic candidate Al Gore responded to a transsexual's question on Gore's support for antidiscrimination protections for transgendered persons, Gore said, "I'll have to learn more about it" (Sobieraj 2000).

LGBT people have made strides in the Democratic Party at the state and local levels as well. Even in states where LGBT people have typically faced greater hurdles and fewer legal protections, the Democratic Party has allowed a place for LGBT people. For example, in Utah the Democratic Party said in 1997 that "it doesn't ask and doesn't care if loyal party members appointed to party committees this summer are homosexual or lesbian" (Bernick 1997). Furthermore, the Utah Democratic Party chairwoman appointed a record number of LGBT persons (fifteen) to party posts in 1997. This occurred even though the Gay and Lesbian Utah Democrats (GLUD) disbanded at the end of 1996. Iowa elected fourteen openly lesbian and gay activists to the state's platform committee for its 2000 Democratic convention, and seven other open gays won election to the Iowa Democratic Party Central Committee. During the 2000 presidential primary, many of the Democratic precinct caucuses also passed a number of gay civil rights and AIDS resolutions.

In Ohio the 2000 presidential election saw increasing involvement of LGBT activists in the Democratic Party. The state party pressed both Gore and Bradley to recruit more LGBT delegates for the national party convention, and the state party for the first time required a contingent of LGBT delegates. Of the 170 Ohio delegates, five were required to be LGBT in 2000. In 1996 Ohio sent one LGBT delegate, who later dropped out, and in 1992 Ohio sent one LGBT delegate to the convention. Lesbian activist Lynn Greer orchestrated the change, and Greer had also convinced delegates to the 1992 convention to wear AIDS ribbons. Many activists in Ohio have viewed Greer's success as part of an increasing involvement of LGBT people in Ohio Democratic politics. Steps to recruit more LGBT delegates for the 2000 Democratic convention also moved forward in New York, California, Iowa, Rhode Island, and Georgia.

The situation in local parties is similar. In Philadelphia the 1998 Democratic City Committee saw thirty-three open gays and lesbians elected to seats, more than doubling the number of LGBT persons on previous Committees (NewsPlanet Staff 1998a). The power of LGBT Democratic activists in Philadelphia is aided by a strong organization in the form of the Liberty City Lesbian and Gay Democratic Club. The Liberty Club even had several of its leaders named as Democratic presidential candidate Bill Bradley's delegates in 2000 and were instrumental in the election of Philadelphia Mayor John Street in 1999. Finally, in Washington, D.C., where LGBT people have made great strides in local politics, eleven LGBT officials sat on the Democratic State Committee in 1998 (Chibbaro 1998a).

Relations with the Republican Party

LGBT political activity within the Republican Party was limited until the 1990s. Until the formation of the LGBT Republican group, the Log Cabin Republicans (LCR)(see Chapter 3), LGBT people were largely unwelcome in national Republican politics. However, LGBT Republicans did make some inroads at the state and local levels. In this section we discuss the history of LGBT activity within the Republican Party at the national, state, and local levels. As we outline below, relations between LGBT activists and the Republican Party have often been tense, with LGBT people often facing intolerance and outright hostility.

Republican Party opposition to homosexuality dates back to at least the 1950s and perhaps earlier. During the 1950s Republicans linked homosexuality to communism, thereby placing homosexuals on the wrong side of Cold War politics. Republican members of Congress also attacked homosexual activist groups. In 1954 Senator Wiley (R-WI) sent a letter to the U.S. postmaster general demanding that a gay magazine (*ONE*) be blocked from using the U.S. mail because of its devotion to the "advancement of sexual perversion" (Streitmatter 1995, 32). The postmaster general complied with the request until the Supreme Court overruled the decision in 1958.

The effort by Republicans to cast homosexuality as a security threat and as immoral created an alliance between Cold Warriors and evangelical Christians in the early 1960s. At the time, evangelical Christians were increasing their involvement within the Republican Party because of the threat to traditional values posed by a Supreme Court ruling on school prayer and the increasing demands of the black civil rights movement. The alliance between Cold Warrior Republicans and Evangelicals was enhanced during the 1970s and 1980s as Republican candidates, including Ronald Reagan and Pat Robertson, courted the religious conservative vote. The strong tie between religious conservatives opposed to LGBT activists reached perhaps its most notorious point during the 1992 Republican convention when religious conservatives used the party platform to express their "traditional family values" viewpoints. The Republican Party's focus on traditional family values has led to the belief that Republicans oppose nontraditional gender roles and homosexuality. Public opinion polls show that Republicans are less likely to support gay civil rights than are Democrats (Adam 1995, 133; Moore 1993, 33; Yang 1998), but Republicans who are political elites, such as members of Congress, are less supportive than the average Republican citizen (Lindaman and Haider-Markel 2000).

Even with the strained relations between the LGBT community and the Republican Party, LGBT Republicans have made their presence felt. The first time there was an organized and visible LGBT presence at a Republican national convention was in 1984, when Ronald Reagan was nominated for a second term. However, this presence did not prevent a conservative faction of the GOP from trying and failing to oust the newly formed Log Cabin Club, a gay Republican group, from the party in 1987. In 1988 cooler heads prevailed and the party's nominee, Vice President George H. W. Bush, endorsed a plan to protect persons with AIDS from discrimination.

The dominance of religious conservatives in the Republican Party base continued in the 1990s, but more moderate Republicans began to accept campaign donations from LGBT activist groups and some began to actively court LGBT voters. LGBT Republicans organized heavily for 1992 and were able to found several new Log Cabin Clubs throughout the country and gain media attention for the first openly gay delegates to the Republican convention.

In 1998 the Republican Party showed some of the first signs of division over LGBT issues. Highly negative public comments by Republican members of Congress and their blocking of President Clinton's appointment of openly gay activist James Hormel as an ambassador worried the moderate wing of the Republican Party. In an interview Senate majority leader Trent Lott had compared homosexuality to alcoholism, kleptomania, and sex addiction. Calls for tolerance increased from both Democrats and Republicans, and seemed to resonate with many Republicans. Indeed, conservative Senator Richard Lugar (R-IN) argued that antigay rhetoric won't "energize the party." Lugar said, "I don't believe the party is likely to grow stronger or our voters more numerous through attacks on minorities, whether they be sexual minorities or religious or racial minorities" (Berke 1998). Ralph Reed, a Republican strategist and former head of the Christian Coalition said, "The Republican Party has tripped over its own shoelaces and found itself on the defensive" and suggested, along with other Republicans, that the antigay language may cost the party votes among moderates and even conservatives who view such attacks as mean-spirited (Berke 1998).

Although Republican presidential candidate Bob Dole refused a donation from a gay Republican group in 1996, during the 2000 presidential campaign, Republican candidate John McCain accepted such donations and even met with the Log Cabin Republicans (LCR). However, Dole endorsed a policy of nondiscrimination for gays during the 1996 campaign and did not specifically use antigay language. LGBT voters may have responded positively to the reduction in antigay rhetoric during the 1996 presidential campaign, as 23 percent of LGB voters supported Republican candidate Dole (Keen 1996).

Although presidential campaign 2000 front-runner Governor George W. Bush said he would not meet with the LCR, he did say he would not ask potential political appointees their sexual orientation. LGBT activists also held positions in the Bush campaign. However, Bush also promised a group of religious conservatives that if elected, he would "not appoint people who espouse a homosexual lifestyle" (Greenberger 2000). And all of the Republican candidates were opposed to openly gay LGBT people serving in the military.

Interestingly, both Bush and McCain made the greatest inroads for Republicans among the LGBT community. For example, the Bush 2000 campaign was able to raise almost $100,000 in Oak Lawn, a Dallas neighborhood said to be the gay cultural capital of north Texas. In that same neighborhood, Democratic candidate Al Gore was able to raise only about $20,000 through December 1999, and Democrat Senator Bill Bradley raised less than half of Gore's total (Underwood 2000). In Houston's main LGBT neighborhood, Montrose, Bush raised over $26,000 by December 1999, more than twice that raised by Gore. Even with the Texas grassroots LGBT support, the LCR of

Texas was contributing its campaign funds to Republican John Mc-Cain. Bush found support in other LGBT areas, including San Francisco, California, where he raised $1.2 million compared to Democrat Bradley's $1.3 million, and Gore's $556,000 (Underwood 2000).

The main LGBT Republican group, the Log Cabin Republicans, held fundraisers in late 1999 for Republican presidential candidate John McCain, raising $40,000 for the senator (Napolitano 2000). Fundraisers were held simultaneously in Boston, Chicago, Minneapolis, New Orleans, New York, Seattle, and Washington, D.C. McCain also met with openly gay Arizona legislator Steve May about May's possible dismissal from the army reserve (Napolitano 2000).

Even so, the National Republican Congressional Committee (NRCC) encouraged Republican candidates in 2000 to "gay-bait," that is, stir up antigay sentiment. For example, the *NRCC Issues Book 2000* instructed candidates to explain their opposition to gay civil rights by arguing that the laws "would allow radical homosexuals to impose their lifestyle choices upon everyone else at our workplaces and schools without simple managerial oversight. The discussion of sexual behavior over the water-cooler at work does not deserve special protection from Washington" (Chibbaro 2000c).

During the 1990s many journalists and academics focused their attention on the rise of religious conservatives within state Republican Party organizations. However, another major trend within state Republican Party organizations during the 1990s was an increase in the number of openly LGBT party activists.

Texas provides an excellent example of the recent changes in LGBT activism within state Republican Party circles. During the 1990s, the Republican Party of Texas refused to allow the LCR of Texas to establish a booth at its state party convention. In 1998 the Texas GOP continued to deny the LCR a booth at the state convention. LGBT protestors outside the convention faced off against counterprotestors as state party spokesman Robert Black compared the LCR to the Ku Klux Klan and said, "We don't allow pedophiles, transvestites or cross-dressers either" (Schmickle 1998). However, almost thirty members of the LCR of Texas attended the Republican Party of Texas state convention in June 1998 as delegates or alternates. This was the greatest number of LGBT persons to ever participate in a Republican Party of Texas state convention. That year was also the first time that LGBT persons (all LCR members) held precinct chair positions in all major Texas urban counties—Austin, Dallas, Houston, and San Antonio.

In Minnesota the state GOP has not traditionally favored LGBT positions on issues. The party platform in 1998 opposed "recognition of same-sex marriage or the establishment of homosexuals as a protected class" (Schmickle 1998). However, Republican candidates for office rarely campaign on these party positions, and in 2000 the party even nominated an openly gay man for the state senate seat that long-time gay activist Democrat Allan Spear had held until his retirement.

LGBT activists in Georgia have also made strides within the state Republican Party. During the 2000 elections the Georgia LCR was able to attract candidates for state offices and party leaders to special dinners.

During the initial selection of delegates for the 2000 presidential convention, Iowa Republicans elected three openly gay delegates, and one delegate was instrumental in his precinct's passage of three gay civil rights resolutions. The 2000 campaign in Iowa also saw the formation of the Log Cabin Republicans of Iowa.

In Virginia, the local Log Cabin Republicans have been involved in congressional, state, and local races, contributing funds and time to campaigns. LCR members have stuffed envelopes, distributed literature, worked phone banks, and worked at the polls on election day on behalf the Republican Party. The local LCR "adopted" four precincts in northern Virginia at the invitation of the local Republican committees, including Arlington, Alexandria, and two precincts in Fairfax County.

Overall, LGBT activists have generally done well in California. However, relations with the California GOP have not been consistent. As far back as 1978 LGBT activists were able to find some influence in the party, when several key Republicans publicly opposed an antigay ballot initiative. By 2000 LGBT activists were able to obtain significant meetings with the state GOP leaders.

Case Study: The 2000 Democratic and Republican National Conventions and LGBT Issues

The Democrats. Although many analysts argued that the 1992 Democratic convention was the most LGBT friendly ever, the 2000 convention may have exemplified the mainstreaming of LGBT politics within the Democratic Party. Several LGBT activists addressed the convention in prime time spots, but LGBT issues in general were not discussed much, and were only alluded to by the Democratic nominees for president and vice president. Although it was not the first time LGBT activists addressed a Democratic convention, the 2000 convention did feature an address by the president of the largest LGBT group, the Human Rights Campaign.

The 2000 Democratic platform stated that the party supported "the full inclusion of gay and lesbian families in the life of the nation," including "an equitable alignment of benefits" (Knickerbocker 2000). Against the protests of some LGBT delegates, convention organizers used a Boy Scout color guard as part of the official program.

The party's presidential nominee, Vice President Al Gore, did not specifically mention sexual orientation or LGBT people in his acceptance speech. However, Gore had made his support clear throughout the campaign.

The Republicans. By 1996 Republicans had toned down their antigay rhetoric in comparison to 1992, but in 2000 the party was able to present an even softer image in its attitude toward LGBT persons, especially LGBTs within the Republican Party. By the time the Republicans held their convention, their precrowned nominee had met with the main LGBT Republican group, and some of the other Republican candidates had improved their ties with LGBT voters. Nonetheless, the Republican nominee, George W. Bush, had noted that "an openly known homosexual is somebody who probably wouldn't share my philosophy" (Knickerbocker 2000). Furthermore, the Republican platform of 2000 stated that the party supports "the traditional definition of 'marriage' as the legal union of one man and one woman," that "homosexuality is incompatible with military service," and that the party "stand[s] united" with the Boy Scouts of America and its positions (Knickerbocker 2000).

For the first time ever an openly LGBT person spoke at the convention—Representative Jim Kolbe (R-AZ). Unfortunately for Kolbe, some delegates bowed their heads in protest when he addressed the convention. Some activists also suggested that a positive aspect of the convention was the fact that Mary Cheney, the lesbian daughter of vice presidential candidate Dick Cheney, sat publicly with her mother and sister. Mary Cheney also helped her father in the campaign and was on the dais during the inauguration.

Although the Republican Party did not officially change any of its positions on LGBT issues, it is notable that the party no longer viewed antigay positions as a means for attracting broad electoral support.

Green Party. The origins of the Greens/Green Party USA began with the formation of the Green Committees of Correspondence (GCoCs) network in 1984. In 1991 a new organization was created from the old, The Greens. The Greens held its first full Congress in August 1991. This congress established the Green Party USA. The Green Party is active in forty-six states and focuses its attention on diverse issues, including "rebuilding the inner cities, fighting nuclear waste dumps, challenging undemocratic governments, creating sustainable alternatives to polluting industries, supporting labor unions, and educating communities about environmental and social justice" (The Greens 2000).

Primarily an environmental party that fields its own political candidates, the Green Party supports sexual equality and justice. Their National Program, which is nonbinding to the party's candidates, contains the following statement related to LGBT people:

> We affirm the beneficial contributions of gay, lesbian, and bisexual people to society and in building our movement. We support and encourage the rights of gay, lesbian, and bisexual people in housing, jobs, benefits, child custody, and all areas of life. We support the legal recognition of gay and lesbian relationships, and urge the repeal of all laws that devalue and criminalize lesbian and gay relationships. We regard heterosexism (the cultural belief that the only legitimate form of sexual expression is between men and women) as a violation of human rights and dignity. We support education in schools on sexuality and sexual orientation. We urge support for and the protection of people with HIV, ARC, and AIDS. We urge an increase in funding for research and development on the prevention and treatment of AIDS, along with an increase in educational efforts on AIDS and its prevention. (The Green Party Website 2000)

Although LGBT persons have been active in the Green Party, few LGBT candidates have run under the Green Party label. However, in 1998 openly gay Scott McLarty did run for the Washington, D.C., city council as a Green Party candidate. And lesbian Green Party candidate Rebecca Kaplan ran for an Oakland, California, at-large city council seat in 2000.

Furthermore, LGB voters seem to offer disproportionate support to Green Party candidates. During the 2000 presidential campaign primaries, LGB voters in California voted for Green Party presidential candidate Ralph Nader by a margin of five to one over heterosexual voters (NGLTF 2000).

The Green Party 2000 presidential candidate Ralph Nader also appeared to strongly support LGBT civil rights, and in particular, Vermont's civil unions law that gives same-sex couples benefits similar to those of married couples. Nader also stated his support for adoption rights, gays in the military, and hate crime laws. However, Nader had not seemed quite so supportive in the past, and spokespersons for the Nader campaign sent conflicting signals on the issue. In a 1996 interview Nader dismissed gay civil rights and pro-choice concerns as "gonadal politics," and openly gay U.S. Representative Barney Frank (D-MA) said that Nader "throughout his career, has steadfastly ignored gay rights" (Fox 2000). However, the overall lack of support for Nader in the 2000 election from LGB voters appeared to stem from the notion that a vote for Nader was a vote for Republican candidate Bush.

Libertarian Party.   The Libertarian Party is the third largest political party in the United States. Libertarians believe in a free market economy, civil liberties and personal freedom, and a foreign policy of nonintervention, peace, and free trade. The party was founded in 1971 by a group of Colorado activists. In 1992 there were more than 700 LP candidates nationwide (Libertarian Party 2000). The party's 1998 platform addresses sexual rights with the following plank:

> We believe that adults have the right to private choice in consensual sexual activity. We oppose any government attempt to dictate, prohibit, control, or encourage any private lifestyle, living arrangement or contractual relationship.
>
> We support repeal of existing laws and policies which are intended to condemn, affirm, encourage, or deny sexual lifestyles or any set of attitudes about such lifestyles. (Libertarian Party Website 2000)

The efforts of LGBT activists to repeal discriminatory laws and protect the rights of LGBT individuals fit well with the Libertarian philosophy and a number of LGBT political candidates have run on the Libertarian Party ticket. However, the Libertarian belief in small government can come into conflict with LGBT activist beliefs concerning the passage of new laws to protect the rights of LGBT individuals.

Libertarian LGBT candidates have included Christopher Cole, who ran for the North Carolina legislature in 1996 and for the U.S. House in 2000; David Atkinson, who was elected to the Provincetown, Massachusetts, board of selectmen in May 1998; and Michael D. Ward, who ran for the Arlington County, Virginia, board of commissioners in 1991. Openly LGBT candidates have also run on the Libertarian ticket for treasurer in Arlington County, Virginia (1991); the Virginia House of Delegates (1991); sheriff in Las Vegas, Nevada (1994); Massachusetts secretary of state (1998); lieutenant governor in Georgia (1998); and for a U.S. House seat from Arizona (1998). (For a list of these candidates and references see the list of LGBT candidates and officeholders at http://lark.cc.ukans.edu/ ~prex/data.html.)

The party's 2000 presidential candidate, Harry Browne, was on the ballot in forty-nine states and the District of Columbia. Browne supported a significantly reduced role for government and stated that "government is not the answer, that individual liberty is" for all issues, including LGBT civil rights issues. Browne consequently supported no government involvement in marriage issues, discrimination, hate crimes, or AIDS. However, Browne did argue that private companies should not discriminate and he supported LGBT persons serving openly in the military.

Reform Party. The Reform Party was created on the back of H. Ross Perot's 1992 presidential candidacy organization, United We Stand America. (A splinter from the Reform Party, the American Reform Party, held its founding convention in October, 1997.) Perot's early focus, as well as the party's, was on the national debt, campaign finance reform, and restricting trade. Perot ran for the presidency again in 1996, but this time as the official Reform Party candidate. Perot's 1992 showing ensured federal funding for 1996, and his 1996 support ensured federal funding for the Reform Party candidate in 2000. The Reform Party held its first national organizing convention in October 1997. In 1998, the Reform Party ran 184 candidates for congressional and state offices.

The Reform Party does not have public stances on LGBT issues and party leaders have sent mixed signals. During the 1992 presidential campaign, H. Ross Perot said that he would not appoint a known homosexual to a cabinet position (Thompson 1994). Although the Reform Party has not adopted specific platform planks related to LGBT people, during its 1997 national convention, the party elected openly gay Jim Mangia as its national secretary. During 1997 the party also adopted a plank that promotes "diversity and tolerance of others" (Johnson 1997b).

The Reform Party has also accepted openly LGBT candidates to run for office under the party's banner. In California, openly gay Reform Party candidate Jim Mangia ran for lieutenant governor. Mangia was assisted in his run by the change in California electoral laws that now allow for open primaries. The new system makes it easier for third party candidates to run for office and may allow third parties to attract more LGBT candidates and voters. During the 1997 elections, the Reform Party also nominated openly gay Bradley Evans for lieutenant governor of Virginia.

However, during the 2000 presidential campaign, party founder H. Ross Perot supported Pat Buchanan's pursuit of the Reform Party's nomination. Buchanan was well known for his anti-abortion, anti-gay, and anti–free trade stances. Socially liberal members of the Reform Party, including Minnesota Governor Jesse Ventura, strongly opposed Buchanan's nomination. In May 2000 the Colorado Reform Party passed a resolution calling for Buchanan to withdraw as the national party's front-running candidate for president after Buchanan made public statements calling homosexuality a "disorder" and stating that he would never choose a running mate or cabinet member with such a "disorder" (McAvoy 2000).

Buchanan eventually won his party's nomination and campaigned on his opposition to same-sex marriage, AIDS funding, and gays in the military. At campaign appearances Buchanan called homosexuality an "unnatural and immoral lifestyle" and said that homosexuality is "the love that will not shut up" (Fox 2000).

Relations with Other Parties

Little has been written on LGBT relations with parties other than the Republican and Democratic Parties. In this section we outline the relations between LGBT activists and the AIDS Cure Party, Constitution Party, the Natural Law Party, the New Party, and Queer Party. We explain the prominence, ideology, and activities of each party as it relates to the LGBT community.

AIDS Cure Party. In 1996 gay activists from ACT UP formed a new political party called the AIDS Cure Party. The new party nominated Steve Michaels as its presidential candidate and Anne Northrop for vice president. The party qualified for the ballot in only a few states and apparently received fewer than 2,000 votes. In 1997 Michaels ran for a city council seat in Ward 6 of Washington, D.C. Michaels finished tenth in the race with only 0.7 percent of the vote (Chibbaro 1997b).

Constitution Party. A number of independent state parties united to form the U.S. Taxpayers Party in 1992. The stated goals of the party were limiting "the Federal Government to its Constitutional boundaries and restoring the foundations of civil government back to the fundamental principles our country was founded upon" (Constitution Party Website 2000). The party's 1992 presidential candidate was on the ballot in twenty-one states, and by 1995 the party became the fifth political party to be formally recognized by the Federal Election Commission as a national political party. At the party's 1999 national nominating convention for the 2000 elections, delegates voted to change the party name to the Constitution Party. By May 2000 the party had made it onto the ballot in thirty-one states for the presidential election.

Through our research we were unable to uncover any evidence of LGBT activity within the Constitution Party. Nor does the party's platform specifically address many issues of concern to LGBT persons. However, the party platform does show a disdain for sexual orientations outside of heterosexuality and strong support for some notion of "family values"—often meaning anti-LGBT. The following platform excerpts are relevant to LGBT people:

> The law of our Creator defines marriage as the union between one man and one woman. The marriage covenant is the foundation of the family. We affirm, therefore, that no government may authorize or define marriage or family relations contrary to what God has instituted . . . . The first duty of civil government is to protect innocent human life. AIDS and HIV is a contagious disease which is dangerous to public health. It should not be treated as a civil rights issue. Under no circumstances should the federal government continue to subsidize activities which have the effect of encouraging perverted or promiscuous sexual conduct.
>
> Criminal penalties should apply to those whose willful acts of omission or commission place members of the public at risk of contracting AIDS or HIV. (Constitution Party Website 2000)

Howard Phillips was the party's candidate for president in 2000 for the third time. Phillips consistently used antigay rhetoric in his campaigns and stated on his 2000 campaign website: "I would revert to the old policy of excluding from military service persons who engage in homosexual conduct, and oppose so-called same-sex marriages. I find nothing in the Constitution which permits the Federal government to interfere with the right of states to prohibit homosexual conduct. I would veto all funding for so-called AIDS education which is in fact a system to promote the propagation of homosexual conduct" (Fox 2000). In 2000 Phillips appeared on the ballot in forty-two states.

Natural Law Party. One of the fastest growing third parties in the United States is the Natural Law Party. The party was founded in 1992 to "bring the light of science into politics." In the 1992 elections the party qualified for the ballot in 32 states, fielded 128 candidates, and became the third party (after the Republicans and Democrats) to be granted national party status by the Federal Election Commission. By 1996 the party ran 400 candidates in 48 states and in 1998 the Party had 142 candidates in 24 states.

On LGBT issues, the Natural Law Party has this to say:

> The Natural Law Party will support any legislation deemed necessary to prevent discrimination and uphold the constitutionally guaranteed rights of all American citizens, including all minorities. At the same time, the Party believes that legislation alone will never be able to eradicate prejudice and bigotry in society. For this we need more effective educational programs . . . . The Natural Law Party also believes that, in principle, government should not attempt to legislate morality or to intervene in the private moral decisions of its citizenry; the Federal Government was not created for this purpose. Therefore, on principle, the Natural Law Party will not draft legislation to discriminate against, nor to actively support, same-sex marriage. (Natural Law Party Website 2000a)

The party's presidential candidate in 2000, John Hagelin, said he would not repeal President Clinton's executive order banning sexual orientation discrimination. Hagelin also opposed the current policy on gays in the military and supported needle exchange programs to prevent the spread of AIDS.

The New Party. The New Party is a progressive political party that is focused on grassroots activism. Starting in 1992 the New Party began building local organizations and running candidates for mostly local and state offices. The party tends to focus on economic and development issues, such as "living wages" and suburban sprawl, but they do campaign on social issues. By 1997 the party had an estimated 10,000 dues-paying members (New Party Website 2000). In its statement of principles, the party states that it supports "an absolute ban on discrimination based on race, gender, age, country of origin, and sexual orientation" (New Party Website 2000).

Socialist Party.   The Socialist Party of the United States has seen dwindling support since World War II. In 2000 the party claimed only 1,000 members and played little role in politics at any level of government. However, the party appeared on the ballot in seven states in 2000. The party "stands for the abolition of every form of domination and exploitation, whether based on social class, gender, race/ethnicity, sexual orientation, or other characteristics" (Fox 2000). In 1980 openly gay David McReynolds ran as the party's presidential candidate and McReynolds ran again in 2000 with political experience spanning fifty years. McReynolds said that his sexual orientation did not affect his campaign, but he did support LGBT rights across a variety of issue areas. However, McReynolds did not support hate crimes legislation, arguing that prosecutors already have too much power. A central focus for McReynolds was the safety of LGBT youth and support for them as they come out.

Queer Party.   Another minor party formed by LGBT activists in Washington, D.C., was the Queer Party. By 2000 the party appeared to have disappeared. Little information is available about this party, but it appears to have been the first LGBT party ever of any significance in the United States. However, the current American electoral system is stacked against third parties, especially those focused on single issues.

Conclusion

Previous research and the case studies presented here suggest that LGBT people will continue to be a significant factor in electoral politics and policy making. Exactly how much influence will depend on the salience of LGBT issues, the closeness of specific electoral contests, and the ability of LGBT voters to both turn out to vote and vote and act as a cohesive group.

Given that the LGBT vote might range between 3 and 10 percent of the voting population in any state or locality, all elected officials in relatively close elections must take LGBT concerns into account. Furthermore, as LGBT activists continue their involvement with political parties and working on political campaigns, they are more likely to be established leaders for LGBT interest groups, be appointed to public office, and gain the experience to run for office on their own. The next chapter examines precisely these issues.

References and Further Reading

Adam, Barry D. 1995. *The Rise of a Gay and Lesbian Movement.* Rev. ed. New York: Twayne Publishers.

"Additional Elections Results." 1998. *NewsPlanet* (10 November).

Adriano, Joneil. 2000. "In a Tightened White House Race, Ralph Nader Could Loom Large." *Lesbian and Gay New York Online,* http://www.lgny.com, Web posting 28 August.

"AIDS Cure Party." 1996. *Ballot Access News* 12(3): 21.

Autman, Samuel. 2000. "Grassroots Campaign Aims to Get Out Gay, Lesbian Vote." *San Diego Union-Tribune* (5 January).

Bailey, Robert W. 1998a. *Gay Politics, Urban Politics: Identity and Economics in an Urban Setting.* New York: Columbia University Press.

———. 1998b. *Out and Voting: The Gay, Lesbian, and Bisexual Vote in Congressional House Elections, 1990–1996.* Washington, DC: National Gay and Lesbian Task Force.

———. 2000. *Out and Voting II: The Gay, Lesbian, and Bisexual Vote in Congressional Elections, 1990–1998.* Washington, DC: National Gay and Lesbian Task Force Policy Institute.

Bandler, James. 2000. "Anger over Civil-union Law Shapes Vt. Governor Race." *Wall Street Journal* (27 September).

Berke, Richard L. 1998. "Intraparty Debate Breaks Out among Republicans over Criticism of Gays." *New York Times News Service* (29 June).

Bernick, Bob, Jr. 1997. "Utah's Top Dem Says Sexual Orientation Is Not an Issue: But Gays and Lesbians Applaud a Record Number of Party Appointments." *The Desert News* (22 August).

Boerner, Heather. 1998. "Gay Votes Help Defeat D'Amato: Exit Poll Finds 77 Percent of Gays Voted for Schumer." *Washington Blade* (6 November).

Bull, Chris. 2000. "Home in the White House; Julian Potter Settles into Her Job as the President's Liaison to Gays and Lesbians." *The Advocate* 14 (March).

Bull, Chris, and John Gallagher. 1996. *Perfect Enemies: The Religious Right, the Gay Movement, and the Politics of the 1990s.* New York: Crown Publishers.

Bumiller, Elisabeth. 1999. "Public Lives: 'Best Little Boy' Is Now a Chief Fundraiser." *New York Times* (19 February).

California Alliance for Pride and Equality. 2000. "CAPE Rides Crest of a Victorious Lavender Wave from Knight Initiative Battle." Press release (8 March).

Carlson, Brian. 1998. "Republican Gubernatorial Forum Focuses on Spending." *Daily Nebraskan* (17 April).

Cassels, Peter. 1999. "Gay Elected Officials Gather in Providence; Annual INLGO Confab Draws 75 Leaders." *Bay Windows* (26 November): 1.

Chibbaro, Lou, Jr. 1997a. "Croft Earns Coalition's Top Rating in Ward 6 Race: Deadlocked Stein Club Doesn't Endorse." *Washington Blade* (14 March).

———. 1997b. "In Ward 6 Race, Michael Finishes in 10th Place." *Washington Blade* (2 May).

———. 1997c. "Gay Republican Lawmaker Forces Vote on Bill; Oregon Representative Bucks Party Line on Employment Bill. *Washington Blade* (9 May).

———. 1997d. "Clinton Taps New Yorker for Small Business Post." *Washington Blade* (17 October).

———. 1998a. "Gay Dems Join Party Leaders." *Washington Blade* (29 May).

———. 1998b. "Record Number of Gays Run in City Elections." *Washington Blade* (4 September).

———. 1999. "Fundraiser with Clinton Expected to Pull $900,000." *Washington Blade* (17 December).

———. 2000a. "Surf's Up for Gore; Vice President Commits to Gay.com Q & A." *Washington Blade* (14 January).

———. 2000b. "Iowa Gay Democrats Split; Bradley May Have Tied Gore among Party's Gays; Observers Unfazed by Third-place Finish for Keyes." *Washington Blade* (28 January).

———. 2000c. "VA Rep. Accused of Gay-baiting in Utah." *Washington Blade* (22 September).

———. 2000d. "Log Cabin Fever: Gay GOP Group Takes Credit for Victory Margin for Presidential Candidate Bush." *Washington Blade* (1 December).

Chibbaro, Lou, Jr., and Lisa Keen. 2000. "Gay Candidate Wins Senate Primary; Vermont State Auditor Advances to General Election against Jeffords." *Washington Blade* (15 September).

Cobb, Kim. 2000. "Political Fallout from Vermont Civil Unions." *New York Times News Service* (16 September).

Coile, Zachary. 1998. "Gay Marriage: Davis and Lungren Opposed, Harman, Checchi in Favor, but Say State Just Isn't Ready." *San Francisco Examiner* (19 April).

The Constitution Party. 2000. *The Constitution Party: National Internet Headquarters,* http://www.ustaxpayers.org/, Web posting 7 January.

D'Emilio, John. 1992. *Making Trouble: Essays on Gay History, Politics, and the University.* New York: Routledge.

Democratic National Committee. 2001. "DNC Welcomes Openly Gay and Lesbian Staff Members." Press release (18 July).

Diamond, Sara. 1995. *Roads to Dominion: Right-Wing Political Movements and Political Power in the United States.* New York: Guilford Press.

Dillon, John. 2000. "`Take Back' Effort Gets a Push by POST." *Rutland Herald* (24 September).

Esteve, Harry. 1997. "House Republicans Bolted Monday from the State Capitol." *The Register-Guard* (15 April).

———. 1998. "Money Can't Always Buy You Election." *The Register-Guard* (2 July).

Fiore, Faye. 1995. "White House AIDS Activist Falls into Political Exile." *Los Angeles Times* (11 September): A1.

Fox, Kara. 2000. "Third-party Candidates Vie for Presidential Votes." *Washington Blade* (27 October).

Friday, Wayne. 2000. "Reform Party Self-destructing?" *Bay Area Reporter* (6 January).

Gay and Lesbian Victory Fund. 1998. "Political Extremists Target Openly Gay Legislator." Press release (April 9).

Georgia Log Cabin Republicans. 2000. *January 19th, 2000, News Update.* Atlanta, GA: Georgia Log Cabin Republicans.

Green, Stephen. 2000. "Analysis: Gays May Hold Key to State for Gore, Bradley Timing of Primary Emphasizes 'Don't Ask, Don't Tell'." *San Diego Union-Tribune* (11 January).

Greenberger, Scott S. 2000. "Bush's Record on Gays Unclear; Mixed Signals Reflect Complexities of Political Situation." *Austin American-Statesman* (17 January).

The Greens/Green Party USA. 2000. The Greens/Green Party USA, Introduction. http://www.greens.org/gpusa/intro.html, Web posting, 7 January.

Haider-Markel, Donald P. 1997. "From Bullhorns to PACs: Lesbian and Gay Politics, Interest Groups, and Policy." Ph.D. diss., University of Wisconsin-Milwaukee.

Haider-Markel, Donald P., and Kenneth J. Meier. 1996. "The Politics of Gay and Lesbian Rights: Expanding the Scope of the Conflict." *Journal of Politics* 58(2): 332–349.

Hertzog, Mark. 1996. *The Lavender Vote: Lesbians, Gay Men, and Bisexuals in American Electoral Politics.* New York: New York University Press.

Hitt, Greg. 2000. "Presidential Candidates Embrace Gay Issues, and Enjoy Donations." *Wall Street Journal* (10 January).

Hoffman, Jack. 2000. "Voters Show Anger over Civil Unions Law." *Rutland Herald* (13 September).

Ivers, Kevin. 1998. "Carpenter Defeated in Oregon: Narrow Loss A Warning Sign to Gay Community, Log Cabin Says, 5/28/98." Press release, Washington, DC: Log Cabin Republicans.

Johnson, David K. 1997. *1971–1997: Twenty-Six Years of Fighting For Equal Rights.* Washington, DC: Gay and Lesbian Activists Alliance.

Johnson, Wendy. 1997a. "17 Gay Candidates Victorious." *Washington Blade* (7 November).

Johnson, Wendy. 1997b. "Reform Party Elects Openly Gay Man as its Secretary." *Washington Blade* (5 December).

Keen, Lisa. 1996. "Where Were Gay Voters? Survey Finds Sharp Drop in Gays at the Polls." *Washington Blade* (8 November).

———. 2000a. "Gays Backing Gore." *Washington Blade* (29 September).

———. 2000b. "Vermont Seeks Civility: Voters Seem to Buck against Hostile Tactics." *Washington Blade* (3 November).

————. 2000c. "Bragging Rights: Gay Vote Margin Big Enough to Swing Races." *Washington Blade* (10 November).

————. 2000d. "Vermont Secure: Governor Wins, Civil Unions Legislation Safe from Repeal." *Washington Blade* (10 November).

Knickerbocker, Brad. 2000. "Election Spotlights Battle over Gay Rights; Conflict Escalates over Issues from Same-sex Unions to Dr. Laura's New TV Show." *Christian Science Monitor* (11 September).

Louisiana Lesbian and Gay Political Action Caucus (LAGPAC). 1998. "Apuzzo to be Guest of Honor at January 23 'Community First' Reception." Press release (29 December). New Orleans: Louisiana Lesbian and Gay Political Action Caucus.

Layman, Geoffrey C., and Edward G. Carmines. 1997. "Cultural Conflict in American Politics: Religious Traditionalism, Postmaterialism, and U.S. Political Behavior." *Journal of Politics* 59(3): 751–777.

Lessy, Harriet. 1999. "Gays Help Street's Transition." *Philadelphia Daily News* (5 December).

Libertarian Party. 2000. Libertarian Party Homepage, http://www.lp.org/, web posting, 6 January.

Lindaman, Kara, and Donald P. Haider-Markel. 2000. "Not All Issues Are Created Equal: Reexamining Issue Evolution in Morality Policy." Paper presented at the annual meeting of the Midwest Political Science Association, April 27–30.

Log Cabin Republicans of Texas. 1998. "Log Cabin Members off to State Party Convention." Press release (31 March). Austin: Log Cabin Republicans of Texas.

Marinucci, Carla. 2000. "Three Supervisors in S.F. Back Bradley; Ammiano, Newsom, Yaki Critical of Gore." *San Francisco Chronicle* (11 January): A15.

Matthews, Christopher. 1997. "Clinton's Historic Gay Rights Speech." *San Francisco Examiner* (13 November).

McAvoy, Tom. 2000. "Colorado Reform Party Fed Up with Buchanan." *Pueblo Chieftain* (17 May).

McNeely, Dave. 1998. "The Parties and Gays." *Austin American-Statesman* (30 June).

Moore, David W. 1993. "Public Polarized on Gay Issue." *Gallop Poll Monthly* (April).

Myers, Steven Lee. 2000. "Despite Gore's Reversal, Candidates Critize 'Litmus Test' for Joint Chiefs." *New York Times* (10 January).

Napolitano, Nick. 1999. "A Night for Celebrating, Sharing, Remembering; Local Transgender Group Holds Holiday Formal." *Washington Blade* (10 December).

————. 2000. "McCain Meets with May, Accepts Log Cabin Donation." *Washington Blade* (14 January).

National Gay and Lesbian Task Force. 2000. "Gay, Lesbian, Bisexual Voters Set Record in California Primary, NGLTF Policy Institute Finds." Press release (9 March). Washington, DC: National Gay and Lesbian Task Force.

Natural Law Party. 2000. Additional platform issues, http://www.natural-law.org/platform/addissues.html. Web posting, 7 January.

Nevins, Buddy. 2000. "Candidates Courting S. Florida's Sizable Gay Voting Bloc." *The Sun-Sentinel* (30 August).

New Party. 2000. "The New Party: A Fair Economy, a Real Democracy, a New Party." http://www.newparty.org/., Web posting, 13 January.

O'Bryan, Will. 2000. "Governors Pack Punch." *Washington Blade* (27 October).

"Open Lesbian Wins Primary in New Hanover County." 2000. *Front Page* (May).

Pagano, Damian. 2000. "Delegation, Stafford Appeal for Tolerance." *Rutland Herald* (1 November).

Paulson, Michael. 2000. "In Wake of Civil Unions, Races Draw National Interest." *Boston Globe* (2 November).

Price, Deb. 2000. "Gay Allies Mobilize Support for Gore." *Detroit News* (28 August).

"Problem Worse Than Statistics Say." 2000. *Associated Press* (5 November). Accessed at http://www.ap.org/.

Puleo, Tom. 2000a. "Civil Unions, a Political Divide." *Hartford Courant* (14 September).

———. 2000b. "Vermont Race a Test of Values." *Hartford Courant* (30 October).

Rayside, David Morton. 1998. *On the Fringe: Gays and Lesbians in Politics.* Ithaca, NY: Cornell University Press.

Rizzo, Katherine. 1999. "Democrats Seek Gays; Party Sets Quota of Five Gay People for Ohio Delegation at 2000 Convention." *Akron Beacon Journal* (9 December).

Rosenstone, Steven J., and John M. Hansen. 1993. *Mobilization, Participation, and Democracy in America.* New York: MacMillan.

Rothaus, Steve. 1999. "Miami Writer Tapped as Democrats' Treasurer." *Miami Herald* (27 January).

Roundy, Bill. 2000a. "Gay Robb Supporters Mobilize across the State; Volunteers Work Phones, Stuff Envelopes, and Help Remind Other Democrats That We're Here." *Washington Blade* (27 October).

———. 2000b. "Gays Could Impact Results in Several U.S. House Races; As Democrats Wage Battle to Control House, Republicans Stress Need to Retain Moderates." *Washington Blade* (27 October).

———. 2000c. "Log Cabin of Northern Virginia Endorses Allen; Republican Group also Supports Bush; 'An Endorsement Is More Than a Pro-forma Entitlement'." *Washington Blade* (27 October).

Schmaler, Tracy. 2000. "Group Holds Forum Fighting Gay 'Behavior'." *Barre Times Argus* (18 October).

Schmickle, Sharon. 1998. "Hormel Nomination Sparked Conflict over Homosexuality." *Star Tribune* (29 June).

Schockman, H. Eric, and Nadine Koch. 1995. "The Continuing Political Incorporation of Gays and Lesbians in California: Attitudes, Motivations, and Political Development." Paper presented at the March meeting of the Western Political Science Association, Portland, Oregon.

Seelye, Katharine. 2000. "Gore Meets with Gay Leaders before Home Stretch in Iowa." *New York Times* (21 January).

Shilts, Randy. 1982. *The Mayor of Castro Street: The Life and Times of Harvey Milk.* New York: St. Martin's Press.

Smith, Rhonda. 1999. "Ammiano Falls Short: Brown Retains Mayor's Seat in S.F." *Washington Blade* (17 December).

Sneyd, Ross. 2000a. "Vt. Gov. Deals with Civil Unions." *Burlington Free Press* (15 September).

———. 2000b. "Same-sex Union an Issue in Vermont." *Boston Globe* (19 October).

Sobieraj, Sandra. 2000. "Gore's Ability Questioned by Voters." *Boston Globe* (12 January).

Streitmatter, Rodger. 1995. *Unspeakable: The Rise of the Gay and Lesbian Press in America.* Boston: Faber and Faber.

Sypert, Tracy. 1998. "Home Court Advantage; Stonewall Democrats Back Davis for Governor." *Frontiers Newsmagazine* 17 (May).

Sypert, Tracy, Marghe Covino, and Karen Ocamb. 1998. "Death of Life Lobby: What Happened? Money Woes, Control Issues Led to Dissolution." *Frontiers Newsmagazine* 17(1).

Thompson, Mark. ed. 1994. *The Long Road to Freedom.* New York: St. Martin's Press.

Underwood, Stephen R. 2000. "Bush Money Tree Growing in Gay Neighborhoods; Gore and Bradley Trailing Badly. *Texas Triangle* (7 January).

"U.S. Political Notes." 1998. *NewsPlanet* (26 May).

Vaid, Urvashi. 1995. *Virtual Equality: The Mainstreaming of Gay and Lesbian Liberation.* New York: Anchor Books.

Walton, Don. 1998. "Equal Rights Groups Condemn Candidate." *Lincoln Journal Star* (18 April).

Wasson, David. 2000. "Move to Moderation Has Backers' Backs Up." *Tampa Tribune* (2 September).

Whereatt, Robert. 1998. "Same-sex Marriage Issue Enters the Governor's Race." *Minneapolis Star Tribune* (15 July).

White, Ben. 2000. "Gay and Lesbian Groups Plan to Step Up Voter Turnout Campaigns." *Washington Post* (22 September).

Wilcox, Clyde. 1992. *God's Warriors: The Christian Right in Twentieth-Century America.* Baltimore, MD: John Hopkins University Press.

Yang, Alan S. 1998. *From Wrongs to Rights: Public Opinion on Gay and Lesbian Americans Moves Toward Equality.* Washington, DC: National Gay and Lesbian Task Force.

5

Being "Out" in Public Life

In any democratic system a central concern is political representation. Group representation may take place through the election of political candidates that belong to a particular racial, ethnic, religious, or gender group; through the election of candidates that don't belong to these groups, but support their interests; or through the appointment of group-affiliated or friendly officials. LGBT concerns over symbolic political representation in the policy process may be even more acute because gays are perhaps the most stigmatized minority group in the United States. Like other groups, LGBT people can try to achieve political representation by electing openly LGBT candidates to public office, ensuring that LGBT people are appointed to official positions, or by influencing the behavior of sympathetic heterosexual and closeted homosexual officials.

However, as with any other career, LGBT persons seeking public office are often hesitant to be open about their sexual orientation. Openness, or being "out," often means revealing one's sexual orientation to friends, family, coworkers, and the like. For public officials, being out means publicly stating one's sexual or gender orientation. But being out for officials may mean discrimination, lack of public support, or even the threat of physical violence. Even so, the public is increasingly less opposed to openly LGBT people holding public office. And as more public officials come out in office or are elected or appointed after being out, opposition appears to be decreasing.

When Representative Michael S. Pisaturo ran for the state house from in Cranston, Rhode Island, in 1994, he was public about his sexual orientation from the start. He discovered that even in Cranston being openly gay worked in his favor. Pisaturo recalled: "People would say, 'I don't agree with gay rights, but you're honest and I like that" (Freyer 1999). Pisaturo has even come to believe that being out can be an asset for politicians. Even so, Pisaturo says he knows of at least six Rhode Island legislators who are secretly gay. Although being gay is only part of Pisaturo's political life, he has been involved in trying to restore AIDS funding, sponsored bills dealing with gay civil rights and same-sex marriage, and publicly supports LGBT organizations. Allan Spear, Minnesota's senate president in 2000, largely agrees with Pisaturo's comments. Spear was elected to the Minnesota Senate in 1972, and came out in 1974. During his three decades in office he has seen little of the backlash experienced by some LGBT candidates. Furthermore, as noted by Annisa Parker, an open lesbian on the Houston City Council, being open may have helped her win by increasing media attention. However, she says, "There aren't many city issues that are gay issues. City government is concerned with potholes and sewers and such, not social and sexual matters" (Freyer 1999).

Some reporters were declaring the 1998 election year as the "year that gay politicians came of age" (Brelis 1998). Massachusetts alone had a record ten openly LGBT candidates running for state or national offices. And these candidates were no longer simply defined as "gay" candidates; instead they were being judged based on their positions on issues. Susan Tracy, an open lesbian candidate for the 8th District U.S. House seat in Massachusetts discovered this when she failed to receive the endorsements of the state's main LGBT group and main LGBT newspapers. Similar problems faced other LGBT candidates in the state as LGBT groups endorsed "gay-friendly" incumbents over openly LGBT challengers. This does not mean that a candidate's sexual orientation is not ever an issue. In fact, for some voters it may always be an issue, even in very liberal areas.

Like racial and ethnic minorities and women before them, successful gay candidates are increasingly discovering that they must speak to a broader constituency. Without the support of heterosexuals, gay candidates cannot expect to be victorious in diverse districts. For example, after a Rhode Island race where openly gay incumbent Representative Michael Pisaturo (D-Cranston) was accused of making gay and lesbian issues his only concern by his losing opponent, Pisa-turo said that his victory was evidence that "gay baiting doesn't work anymore and a candidate's sexual orientation is much less important to voters than policy positions and advocacy on the issues of the district." Nonetheless, Representative Pisaturo went on to say, "I could not have run solely on lesbian and gay issues and expected to win" (Boyce 1998).

Opponents of gay civil rights continue in their attempts to marginalize LGBT candidates and portray them as representing a special interest group. The president of the anti-LGBT political action committee, Campaign for Working Families, argues that gay candidates are running for office to increase their efforts at "promoting homosexuality as an acceptable alternative lifestyle" (Polman 1998). During the 1994 race for New York attorney general, Republican Dennis Vacco repeatedly insisted that his openly lesbian opponent, Karen Burstein, represented special and narrow interests. Vacco argued: "I have no problems with that sort of agenda, but I think the people of the state should know that that's her agenda" (Polman 1998). Vacco won the race, but lost four years later after being accused of pursuing a very narrow conservative political agenda. In Connecticut openly bisexual state Representative Evelyn Mantilla won a landslide victory in 1998 even though her challenger, Reverend Gabriel José Carrera, tried to appeal to Latino voters by arguing that Mantilla's bisexuality and support of lesbian and gay issues ran contrary to their values. During Representative Tammy Baldwin's (D-WI) historic 1998 campaign, her sexual orientation was an issue during the primary, but not during the general election. Ron Greer, a Republican candidate for the congressional seat, raised Baldwin's orientation during the primary as a way to mobilize religious conservatives in the district. Greer lost the primary and Baldwin's opponent in the general election was far more moderate. In the relatively liberal Madison, Wisconsin, district, Baldwin's openness mattered less than her party affiliation and positions on the issues.

Although the number of elected and nonelected openly LGBT public officials has dramatically increased in the past decade, the overall numbers are still relatively small. In 1987 activists counted only 20 openly LGBT elected officials in the country (Freyer 1999). And prior to 1990 a total of 50 openly LGBT officials had served in public offices across America (Haider-Markel 1997). In 1991 there were only 52 openly LGBT elected officials, and by April of 1998 there were at least 146 LGBT elected officials holding office in 27 states and the District of Columbia (Niedowski 1998; Polman 1998).

Of the 500,000 or so elected offices in the country, only about 180 were held by openly LGBT persons in 2000. Furthermore, of the several million appointed public offices, we estimate that less than 0.5 percent of them are held by openly LGBT persons.

Nonetheless, there are in 2001 three openly LGBT members of Congress, and many local and state LGBT officials are reelected as long as they continue to seek office. Interestingly, the relatively conservative state of Arizona has been a leader in the election of openly LGBT officials, with a gay member of Congress, two openly gay state legislators, and a city (Tempe) that is the largest city in the country with an openly LGBT mayor. In 2000 California had the most openly LGBT officials with thirty-six, and New York was second with seventeen.

More LGBT candidates are also running for office. The Gay and Lesbian Victory Fund, an LGBT political action committee (PAC) that supports only openly LGBT candidates, had 40 LGBT candidates ask for funds during the 1991–1992 election cycle. During the 1995–1996 election cycle, 277 LGBT candidates sought assistance from the Victory Fund (Polman 1998). The numbers are somewhat smaller for the overall number of openly LGBT candidates actually appearing on the ballot. In 1996 there were 72 openly LGBT candidates on the ballot, though that number dropped to 63 for the 1998 midterm elections. In 2000 the number of LGBT candidates increased 58 percent over 1996 to 114. The 2000 election also had a number of interesting candidates, including the first openly gay major party nominee for the U.S. Senate, three incumbent members of Congress and seven challengers for congressional seats, a third-party presidential nominee, 32 state legislators seeking reelection, and 31 challengers for state legislative seats (Freiberg 2000).

Public Opinion

We know that a significant portion of the public has unfavorable feelings toward homosexuals and LGBT persons generally. But do these feelings influence public support for LGBT candidates and other public officials? In other words, does the sexual orientation of candidates and public officials influence public support?

It is not enough to use polls that show how the public feels about homosexuals or homosexuality. Citizen views may or may not influence voting behavior or policy stances. But candidate positions clearly influence voter choices. For example, in a November 12, 1998,

New Jersey poll by the Quinnipiac College Polling Institute, 42 percent of respondents said that their support for a candidate would be influenced by his or her opinion on gay rights (Folio Bound VIEWS 1999). Furthermore, citizen preferences on gay civil rights policy are correlated with attitudes toward gays and homosexuality. Based on existing research, we might expect that voting behavior toward LGBT candidates would be influenced by attitudes toward gays, but this conclusion might be partially misleading. Anecdotal evidence does suggest that the sexual orientation of openly gay and lesbian candidates is a factor in their campaigns (for example see DeBold 1994), but no one knows for sure if sexual orientation of the candidates influences real-world voting behavior or election outcomes.

The only published research on this topic is by Rebekah Herrick and Sue Thomas (1999). Using an experimental research design, the authors set up hypothetical elections in which respondents were asked to state voting preferences and their perceptions of candidates. Controlling for a variety of other factors, including gender and ideology, they found that a candidate's sexual orientation does have a slight influence on voting preference and on perceptions of a candidate's electoral viability (ability to win the election). Interestingly, lesbians were not viewed any more negatively than gay men, a finding that is consistent with studies that suggest that voters rarely vote based on gender (Fox 1997).

Another way to look at this question is to examine Gallup poll questions on voting for a presidential candidate if the candidate is homosexual. In 1978, 1983, and 1999 Gallup asked: "Between now and the [year] political conventions, there will be discussion about the qualifications of presidential candidates—their education, age, religion, race, and so on. If your party nominated a generally well-qualified person for president who happened to be a homosexual, would you vote for that person?" In 1978 only 26 percent of respondents said yes, in 1983 29 percent said yes, but by 1999 59 percent said they would vote for a homosexual candidate for president (Newport 1999). The increase in support between 1983 and 1999 was large and significant, but support for a homosexual candidate has increased at a much slower rate than for women, blacks, Catholics, and Jews (Newport 1999). Other polls show even more support for LGBT candidates. For example, a 1999 poll asked respondents if they would support gay candidates for local or state offices. Over 77 percent said they would (Cassels 1999).

Of course, support for LGBT candidates varies by state. A 1994 California poll by Political Media Research found that 2 percent of respondents would be more likely to vote for a lesbian or gay candidate, 41 percent would be less likely, and 55 percent said it would have no effect on their vote (Folio Bound VIEWS 1999). A 1989 New Jersey poll by *The Record* found that only 23 percent of respondents said that sexual orientation should be considered when the person is a gay man running for political office, and 65 percent said it should not be considered (Folio Bound VIEWS 1999). In 1994 Staten Island, New York, borough President Guy Molinari said that someone who is gay or lesbian is not fit for public office. During a *New York Times/CBS News* state poll following the comment, respondents who knew about Molinari's statement were asked if the statement bothered them. Over 60 percent of respondents said the comments bothered them, but 38 percent said the comments did not bother them (Folio Bound VIEWS 1999).

However, respondents who answer in the manner they think is most appropriate may inflate the survey numbers. Also, as of yet no one has tested these questions in a real-world political campaign. Thus, we cannot draw firm conclusions about the effect of sexual orientation on vote choice. We can say that if a respondent is more conservative, lives in a rural area, is older, or is more religious, he or she is less likely to support an LGBT candidate. How aggressive or "out" a candidate is has not been examined. However, the experimental study cited above does suggest that voters perceive gay candidates as more supportive of gay rights and more interested in gay rights issues. This suggests that "aggressiveness" is not likely to matter too much—voters will make their own assumptions. However, gay politicians consistently say that gay candidates must focus on broader issues in order to win elections.

As the public becomes more accustomed to LGBT candidates in all parts of the country, and as a larger pool of LGBT officials gain experience in public office, we should see greater numbers of LGBT candidates winning state and national elections. However, as with other minority groups, this will likely be a long process with many setbacks. Below we outline the history and future of openly LGBT elected and nonelected officials.

Case Study: Outing Assistant Defense Secretary Pete Williams

As AIDS continued to take its toll on gay men in the late 1980s and early 1990s, a number of activists began discussing a political strategy of publicly revealing the sexual orientation of public figures that were known homosexuals as well as hypocritical in their public versus private lives. The controversial practice came to be known as "outing." In this section we briefly discuss a key case of outing a public official.

During the 1991 Gulf War Assistant Defense Secretary for Public Affairs Pete Williams played a significant role in the Bush administration by providing regular press briefings and had the respect of all officials with whom he worked. Williams had spent ten years as a reporter and went to Washington as a press secretary for then-U.S. Representative Dick Cheney (R-WY). Williams followed Cheney when Cheney became secretary of defense in the Bush administration. Many Washington insiders had known for some time that Williams was a gay man, but Williams had never publicly discussed his sexual orientation. Such a revelation would not have gone over well in the Bush administration, especially because religious conservatives already viewed President Bush as too moderate.

LGBT activists began the outing of Pete Williams when Queer Nation held a protest outside a Washington, D.C., bar, but Michelangelo Signorile, a reporter for the *Advocate,* was the one person who dug up the most convincing evidence after talking with a number of Williams's previous boyfriends. The first revelation that Williams was gay came shortly thereafter in a newspaper column called "Washington Merry-Go-Round," written by syndicated columnist Jack Anderson for August 2, 1991, publication. Anderson wrote that a "radical homosexual group" was about to out Williams. Although many newspapers refused to carry the column, the *Detroit News* and the *Philadelphia Inquirer* both wrote stories on Williams with their own staff, and newspapers in Williams's native Wyoming had no problem running the Anderson column. The national LGBT magazine, the *Advocate,* wrote a key story outing Williams in its August 27 issue and although the national television networks refused to cover the story, several local affiliates and CNBC did. On August 4 Sam Donaldson interviewed Defense Secretary Dick Cheney on *This Week With David Brinkley* and asked him: "Well, I take it Mr. Secretary, that this individual, who must defend department regulations [on homosexuals in the military] as a spokesman, is not going to be asked to resign?" To which Cheney replied, "Absolutely not" (O'Brien 1991, 11). But neither man identified Williams by name.

Nonetheless, Williams refused to discuss the issue. In fact, the only time Williams came close to discussing the issue was on August 6 at a regular briefing when he said: "As a government spokesperson, I stand here and talk about government policy. I am not paid to discuss my personal opinions about that [military ban on homosexuals] policy or talk about my personal life, and I don't intend to" (O'Brien 1991, 12).

Editors and writers who broke the story argue that they never intended for Williams to lose his job, and apparently Bush administration officials never considered firing Williams. However, the practice of outing public officials—violating their privacy—always has the potential to upset that person's personal relationships. Indeed, a survey of the *Advocate*'s readers suggested that 45 percent opposed the magazine's outing of Williams (Rouilard 1991). LGBT activists viewed the outing as important because it helped bring attention to the military policy on homosexuals. This outcome may in fact be true. During the 1992 presidential campaign Democratic presidential candidate Bill Clinton promised to remove the ban, and although his efforts failed once elected, the policy was revised.

Pete Williams's outing in 1991 helped pique the debate within the LGBT movement over the outing of closeted public figures. The issue has not yet been resolved, and there have been several important outing, or threat of outing, cases since then, including the *Advocate*'s threat to out U.S. Representative Jim Kolbe (R-AZ) after Kolbe voted for the anti-LGBT Defense of Marriage Act. Kolbe publicly came out before the *Advocate* could run the story, and was reelected. But both sides of the outing debate have good points, with proponents arguing that public figures taking anti-LGBT positions should not be allowed to maintain a hypocritical closeted private life, and opponents arguing that LGBT people should understand the importance of the right to privacy more than almost any segment of society. Furthermore, some conservatives have chosen to out public officials in order to shame or embarrass them, perhaps defeating the purpose of gay activists who out public officials. The debate is not likely to be resolved in the near future.

Why Does It Matter?
LGBT Officials and Political Representation

It seems appropriate to ask the question of whether it matters to have openly LGBT elected officials. In other words, do LGBT elected officials represent the interests of the LGBT community? All government officials are elected, in large part, based on their party affiliations, group affiliations, and issue positions. As such, constituents can expect representation based on the extent to which their affiliations and positions coincide with those of their elected officials. When an elected official belongs to a particular ethnic, racial, or religious group, the group can be said to have achieved symbolic or descriptive representation. If the official spends at least part of his or her time representing the policy interests of his or her community, she or he will have achieved substantive representation.

Substantive representation, however, is by no means certain, and it can also occur without the election of gay officials. For example, heterosexual Representative Bella Abzug (D-NY), the mother of a lesbian, acted as a policy entrepreneur on the issue of gay civil rights by introducing the first gay civil rights bill in Congress in 1974 and being the main sponsor of similar legislation each year until she left the House in 1977.

Although elected LGBT officials may represent the interests of their group, sympathetic non-LGBT officials may also enact or support policies LGBT activists favor. Furthermore, LGBT officials are likely to face added electoral pressure to focus on non-LGBT issues. How can we determine if LGBT elected officials represent the issues of their group?

In the past researchers have examined whether or not elected officials from minority groups have influenced policy related to minorities. Some researchers discovered that the election of blacks increased policy benefits to the black community. In the 1980s and 1990s, researchers continued to find significant links between the election of minorities and women and policies adopted by local and state governments. For example, Sue Thomas (1994) discovered that the election of women to state legislatures led to more policy initiatives specific to women. Similarly, Rufus Browning, Dale Marshall, and David Tabb (1984), found that the election of blacks and Hispanics to city governments contributed to greater inclusion of these minority groups on citizen boards and commissions, and increased minority contracting by government. Peter Eisinger (1982) and Grace Hall Saltzstein (1989) concluded that election of black city council members and mayors increased black hiring in police departments and resulted in police policies more favorable to blacks. And the prominence of black and Hispanic city council members enhanced group representation in public employment.

So what about LGBT elected officials—do they help pass policies that benefit the LGBT community? Both the anecdotal and empirical evidence suggest yes. For example, in Illinois, gay state Representative Larry McKeon (D-Chicago) sponsored bills in 1997 and

1998 that would have banned discrimination in employment and housing based on sexual orientation. McKeon actively fought for both bills, testifying before legislative committees and building a nonpartisan coalition of supportive legislators. During the 1997 Washington legislative session the only openly gay state official, Representative Ed Murray (D-43-Seattle), introduced several progay measures, including a bill to allow same-sex marriages, a bill banning employment discrimination based on sexual orientation, and a bill for domestic partnership benefits for state employees. In Santa Barbara, California, council member Tom Roberts, gay and Republican, was the main force behind the enactment of a 1997 domestic partner policy providing benefits to city employees. Roberts was re-elected following these efforts, establishing precedent that gay officials can achieve substantive representation without alienating their broader constituency. In Minnesota openly gay state Senator Allan Spear was the primary sponsor of S 2183, a 1988 bill that would add sexual orientation to the state's 1983 hate crime law. Even though it faced opposition from several conservative legislators, S 2183 passed easily in the senate by forty-seven to seven. Spear, the longest-serving openly gay legislator in the country, was also active in passing the state's antidiscrimination law in 1991 and in delaying the state's adoption of a ban on same-sex marriage. Thus, there is considerable anecdotal evidence that openly LGBT officials can offer leadership to the LGBT community, place LGBT issues on the political agenda, and even help ensure that public policy reflects the concerns of the LGBT community.

In the only study of its kind, Donald Haider-Markel, Mark Joslyn, and Chad Kniss (2000) found that the presence of openly lesbian and gay local elected officials increases the likelihood that a locality will adopt both domestic partner registries and benefits, such as health insurance for their unmarried partners. The study also found that sympathetic non-LGBT officials, the mobilization of the LGBT community, the size of the conservative religious population, and the tolerance of the general population also influence the adoption of these policies. The results suggest that the election of gay officials is not simply a symbolic action, as they actively represent the interests of their community. In some policy arenas this substantive political representation may make the difference in policy adoption, but in others gay officials are one political influence among many. Whether as a symbolic force or legislative entrepreneurs, elected gays and lesbians are important factors toward achieving the policy goals of the LGBT community. Haider-Markel, Joslyn, and Kniss (2000) also suggest that gays should not ignore alliances with heterosexual officials interested in gay concerns. This finding is especially relevant to gays as a group as they have achieved a minimal level of success in electing identified members and most of these gains have been at the local level. Although the number of gay officials is on the rise, LGBT activities often remain dependent upon the judgments of heterosexual elected officials.

Elected Officials

In this section we examine openly LGBT elected officials at all levels of government and in all branches of government. Clearly there are and have been LGBT people elected to positions who are not discussed here. We do not discuss elected officials based on speculation about their sexual orientation. Only openly LGBT officials are of concern for this discussion, and perhaps for the movement as well—only open LGBT people can serve as role models and speak to LGBT issues convincingly from personal experience.

Executive Branch Officials

National Approach (The Lack Thereof). In the United States the only nationally elected executive officials are the president and vice president. Although there have been a few LGBT third-party candidates for these offices, no openly LGBT candidates have ever been elected to the national executive branch. And, as the discussion above suggests, it will likely be some time before this occurs. (Historical debate over whether bachelor president James Buchanan or other historical presidents may have been homosexual are somewhat beside the point—whether they were or not, they were certainly not open about it.)

However, it should be noted that the first openly LGBT candidates for president and vice president of the United States nominated by any party were David McReynolds and Mel Boozer, endorsed in 1980 by the Socialist Party USA for president and vice president, respectively. Further, at the 1980 Democratic National Convention, Boozer was nominated for vice president on the Democratic ticket. The nomination failed.

State.   At the state level the numbers of openly LGBT public officials are few. In fact, Ed Flanagan, Vermont's auditor of accounts, is
in 2000 the only openly LGBT person ever to be elected to a
statewide office by a vote of the people. Flanagan was first elected
to his office in 1992, but he did not come out as openly gay until
1995. After coming out Flanagan was reelected in 1996 and 1998.
In 2000 Flanagan won the Vermont Democratic primary race for
the U.S. Senate, becoming the first LGBT candidate for the U.S. Senate endorsed on a major party ticket, but he lost the general election to a popular Republican, Jim Jeffords (who became an independent in 2001).

In Maine openly lesbian Dale McCormick served in the executive
branch as state treasurer from 1996 to 1998, but she was appointed to
her position by a vote of the state legislature. Prior to being appointed to her executive position, McCormick served three terms as
an open lesbian in the state senate, and was forced out by term limits. In California, Tony Miller was appointed as acting secretary of
state in 1994. Miller ran for a term in the office but lost the general
election.

Of known openly LGBT candidates, at least ten have run unsuccessfully for executive branch offices in the states, all since 1994.
These candidates have run for positions as secretary of state, governor, lieutenant governor, attorney general, and state treasurer. They
have also run as Democrats, Republicans, Libertarians, Reform Party,
and Independents. For example, in New York Karen Burstein won the
Democratic primary for attorney general in 1994, but lost the general
election. Mike Duffy won the 1998 Republican primary for Massachusetts state treasurer but lost in the general election.

Local.   At the local level LGBT candidates have been most successful in achieving executive branch positions. Most often local LGBT
elected officials are mayors, but there are two sheriffs—Margo Frasier
in Travis County, Texas, and Anne Strasdauskas in Baltimore County,
Maryland. The first LGBT deputy sheriff or sheriff elected in the
United States was Rudi Cox in San Francisco in March 1975. San
Francisco has also elected LGBT candidates to two other executive
positions, Richard Gordon to the Criminal Justice Council in 1981
and Susan Leal as city treasurer in 1997.

The first openly LGBT mayors in the country were all elected in
1983 and include Robert Gentry in Laguna Beach, California; John
Laird in Santa Cruz, California; and Richard Heyman in Key West,

Florida. Valerie Terrigno became the first lesbian mayor in the country in 1984 when her fellow city council members elected her mayor of West Hollywood, California. Since 1983 twenty LGBT individuals have served at least one term as mayor, and Ken Reeves of Cambridge, Massachusetts, served an additional term as vice mayor. California has boasted the most LGBT mayors, but most regions have at least one. The cities and towns these mayors have presided over range in size from about 700 (Bill Crews in Melbourne, Iowa) to over 160,000 (Neil Giuliano in Tempe, Arizona). In 2001 we were able to confirm that there are at least ten openly LGBT mayors around the country. Although some LGBT mayors are elected to a city council, and then elected by the council to serve as mayor, most have either been directly elected or have received the most votes in an at-large city council election, making them mayor. Further, most LGBT partisan mayors have been Democrats, but more recent trends have brought a few Republican LGBT mayors into office, including Dan Stewart, elected mayor of Plattsburgh, New York, in 1999 and who received considerable attention from the state's Republican Party during the 2000 elections.

Case Study: Mayor Neil Giuliano

In 2001 Republican Neil Giuliano was serving the last part of his fourth term as mayor of Tempe, Arizona. Giuliano was first elected mayor in 1994, but did not publicly declare his sexual orientation until September 1997. After coming out Giuliano was easily reelected in 1998 and 2000. Giuliano rarely faced antigay rhetoric during his campaigns, but did have some campaign signs defaced in 1998. Until the fall of 2000 Giuliano was a consistently popular mayor, bringing new investment to the city while balancing environmental concerns. Members of both parties praised his work and influence with state officials. But in October 2000, a group of citizens began a recall effort against Giuliano, arguing that he abused his power by trying to prevent city employees from donating to the Boy Scouts through the United Way. Giuliano had tried to block donations because the Boy Scouts ban homosexuals from their organization. A week after his initial statement, Giuliano also suggested that the city cut back its relationship with Valley of the Sun United Way, which channeled about $491,000 per year to the Boy Scouts. Shortly thereafter, Giuliano uncharacteristically flip-flopped and suggested that the city maintain its relationship with the United Way. Referring to his actions, the mayor said, "I made a mistake and I have asked for forgiveness" (Diaz 2000). All of the actions led to the recall effort.

The recall election was September 11, 2001, with the main challenger being Gene Ganssle. During the campaign, Ganssle and others at times appeared to try to make the recall election about Giuliano's sexual orientation, suggesting that his maneuvers were based on "personal orientations." Political pundits suggested that the recall effort might have put an end to any of Giuliano's aspirations to higher political office, but Giuliano survived the recall election, garnering 68 percent of the vote (Krisberg 2001).

Legislative Branch Officials

National. It is often said that if all of the LGBT members of Congress were open about their sexual orientation, they would have enough members to form their own caucus. However, only three members are openly LGBT in the year 2001. These members are Representatives Tammy Baldwin (D-WI), Barney Frank (D-MA), and Jim Kolbe (R-AZ). No openly LGBT person has yet been elected to the U.S. Senate, but the numbers of openly LGBT candidates for both the House and the Senate have been on the increase for the past ten years.

Frank Kameny was the first openly LGBT person to run for the U.S. Congress. Kameny ran for the Washington, D.C., U.S. House Delegate position in 1971. Kameny only received 1.6 percent of the vote, but his campaign provided the impetus for a long-term local LGBT group in Washington (Johnson 1997, 2). Since Kameny lost his race, at least another thirty openly LGBT candidates have run for Congress, with eighteen of those running since 1998. The other recent trend is that more lesbians are running for Congress than ever before, and all candidates are more likely to have the endorsements of major parties than they did in the past. Not surprisingly, more recent candidates are also more likely to have held elective office prior to their run for Congress.

The first openly gay member of Congress was Representative Gerry Studds (D-MA). Studds was not openly gay when he was first elected but revealed that he was gay in July 1983. After coming out he was re-elected every election cycle through 1994. Studds chose to retire in 1996. Representative Barney Frank (D-MA) was the second openly gay member of Congress after he came out in May 1987; he has been reelected every two years since. Frank is perhaps the best-known LGBT elected official in the country. In a 2001 interview Frank was asked about being an openly gay official and if he thought he could win a race for Congress as an openly gay nonincumbent. Frank responded:

> Well, I would certainly want to be [out]. I mean one of the stupidest things I ever did was to wait so long. I didn't realize this at the time—that I did stupid things because I wasn't out. I think now in my district, you could win. I'm not sure. . . . I think if you probably ran for the first time in most districts as a gay or lesbian person—you hadn't any previous record—I don't know that it would stop you. It would still be a disadvantage in this sense: People are skeptical about voting for somebody else at first. And what happens is the opponents have a sophisticated way of going after you by saying, "Well, it's OK that she's a lesbian, but, you know, that's all she's going to worry about." When people vote for a legislator, they want to feel that they're voting for their advocate, somebody who's going to fight for them. And they're a little nervous if they think you may be fighting for a group that doesn't include them. Someone now who was running who was openly gay for Congress in Massachusetts—yeah, there are districts you could win. It would be a disadvantage, but it wouldn't be a fatal one, necessarily. (Alsdorf 2000a)

Perhaps the most homophobic incident involving Frank came in 1995 when Representative Dick Armey (R-TX) referred to Frank as "Barney Fag" in a speech on the floor of the House. Armey immediately corrected himself, saying it was a slip of the tongue. When Frank was asked about life in the House as openly gay, the extent of homophobia, and if he is able to work with homophobic members, Frank had this to say:

> Usually not. I'm not interested in doing so. Now, we get along pretty well with most of the people, and you certainly have to accept disagreements. But I've said several times, we have a rule around here that you're not supposed to take things personally, but I take personal things personally. And, no, I do not have any interest in being civil to Bob Barr (R-GA) or Dan Burton (R-IN) or Trent Lott (R-MS). I don't work with Republican Senators just because we don't do that. But that would have been an obstacle. I do not say, "Oh, well, that's just politics" when people make personally bigoted remarks. Dick Armey and I had worked together on some things. We have not had any kind of working relationship since his "Barney Fag" comment. (Alsdorf 2000a)

Following Frank, two Republican members of Congress came out in the 1990s. Before election day in 1994, Representative Steve Gunderson (R-WI) became the first openly gay Republican member of Congress when he revealed his sexual orientation, apparently simply because he no longer wanted to hide his private life. Gunderson was safely reelected in 1994, but chose not to run again in 1996. Although there was some speculation that Gunderson retired because he had been receiving a cold shoulder from Republican leaders in Congress, Gunderson denied this. However, he had been warned that conservative religious groups planned to run a "smear campaign" against him if he ran in 1996. His life and experiences in Congress and with his long-term partner are described in his coauthored book, *House and Home: The Political and Personal Journey of a Gay Republican Congressman and the Man with Whom He Created a Family.* As a member of Congress, Gunderson was perhaps best known for fighting for AIDS research funding and medical care.

Just as Gunderson announced his retirement in 1996, Representative Jim Kolbe (R-AZ) was faced with a decision, to publicly announce that he was in fact a gay man, or to wait and answer questions following an article outing him as gay that was set to appear in the *Advocate.* The magazine had decided to run the story outing Kolbe after Kolbe voted for a law banning federal recognition of same-sex marriages for the purpose of federal benefits, called the Defense of Marriage Act. Kolbe decided it would be best if he made the announcement himself, before the magazine did. Kolbe was not happy about being forced to reveal he was gay and said that "The fact that I'm gay makes no more difference than my being right-handed, blue-eyed and balding . . . I'm certainly not a poster boy [for gay causes]" (Davidson 1996). Nevertheless, after coming out Kolbe said he received widespread support in Congress and at home and indicated that he thinks the Republican Party is the party for LGBT people because "[t]he Republican Party was founded on a belief in personal liberties and freedom" (Davidson 1996). Since coming out Kolbe has continued to be an effective member of Congress, with only a few negative incidents. In October 1996 during his reelection campaign, some religious conservatives posted signs in his district that said Kolbe had AIDS. And although Kolbe became the first open LGBT elected official to address a GOP convention in 2000 (Log Cabin Republican Steve Fong spoke for one minute at the 1996 convention, making him the first LGBT person to ever address a Republican National Convention), members of the Texas delegation protested by refusing to stand and remaining seated with their heads bowed in prayer as Kolbe spoke for less than five minutes on free trade—an issue on which he is a noted expert.

Tammy Baldwin made history in 1998 during an election year that might have been called "the year of the lesbian," because Baldwin and three other lesbians ran for seats in the U.S. House. Not only did Baldwin (D-WI) make history as the first lesbian elected to Congress, but she also became the first woman elected to Congress from Wisconsin, and the first nonincumbent LGBT person elected to Congress. Baldwin served two terms on the Dane County, Wisconsin, Board of Supervisors and became the first LGBT person elected to the Wisconsin legislature, serving three terms in the state assembly before being elected to Congress. She was reelected to Congress in 2000. In a speech at the April 2000 LGBT march on Washington, D.C., Baldwin offered the following as to why she joined this march and those in 1987 and 1993:

> I can say with conviction: Never doubt that there is reason to be hopeful. Never doubt that Congress will pass legislation that expands the definition of hate crimes. Never doubt that the states will grant us equal rights, including all the rights afforded couples through marriage. Never doubt that we will enact legislation ensuring nondiscrimination in the workplace. Never doubt that America will one day realize that her gay, bisexual, and transgendered sons and daughters want nothing more—and deserve nothing less—than the rights accorded every other citizen. But we must make it so—by daring to dream of a world in which we are free . . . . Never doubt that we will create this world, because, my friends, we are fortunate to live in a democracy, and in a democracy, we decide what's possible. (Baldwin 2000)

When asked about how she feels about being labeled an openly lesbian legislator, Baldwin responded:

> Well, I've always looked at it as both an opportunity and a challenge. The opportunity is immense—the opportunity to inspire, to potentially serve as a role model. Everyone tells you you can't, and people told me I can't because we'd never elected a woman to Congress before, and we'd never elected a lesbian to Congress before. So I symbolically serve as a reminder that "Yes, we can. They're wrong, those naysayers." But beyond that, to address the challenge, it should be quite clear that in a constituency of 600,000 people they want a representative who understands them and their issues and who is equipped to address a broad array of very important issues. So the challenge, when you see that type

of reference in the media, is to persuade people that I'm not just about one issue. While civil rights is a critical issue to me, so is health care for all, so is affordable prescription drugs for senior citizens, so is a better farm economy for the farmers that I represent, and so on. And that has always created a challenge when I'm identified only by one facet of my being. (Alsdorf 2000c)

During her two terms Baldwin has focused considerable attention on health care and education, with ties to civil rights issues. Opposition to her as a lesbian appears minimal, and it's clear that Baldwin has opened a historic path that other LGBT candidates are likely to follow.

One historic candidate for the U.S. House in 2000 was Karen Kerin—the first transsexual to run for national office. Kerin ran for and won the Republican Party's nomination for the at-large Vermont seat in the U.S. House. The Republican Party had neglected to find a challenger to face popular independent incumbent Bernie Sanders, so Kerin decided she would run for the nomination. Virtually unopposed, Kerin won the primary. However, her chances of a victory over Sanders were slim. To make matters worse, the media and some Republican officials could not get past the transgender issue. Kerin described the situation: "The GOP has not repudiated me and I certainly have not repudiated them" (Derby 2000). According to the Vermont secretary of state, in the general election Kerin received 51,977 votes, or 18 percent.

The fifty-six-year-old Kerin was raised in Montpelier, Vermont, as Charles Kerin and received her engineering degree from the University of Vermont in 1971. Kerin had a sex reassignment surgery operation in the early 1990s. In 1994 she lost a Republican primary in her attempt to represent Montpelier in Vermont's House of Representatives. Kerin married a woman in 1996, receiving a marriage license because it was determined that her birth certificate still listed her as a male. In 1997 she graduated from the Vermont Law School and soon became director of a nonprofit group known as the World Institute of Human Rights and International Law. Kerin focused her 2000 campaign on the budget and arms treaties, arguing that Sanders lacked fiscal restraint: "The youngest generations have every right to be disgusted and discouraged over their future being mortgaged with still growing national debt" (Derby 2000).

State. At the state level the number of LGBT legislative officials is also on the increase. The first openly LGBT state legislators were

Elaine Noble (Massachusetts house) and Allan Spear (Minnesota senate). Noble came out first in 1974 as an open lesbian and served two terms. Spear was first elected to the state senate in 1972 and came out in 1974, serving until he retired in 2000. Both Spear and Noble took incredible political risks by coming out, but voters seemed happy to reelect them both. In addition, the first transgender state legislator in the country was Althea Garrison, elected in 1992 to the Massachusetts House of Representatives.

In 1988 there were only three sitting openly LGBT state legislators, but by 1998 there were twenty-six openly LGBT officials in sixteen states. The state Democratic Party Chair in Vermont, Steve Howard, is also openly gay and is thought to be the first openly gay person to head one of the major parties in a state. During the November 1998 elections, sixty-one LGBT candidates ran for a variety of state and local offices around the county. Of these candidates, sixteen were incumbents seeking reelection to state offices and twenty were LGBT candidates challenging incumbents for state offices (Freiberg 1998). By 2001 there were forty-three openly LGBT state legislators in twenty-one states, a historic high. In some states, such as Rhode Island, Utah, and Montana, these officials were the only openly LGBT officials in the state.

Overall there have only been sixty-eight openly gay or lesbian state legislators since 1974. Most of these officials have served in the lower legislative chamber (usually called the house or assembly), which tend to be composed of smaller districts. Furthermore, nearly all of these legislators have served in urban districts. Although exact figures are not known, by 2001 at least ninety-five LGBT candidates had run for state offices and lost, with the numbers increasing virtually every election cycle. By all accounts 1998 and 2000 were banner years for LGBT candidates running for state legislative seats. In those two years alone, at least fifty-six LGBT candidates ran for state legislative seats, twenty-three in 1998 and thirty-four in 2000.

Some states have seen a greater increase in LGBT legislators than others. In New Hampshire, a concerted effort was made by openly LGBT Democratic leaders to recruit more gay candidates for 2000 and openly LGBT legislators formed the country's first state legislative caucus of gay and gay-friendly legislators in 1999. A result of these efforts was that five openly LGBT legislators sought reelection and seven more LGBT persons ran for state legislative seats. In addition, state legislator Ray Buckley claimed there were four Republicans running that were closeted (Freiberg 2000). And in neighboring Vermont, six LGBT candidates ran for the state legislature as challengers in 2000. Historically New Hampshire has had the most LGBT legislators with seven, Oregon and Maine follow with six, and California and Massachusetts have both had five.

Although the total number of LGBT candidates for state legislative office and the number of LGBT state legislative officials is still relatively small, LGBT people are clearly making dramatic inroads in state legislatures. Furthermore, these officials are having an impact on policy once elected.

One classic example is Allan Spear, who served as openly gay in the Minnesota Senate from 1974 until his retirement in 2000. Spear served as a liberal member of the Minnesota Democratic Farmer-Labor Party, but had the respect of all legislators. When Spear came out in 1974, he told a newspaper reporter how "lousy" he had felt in 1973 as the legislature debated a gay civil rights bill and he remained silent (Grow 2000). Indeed, Spear views one of his greatest victories as the passage of a comprehensive civil rights law in 1993 that included sexual orientation as well as gender orientation. Spear sponsored the bill in the senate, with openly lesbian Representative Karen Clark (D-FL) sponsoring the bill in the house. During debate on the bill some state senators continued to argue that the law was unnecessary because "homosexuality is a choice, not a condition of birth." Spear responded with a speech on the senate floor in which he pointed out: "Let me tell you, I'm a 55-year-old Gay man and I am not just going through a phase. I can also assure you that my sexual orientation is not something I chose, like choosing to wear a blue shirt and a red tie today" (Grow 2000). That same year his colleagues elected Spear as president of the senate. Some suggest that Spear's greatest contribution was as a role model of a gay person. As one legislator described it, Spear "did a great job in the educating process. Homosexuality was something I'd barely heard of in my little town. It wasn't talked about. Here we had Allan Spear. He was a good person, no different from the rest of us. We all needed that education" (Grow 2000). Perhaps best known for witty and educational speeches, Spear became a policy wonk in the area of criminal justice. Spear served twenty-six years as openly LGBT, making him the longest-serving elected LGBT official in the country.

Local.   Local legislatures mostly consist of city and county councils, commissions, and boards. Regardless of the name, these local legislatures deal with a multitude of issues that can influence the lives of LGBT people. However, the powers granted to local government are determined by each state, and local government authority varies considerably from state to state.

LGBT candidates have increasingly sought positions on local legislatures and local legislatures have seen the greatest LGBT official representation of any elected political office. At least 130 openly LGBT persons have occupied seats on local legislatures and representation has increased over time. In 1980 only two LGBT officials sat on local legislatures, by 1990 that number had reached twenty-one, and by 2001 representation increased to fifty. The first openly LGBT elected official (for any office) in the country was Kathy Kozachenko, who was elected to the Ann Arbor, Michigan, city council in April 1974. Only a few LGBT officials followed her to local legislative seats through the 1980s. However, in 1984 residents of newly incorporated West Hollywood, California, did elect a majority LGBT council for a short period. It was in the 1990s that the number of local LGBT officeholders really took off, with California, New York, Massachusetts, and Wisconsin electing the greatest number. It was also in the 1990s when many states elected their first LGBT officials to any office, and these positions were most often on local legislatures. Of course the number of openly LGBT candidates for local legislatures has gone up as well, with at least additional 126 candidates running failed campaigns between 1961 and 2001. Indeed, the first openly LGBT candidate to run for any office in the United States was Jose Sarria, who ran for the San Francisco, California, board of supervisors in 1961.

One example of local legislators elected in the 1990s is Jim McGill, a member of the borough council in Wilkinsburg, Pennsylvania. McGill was first elected to the council in 1993 and reelected in 1997 with the endorsement of the Gay and Lesbian Victory Fund. McGill has spent some time on LGBT-related issues—he successfully initiated an amendment that bans hiring discrimination based on sexual orientation—but most of his time is spent as chairperson of the codes, zoning, and traffic committee, or on the public works, public property, community health, and sanitation committee.

LGBT officials on local legislatures have made a significant difference on policies related to LGBT rights. These officials have helped to ensure that LGBT issues reach the political agenda and become law. For example, one study found that the presence of openly LGBT officials on local legislatures increases the likelihood that localities will adopt policies benefiting domestic partners (Haider-Markel, Joslyn, and Kniss 2000). But anecdotal evidence abounds as well. For example, San Francisco's first openly gay official, Harvey Milk, was the principal policy entrepreneur in the city's adoption of an antidiscrimination policy for lesbians and gays. Christine Kehoe, San Diego's first lesbian city council member, successfully sponsored legislation providing insurance to domestic partners of city employees in 1994. Kehoe was also reelected with ease. LGBT officials also spearheaded passage of domestic partner policies in Ann Arbor (Michigan), Chapel Hill (North Carolina), San Francisco, Seattle, and West Hollywood (California).

Other types of local bodies also have LGBT representatives, including school boards, community college districts, special commissions, neighborhood committees, planning boards, and local party organizations. All told by 2001 at least sixty-eight openly LGBT officials have held positions on these bodies and another forty openly LGBT candidates have run for these offices and lost.

Although many of these local bodies do not wield considerable political power, they do potentially impact the lives of LGBT people in important ways. For example, LGBT representation on local school boards can make a considerable difference on school antidiscrimination policy and the treatment of LGBT students—and this issue has increasingly appeared on the radar screen of local school districts. And as Chapter 4 makes clear, election to local political party committees can have a significant impact on how parties address LGBT issues.

Case Study: The Assassination of Harvey Milk

Perhaps the most famous and most significant openly LGBT official ever elected in the United States was Harvey Milk. In 1977 Harvey Milk was elected to the San Francisco Board of Supervisors. Although he was not the first LGBT person elected in the country, he was the first LGBT person elected in San Francisco. His election and assassination brought to an end a decade-long struggle for LGBT people in San Francisco and began a new period of activism. After Milk was elected he received a number of threats on his life, but the threats were largely ignored. In 1999 openly gay San Francisco Board of Supervisors President Tom Ammiano was threatened as he campaigned in a run-off election to become mayor. Some viewed Ammiano as the "political heir to Milk because of his progressive views and grass-roots style" (Coile 1999). This threat, however, was taken seriously, and police increased their security around Ammiano. One activist said of the threat: "The fact that, even in San Francisco in 1999, a good Gay candidate cannot run for mayor without his very life being threatened is a sad commentary indeed. . . . The bias-motivated threat against Tom reminds us that we have far to go until all Americans can live free from discrimination" (Chibbaro 1999f). However, the fact that police took the threat so seriously may in fact indicate how far we have come since 1977, when threats, eventually carried out, against Harvey Milk evoked little response from police.

Milk's career, but not his legacy, was cut short in 1978. To the horror of San Franciscans, former Board Supervisor Dan White assassinated Milk along with Mayor George Moscone in City Hall on November 27, 1978. One of the last people to see Milk alive was Jim Rivaldo. Rivaldo recalled Milk and his assassination: "I don't have the same deep level of sadness other people do about Harvey's death. He certainly accomplished what he hoped to accomplish. Here was a guy who was a total scruffy hippie with a little camera store, a guy no one in City Hall would listen to before he was elected. Three years later he was lying in state in City Hall with everyone passing by crying" (Morse 1999).

Harvey Milk began his career in electoral politics in 1973 when he ran for a seat on the San Francisco Board of Supervisors. Milk had no money to run, but was convinced he could gain support from the LGBT community and liberals. Although gay issues provided Milk with some inspiration to run, he was also motivated by government regulations on small business and lack of funding for public schools. Even though Milk had considerable populist appeal, divisions in the gay community sunk his campaign, as gay leaders such as Jim Foster sought to discredit Milk. In that first election Milk came in tenth, with 17,000 votes, out of 32 candidates. Following his defeat, Milk cut his hair and vowed to never again smoke marijuana or go to a gay bathhouse, saying, "you have to play the game, you know" (Shilts 1982, 80).

In March 1975 Milk announced that he was making his second run for the San Francisco Board of Supervisors. By this time Milk had adopted the unofficial title of "Mayor of Castro Street." In the interim between campaigns, Milk had helped organize the boycott of Coors beer because of the company's antigay and antiunion positions, and its discriminatory practices against Hispanics. This activity had provided Milk with a wider base of support than he had enjoyed in his previous run. Especially key for Milk was obtaining the backing of the labor unions. However, even with this diverse support, Milk faced strong opposition from moderate gays in the community, who viewed Milk as a "nut." He tried to point out to moderate LGBT groups that all their support for moderate candidates had failed to result in a single gay appointment or the passage of a gay civil rights law. Milk argued, "Let them come to us. The time of being political groupies has ended. The time to become strong has begun" (Shilts 1982, 104). So it was with mixed support that Milk came in seventh in the supervisor's race, one spot away from obtaining a seat.

By 1976 Harvey Milk had not lost his political ambitions. To the contrary, a wave of openness had swept the country concerning the sexual orientation of public officials. Most importantly, two state legislators had come out and publicly declared their homosexuality. Mayor Moscone kept his promise and appointed Milk to the city's Board of Permit Appeals. However, Milk was soon fired from the position when he decided to run for the California 16th District Assembly seat. Most importantly, many gay leaders endorsed Milk's opponent and vehemently attacked Milk, arguing he would be shunned in the state legislature. Even so, Milk argued in his stump speech that "a gay official is needed not only for our protection, but to set an example for younger gays that says the system works. . . . we've got to give them hope" (Shilts 1982, 143). In the end Milk lost by 3,600 votes out of 33,000. Milk took the defeat hard, but vowed to fight on (Shilts 1982, 149).

Along with friends from the Castro district, Milk helped form a new group called the San Francisco Gay Democratic Club to provide an alternative to the more moderate Toklas Club, which some argued had gotten too cozy with the Democratic machine without asking for much in return. The new group was especially focused on ensuring that gay interests were represented in local government by openly gay appointed and elected officials, rather than sympathetic heterosexuals.

In 1977 Milk announced his candidacy for the new 5th District seat on the San Francisco Board of Supervisors. He faced at least one openly gay opponent, moderate Rick Stokes, but ran a campaign in the style of an incumbent. Milk was again able to obtain significant endorsements from labor, but this time he also gained support from key ethnic groups and even a gay Republican group. Milk also hired openly lesbian Anne Kronenberg as his campaign manager, the first real manager he ever had. Even so, Milk never slowed his campaign, working every voter to the end. On election night Milk roared to victory, winning two-to-one over his closest opponents. Nevertheless, part of Milk's celebration included sending the mayor a list of people to be considered for his seat should something happen and to tape three messages titled "In case," one of which included the ominous phrase, "if a bullet should enter my brain, let that bullet destroy every closet door" (Shilts 1982, 184).

Milk faced a conservative majority on the 1978 Board of Supervisors. However, Milk did have an ally in Mayor Moscone, who was regarded as the first heterosexual politician to make strong ties with the LGBT community. Milk worked tirelessly as supervisor until his last day in the position. Milk had focused on LGBT issues, but also on many other issues, mostly those addressing the concerns of the disenfranchised. On the board a frequent opponent of Milk was Supervisor Dan White. White often voted against the mayor's proposals as well as those from Milk. However, White faced financial crisis from the low-paying elected position and soon had to resign to tend to his business. However, the police union and real estate developers soon encouraged White to ask for his seat back, in part to oppose the likes of Milk. On the day the mayor was to announce whom he would appoint to White's seat, November 27, 1978, White showed up at City Hall with a 0.38 calibre Smith and Wesson. White first went to see Mayor Moscone. Moscone was shot several times before he died. Milk faced the same fate. White had raced down the hall, asked Milk to come with him to White's former office, and then unloaded his gun, killing Milk (Shilts 1982, 268–270).

Although Milk's ashes were scattered at sea, plans to place an urn in the Congressional Cemetery initiated in 1987 were finally achieved in 1997. Activists argued that Milk, a navy veteran, had the right to burial and a ceremony in the government cemetery. The issue has yet to be fully decided, but Milk's path-breaking career continues to impact LGBT politics and openly LGBT candidates for public office.

Judicial Branch Officials

There have been far fewer openly LGBT candidates for judicial offices, and even fewer that have obtained these offices. This could be because judicial elections generally receive little media or public attention, making it less likely that a LGBT candidate would even be noted. Not surprisingly, most candidates have been at the local level, but there have been a few at the state level. Below we briefly describe these officials.

National. In the United States no federal judges or judicial officials are elected, instead they are all appointed by the president and confirmed by the Senate. There are no records of any openly LGBT persons serving as federal judges or judicial officials, but given the growing ranks of LGBT judges at the state and local levels, it is likely only a matter of time before one is appointed to a federal bench or as judicial official.

State. Although there are many judicial positions at the state level, we were unable to identify any openly LGBT elected officials in state-level judicial positions. However, a number of LGBT judicial officials at the local level were actually first appointed by governors to positions they later had to face retention elections to hold. (Retention elections are elections in which voters simply vote "yes" or "no" for an officeholder to maintain a position to which he or she was appointed. There are no challenger candidates.)

Local. All told there have been at least thirty-seven openly LGBT judicial officials in the United States. Most of these officials have been judges and some of them have been appointed to elective positions without facing an actual election. An additional nineteen LGBT candidates have run for local judicial positions and lost. California has all the firsts for these offices. The first openly gay judge was Stephen Lachs, appointed by the governor to Los Angeles Superior Court in 1979. The first openly lesbian judge in the United States was appointed by the governor to the San Francisco Municipal Court in 1981, and the first open lesbian to be elected to a state judicial position was Donna Hitchens, who was elected to the San Francisco Superior Court in 1989.

California and New York have the most elected LGBT judicial officials, but even South Carolina and North Carolina have at least one. Although social science research clearly suggests that personal ideology, race, and gender, among other factors, influence the decisions of judicial officials (Wrightsman 1999), such studies have not been conducted with LGBT officials. However, based on the findings of previous research it seems likely that sexual orientation does influence judicial decision making, suggesting that having openly LGBT judicial officials can have a significant impact on cases involving LGBT people, including the areas of family law, adoption, and survivor benefits, among many others.

Appointed Officials

Just as LGBT persons have increasingly achieved elected office in the past twenty years, so too have LGBT people been appointed to public offices in increasing numbers. Indeed, although no accurate figures exist, it is safe to say that LGBT people have served openly and more often in appointed rather than elected positions at all levels of government. Clearly, many LGBT people may serve as assistants to governors and presidents before an LGBT person is elected to such a position.

In this section we outline the scope of LGBT appointments at the national, state, and local levels to show the diversity of positions, people, and experiences. However, readers should be aware that appointed positions are often relatively low profile, and any lists of openly LGBT officials will always miss some individuals. Unless otherwise noted, information in this section can be accessed at http://lark.cc.ukans.edu/~pres/data. html.

National

Executive Branch. Although the executive branch of the federal government is massive, and each president can make roughly 5,000 appointments, not including White House staff, few presidents have appointed LGBT officials. However, this is not to say that LGBT people have not been appointed. President Clinton has been the most important president in terms of appointing *openly* LGBT people. However, even Presidents Reagan and George Bush Sr. were known to have appointed LGBT officials, but none of these officials were openly and publicly LGBT, meaning that none of these appointees provided a positive role model of LGBT Americans.

Of an estimated 1,850 executive branch appointments by Clinton, an estimated 100 went to LGBT people between 1993 and 1997. However, the names of only 26 of these appointees were ever released and only 5 of these appointments required Senate confirmation (Bull 1997). Ten of the appointees were named to middle-level, staff assistant level, and nonpaid advisory committee positions at the White

House or White House complex (Chibbaro 1997a). LGBT appointments were so frequent in the Clinton administration largely because
Clinton seemed to recognize the important role LGBT voters played
in 1992 and 1996, but also because national LGBT groups pressured
Clinton to continue making LGBT appointments, even into his second term. By the time Clinton left office in January 2001, he claimed
to have appointed at least 150 LGBT officials, but no accounting of
all these officials was ever provided.

Not all of these appointments went smoothly, especially those that
required confirmation by the Senate. The case of James Hormel is discussed in detail below, but a less often cited case was Roberta Achtenberg. President Clinton appointed Achtenberg to be assistant secretary of fair housing and equal opportunity at the Department of
Housing and Urban Development in 1993, a position requiring Senate confirmation. The main opposition came from Senator Jesse
Helms (R-NC), who went so overboard in his public comments about
Achtenberg that he apparently alienated members of his own party.
In a press interview about the nomination, Senator Helms stated that
he was opposing the nomination of Achtenberg because she was a
"damn lesbian" and in another related interview he argued that
Achtenberg is "not your garden-variety lesbian—she's a militant ac-
tivist-mean lesbian, working her whole career to advance the homosexual agenda" (Chibbaro 2001). Perhaps partly because of the comments from Senator Helms, the Senate voted fifty-eight to thirty-one
to approve Achtenberg's nomination.

When President Clinton took office in 1993, he created the first office ever to serve as the president's liaison to the LGBT community.
Marsha Scott, a White House aide, was first appointed to the liaison
position. In 1999 openly lesbian Julian Potter was appointed as the
White House LGBT liaison at the request of Vice President Al Gore.
Potter had worked for Gore for several years. Potter brought with her
experience on presidential campaigns and in New York City politics,
an advanced-degree education in public policy, and her experience in
appointed positions at the Department of Housing and Urban Development. In one interview Potter described herself and her role, "I really feel I know the United States. You need people here in Washington who know what's going on out there. I think it's important in
this job to reach out to people, to women, to gay, lesbian, bi and
transgendered people in more rural communities and small cities,
and to youth—you know, there are a lot of GLBT youth out there,
outside the big cities. We have to connect with all these people" (Barlow 1999). Potter also pointed out that her main goal was to connect

federal government programs with local LGBT community groups, and let local groups know what was available.

Another key openly LGBT official in the Clinton White House was Virginia Apuzzo, who was a senior White House aide. Apuzzo was active in LGBT politics for parts of two decades and served as an assistant to New York Governor Mario Cuomo before joining the Clinton team. She saw her role as important, arguing, "There is no question we have to keep striving for more diverse representation around a table where decisions affecting our lives are being made. At the same time we should never lose sight of the fact that we are putting together a critical mass at the center of power, where there have never been openly gay people" (Bull 1997). When Clinton appointed Apuzzo in September 1997, she became the highest-ranking openly gay official ever to serve in the White House. Apuzzo was one of eighteen top assistants with direct access to the president.

Perhaps one of the most influential LGBT appointees in the Clinton administration was Richard Socarides, who had served as White House liaison to the gay community from 1996 to 1999. Previously Socarides served as the Labor Department's liaison to the White House from 1993 to 1995. Leaders of LGBT groups "credited Socarides with playing a pivotal role in helping the Clinton administration build unprecedented ties to the gay community" and argued that Socarides had detailed knowledge of LGBT and AIDS issues (Chibbaro 1999d). But Socarides also had his critics. Some LGBT activists argued that Socarides had not pushed the administration far enough, and that Socarides had spent too much time apologizing for White House inaction. Winnie Stachelberg, political director of the Human Rights Campaign, "called Socarides's job one of the hardest in town because, said Stachelberg, he had to walk a thin line between serving both the president and the Gay community at a time when some in the White House feared that Gay issues would hurt Clinton politically." She added, "He has done an excellent job. He will be missed" (Chibbaro 1999d). After Clinton was reelected in 1996, Socarides pushed hard on LGBT issues, convincing Clinton to be more supportive of the Employment Non-Discrimination Act, a national gay civil rights bill; influencing the president's decision to sign an executive order banning sexual orientation discrimination against federal workers; and convincing the president to hold a White House conference on hate crimes. Further, Socarides played an important role in persuading Clinton to call for a gay civil rights bill and the Hate Crimes Prevention Act in his 1998 State of the Union address. Socarides also engaged in non-LGBT-related duties, including serving as White House coordinator of the international NATO conference held in Washington in 1999. Interestingly, Socarides is the son of Charles Socarides, a prominent psychologist well known for promoting a view of homosexuality as pathological. In this regard, Socarides is but one of a number of openly LGBT children of political conservatives including right-wing activist Phyllis Schlafly and Vice President Dick Cheney.

Of course, appointed positions for openly LGBT people become more important and controversial when the U.S. Senate must confirm those positions, which is required for many cabinet level and agency appointments. One openly LGBT official who was appointed by President Clinton and confirmed by the Senate was Robert Raben, an openly gay attorney, as assistant U.S. attorney general for legislative affairs. Raben had served as a high-level aide to U.S. Representative Barney Frank (D-MA). The Senate confirmed Raben's nomination by unanimous consent in October 1999. However, unlike previous openly LGBT appointees, neither the White House nor LGBT groups identified Raben as openly LGBT while the Senate deliberated the nomination. Furthermore, the issue was not raised during confirmation hearings, even though James Hormel's nomination as ambassador was being held up at the time precisely because he was viewed as a gay activist. In his capacity as an assistant attorney general, Raben reported directly to Janet Reno and his duties largely included serving as the Justice Department's chief lobbyist on Capitol Hill. One of Raben's main lobbying tasks was to coordinate support for the Hate Crimes Prevention Act and the Employment Non-Discrimination Act, a bill banning discrimination based on sexual orientation, as well as to serve as the Justice Department's chief lobbyist during Senate confirmation proceedings for the president's appointments of judges and federal prosecutors (Chibbaro 1999e).

Even though there have clearly been many LGBT appointments in the Clinton administration, one might ask if LGBT officials have made an impact in their positions. Anecdotal evidence suggests that this representation is not just symbolic, and does make a difference beyond providing a positive role model for LGBT people.

For example, Harold J. Creel was appointed to the Federal Maritime Commission in 1994 by President Clinton with Senate approval, and was appointed to be chair of the commission in 1996. In August 1997 Creel issued a directive that banned sexual orientation discrimination against the commission's employees. The directive outlined a procedure for handling discrimination complaints and was one of the comprehensive directives for prohibiting discrimination against federal workers to be issued since 1993, when President Clinton asked agencies to issue such directives (Chibbaro 1997b).

However, not all were happy with the ability of openly LGBT officials to get things done during the Clinton presidency. Indeed, some of the LGBT officials were unhappy with progress during the Clinton administration. For example, Bob Hattoy, a Clinton appointee who served as White House liaison for the Interior Department on environmental issues staring in 1994, argued that he was the only official speaking out on AIDS and that his message left him an outsider in the administration (Fiore 1995). Hattoy came to his position as an HIV-positive gay man who had been rising in the ranks of Democratic politics. And although some agreed with Hattoy's assessments of Clinton's failures on AIDS, others saw Hattoy himself as the problem.

Hattoy had campaigned with Clinton and joined the White House staff as associate director of White House personnel. At the time Hattoy had the administration's ear and used his position to push Clinton to do more on AIDS. However, within months Hattoy was publicly criticizing the White House on AIDS policy and the gays-in-the-military issue. The White House press secretary chided him and the *New York Times* called him "a time bomb" (Fiore 1995). So Hattoy was transferred to the Department of Interior. Hattoy described his own situation and the AIDS issue, "I didn't come to Washington to be a faceless federal bureaucrat. I came to Washington to be a bureaucrat in your face. If a foreign enemy were killing that many people, we'd be calling out the Marines" (Fiore 1995). Of Hattoy, one official said, "People are afraid of Bob because of his fearlessness and the quotability. Bob has created this persona for himself that he is going to hold their feet to the fire and let them know it when they fall short" (Fiore 1995). Faced with such critics, Hattoy says that AIDS is the real issue, arguing "I'll compromise a little on environmental stuff, everything is not a bottom-line thing for me. But AIDS is a bottom-line life or death thing for me and hundreds of thousands of Americans. And no one else at the White House is speaking out on this. No one else is" (Fiore 1995).

Although President George W. Bush suggested during the 2000 presidential campaign that he was unlikely to hire openly LGBT people for his administration, in April 2001 he became the first Republican president to appoint an openly LGBT official. Bush appointed Scott Evertz to be the director of the White House Office of National AIDS policy. Evertz led the Wisconsin Log Cabin Republicans and had worked for years on AIDS policy. However, when announcing the appointment, White House officials made no mention of Evertz's sexual orientation and said that President Bush did not consider sexual orientation a factor in the appointment. President Bush followed a similar strategy in August 2001 when he tapped gay Republican activist Donald A. Capoccia to be an unpaid member of the U.S. Commission on Fine Arts. Even so, the Republican appointments bode well for future LGBT appointments in the executive branch.

LGBT people are increasingly attaining positions within the national Democratic Party as well. Although these are not positions appointed by elected officials, they are similar in terms of stature and influence. For example, in July 2001 Christine Kenngott was named as the new deputy director of marketing for the Democratic National Committee (DNC). Kenngott had been involved in politics since 1992, raising millions of dollars for Democrats working as a project manager in the DNC Marketing Department. In 1993 she began working for the Democratic Congressional Campaign Committee (DCCC) as deputy director of marketing for the 1994 election cycle. By 1996 she was the deputy director of marketing for the Clinton-Gore presidential campaign and after the election became the deputy director of ticketing for the 1997 Presidential Inaugural Committee. In 2000 Kenngott was the director of marketing for the Gore/Lieberman presidential campaign. As an open lesbian, she has worked to increase the awareness of the gay and lesbian presence in the Democratic Party. However, in 1999 Andrew Tobias was tapped by President Clinton to take the highest position attained by an LGBT person in the DNC.

Legislative Branch. An unknown number of LGBT people have served members of Congress and worked for congressional committees. Many have done so without being openly LGBT, but in the 1990s more LGBT staffers began to come out. A number of LGBT staffers formed the Lesbian and Gay Congressional Staff Association, including Victor Castillo. Castillo appeared in an ad for the group and wrote part of the text, saying "When gay people hide the 'real' us we unwittingly reinforce misperceptions about gays and contribute to our own oppression. Although being 'out' may lead to an occasional uncomfortable situation, none could be as uncomfortable as hiding a part of the real me in a closet again. Being out is not a crusade for me; it's simply part of who I am" (Sypert 1997). In 1993 the association had eighty members, but that dropped to forty following the 1994 midterm elections, with a mailing list of 140 (Sypert 1997). Even so, the new Republican majority granted the group the same rights and access to space as other staffing groups.

Another example is Paul Yandura, who originally went to Washington on a scholarship, but soon found a position as an intern for House Minority Leader Richard Gephardt (D-MO). Within months Yandura was hired by the White House Office of Political Affairs, and then as a staff member by President Clinton's liaison to the gay and lesbian community in 1994. During Clinton's 1996 reelection campaign, Yandura served as the national lesbian/gay outreach director and in 1997 became an AIDS specialist for the Clinton administration, by working both for the Office on National AIDS Policy and the Department of Housing and Urban Development's Housing Opportunities for People with AIDS program (Sypert 1997).

Victor Castillo had a somewhat different experience. He began his career as a legislative staffer by working for Bob Filner's campaign for the San Diego city council in 1991. Prior to that Castillo had served on both LGBT and non-LGBT groups, and worked for Senator Dianne Feinstein's (D-CA) 1990 gubernatorial campaign. Castillo followed Representative Filner (D-CA) to Congress. Castillo's experience demonstrates the impact of being out in public life. Castillo relates a story of a congressional coworker who stopped by one day to tell him a close friend had just come out to her. The woman explained that she accepted the friend easily, even though she thought she would have reacted very differently a few years before. Castillo recalled, "She said, 'I asked myself what's the difference, then it occurred to me: It's Victor. It's you. You changed my impression'" (Sypert 1997). Furthermore, Castillo argues that being out helped him in his career by helping his boss, Bob Filner, "One of the benefits in hiring me was that I was gay and openly gay. As a gay man I'm able to give him insight into gay and lesbian issues, the same kind of insight I can give him as a Latino man" (Sypert 1997). Working for Filner, Castillo focuses on transportation and labor issues, but also takes the lead on gay and lesbian concerns.

But not all congressional staffers had an easy time coming out or being out in their positions. Rodney Walker was press secretary for Senator J. Bennett Johnston (D-LA) from 1991 to 1995 and for most of that time he remained in the closet. Walker says he was afraid of being out in his office; "I was very concerned that I would be seen as a person who had an agenda that was not the senator's. I was afraid they would think I wasn't devoted to his interests" (Sypert 1997). But when Walker began dating another congressional staffer from the Louisiana delegation his sexual orientation became difficult to hide. As a result, Walker began coming out to his coworkers in 1995. Later that year he accepted a position as press secretary for Representative John Conyers Jr. (D-MI), and he told Conyers about his sexual orientation soon after he took the job. Soon after, the Defense of Marriage Act was being debated in Congress and Walker recalled the effect of the debate on LGBT staffers. "When that nasty debate began, I sensed immediately that some gays, especially those who worked in conservative offices, they weren't going to hang out with me any more. A lot of gays who were not completely out began to hide and downplay their sexuality during that debate. People who had their closet doors open, shut them" (Sypert 1997).

Other LGBT staffers working for conservative members of Congress have had similar experiences. Some remain closeted even as they exchange ideas and politics in gay bars in the capital city. Tracey L. St. Pierre, a top aide to Representative Charles T. Canady (R-FL) who helped pass DOMA in 1996, resigned her post and argued, "There are scores of gay people in the Republican Party who are looking for safe passage out of the closet" (Yang 1997). St. Pierre says that LGBT staffers work for some of the most socially conservative members of Congress as chiefs of staff, in party campaign committees, and in GOP leadership offices. One such staffer said, "If there is a gene that determines your sexual orientation, it's not working in conjunction with the one that determines your political affiliation. I'm certain [Republican lawmakers] don't realize the number of gay people who work in Republican offices, whose members depend on them for advice, to get them reelected" (Yang 1997). Although many remain closeted, they do often work through informal networks and groups, which at times have grown quite large. Some are like the late Terry Dolan, the conservative activist who publicly denied he was gay and led a double life until his death (Yang 1997). But the key argument made by many Republican staffers is that LGBT people must remain in the party and change attitudes by example. Brian O'Leary Bennett, who worked for Representative Robert K. Dornan (R-CA) for twelve years, even though Dornan commonly referred to gay men as "sodomites," said, "If we run from the Republican Party, who's going to enlighten them?" (Yang 1997).

It would perhaps be easiest to work for a legislator who is openly LGBT. One such high-level aide was Robert Raben, who served under U.S. Representative Barney Frank (D-MA) for six years. During that time Raben was one of the founders of the Lesbian and Gay Congressional Staff Association. Raben had served as a private attorney until 1993 when he was hired by Frank to serve as legal counsel to Frank's staff. Raben's job included research, "coalition building," and meeting with constituents (Sypert 1997). By 1995 Frank requested that Raben be hired as the Democratic counsel to the House Judiciary Committee's Subcommittee on the Constitution. Raben later served as Democratic counsel to the Judiciary Subcommittee on Courts and Intellectual Property. Many thought highly of Raben's service and later recommended him during his confirmation hearings as a Clinton appointee. Representative Henry Hyde (R-IN) wrote, "Throughout his tenure with the Judiciary Committee, Robert has distinguished himself with a commitment to his profession and a dedication to serving the members. Robert has demonstrated a superior ability to work in conjunction with the majority, and where there are differences of opinion, [he] disagrees respectfully and constructively" (Chibbaro 1999e). Twelve other Republican members of the House Judiciary Committee signed on to Hyde's letter endorsing Raben.

In 1996 as Congress considered the Defense of Marriage Act, Raben was serving as counsel for the House Constitution Committee. Rabin described it as "a long and ugly battle and it really went to the very heart of what our personal lives are organized around. In the committee markup there was a very poignant interchange between Sonny Bono and Barney Frank in the consideration of the bill. Mr. Bono [whose daughter, Chastity, is a lesbian] was struggling. And he reached across the aisle and genuinely said, 'Barney, you're a person I care about and I want to understand, but I'm not there yet.' Maxine Waters (D-CA) was in the room and she took his hand and said, 'Mr. Bono, I appreciate your willingness to struggle with this and we'll be here when you're ready'" (Sypert 1997).

Steve Morin is one of the most accomplished LGBT staffers to have worked on Capitol Hill. From 1988 to 1997 Morin played some role in nearly every AIDS-related bill that surfaced, from the Ryan White CARE Act to attempts to repeal laws blocking HIV-positive persons from immigrating to the United States (Wright 1997). Morin came to the capital as a legislative assistant on AIDS issues for Representative Nancy Pelosi (D-CA). From 1994 on, Morin helped draft the Labor, Health and Human Services (HHS) appropriations bill, which provides funding for the National Institutes of Health (NIH) and the U.S. Centers for Disease Control and Prevention (CDC), the bureaucracies that run programs such as the AIDS Drug Assistance Program (ADAP), the Ryan White CARE Act programs, and all NIH and CDC AIDS research (Wright 1997). Morin also helped draft the bill that created the Housing Opportunities for People with AIDS (HOPWA) program and assisted in the oversight hearings of the late 1980s that pushed the Food and Drug Administration to place a greater priority on AIDS drug development. Morin says that Clinton appointees had led to a "major sea change" in AIDS policy, and Morin himself had served as the new administration's transition team person for the CDC. Morin said of the experience, "The CDC at the time had a very conservative administration. We had been battling with them for some period of time. To have an openly Gay man chair the transition team was a major message to them that the times had changed" (Wright 1997). After the Republican takeover of Congress in 1995, Morin argues that some bipartisan legislation passed on AIDS issues, even though other LGBT legislation stalled.

Case Study: Federal-level Appointments—James Hormel

In October 1997 President Clinton nominated San Francisco openly gay activist and philanthropist James Hormel, heir to the Hormel Meat Company fortune, as U.S. ambassador to Luxembourg. No openly LGBT person had ever been nominated or appointed to such a position. From the beginning it was clear that this nomination would not face easy confirmation in the Senate. The Senate Foreign Relations Committee, which handles such nominations, was chaired by ultraconservative Jesse Helms (R-NC). Senator Helms had shown his opposition to supporters of liberal causes, such as legalization of medical marijuana, abortion rights, and gay rights, by blocking the nomination of Massachusetts Governor William Weld for ambassador to Mexico. Helms had simply refused to hold hearings or a vote on the issue, preventing the Senate from considering Weld's nomination (Coile 1997). Helms had also used the opportunity to attack LGBT civil rights, as he did during the confirmation hearings for another Clinton appointee, openly lesbian Roberta Achtenberg. (There was also the possibility that Hormel, who had given at least $125,000 to the Clinton reelection campaign and Democratic National Committee in 1996 might be named in the campaign finance scandals surrounding the 1996 campaign.)

Clinton had considered Hormel for ambassador to Fiji in 1994. Hormel was dropped from consideration over protests from Fiji officials. However, Hormel had been a member of the 1995 U.S. delegation to the United Nations Human Rights Commission. And Senator Helms's committee did approve Hormel's 1996 nomination as an alternate U.S. delegate to the United Nations General Assembly. Commenting on the nomination, David Mixner, a long-time gay political strategist, said he had confidence Hormel would make it through, "Call me an optimist, but I don't think they'll allow [Helms] to hold things up on the basis of discrimination" (Coile 1997). But that is precisely what happened.

Hormel's confirmation process stalled in Senator Helms's Foreign Relations Committee, as many early newspaper reports speculated it would. But the committee did pass the nomination to the full Senate by the end of 1997. As Hormel came up for active consideration in the Senate during January 1998, Senator James Inhofe (R-OK), with urging from religious groups, placed a "hold" on the nomination as part of a Senate norm that allows a single senator to block presidential appointments. Senate Majority Leader Trent Lott (R-MS) agreed with the hold and appears to have led the opposition to a floor vote on Hormel's confirmation. Senator Lott stated publicly that he would not allow a floor vote and later said that homosexuals are sinners, like alcoholics or kleptomaniacs (Chibbaro 1999b). The antigay rhetoric heated up further when Representative Dick Armey (R-TX), the House majority leader, defended Senator Lott, citing the biblical passage I Corinthians, which condemns "fornicators," "idolaters," the "effeminate," and "adulterers" (Chibbaro 1999b). Armey went on to say that "[t]he Bible is very clear on [homosexuality] both myself and Senator Lott believe very strongly in the Bible" (Chibbaro 1999b).

By June 1998 some high-profile Republicans began to publicly criticize the Republican senators, including Helms, who were holding up the nomination process. For example, in a letter to Senate Majority Leader Trent Lott (R-MS), Senator Alfonse D'Amato (R-NY) wrote: "I fear Mr. Hormel's nomination is being obstructed for one reason, and one reason only: the fact that he is Gay. In this day and age, when people ably serve our country in so many capacities without regard to sexual orientation for the United States Senate to deny an appointment on that basis is simply wrong. On a personal level, I am embarrassed that our Republican Party, party of Lincoln, is seen to be the force behind this injustice" (Chibbaro 1998b). In a television interview response, Senator Don Nickles (R-OK) said of Hormel's role in gay politics that Hormel "has promoted a lifestyle and promoted it in a big way. One might have that lifestyle, but if one promotes it as acceptable behavior, I don't think they should be a representative of this country. I think it's immoral behavior" (Chibbaro 1998b). At the time, Hormel's supporters had the votes of fifty-nine senators, one short of the sixty they needed to call for a vote on the floor of the Senate.

President Clinton finally broke the deadlock in June 1999 by appointing Hormel to the ambassador post while Congress was in recess. The move was an exercise of the president's constitutional power and although rare, was a procedure used by many previous presidents. Any presidential appointment made while Congress is in recess installs the appointee to the post until the end of the next session of Congress. For

Hormel, this meant he would be ambassador until October 2000—in effect, for the rest of Clinton's second term. Senate Republicans and religious conservative activists were upset by the appointment, with a spokesman for the Family Research Council arguing: "This appointment was not going to fly, so he imposed it on the country. And it means that [Clinton's] using this nation to make the case to the world for sodomy and adultery" (Seelye 1999). Senator Inhofe again responded negatively, saying that he would place holds on all Clinton nominees in retaliation. And although the Senate could have reversed Clinton's decision with a floor vote disapproving of the nomination, calls for such a vote by Republicans never moved forward. Hormel was sworn in on June 29, 1999, by Secretary of State Madeleine Albright as supporters and family watched. Hormel took his oath with his hand on a Bible held by his partner, Timothy Wu. Some religious conservative groups did conduct a small protest outside of the State Department (Chibbaro 1999c).

However, once Hormel took his post, most of the uproar dissipated, and in Luxembourg Hormel's sexual orientation was a nonissue. The German Ambassador to Luxembourg, Horst Pakowski said that although the close-knit diplomatic corps in Luxembourg were wary of the controversy surrounding Hormel, they were soon "overwhelmed by his seriousness and his charm. . . . [H]e is very open to the great problems of a small country" (Kupfer 2000). During interviews following his arrival in Luxembourg, Hormel spoke of his nomination process as a "painful personal experience" and said that "[a] very clear message that came out of the process was that there continues to be de facto discrimination. It was an incredibly adversarial situation. There were accusations that had no relation to reality" (Kupfer 2000). Even though the process was painful, Hormel said he never moved to withdraw his name from the confirmation process. He said, "A lot of people, including members of my family, said: 'Why are you doing this to yourself?' It could have been discouraging, but at the same time, I had enormous encouragement from people who regarded me as highly qualified" (Kupfer 2000).

Finally, when Hormel was asked whether he thought his historic appointment would encourage other LGBT people, Hormel said "I would love to think that someone, somewhere is saying, 'Gee, maybe I can do that, too.' I think we live by example, and I want to be the best possible example I can be" (Kupfer 2000). Overall, Hormel's appointment by President Clinton illustrates both the problems that appointed gay public officials face, as well as the personal and public rewards for LGBT people in government service.

State

At the state level we were only able to identify openly LGBT officials in the executive branch or on special commissions associated with the executive branch. Although there are surely openly LGBT officials in appointed legislative and judicial positions, those positions have lower profiles, making it difficult to track individuals. Thus, this section is largely limited to executive branch, special commission, and political party positions.

At least thirty-six state-level appointed positions have been filled by openly LGBT people, but perhaps three times this number have served with little notice. These positions are quite varied, including positions on boards of trustees for state university systems, coastal commissions, human rights commissions, governors' transition teams, and boards of medical examiners.

One example comes from Minnesota. Reform Party Governor Jesse Ventura selected Steven Bosacker to lead his transition team following Ventura's 1998 upset gubernatorial victory. Governor Ventura then asked Bosacker to be his chief of staff in 1999. Before serving in the governor's administration, Bosacker had served for four years as executive director for the University of Minnesota Board of Regents. During the 1998 transition Representative Tim Penny (D-MN) recommended Bosacker to Ventura. Bosacker had served as a top aide to Penny for ten years.

In Illinois Governor George Ryan repaid the LGBT community's support of his campaign by appointing Glen Good to serve as assistant director of central management services for the governor's office in 1999. Good was the first openly LGBT person appointed to a cabinet-level position in the state and was confirmed unanimously by the state senate. During his confirmation hearing, Good did not face any questions about his sexual orientation and received positive feedback in his private meetings with leaders of the Republican-controlled chamber. As an assistant director, Good provided oversight of more than 4,000 state employees in two Chicago facilities. Governor Ryan appointed Good along with Dan Sprehe, with Sprehe being appointed to the Illinois Human Rights Commission. Along with several other appointments of LGBT officials by the governor, three openly gay men served on Ryan's transition team. Both Good and Sprehe had served as leaders of a mostly LGBT group, Progressives in Politics, that had worked to bring out LGBT voters in support of Ryan and other candidates in the 1998 election (Weisberg 1999).

Local

By our count openly LGBT people have been appointed to at least 110 positions in local government (including Washington, D.C., local government), but the actual count is probably as much as twice this number. These positions include judgeships (in which the judge never faces an election); deputy mayors; and advisory committee seats for specific issues, such as health, citizen/police review boards, liaisons to the gay community, human rights commissions, and zoning boards.

As Chapter 4 pointed out, LGBT activists have come to play increasingly important roles in campaigns for local office. Involvement in these campaigns has sometimes led to positions within the public official's office, or at least on the transition team that prepares to take over an office. For example, after John Street was elected mayor of Philadelphia in 1999, he was quick to select lesbians and gays from his campaign to work on his transition team. All told, Street had fourteen openly LGBT persons work on his transition team (Lessy 1999).

In Houston, Matthew P. Eastus became a significant player in city politics in the 1990s. In 1998 Houston's mayor appointed Eastus special liaison to the gay and lesbian community, fulfilling a campaign promise. In his position Eastus, a lawyer, spoke for the LGBT community in the mayor's office, but also ensured that the LGBT community had an understanding of the mayor's policies and positions. Even though Eastus had not been an activist in the LGBT community, many leaders in the community gave him leeway in his official position. Eastus began his position by meeting with representatives of the main LGBT groups in Houston and relaying the views of these groups to the mayor (Dyer 1998).

One example of a local legislative aide is Victor Castillo, who served as an aide to San Diego Councilman Bob Filner after working on Filner's campaign. Castillo served on the Dignity Ordinance Task Force and helped design the antidiscrimination ordinance that covered sexual orientation and was eventually adopted by the city (Sypert 1997).

Unofficial Public Figures and Movement Leaders

Although LGBT representation in the political process through elected and appointed positions is important, nonpolitical public figures can also have a significant impact on the lives of LGBT people.

In particular, key individuals acting on their own, organizational leaders, and celebrities from the entertainment industry can play active roles in elections and the policy-making process by providing positive role models and in educating the public. In this section we discuss examples of some of these "unofficial officeholders" from across the political spectrum, the impact they've had on the LGBT movement, elections and government, and culture. The figures discussed include a random sample of important leaders, including several that tend to work behind the scenes or are less frequently presented as leaders of the LGBT movement.

Opinion Leaders

David Mixner. Perhaps one of the most important, as well as controversial, opinion leaders in the LGBT community is David Mixner. Mixner is a long-time gay activist who had a long-standing friendship with Bill Clinton. In 1992 Mixner was credited with raising $3.5 million dollars for then-candidate Clinton and the Democratic Party (Polman 2000). Mixner's efforts in 1992 may have helped ensure that the LGBT community became a political force in the 1990s, rather than a traditional splinter group in Democratic Party politics. Mixner himself pointed to the importance of gay issues in the 2000 Democratic presidential primaries, which he argues was a result of candidates recognizing the size of the LGBT vote in key states like New York, California, and Ohio, but also in Iowa and New Hampshire (Polman 2000). Mixner also notes how LGBT activists matched his 1992 record in just a few events for the 2000 race.

Lynn Cothren. One important opinion leader who speaks for more than one community is Lynn Cothren. Cothren has served as a personal aide to Coretta Scott King, widow of Martin Luther King Jr., for over fifteen years. In his position Cothren has helped to highlight the similarities between the LGBT movement and the black civil rights movement, as well as provide a conduit between the two communities. Cothren tends to be modest about his influence, but compares his position to that of Bayard Rustin, the openly gay man who organized the 1963 March on Washington. Cothren arranges Mrs. King's media interviews and travel schedule, often traveling with her. Cothren says, "My typical days are never the same, it's dictated by whatever's going on in the world" (Sypert 1997). And he describes being open and working for Mrs. King as a nonissue; "It's not something where I necessarily think I have to wear a badge saying I'm queer at work. I'm not the paid queer here. I never have been" (Sypert 1997). Cothren also addresses LGBT issues in his personal time. He even helped organize the boycott in Atlanta against the Cracker Barrel restaurant chain for antigay discrimination.

Andrew Sullivan. Perhaps the most controversial LGBT opinion leader representing a conservative perspective is Andrew Sullivan. Sullivan grew up in England and first gained notice when he was selected as an openly gay editor of the neoconservative magazine *The New Republic* in 1991. Sullivan has written several books and articles outlining his views of homosexuality, sex, relationships, and society. These include his controversial 1993 article in *The New Republic,* "The Politics of Homosexuality"; *Virtually Normal: An Argument About Homosexuality* (1995); and *Love Undetectable: Notes on Friendship, Sex and Survival* (1999). As outlined in greater detail in Chapter 1, Sullivan has argued that there are four paradigms for interpreting homosexuality as represented by what he calls the prohibitionists, the liberationists, the conservatives, and the liberals. Sullivan went on to suggest a fifth perspective, reflecting his own beliefs, that focuses on personal responsibility and that he calls "public equality, private freedom." Detractors simply refer to Sullivan's perspective as assimilationist. Although many of Sullivan's ideas seem relatively tame or accepted (e.g., the government should protect gays from discrimination), he has come under fire for his accusations against what he calls the gay liberationists. Sullivan argues that the liberationists have been giving the LGBT community a bad name by promoting sexual promiscuity since the 1970s. Indeed, gay newspaper editor Jeff Epperly suggested that Sullivan's motto should be: "I love gay sex, but hate gay people" (Kurtz 2001). Sullivan seems to take joy in these attacks, stating, "I'm not looking for people to agree with me. I'd be bored out of my brain" (Kurtz 2001).

In 1996 Sullivan resigned as editor of *The New Republic* and chose to publicly state he had HIV. Many observers thought Sullivan's career was over, but he continued to write columns and contribute to magazines and to start his own website (AndrewSullivan.com), as well as complete his 1999 book. Sullivan has mingled with power brokers as diverse as the Reverend Pat Robertson, the Kennedy family, Senator John McCain (R-AZ), and national gay interest group leaders, while still participating in the gay subculture of late-night discos. In 2001 Sullivan faced perhaps his biggest controversy yet when he was linked to a classified ad on a website for unprotected gay sex called "bare backing." Sullivan was viewed as a hypocrite because he had long criticized promiscuous and unsafe sexual behavior.

Michelangelo Signorile. This man is best known as the "father" or "pope" of "outing." In 1990 Signorile had begun a campaign to publicly identify closeted homosexuals in the public sphere, including elected officials. *Time* magazine coined the term "outing" to describe Signorile's activities, as well as those of other gay activists. At the time Signorile was a writer for *Outweek* and a columnist for *The Advocate*. Signorile was a key figure in the outing of Defense Department Spokesman Pete Williams in spreading the rumor that millionaire Malcolm Forbes was gay. Signorile has written for a variety of media outlets on topics ranging from the Mormon Church and gay pro-lifers. He has also written three books on homosexuality, including *Queer in America* (1993); *Outing Yourself* (1995); and *Life Outside: The Signorile Report on Gay Men: Sex, Drugs, Muscles and the Passages of Life* (1997).

Signorile grew up in New York City and studied journalism at Syracuse University. In the 1980s Signorile joined ACT UP to fight AIDS and used his training to gain media attention for the group. Dissatisfied with the lack of gay issues on ACT UP's agenda, Signorile founded the group Queer Nation, which made headlines by creating posters outing celebrities.

Organizational Leaders

Dale Jennings. Known by some as the "Rosa Parks" of the LGBT movement, Dale Jennings was born in Amarillo, Texas, on October 21, 1917. After high school, Jennings moved to Los Angeles where he wrote, produced, and directed stage plays. Jennings served in the army from 1942 to 1946. In 1950 Jennings and Harry Hay cofounded the Mattachine Society in Los Angeles, the first homophile organization. And in 1952 he cofounded ONE, Inc., which began publishing *ONE Magazine,* a magazine for homosexual rights (White 2000). The Los Angeles postmaster deemed the publication obscene in 1954 and confiscated magazines sent to subscribers. *ONE* sued the postmaster, leading to a 1958 U.S. Supreme Court ruling that a magazine calling for equality for homosexuals is not obscene and that the Post Office should not interfere with its mailing. The ruling allowed for the LGBT press to grow throughout the 1960s and 1970s.

Jennings also stood up for his rights with police. In the early 1950s Jennings was followed home by a plainclothes vice officer who arrested him in his apartment under an indecent behavior charge. Jennings chose to fight the charge with a defense funded by the Mattachine Society. In 1952 Jennings faced a ten-day trial by jury and was acquitted of all charges. The case provided the impetus to begin removing so-called antisodomy or "crimes against nature" laws throughout the United States and highlighted, for the first time, police harassment of gays. Jennings continued fighting for gay civil rights until his death in May 2000 (White 2000).

Deanna Duby, Director of Education Policy for People for the American Way. Deanna Duby worked as a lawyer in a private law firm before coming out. Once she did come out, she asked herself "Why am I playing a role [professionally] when the things I really care about I do in my off hours?" (Sypert 1997). She soon left the corporate law firm and went to work for a lesbian law firm, focusing on cases involving civil rights and domestic violence. After four years Duby was hired as director of education policy for People for the American Way, a progressive organization focused on civil rights and social justice issues. In her position Duby focuses on ensuring that public schools become more hospitable to LGBT students, but has also fought against private school vouchers. She says, "I see what happens to kids and how they're harassed. We are slowly, but surely, beginning to recognize that there are a lot of gay and lesbian people out there. We cannot any longer deny that or pretend they are not there. . . . [Y]ou cannot allow kids to be harassed. You have to protect them. Schools have to deal with it" (Sypert 1997). Duby also works on the group's annual publication *Hostile Climate,* a state-by-state report of antigay activity, and conducts research for her group's lobbying efforts.

Kevin Ivers, Log Cabin Republicans' Director of Public Affairs. In an interview during the 2000 presidential campaign, Ivers was very upbeat about the ability of the Log Cabin Republicans (LCR) to work within the Republican Party. Ivers described Republican candidate George W. Bush's meeting with gay Republicans as historic, even though Bush only met with gay Republicans who publicly supported his campaign. Ivers said that the LCR would endorse Bush if the candidate declared that he was opposed to discrimination in the workplace and if he was committed to AIDS funding. When asked about people who say that "gay Republican" is an oxymoron, Ivers responded:

> Well, I've seen some documentary films from 30 years ago where people say that "gay Texan" and "gay Utahan" were oxymorons. And that you

were not truly gay unless you abandoned your hometown and moved to San Francisco and became a radical . . . . I think the fact that that's laughed at today says a lot about how the more gay identity evolves and comes out of the closet, the more we get back to the fundamental reality that gay people are everywhere, and gay people come with all points of view, all walks of life, all races. For me, it all comes down to what the voting public is saying, the data from the exit polls. And one in three gays have been voting Republican consistently in every general election since 1994. That tells me that there are a lot of gay people out there who are Republicans, or who are inclined to vote Republican if the candidate reaches out to the gay community . . . . So there's a lot about conventional wisdom that always tends to be a little wrong and a little behind the times. But what's more, I think the people who would say that gay and Republican are an oxymoron are probably living a very isolated ghetto existence. And they don't seem to be in touch with what's really going on out there in the country. (Alsdorf 2000b)

Michael Colby, Executive Director of the National Stonewall Democratic Federation. Michael Colby grew up in New Hampshire and held several positions in the media before becoming the communications director for the New Hampshire state senate. Colby's other political activities included being elected as an openly gay delegate to represent his state at the 2000 Democratic National Convention, serving on the executive committee of the New Hampshire Democratic Party; the Merrimack County, New Hampshire, Democratic Committee; and the City Democratic Committee of Concord, as well as being a founding member of the Granite State Stonewall Gay and Lesbian Caucus (Chibbaro 2000). In 2000 Colby was selected to head the National Stonewall Democratic Federation (NSDF).

As head of NSDF Colby coordinates the efforts of fifty affiliated LGBT Democratic clubs around the country, focusing on the election of LGBT-friendly Democrats to all levels of government. The group played a key role in mobilizing the LGBT vote for the 2000 presidential election and participated in the drafting of the Democratic Party's 2000 platform.

Rich Tafel: Executive Director of the Log Cabin Republicans. Rich Tafel grew up in the Philadelphia suburbs and studied at East Stroudsburg University and Harvard. In 1990 Tafel was elected volunteer president of a national federation of Log Cabin Clubs. During the 1992 elections he helped mobilize and coordinate Log Cabin chapters while serving as director of the Massachusetts Adolescent Health Services in the administration of Governor William Weld. When the Log Cabin Republicans (LCR) was incorporated as a 501(c)(4) organization, Tafel opened the first Log Cabin national office in Washington, D.C., and was hired as executive director. He has served longer than any sitting executive director of a major national gay political organization and renewed his contract in 2000 (Ivers 2000).

In 1995 the Liberty Education Fund (LEF) was founded by the LCR as an educational and research organization, with a focus on closing the gap between the gay community and conservative Americans. The organization is nonpartisan and Tafel was selected as its president. In 2000 the organization created a Policy Institute initiated by Tafel.

Tafel has raised high praise from many corners. Robert Stears, chairman of the LCR Board of Directors described Tafel as a visionary leader who "has taken Log Cabin Republicans from obscurity to a household name and a major player in national politics" (Ivers 2000). Robert Kabel, Chairman of the LEF Board of Directors described Tafel's achievements: "The conservative gay movement has truly come of age, thanks in no small part to Rich Tafel's leadership. He has not only awakened a national political movement that has become a force to be reckoned with, but he has helped create a philosophical, moral and spiritual shift in our community that has changed the course of our movement for the better" (Ivers 2000). Finally, openly gay Congressman Jim Kolbe (R-AZ) said of Tafel, "Since he came to Washington in 1993, Rich has been an important and courageous leader in the Republican Party, and a force for positive change" (Ivers 2000).

Even with a considerable record of success in moving Republican Party moderates toward the LCR's perspective, Tafel came under fire in 2000 for refusing to meet with Republican presidential candidate George W. Bush under Bush's terms and for publicly supporting Republican presidential candidate John McCain even though the LCR had not endorsed a candidate.

Case Study: Ellen DeGeneres, LGBT Celebrity

On April 30, 1997, the comedian Ellen DeGeneres made television history by coming out as a lesbian and having her character, Ellen Morgan, on the television show *Ellen,* come out as well. Prior to 1997 the character Ellen Morgan had been a heterosexual female who owned a bookstore and faced everyday struggles with friends, family, and the occasional boyfriend. The show first aired in 1994.

The "coming out" episode and subsequent episodes focused heavily on Ellen as a lesbian and evoked considerable praise as well as controversy. The story made the cover of *Time* and was a hot media topic for weeks. For the episode ABC refused advertising from the Human Rights Campaign, citing a policy against issue advertising. Chrysler, General Motors, and Johnson & Johnson, which normally ran ads during the show, decided to pull their advertising for the coming-out episode. A spokesperson for the Family Research Council said, "Homosexuality exists in our society, but to glamorize it and attempt to make a joke out of something that is much more significant is an unfortunate choice for Disney [the owner of ABC television network]" (Lochhead 1997).

LGBT people around the country held "coming-out" parties for the April 30 event. The Human Rights Campaign had even created a "party kit" for the event, and mailed 1,400 of them two weeks before the show. The group Gay and Lesbian Alliance Against Defamation (GLAAD) used the event to encourage members to hold parties as part of a membership drive. GLAAD and the HRC also sponsored public viewings in a few large cities. The director of the HRC, Elizabeth Birch, viewed the event as a great opportunity for public education, stating: "We couldn't have dreamed for a better vehicle. Clearly, "Ellen" stands on the shoulders of tremendous work (for gay rights) that has gone on in this country, particularly in recent years. It's hard to miss the fact that this is a monumental move on her part in terms of basic American pop culture. America has never quite seen anything like this, where the girl next door comes out" (Lochhead 1997). Both proponents and opponents seemed to agree that having an openly LGBT lead character on a prime-time network sitcom could increase public acceptance of LGBT people. And although direct causation cannot be established, tolerance of LGBT people has increased since the show aired in 1997. In 2001 CBS announced that it would be carrying a new sitcom featuring DeGeneres called *The Ellen Show,* described as having the comedy without the politics. Nonetheless, DeGeneres's character is a lesbian.

Conclusion

This chapter examined LGBT participation in official government positions, perhaps the most important type of participation in any political system, as well as other important leaders and role models in the LGBT movement. Some important conclusions can be drawn by this investigation.

First, openly LGBT officials, both elected and appointed, are on the increase, with the most dramatic increases occurring in the past five years at all levels of government.

Second, the increases in LGBT representation have been wide-ranging, including a considerable increase in openly LGBT members of Congress and appointments of LGBT people in the executive branch. As more LGBT people seek public office at the local and state level, they will gain experience to further increase representation at the national level.

Third, increased representation is important for policy change. Although symbolic representation has value, recent research suggests that increased LGBT representation is also associated with the adoptions of policies that benefit LGBT people.

Finally, some leaders of the LGBT movement are not elected officials, but do the important work of mobilizing the LGBT community, educating the public, and educating public officials. Although these leaders are often less noticeable, their work is perhaps the most important for the LGBT movement because they organize the community, build organizations, work within broader coalitions, and represent the LGBT community through a broad array of roles.

References and Further Reading

Alsdorf, Matt. 2000a. "An Interview with Barney Frank." *PlanetOut News* (28 April).

———. 2000b. "An Interview with Kevin Ivers of the Log Cabin Republicans." *PlanetOut News* (1 May).

———. 2000c. "An Interview with Tammy Baldwin." *PlanetOut News* (28 April).

Baldwin, Tammy. 2000. "Speech: Keep Flame Alive for Rights." *Capital Times* (15 May).

Barlow, Gary. 1999. "New White House GLBT Liaison Chats with Windy City Times." *Windy City Times* (23 December).

Becker, Elizabeth. 2001. "Gay Republican Will run White House AIDS Office." *New York Times* (9 April).

Belser, Ann. "Gayness Discounted as Local Political Issue." *Post Gazette* (12 November).

Berrill, Kevin T. 1992. *Countering Anti-Gay Violence through Legislation.* Washington, DC: National Gay and Lesbian Task Force Policy Institute.

"Bill Would Aid Homosexuals." 1998. *St. Louis Post-Dispatch* (20 March).

Boyce, Ed. 1998. "RI Gov. Almond Wins Re-election; Democrat York's Defeat Blamed on Ignoring 'Core Constituencies'." *Newsweekly* 8(11).

Brelis, Matthew. 1998. "From Closet to Campaign Trail: Being Gay Once Defined a Candidate. Now the Issues Do." *Boston Globe* (30 August).

Browning, Rufus P., Dale R. Marshall, and David H. Tabb. 1984. *Protest Is Not Enough: The Struggle of Blacks and Hispanics for Equality in Urban Politics.* Berkeley: University of California Press.

Bull, Chris. 1997. "Direct Line to the President: The White House Responds to Activists' Criticisms with a New Wave of Openly Gay Appointments." *The Advocate* (31 October).

———. 2000. "Home in the White House; Julian Potter Settles into Her Job as the President's Liaison to Gays and Lesbians. *The Advocate* (14 March).

Button, James W., Barbara A. Rienzo, and Kenneth D. Wald. 1997. *Private Lives, Public Conflicts: Battles over Gay Rights in American Communities.* Washington, DC: CQ Press.

Campbell, David, and Joe R. Feagin. 1977. "Black Politics in the South: A Descriptive Analysis." *Journal of Politics* 37: 129–159.

Cassels, Peter. 1999. "Gay Elected Officials Gather in Providence: Annual INLGO Confab Draws 75 Leaders." *Bay Windows* (26 November): 1.

Chibbaro, Lou Jr. 1997a. "Clinton May Appoint Gay Ambassador: Several Other High-Level Appointments Promised." *Washington Blade* (27 June).

———. 1997b. "Maritime Commission Issues Sweeping Directive: Gay Chairperson's Ruling Is One of the Nation's Most Far-Reaching." *Washington Blade* (12 September).

———. 1998a. "Bella Abzug Dies at 77: Introduced First Federal Gay Civil Rights Bill." *Washington Blade* (3 April).

———. 1998b. "Capitol Hill Update: D'Amato Criticizes GOP Senators for Blocking Appointment of Gay Ambassador." *Washington Blade* (26 June).

———. 1999a. "Budgets Up, Donors Down: Biennial Survey Shows New Numbers at National Groups." *Washington Blade* (11 June).

———. 1999b. "Clinton Utilizes Recess Power: After Long Delay, Hormel to Serve." *Washington Blade* (11 June).

———. 1999c. "Hormel Sworn in as Ambassador; Albright: Nice Guy Finishes First." *Washington Blade* (2 July).

———. 1999d. "Socarides Leaving White House: Clinton's Liaison Credited with Building Unprecedented Ties." *Washington Blade* (24 September).

———. 1999e. "Senate Confirms Gay Assistant Attorney General: Robert Raben Slips below Radar during Six Months Following President's Nomination." *Washington Blade* (15 October).

———. 1999f. "Ammiano Threatened: San Francisco Police Step Up Security." *Washington Blade* (19 November).

———. 2000. "Colby Takes Helm of Gay Democratic Organization." *Washington Blade* (16 June).

———. 2001. "Helms Calls It Quits: Anti-Gay Senator from N.C. Announces His Retirement." *Washington Blade* (24 August).

Coile, Zachary. 1997. "Clinton Nominates Gay as Ambassador." *San Francisco Examiner* (8 October).

———. 1999. "Memorial March Becomes Ammiano Campaign Rally: Ceremony Honoring Moscone and Milk Goes Sharply Partisan." *San Francisco Examiner* (28 November).

Cole, Leonard. 1976. *Blacks in Power: A Comparative Study of Black and White Elected Officials.* Princeton, NJ: Princeton University Press.

Davidson, Miriam. 1996. "I'm No Poster Boy." *Arizona Republic* (3 August).

DeBold, Kathleen, ed. 1994. *Out for Office: Campaigning in the Gay Nineties.* Washington, DC: Gay and Lesbian Victory Fund.

Derby, Diane. 2000. "Kerin's Congressional Bid Tests GOP on Gender, Issues." *Rutland Herald* (8 June).

Diaz, Elvia. 2000. "Recall May Shoot Down Rising Star." *Arizona Republic* (7 October).

Dyer, R. A. 1998. "Mayor's New Gay Liaison Vows to Prove Work, Worth." *Houston Chronicle* (3 May).

Eisinger, Peter K. 1982. "Black Employment in Municipal Jobs: The Impact of Black Political Power." *American Political Science Review* 76(2): 380–392.

Epstein, Edward. 1997. "Memorials Honor Slain Harvey Milk: 20th Anniversary of His Election as Supervisor." *San Francisco Chronicle* (7 November).

Fiore, Faye. 1995. "White House AIDS Activist Falls into Political Exile." *Los Angeles Times* (11 September): A1.

Fishbein, Martin, and Icek Azjen. 1975. *Belief, Attitude, Intention, and Behavior.* Reading, MA: Addison-Wesley.

Fox, Richard Logan. 1997. *Gender Dynamics in Congressional Elections.* Thousand Oaks, CA: Sage Publications.

Folio Bound VIEWS. 1999. *Polling the Nations, 1986–1998.* Silver Spring, MD: ORS Publishing. CD ROM.

Frank, Barney. 1994. "Reaching a Broader Audience." In *Out for Office: Campaigning in the Gay Nineties,* edited by Kathleen DeBold. Washington, DC: Gay and Lesbian Victory Fund.

Freiberg, Peter. 2000. "A Vote of Confidence: Openly Gay Candidates Nearly Double Compared to Number on 1998 Ballots." *Washington Blade* (27 October).

Freyer, Felice J. 1999. "Officials Say Being Openly Gay Isn't a Detriment." *Providence Journal-Bulletin* (21 November).

Gay and Lesbian Victory Fund. 1998. "Political Extremists Target Openly Gay Legislator." Press release (April 9). Washington, DC: Gay and Lesbian Victory Fund.

Gray, Ellen. 1997. "Television Today: ABC's Dilemma: Whose 'Ellen' Is It, Anyway?" *Philadelphia Daily News* (14 April).

Grow, Doug. 2000. "Allan Spear, Gay Senator Who Educated Minnesota, Retiring." *Minneapolis Star Tribune* (17 May).

Gunderson, Steve, Rob Morris, and Bruce Bawer. 1996. *House and Home: The Political and Personal Journey of a Gay Republican Congressman and the Man with Whom He Created a Family.* New York: Dutton.

Haider-Markel, Donald P. 1997. "From Bullhorns to Pacs: Lesbian and Gay Politics, Interest Groups, and Policy." Ph.D. diss., University of Wisconsin-Milwaukee.

———. 1998. "Policy Entrepreneurs and the Political Representation of Minority Group Interests: The Case of Domestic Partner Policies." Paper presented at the annual meeting of the Midwest Political Science Association, April 23–25.

———. 2000. "Lesbian and Gay Politics in the States: Interest Groups, Electoral Politics, and Public Policy." In *The Politics of Gay Rights,* edited by

Craig Rimmerman, Kenneth Wald, and Clyde Wilcox. Chicago: University of Chicago Press.

Haider-Markel, Donald P., Mark R. Joslyn, and Chad J. Kniss. 2000. "Minority Group Interests and Political Representation: Gay Elected Officials in the Policy Process." *The Journal of Politics* 62(2): 568–577.

Herrick, Rebekah, and Sue Thomas. 1999. "The Effects of Sexual Orientation on Citizen Perceptions of Candidate Viability." In *Gays and Lesbians in the Democratic Process,* edited by Ellen D. B. Riggle and Barry Tadlock. New York: Columbia University Press.

Ivers, Kevin. 2000. "LCR Executive Director Rich Tafel Renews Contract." Press release (June 13). Washington, DC: Log Cabin Republicans.

Johnson, David K. 1997. *1971–1997: Twenty-Six Years of Fighting For Equal Rights.* Washington, DC: Gay and Lesbian Activists Alliance.

Keech, William R. 1968. *The Impact of Negro Voting: The Role of the Vote in the Quest for Equality.* Chicago: Rand McNally.

Kingdon, John. 1989. *Congressmen's Voting Decisions.* 3d ed. New York: Harper and Row.

Krisberg, Kim. 2001. Giuliano Wins; Mayoral Recall Effort Fails; Lesbian Loses Bid in Mass." *Washington Blade* (September 14).

Kupfer, Peter. 2000. "Gay Ambassador Finds Acceptance in New Post: He Tackles Luxembourg Job after Senate Battle." *Dallas Morning News* (9 September).

Kurtz, Howard. 2001. "The Comeback Columnist: Andrew Sullivan Continues to Defy All Expectations." *Washington Post* (19 April): C1.

Lessy, Harriet. 1999. "Gays Help Street's Transition." *Philadelphia Daily News* (5 December).

Levine, Charles H. 1974. *Racial Conflict and the American Mayor.* Lexington, MA: Lexington Books.

Lochhead, Carolyn. 1997. "Toasting 'Ellen' at Home: Coming-Out Parties Planned around U.S." *San Francisco Chronicle* (14 April).

Luttbeg, Norman R. 1991. "Political Attitudes: A Historical Artifact or a Concept of Continuing Importance to Political Science?" In *Political Science: Looking to the Future,* edited by William Crotty. Evanston, IL: Northwestern University Press.

Mladenka, Kenneth R. 1989. "Blacks and Hispanics in Urban Politics." *American Political Science Review* 83(1) :165–191.

Morse, Rob. 1999. "Same Old City, but Different, 21 Years after Horror." *San Francisco Examiner* (26 November).

Newport, Frank. 1999. "Americans Today Much More Accepting of a Woman, Black, Catholic, or Jew as President." *Gallup News Service* (29 March).

———. 2001. "American Attitudes toward Homosexuality Continue to Become More Tolerant." *Gallup News Service* (4 June).

Niedowski, Erika. 1998. "Four Walk Out of the Closet and Toward the House." *Congressional Quarterly* (April 28).

O'Brien, Sue. 1991. "Privacy." *The Quill* 79(9): 9–15.

Palmieri, Jennifer. 2001. "DNC Welcomes Openly Gay and Lesbian Staff Members." Press release (18 July). Washington, DC: Democratic National Committee.

Polman, Dick. 1998. "Openly Gay Candidates the Hot Topic in U.S. Politics: Seeing a More Tolerant America, They Want Straight Voters to Know They Share Concerns." *Philadelphia Inquirer* (3 May).

———. 2000. "New Clout for Gays in Fall Election." *Philadelphia Inquirer* (17 January).

Price, Deb. 1997. "New Gay Rights Projects Need Some Support from New Jersey's Re-Elected Gov. Whitman." *Detroit News* (7 November).

Rayside, David Morton. 1998. *On the Fringe: Gays and Lesbians in Politics.* Ithaca, NY: Cornell University Press.

Riggle, D. B., and Barry L. Tadlock, eds. 1999. *Gays and Lesbians in the Democratic Process,* New York: Columbia University Press.

Rouilard, Richard. 1991. "If You Can't Name the Name, Then Don't Play the Closet Game." *The Advocate* (8 October): 7.

Saltzstein, Grace Hall. 1989. "Black Mayors and Police Policies." *Journal of Politics* 51(3): 525–544.

Seelye, Katharine. "Clinton Appoints Gay Man as Ambassador as Congress Is Away." *New York Times,* 5 June 1999.

Sherrill, Kenneth S. 1996. "The Political Power of Lesbians, Gays, and Bisexuals." *Political Science and Politics* 29: 469–473.

Shilts, Randy. 1982. *The Mayor of Castro Street: The Life and Times of Harvey Milk.* New York: St. Martin's Press.

Swain, Carol. 1993. *Black Faces, Black Interests.* Cambridge, MA: Harvard University Press.

Sypert, Tracy. 1997. Capitol assets: Working the political angle. *Frontiers Newsmagazine* (17 October).

Thomas, Sue. 1994. *How Women Legislate.* New York: Oxford University Press.

Vaid, Urvashi. 1995. *Virtual Equality: The Mainstreaming of Gay and Lesbian Liberation.* New York: Anchor Books.

"Ventura's Chief of Staff Cited for Indecent Conduct." 2000. *St. Paul Pioneer Press* (1 November).

Weisberg, Louis. 1999. "Gay Man Gets Cabinet-Level Post in Ryan's Office." *Windy City Times* (11 March).

White, Todd. 2000. "Dale Jennings, Known as the 'Rosa Parks' of the Gay Rights Movement, Dies at 82." Press release (24 May). Los Angeles: ONE Institute.

Wilcox, Clyde, and Robin Wolpert. 2000. "Gay Rights in the Public Sphere: Public Opinion on Gay and Lesbian Equality." In *The Politics of Gay Rights,* edited by Craig A. Rimmerman, Kenneth D. Wald, and Clyde Wilcox. Chicago: University of Chicago Press.

Wright, Kai. 1997. "'It's Always a Battle': After Ten Years of Working on Aids Funding, Steve Morin Leaves the Hill." *Washington Blade* (24 October).

Wrightsman, Lawrence S. 1999. *Judicial Decision Making: Is Psychology Relevant?* New York: Kluwer Academic/Plenum Publishers.

Yang, John E. 1997. "Gays in a Conservative Closet: Some GOP Congressional Aides Experience Dissonance between Personal, Political." *Washington Post* (7 November)

Documents

Bowers v. Hardwick and the Zone of Privacy

In 1986 the U.S. Supreme Court dealt a major setback to the LGBT rights movement. During the previous several decades, particularly during the tenures of Chief Justices Earl Warren (1953–1969) and Warren Burger (1969–1986), the Supreme Court had championed civil rights, reinforced the rights of the accused, and propounded the right of citizens to a zone of privacy. This zone of privacy, inferred from the Fourth Amendment's protections against unreasonable search and seizure, led the Court to rule that married individuals had a privacy right to practice contraception (Griswold v. Connecticut, 1965) and that women had the right to terminate a pregnancy (Roe v. Wade, 1973).

When presented with a challenge to the Georgia state law criminalizing sodomy in the case described below, many anticipated that the Court would extend the precedents of Griswold and Roe and rule that the law unconstitutionally violated the privacy rights of defendant Michael Hardwick, a gay man. However, by 1987, the Court had begun a long-term shift to the political right, and the nation was gripped by near-hysteria over the AIDS epidemic. The Court upheld the law's constitutionality in a ruling that signaled an end to the expansion of privacy rights and perpetuated the criminalization of same-sex consensual sexual activity between adults. As can be seen in the excerpt below, the slim five-to-four majority (Justice Lewis Powell later admitted that he wished he had not voted to uphold the statute) ruled that "in constitutional terms there is no such thing as a fundamental right to commit homosexual sodomy." Notably, the ruling must reach back to ancient and Medieval precedents, rather than contemporary jurisprudence, for its justification.

Although Bowers v. Hardwick was a major blow to hopes for equality under the law, individual state supreme courts and legislators have continued to decriminalize sodomy. Likewise, the Bowers precedent did not prevent the

Supreme Court from issuing a pro-LGBT decision in the later and perhaps more important case of Romer v. Evans *(see below). In an ironic footnote, the Georgia attorney general who prosecuted Hardwick, Michael Bowers, later admitted during a failed run for governor that during the case he himself had been committing adultery, which was also illegal under Georgia state law.*

U.S. Supreme Court
BOWERS v. HARDWICK, 478 U.S. 186 (1986)
478 U.S. 186
BOWERS, ATTORNEY GENERAL OF GEORGIA v. HARDWICK ET AL. CERTIORARI TO THE UNITED STATES COURT OF APPEALS FOR THE ELEVENTH CIRCUIT No. 85–140. Argued March 31, 1986. Decided June 30, 1986.

After being charged with violating the Georgia statute criminalizing sodomy by committing that act with another adult male in the bedroom of his home, respondent Hardwick (respondent) brought suit in Federal District Court, challenging the constitutionality of the statute insofar as it criminalized consensual sodomy. The court granted the defendants' motion to dismiss for failure to state a claim. The Court of Appeals reversed and remanded, holding that the Georgia statute violated respondent's fundamental rights.

Held:

The Georgia statute is constitutional. Pp. 190–196.

(a) The Constitution does not confer a fundamental right upon homosexuals to engage in sodomy. None of the fundamental rights announced in this Court's prior cases involving family relationships, marriage, or procreation bear any resemblance to the right asserted in this case. And any claim that those cases stand for the proposition that any kind of private sexual conduct between consenting adults is constitutionally insulated from state proscription is unsupportable. Pp. 190–191.

(b) Against a background in which many States have criminalized sodomy and still do, to claim that a right to engage in such conduct is "deeply rooted in this Nation's history and tradition" or "implicit in the concept of ordered liberty" is, at best, facetious. Pp. 191–194.

(c) There should be great resistance to expand the reach of the Due Process Clauses to cover new fundamental rights. Otherwise, the Judiciary necessarily would take upon itself further authority to govern the country without constitutional authority. The claimed right in this case falls far short of overcoming this resistance. Pp. 194–195.

(d) The fact that homosexual conduct occurs in the privacy of the home does not affect the result. *Stanley v. Georgia,* 394 U.S. 557, distinguished. Pp. 195–196.

(e) Sodomy laws should not be invalidated on the asserted basis that majority belief that sodomy is immoral is an inadequate rationale to support the laws. P. 196.

760 F.2d 1202, reversed. [478 U.S. 186, 187]

WHITE, J., delivered the opinion of the Court, in which BURGER, C. J., and POWELL, REHNQUIST, and O'CONNOR, JJ., joined. BURGER, C. J., post, p. 196, and POWELL, J., post, p. 197, filed concurring opinions. BLACKMUN, J., filed a dissenting opinion, in which BRENNAN, MARSHALL, and STEVENS, JJ., joined, post, p. 199. STEVENS, J., filed a dissenting opinion, in which BRENNAN and MARSHALL, JJ., joined, post, p. 214.

This case does not require a judgment on whether laws against sodomy between consenting adults in general, or between homosexuals in particular, are wise or desirable. It raises no question about the right or propriety of state legislative decisions to repeal their laws that criminalize homosexual sodomy, or of state-court decisions invalidating those laws on state constitutional grounds. The issue presented is whether the Federal Constitution confers a fundamental right upon homosexuals to engage in sodomy and hence invalidates the laws of the many States that still make such conduct illegal and have done so for a very long time. The case also calls for some judgment about the limits of the Court's role in carrying out its constitutional mandate. . . .

We first register our disagreement with the Court of Appeals and with respondent that the Court's prior cases have construed the Constitution to confer a right of privacy that extends to homosexual sodomy and for all intents and purposes have decided this case. . . . Accepting the decisions in these cases and the above description of them, we think it evident that none of the rights announced in those cases bears any resemblance to the [478 U.S. 186, 191] claimed constitutional right of homosexuals to engage in acts of sodomy that is asserted in this case. No connection between family, marriage, or procreation on the one hand and homosexual activity on the other has been demonstrated, either by the Court of Appeals or by respondent. Moreover, any claim that these cases nevertheless stand for the proposition that any kind of private sexual conduct between consenting adults is constitutionally insulated from state proscription is unsupportable. . . .

Precedent aside, however, respondent would have us announce, as the Court of Appeals did, a fundamental right to engage in homosexual sodomy. This we are quite unwilling to do. . . .

It is obvious to us that neither of these formulations would extend a fundamental right to homosexuals to engage in acts of consensual sodomy. Proscriptions against that conduct have ancient roots. See generally Survey on the Constitutional Right to Privacy in the Context of Homosexual Activity, 40 U. Miami L. Rev. 521, 525 (1986). Sodomy was a criminal offense at common law and was forbidden by the laws of the original 13 States when they ratified the Bill of Rights. In 1868, when the Fourteenth Amendment was [478 U.S. 186, 193] ratified, all but 5 of the 37 States in the Union had criminal sodomy laws. In fact, until 1961, all 50 States outlawed sodomy, and today, 24 States and the District of Columbia [478 U.S. 186, 194] continue to provide criminal penalties for sodomy performed in private and between consenting adults. See Survey, U. Miami

L. Rev., supra, at 524, n. 9. Against this background, to claim that a right to engage in such conduct is "deeply rooted in this Nation's history and tradition" or "implicit in the concept of ordered liberty" is, at best, facetious. . .

Even if the conduct at issue here is not a fundamental right, respondent asserts that there must be a rational basis for the law and that there is none in this case other than the presumed belief of a majority of the electorate in Georgia that homosexual sodomy is immoral and unacceptable. This is said to be an inadequate rationale to support the law. The law, however, is constantly based on notions of morality, and if all laws representing essentially moral choices are to be invalidated under the Due Process Clause, the courts will be very busy indeed. Even respondent makes no such claim, but insists that majority sentiments about the morality of homosexuality should be declared inadequate. We do not agree, and are unpersuaded that the sodomy laws of some 25 States should be invalidated on this basis.

Accordingly, the judgment of the Court of Appeals is

Reversed.

CHIEF JUSTICE BURGER, concurring.

I join the Court's opinion, but I write separately to underscore my view that in constitutional terms there is no such thing as a fundamental right to commit homosexual sodomy.

As the Court notes, ante, at 192, the proscriptions against sodomy have very "ancient roots." Decisions of individuals relating to homosexual conduct have been subject to state intervention throughout the history of Western civilization. Condemnation of those practices is firmly rooted in Judeo-Christian moral and ethical standards. Homosexual sodomy was a capital crime under Roman law. See Code Theod. 9.7.6; Code Just. 9.9.31. See also D. Bailey, Homosexuality [478 U.S. 186, 197] and the Western Christian Tradition 70–81 (1975). During the English Reformation when powers of the ecclesiastical courts were transferred to the King's Courts, the first English statute criminalizing sodomy was passed. 25 Hen. VIII, ch. 6. Blackstone described "the infamous crime against nature" as an offense of "deeper malignity" than rape, a heinous act "the very mention of which is a disgrace to human nature," and "a crime not fit to be named." 4 W. Blackstone, Commentaries *215. The common law of England, including its prohibition of sodomy, became the received law of Georgia and the other Colonies. In 1816 the Georgia Legislature passed the statute at issue here, and that statute has been continuously in force in one form or another since that time. To hold that the act of homosexual sodomy is somehow protected as a fundamental right would be to cast aside millennia of moral teaching.

This is essentially not a question of personal "preferences" but rather of the legislative authority of the State. I find nothing in the Constitution depriving a State of the power to enact the statute challenged here.

JUSTICE BLACKMUN, with whom JUSTICE BRENNAN, JUSTICE MAR-SHALL, and JUSTICE STEVENS join, dissenting.

. . . [T]this case is about "the most comprehensive of rights and the right most valued by civilized men," namely, "the right to be let alone." *Olmstead v. United States,* 277 U.S. 438, 478 (1928) (Brandeis, J., dissenting). The statute at issue, Ga. Code Ann. 16–6–2 (1984), denies individuals the right to decide for themselves whether to engage in particular forms of private, consensual sexual activity. The Court concludes that 16–6–2 is valid essentially because "the laws of . . . many States . . . still make such conduct illegal and have done so for a very long time." Ante, at 190. But the fact that the moral judgments expressed by statutes like 16–6–2 may be "'natural and familiar . . . ought not to conclude our judgment upon the question whether statutes embodying them conflict with the Constitution of the United States.'" *Roe v. Wade,* 410 U.S. 113, 117 (1973), quoting *Lochner v. New York,* 198 U.S. 45, 76 (1905) (Holmes, J., dissenting). Like Justice Holmes, I believe that "[i]t is revolting to have no better reason for a rule of law than that so it was laid down in the time of Henry IV. It is still more revolting if the grounds upon which it was laid down have vanished long since, and the rule simply persists from blind imitation of the past." Holmes, The Path of the Law, 10 Harv. L. Rev. 457, 469 (1897). I believe we must analyze respondent Hardwick's claim in the light of the values that underlie the constitutional right to privacy. If that right means anything, it means that, before Georgia can prosecute its citizens for making choices about the most intimate [478 U.S. 186, 200] aspects of their lives, it must do more than assert that the choice they have made is an "'abominable crime not fit to be named among Christians.'" *Herring v. State,* 119 Ga. 709, 721, 46 S. E. 876, 882 (1904).

Romer v. Evans and Equal Protection under the Law

In the early 1990s, two of the fastest rising forces in American politics were those of the LGBT community and those of the so-called religious right. Composed primarily of socially conservative members of fundamentalist and evangelical Protestant churches, the religious right had traditionally shunned involvement in politics. However, the leftward shift in U.S. politics in the 1960s and 1970s, and the attendant challenges to traditional values, activated the religious right from political dormancy into militant action, as most prominently represented by the Moral Majority during the 1980s and the Christian Coalition in the 1990s.

Along with abortion, LGBT rights has been one of the two major concerns of the religious right. They have employed a wide variety of political strategies to rollback LGBT advances or to forestall further advances, but have had limited success in the courts or through legislatures. For this reason, religious right organizations spearheaded populist movements for anti-LGBT measures through the initiative and referendum process. In the fall of 1992, amidst a call for a

"Culture War" at the Republican National Convention, voters in Oregon and Colorado were presented with anti-LGBT ballot measures. The harsh, condemnatory Proposition 9 in Oregon failed narrowly, but Amendment 2 in Colorado passed narrowly.

As an amendment to the state constitution, Amendment 2 would have overridden any attempts to protect individuals on the basis of their sexual orientation. The immediate effect of the amendment would have been to reverse ordinances in Denver and other cities prohibiting discrimination on the basis of sexual orientation. A more far-reaching effect, however, might have been to create a permanent "second class citizenship" for LGBT people by cutting off their ability to petition the government. Lower courts issued injunctions preventing the implementation of the amendment on the grounds that it violated the federal Fourteenth Amendment's guarantees of equal rights to all citizens. In 1996 the U.S. Supreme Court struck down Amendment 2 in the case of Romer v. Evans, *stating that "Amendment 2 classifies homosexuals not to further a proper legislative end but to make them unequal to everyone else. This Colorado cannot do. A State cannot so deem a class of persons a stranger to its laws. Amendment 2 violates the Equal Protection Clause."*

Some experts now feel that the seemingly conflicting precedents of Romer *in 1996 and* Bowers v. Hardwick *in 1986, which upheld the constitutionality of antisodomy laws, leave LGBT people in legal limbo. Others feel that* Romer *has in practical terms begun to eclipse* Bowers, *even though the latter has never actually been overruled.*

U.S. Supreme Court
ROMER v. EVANS, 517 U.S. 620 (1996)
ROY ROMER, GOVERNOR OF COLORADO, ET AL. PETITIONERS v. RICHARD G. EVANS ET AL. CERTIORARI TO THE SUPREME COURT OF COLORADO No. 94–1039 Argued October 10, 1995. Decided May 20, 1996.

After various Colorado municipalities passed ordinances banning discrimination based on sexual orientation in housing, employment, education, public accommodations, health and welfare services, and other transactions and activities, Colorado voters adopted by statewide referendum "Amendment 2" to the State Constitution, which precludes all legislative, executive, or judicial action at any level of state or local government designed to protect the status of persons based on their "homosexual, lesbian or bisexual orientation, conduct, practices or relationships." Respondents, who include aggrieved homosexuals and municipalities, commenced this litigation in state court against petitioner state parties to declare Amendment 2 invalid and enjoin its enforcement. The trial court's grant of a preliminary injunction was sustained by the Colorado Supreme Court, which held that Amendment 2 was subject to strict scrutiny under the Equal Protection Clause of the Fourteenth Amendment because it infringed the fundamental right of gays and lesbians to participate in the political process. On remand, the trial court found that the Amendment failed to satisfy strict scrutiny. It enjoined Amendment 2's enforcement, and the State Supreme Court affirmed.

Held:

Amendment 2 violates the Equal Protection Clause. Pp. 4–14.

(a) The State's principal argument that Amendment 2 puts gays and lesbians in the same position as all other persons by denying them special rights is rejected as implausible. The extent of the change in legal status effected by this law is evident from the authoritative construction of Colorado's Supreme Court—which establishes that the amendment's immediate effect is to repeal all existing statutes, regulations, ordinances, and policies of state and local entities barring discrimination based on sexual orientation, and that its ultimate effect is to prohibit any governmental entity from adopting similar, or more protective, measures in the future absent state constitutional amendment—and from a review of the terms, structure, Page II and operation of the ordinances that would be repealed and prohibited by Amendment 2. Even if, as the State contends, homosexuals can find protection in laws and policies of general application, Amendment 2 goes well beyond merely depriving them of special rights. It imposes a broad disability upon those persons alone, forbidding them, but no others, to seek specific legal protection from injuries caused by discrimination in a wide range of public and private transactions. Pp. 4–9.

(b) In order to reconcile the Fourteenth Amendment's promise that no person shall be denied equal protection with the practical reality that most legislation classifies for one purpose or another, the Court has stated that it will uphold a law that neither burdens a fundamental right nor targets a suspect class so long as the legislative classification bears a rational relation to some independent and legitimate legislative end. See, e.g., *Heller v. Doe,* 509 U.S. 312, 319–320. Amendment 2 fails, indeed defies, even this conventional inquiry. First, the amendment is at once too narrow and too broad, identifying persons by a single trait and then denying them the possibility of protection across the board. This disqualification of a class of persons from the right to obtain specific protection from the law is unprecedented and is itself a denial of equal protection in the most literal sense. Second, the sheer breadth of Amendment 2, which makes a general announcement that gays and lesbians shall not have any particular protections from the law, is so far removed from the reasons offered for it, i.e., respect for other citizens' freedom of association, particularly landlords or employers who have personal or religious objections to homosexuality, and the State's interest in conserving resources to fight discrimination against other groups, that the amendment cannot be explained by reference to those reasons; the Amendment raises the inevitable inference that it is born of animosity toward the class that it affects. Amendment 2 cannot be said to be directed to an identifiable legitimate purpose or discrete objective. It is a status-based classification of persons undertaken for its own sake, something the Equal Protection Clause does not permit. Pp. 9–14.

882 P.2d 1335, affirmed.

KENNEDY, J., delivered the opinion of the Court, in which STEVENS, O'CONNOR, SOUTER, GINSBURG, and BREYER, JJ., joined. SCALIA, J., filed a dissenting opinion, in which REHNQUIST, C. J., and THOMAS, J., joined. [ROMER v. EVANS, ___ U.S. ___ (1996), 1]

JUSTICE KENNEDY delivered the opinion of the Court.

One century ago, the first Justice Harlan admonished this Court that the Constitution "neither knows nor tolerates classes among citizens." *Plessy v. Ferguson,* 163 U.S. 537, 559 (1896) (dissenting opinion). Unheeded then, those words now are understood to state a commitment to the law's neutrality where the rights of persons are at stake. The Equal Protection Clause enforces this principle and today requires us to hold invalid a provision of Colorado's Constitution . . . .

Amendment 2 . . .is at once too narrow and too broad. It identifies persons by a single trait and then denies them protection across the board. The resulting disqualification of a class of persons from the right to seek specific protection from the law [ROMER v. EVANS, 517 U.S. 620 (1996), 11] is unprecedented in our jurisprudence. The absence of precedent for Amendment 2 is itself instructive; "[d]iscriminations of an unusual character especially suggest careful consideration to determine whether they are obnoxious to the constitutional provision." *Louisville Gas & Elec. Co. v. Coleman,* 277 U.S. 32, 37–38 (1928).

It is not within our constitutional tradition to enact laws of this sort. Central both to the idea of the rule of law and to our own Constitution's guarantee of equal protection is the principle that government and each of its parts remain open on impartial terms to all who seek its assistance. "'Equal protection of the laws is not achieved through indiscriminate imposition of inequalities.'" *Sweatt v. Painter,* 339 U.S. 629, 635 (1950) (quoting *Shelley v. Kraemer,* 334 U.S. 1, 22 (1948)). Respect for this principle explains why laws singling out a certain class of citizens for disfavored legal status or general hardships are rare. A law declaring that in general it shall be more difficult for one group of citizens than for all others to seek aid from the government is itself a denial of equal protection of the laws in the most literal sense. . . .

A second and related point is that laws of the kind now before us raise the inevitable inference that the disadvantage imposed is born of animosity toward the class of persons affected. "[I]f the constitutional conception of 'equal protection of the laws' means anything, it must at the very least mean that a bare . . . desire to harm a politically unpopular group cannot constitute a legitimate governmental interest." *Department of Agriculture v. Moreno,* 413 U.S. 528, 534 (1973). Even laws enacted for broad and ambitious purposes often can be explained by reference to legitimate public policies which justify the incidental disadvantages they impose on certain persons. Amendment 2, however, in making a general announcement that gays and lesbians shall not have any particular protections from the law, inflicts on them immediate, continuing, and real injuries that outrun and belie any legitimate justifications that may be claimed for it. We conclude that, in addition to the far-reaching deficiencies of Amendment 2 that we have noted, the principles it offends, in another sense, are conventional and venerable; a law must bear a rational relationship to a legitimate governmental purpose, *Kadrmas v. Dickinson Public Schools,* 487 U.S. 450, 462 (1988), and Amendment 2 does not.

The primary rationale the State offers for Amendment 2 is respect for other citizens' freedom of association, and in [ROMER v. EVANS, 517 U.S. 620 (1996), 13] particular the liberties of landlords or employers who have personal or religious objections to homosexuality. Colorado also cites its interest in conserving resources to fight discrimination against other groups. The breadth of the Amendment is so far removed from these particular justifications that we find it impossible to credit them. We cannot say that Amendment 2 is directed to any identifiable legitimate purpose or discrete objective. It is a status-based enactment divorced from any factual context from which we could discern a relationship to legitimate state interests; it is a classification of persons undertaken for its own sake, something the Equal Protection Clause does not permit. "[C]lass legislation . . . [is] obnoxious to the prohibitions of the Fourteenth Amendment. . . ." *Civil Rights Cases,* 109 U.S., at 24.

We must conclude that Amendment 2 classifies homosexuals not to further a proper legislative end but to make them unequal to everyone else. This Colorado cannot do. A State cannot so deem a class of persons a stranger to its laws. Amendment 2 violates the Equal Protection Clause, and the judgment of the Supreme Court of Colorado is affirmed.

It is so ordered. [ROMER v. EVANS, 517 U.S. 620 (1996), 1]

JUSTICE SCALIA, with whom THE CHIEF JUSTICE and JUSTICE THOMAS join, dissenting.

The Court has mistaken a Kulturkampf for a fit of spite. The constitutional amendment before us here is not the manifestation of a "'bare . . . desire to harm'" homosexuals, ante, at 13, but is rather a modest attempt by seemingly tolerant Coloradans to preserve traditional sexual mores against the efforts of a politically powerful minority to revise those mores through use of the laws. That objective, and the means chosen to achieve it, are not only unimpeachable under any constitutional doctrine hitherto pronounced (hence the opinion's heavy reliance upon principles of righteousness rather than judicial holdings); they have been specifically approved by the Congress of the United States and by this Court.

In holding that homosexuality cannot be singled out for disfavorable treatment, the Court contradicts a decision, unchallenged here, pronounced only 10 years ago, see *Bowers v. Hardwick,* 478 U.S. 186 (1986), and places the prestige of this institution behind the proposition that opposition to homosexuality is as reprehensible as racial or religious bias. Whether it is or not is precisely the cultural debate that gave rise to the Colorado constitutional amendment (and to the preferential laws against which the amendment was directed). Since the Constitution of the United States says nothing about [ROMER v. EVANS, 517 U.S. 620 (1996), 2] this subject, it is left to be resolved by normal democratic means, including the democratic adoption of provisions in state constitutions. This Court has no business imposing upon all Americans the resolution favored by the elite class from which the Members of this institution are selected, pronouncing that "animosity" toward homosexuality, ante, at 13, is evil. I vigorously dissent.

* * *

Today's opinion has no foundation in American constitutional law, and barely pretends to. The people of Colorado have adopted an entirely reasonable provision which does not even disfavor homosexuals in any substantive sense, but merely denies them preferential treatment. Amendment 2 is designed to prevent piecemeal deterioration of the sexual morality favored by a majority of Coloradans, and is not only an appropriate means to that legitimate end, but a means that Americans have employed before. Striking it down is an act, not of judicial judgment, but of political will. I dissent.

Baker v. State (of Vermont) and Same-Sex Marriage

By the 1990s, with antisodomy laws on the wane, two of the major remaining forms of government-sanctioned discrimination on the basis of sexual orientation were in the areas of military service and same-sex marriage. During the 1992 presidential campaign, Bill Clinton promised to reverse the ban on "gays in the military" but was outflanked by public opinion and strong opposition in Congress. Because military policy is made only at the national level, and because the courts tend to defer to the executive and legislative branches in the area of military policy, few steps have been taken in this area besides a failed policy of "don't ask, don't tell, don't pursue."

By contrast, marriage law is made by individual states, allowing a variety of legal challenges to laws which extend the right to civil marriage only to opposite-sex couples. In the case of Baehr v. Miike *in Hawaii, the Hawaii State Supreme Court ruled that it was discriminatory to exclude same-sex couples from marriage but was overruled by a hastily passed constitutional amendment giving the state legislature the right to regulate marriage. While national attention was focused on Hawaii, however, the Vermont Supreme Court ruled in a similar case that the state had to provide equal access to marriage and its benefits to same-sex couples. It allowed the legislature, however, to decide between broadening the existing marriage statutes and creating a new "civil union," the latter option being the one enacted.*

Because marriages performed in one state are normally recognized in all others as well as by the federal government, a spate of "Defense of Marriage Acts" (DOMAs) were passed by a variety of state legislatures, as well as by the U.S. Congress with the signature of President Clinton. These laws are designed to allow state and federal governments to deny recognition to same-sex marriages de-

spite the clause in the U.S. Constitution requiring each state to give "full faith and credit" to the acts of others. At press time, it was unclear whether DOMAs could be successfully challenged in Court, although one stumbling block seemed likely to be that Vermont does not actually have same-sex "marriages" but rather have created the new, parallel institution of "civil union." Nonetheless, as a number of western European countries have legalized same-sex marriages or "civil unions," many cities and private corporations provide benefits for same-sex "domestic partners," a trend towards same-sex marriage may well continue.

Baker v. State (98–032) [Filed 20-Dec–1999] ENTRY ORDER SUPREME COURT DOCKET NO. 98–032 NOVEMBER TERM, 1998 Stan Baker, et al.} APPEALED FROM:} } v. } Chittenden Superior Court } State of Vermont, et al. } } DOCKET NO. 1009–97CnC

May the State of Vermont exclude same-sex couples from the benefits and protections that its laws provide to opposite-sex married couples? That is the fundamental question we address in this appeal, a question that the Court well knows arouses deeply-felt religious, moral, and political beliefs. Our constitutional responsibility to consider the legal merits of issues properly before us provides no exception for the controversial case. The issue before the Court, moreover, does not turn on the religious or moral debate over intimate same-sex relationships, but rather on the statutory and constitutional basis for the exclusion of same-sex couples from the secular benefits and protections offered married couples.

We conclude that under the Common Benefits Clause of the Vermont Constitution, which, in pertinent part, reads, That government is, or ought to be, instituted for the common benefit, protection, and security of the people, nation, or community, and not for the particular emolument or advantage of any single person, family, or set of persons, who are a part only of that community, Vt. Const., ch. I, art 7., plaintiffs may not be deprived of the statutory benefits and protections afforded persons of the opposite sex who choose to marry. We hold that the State is constitutionally required to extend to same-sex couples the common benefits and protections that flow from marriage under Vermont law. Whether this ultimately takes the form of inclusion within the marriage laws themselves or a parallel "domestic partnership" system or some equivalent statutory alternative, rests with the Legislature. Whatever system is chosen, however, must conform with the constitutional imperative to afford all Vermonters the common benefit, protection, and security of the law.

Plaintiffs are three same-sex couples who have lived together in committed relationships for periods ranging from four to twenty-five years. Two of the couples have raised children together. Each couple applied for a marriage license from their respective town clerk, and each was refused a license as ineligible under the applicable state marriage laws. Plaintiffs thereupon filed this lawsuit against defendants—the State of Vermont, the Towns of Milton and Shelburne, and the City of South Burlington—seeking a declaratory judgment that the refusal to issue them a license violated the marriage statutes and the Vermont Constitution. The State, joined by Shelburne and South Burlington, moved to dismiss the action on the ground that plaintiffs had failed to state a claim for which relief could be granted. The Town of Milton answered the complaint and subsequently moved for judgment on the pleadings. Plaintiffs opposed the motions and cross-moved for judgment on the pleadings. The trial court granted the State's and the Town of Milton's motions, denied plaintiffs' motion, and dismissed the complaint. The court ruled that the marriage statutes could not be construed to permit the issuance of a license to same-sex couples. The court further ruled that the marriage statutes were constitutional because they rationally furthered the State's interest in promoting "the link between procreation and child rearing." This appeal followed. (FN1)

III. Conclusion

While many have noted the symbolic or spiritual significance of the marital relation, it is plaintiffs' claim to the secular benefits and protections of a singularly human relationship that, in our view, characterizes this case. The State's interest in extending official recognition and legal protection to the professed commitment of two individuals to a lasting relationship of mutual affection is predicated on the belief that legal support of a couple's commitment provides stability for the individuals, their family, and the broader community. Although plaintiffs' interest in seeking state recognition and protection of their mutual commitment may—in view of divorce statistics—represent "the triumph of hope over experience," the essential aspect of their claim is simply and fundamentally for inclusion in the family of State-sanctioned human relations. The past provides many instances where the law refused to see a human being when it should have. See, e.g., *Dred Scott,* 60 U.S. at 407 (concluding that African slaves and their descendants had "no rights which the white man was bound to respect"). The future may provide instances where the law will be asked to see a human when it should not. See, e.g., G. Smith, Judicial Decisionmaking in the Age of Biotechnology, 13 Notre Dame J. Ethics & Pub. Policy 93, 114 (1999) (noting concerns that genetically engineering humans may threaten very nature of human individuality and identity). The challenge for future generations will be to define what is most essentially human. The extension of the Common Benefits Clause to acknowledge plaintiffs as Vermonters who seek nothing more, nor less, than legal protection and security for their avowed commitment to an intimate and lasting human relationship is simply, when all is said and done, a recognition of our common humanity. The judgment of the superior court upholding the constitutionality of the Vermont marriage statutes under Chapter I, Article 7 of the Vermont Constitution is reversed. The effect of the Court's decision is suspended, and jurisdiction is retained in this Court, to permit the Legislature to consider and enact legislation consistent with the constitutional mandate described herein.

FOR THE COURT
Chief Justice

The Denver Principles, ACT UP, and the Politics of AIDS

Written during the period June 9–12, 1983, the Denver Principles in many ways represent the Declaration of Independence and the Bill of Rights rolled into one for people with AIDS (PWAs). Little was known—and much was feared—about HIV/AIDS in June 1983, considering that the first cases of AIDS had been identified less than two years earlier, and HIV had been discovered scarcely six months prior.

The Principles grew out of a casual meeting in a hotel hospitality suite of about a dozen PWAs at the National Lesbian and Gay Health Conference in Denver. Struck that all of them had been treated as helpless victims, the group called upon two of the men—early AIDS activists Bobbi Campbell of San Francisco and Michael Callen of New York City—to draft a statement of principles based upon their discussions.

The preamble set the tone: "We condemn attempts to label us as 'victims,' which implies defeat, and we are only occasionally 'patients,' which implies passivity, helplessness, and dependence upon the care of others. We are 'people with AIDS.'" The seventeen principles themselves were clustered around the themes of recommendations for health care professionals, "all people," and people with AIDS, and the rights of people with AIDS. Together, they form the cornerstone of the PWA self-empowerment movement.

From this launching point, the PWA movement would go on to dramatically redefine the doctor-patient relationship and set a powerful example for breast-cancer and other health consumer movements. Although much scapegoating, blame, and generalization have followed in the years since 1983, the Principles provided the basis for active resistance to AIDS phobia. Many of the drafters would go on to become internationally prominent advocates of the rights of people with HIV/AIDS, as well as founding members of the National Association of People with AIDS (NAPWA).

The Principles also set the stage for the emergence of such AIDS protest and activist groups as ACT UP, one of the most significant social movements of the 1980s and 1990s. With a combination of media-savvy tactics, confrontational direct action fueled by fear and anger, and decentralized organization, ACT UP galvanized action against an epidemic that had been neglected for over half a decade. As reflected in the first flyer for an action by ACT UP (then still known as "The AIDS Network") printed below, ACT UP's concerns were both pragmatic, such as quicker release of experimental drugs, and ideological, such as combating homophobia and sexism.

THE DENVER PRINCIPLES

(Statement from the advisory committee of the People with AIDS)

We condemn attempts to label us as "victims," a term which implies defeat, and we are only occasionally "patients," a term which implies passivity, helplessness, and dependence upon the care of others. We are "People With AIDS."

RECOMMENDATIONS FOR ALL PEOPLE

1. Support us in our struggle against those who would fire us from our jobs, evict us from our homes, refuse to touch us or separate us from our loved ones, our community or our peers, since available evidence does not support the view that AIDS can be spread by casual, social contact.

2. Do not scapegoat people with AIDS, blame us for the epidemic or generalize about our lifestyles.

RECOMMENDATIONS FOR PEOPLE WITH AIDS

1. Form caucuses to choose their own representatives, to deal with the media, to choose their own agenda and to plan their own strategies.

2. Be involved at every level of decision-making and specifically serve on the boards of directors of provider organizations.

3. Be included in all AIDS forums with equal credibility as other participants, to share their own experiences and knowledge.

4. Substitute low-risk sexual behaviors for those which could endanger themselves or their partners; we feel people with AIDS have an ethical responsibility to inform their potential sexual partners of their health status.

RIGHTS OF PEOPLE WITH AIDS

1. To as full and satisfying sexual and emotional lives as anyone else.

2. To quality medical treatment and quality social service provision without discrimination of any form including sexual orientation, gender, diagnosis, economic status or race.

3. To full explanations of all medical procedures and risks, to choose or refuse their treatment modalities, to refuse to participate in research without jeopardizing their treatment and to make informed decisions about their lives.

4. To privacy, to confidentiality of medical records, to human respect and to choose who their significant others are.

5. To die—and to LIVE—in dignity.

Flyer of the first ACT UP action March 24, 1987, Wall Street, New York City

NO MORE BUSINESS AS USUAL!

Come to Wall Street in front of Trinity Church at 7 AM Tuesday March 24 for a

MASSIVE AIDS DEMONSTRATION

To demand the following

1. Immediate release by the Federal Food & Drug Administration of drugs that might help save our lives.

These drugs include: Ribavirin (ICN Pharmaceuticals); Ampligen (HMR Research Co.); Glucan (Tulane University School of Medicine); DTC (Merieux); DDC (Hoffman-LaRoche); AS 101 (National Patent Development Corp.); MTP-PE (Ciba-Geigy); AL 721 (Praxis Pharmaceuticals).

2. Immediate abolishment of cruel double-blind studies wherein some get the new drugs and some don't.

3. Immediate release of these drugs to everyone with AIDS or ARC.

4. Immediate availability of these drugs at affordable prices. Curb your greed!

5. Immediate massive public education to stop the spread of AIDS.

6. Immediate policy to prohibit discrimination in AIDS treatment, insurance, employment, housing.

7. Immediate establishment of a coordinated, comprehensive, and compassionate national policy on AIDS.

President Reagan, nobody is in charge!

AIDS IS THE BIGGEST KILLER IN NEW YORK CITY OF YOUNG MEN AND WOMEN.

Tell your friends. Spread the word. Come protest together.

7 AM . . . March 24 . . . You must be on time!

AIDS IS EVERYBODY'S BUSINESS NOW.

The AIDS Network is an ad hoc and broad-based community of AIDS-related organizations and individuals.

Executive Orders Barring Discrimination

As of this writing, no legislation has been passed at the national level to prohibit discrimination on the basis of sexual orientation in employment, housing, or other areas. The Employment Non-Discrimination Act (ENDA), which would codify such protections, has not been enacted into law. However, President Clinton issued two Executive Orders to much the same end. The first, on June 2, 1998, amended Executive Order 11478 (full amendment below) to add "sexual orientation" as a protected category for all civilian employees of the federal government. Executive Order 13160 of June 23, 2000, (excerpted below) required nondiscrimination on the basis of sexual orientation, among other characteristics, in federally conducted education and training programs.

Federal Register / Vol. 63, No. 105 / Tuesday, June 2, 1998 / Presidential Documents 30097

Presidential Documents

Executive Order 13087 of May 28, 1998

Further Amendment to Executive Order 11478, Equal Employment Opportunity in the Federal Government

By the authority vested in me as President by the Constitution and the laws of the United States, and in order to provide for a uniform policy for the Federal Government to prohibit discrimination based on sexual orientation, it is hereby ordered that Executive Order 11478, as amended, is further amended as follows:

Section 1. The first sentence of section 1 is amended by substituting "age, or sexual orientation" for "or age."

Sec. 2. The second sentence of section 1 is amended by striking the period and adding at the end of the sentence ", to the extent permitted by law.,"

WILLIAM J. CLINTON
THE WHITE HOUSE,
May 28, 1998.

Federal Register / Vol. 65, No. 124 / Tuesday, June 27, 2000 / Presidential Documents 39775

Presidential Documents

Executive Order 13160 of June 23, 2000

Nondiscrimination on the Basis of Race, Sex, Color, National Origin, Disability, Religion, Age, Sexual Orientation, and Status as a Parent in Federally Conducted Education and Training Programs

By the authority vested in me as President by the Constitution and the laws of the United States of America, including sections 921–932 of title 20, United States Code; section 2164 of title 10, United States Code; section 2001 *et seq.*, of title 25, United States Code; section 7301 of title 5, United States Code; and section 301 of title 3, United States Code, and to achieve equal opportunity in Federally conducted education and training programs and activities, it is hereby ordered as follows:

Section 1. *Statement of policy on education programs and activities conducted by executive departments and agencies.*

1–101. The Federal Government must hold itself to at least the same principles of nondiscrimination in educational opportunities as it applies to the education programs and activities of State and local governments, and to private institutions receiving Federal financial assistance. Existing laws and regulations prohibit certain forms of discrimination in Federally conducted education and training programs and activities—including discrimination against people with disabilities, prohibited by the Rehabilitation Act of 1973, 29 U.S.C. 701 *et seq.*, as amended, employment discrimination on the basis of race, color, national origin, sex, or religion, prohibited by Title VII of the Civil Rights Act of 1964, 42 U.S.C. 2000e–17, as amended, discrimination on the basis of race, color, national origin, or religion in educational programs receiving Federal assistance, under Title VI of the Civil Rights Acts of 1964, 42 U.S.C. 2000d, and sex-based discrimination in education programs receiving Federal assistance under Title IX of the Education Amendments of 1972, 20 U.S.C. 1681 *et seq.* Through this Executive Order, discrimination on the basis of race, sex, color, national origin, disability, religion, age, sexual orientation, and status as a parent will be prohibited in Federally conducted education and training programs and activities.

1–102. No individual, on the basis of race, sex, color, national origin, disability, religion, age, sexual orientation, or status as a parent, shall be excluded from participation in, be denied the benefits of, or be subjected to discrimination in, a Federally conducted education or training program or activity.

Sec. 2. *Definitions.*

2–201. "Federally conducted education and training programs and activities" includes programs and activities conducted, operated, or undertaken by an executive department or agency.

2–202. "Education and training programs and activities" include, but are not limited to, formal schools, extracurricular activities, academic programs, occupational training, scholarships and fellowships, student internships, training for industry members, summer enrichment camps, and teacher training programs.

2–203. The Attorney General is authorized to make a final determination as to whether a program falls within the scope of education and training programs and activities covered by this order, under subsection 2–202, or is excluded from coverage, under section 3.

2–204. "Military education or training programs" are those education and training programs.

Sec. 3. *Exemption from coverage.*

3–301. This order does not apply to members of the armed forces, military education or training programs, or authorized intelligence activities. Members of the armed forces, including students at military academies, will continue to be covered by regulations that currently bar specified forms of discrimination that are now enforced by the Department of Defense and the individual service branches. The Department of Defense shall develop procedures to protect the rights of and to provide redress to civilians not otherwise protected by existing Federal law from discrimination on the basis of race, sex, color, national origin, disability, religion, age, sexual orientation, or status as a parent and who participate in military education or training programs or activities conducted by the Department of Defense.

THE WHITE HOUSE, *June 23, 2000.*

WILLIAM J. CLINTON

Pride Proclamation

For years, it has been a tradition for some political figures to write letters of support or issue proclamations to mark the LGBT pride celebrations held each June throughout the country. For the first time, in 1998, however, a president of the United States wrote such a letter; in 2000 (see below), President Bill Clinton issued a formal proclamation.

THE WHITE HOUSE
Office of the Press Secretary
For Immediate Release
June 2, 2000
GAY AND LESBIAN PRIDE MONTH, 2000
BY THE PRESIDENT OF THE UNITED STATES OF AMERICA

A PROCLAMATION

Gay and lesbian Americans have made important and lasting contributions to our Nation in every field of endeavor. Too often, however, gays and lesbians face prejudice and discrimination; too many have had to hide or deny their sexual orientation in order to keep their jobs or to live safely in their communities.

In recent years, we have made some progress righting these wrongs. Since the Stonewall uprising in New York City more than 30 years ago, the gay and lesbian rights movement has united gays and lesbians, their families and friends, and all those committed to justice and equality in a crusade to outlaw discriminatory laws and practices and to protect gays and lesbians from prejudice and persecution.

I am proud of the part that my Administration has played to achieve these goals. Today, more openly gay and lesbian individuals serve in senior posts throughout the Federal Government than during any other Administration. To build on our progress, in 1998 I issued an Executive Order to prohibit discrimination in the Federal civilian workforce based on sexual orientation, and my Administration continues to fight for the Employment Non-Discrimination Act, which would outlaw discrimination in the workplace based on sexual orientation.

Yet many challenges still lie before us. As we have learned from recent tragedies, prejudice against gays and lesbians can still erupt into acts of hatred and violence. I continue to call upon the Congress to pass meaningful hate crimes legislation to strengthen the Department of Justice's ability to prosecute hate crimes committed due to the victim's sexual orientation.

With each passing year the American people become more receptive to diversity and more open to those who are different from themselves. Our Nation is at last realizing that gays and lesbians must no longer be "strangers among friends," as the civil rights pioneer David Mixner once noted. Rather, we must finally recognize these Americans for what they are: our colleagues and neighbors, daughters and sons, sisters and brothers, friends and partners.

This June, recognizing the joys and sorrows that the gay and lesbian movement has witnessed and the work that remains to be done, we observe Gay and Lesbian Pride Month and celebrate the progress we have made in creating a society more inclusive and accepting of gays and lesbians. I hope that in this new millennium we will continue to break down the walls of fear and prejudice and work to build a bridge to understanding and tolerance, until gays and lesbians are afforded the same rights and responsibilities as all Americans.

NOW, THEREFORE, I, WILLIAM J. CLINTON, President of the United States of America, by virtue of the authority vested in me by the Constitution and laws of the United States, do hereby proclaim June 2000 as Gay and Lesbian Pride Month. I encourage all Americans to observe this month with appropriate programs, ceremonies, and activities that celebrate our diversity and recognize the gay and lesbian Americans whose many and varied contributions have enriched our national life.

IN WITNESS WHEREOF, I have hereunto set my hand this second day of June, in the year of our Lord two thousand, and of the Independence of the United States of America the two hundred and twenty-fourth.

WILLIAM J. CLINTON

Coming Out Statement of
U.S. Representative Jim Kolbe

U.S. Representative Jim Kolbe, Republican of Arizona, publicly revealed his homosexuality on August 1, 1996, making him the first Republican holding national office to do so. The statement came after Kolbe's sexual orientation was about to be revealed by some LGBT activists after he voted to support the federal Defense of Marriage Act, which allowed the federal and all state governments to refuse to recognize same-sex marriages performed in any U.S. state. Below are his remarks, reflecting the tensions between the demands of public life and the realities of public life as well as how far LGBT people have come, yet still have to go, before being accepted as elected officials. He was reelected to office in 1998 and 2000, during which year he became the first openly gay person to speak at a Republican National Convention. As of this writing, Kolbe remains in office.

Twenty years ago, when I first sought public office, I made a decision that my commitment to civic involvement would mean my public life would have to come ahead of my personal and private life.

I have, in the intervening 20 years, sought to fulfill my public responsibilities in a manner that benefits all those I have represented in either the Arizona Legislature or in Congress. I will continue that commitment as long as I am in public service.

I look back on what I have accomplished for Southern Arizona since I came to Congress nearly 12 years ago, and I am proud of the record I have compiled. I have led the fight to keep Arizona and America's economy strong and growing by opening new markets around the world; NAFTA was the capstone of this vision. I have fought to lower the crushing tax burden on our families by reducing taxes. I have worked for six years as a member of the budget committee to achieve a balanced budget so we can relieve our children of the burden of a crushing national debt. I have worked to keep Arizona's reputation as the astronomy capital of the world by assuring that new advances in astronomy will go forward here. I have argued and won funds to protect our natural heritage, including the expansion of Saguaro National Park. And, just this week we achieved the most sweeping, most important reform of welfare in decades. There is, of course, much more, but this is a record I believe I can point to with justifiable pride.

I am just as proud of my record in the area of human rights and individual rights. I abhor and vigorously oppose discrimination in the workplace based on race, religion, gender, or sexual orientation—any treatment that is not based on merit. I fought to repeal the provision in law which requires an automatic discharge of any armed services member who is HIV-positive. I support health benefits for domestic partners.

I also believe that if the citizens of Hawaii believe it to be in their public interest to permit same-sex marriages, they should be permitted to do so. By the same token, other states—as Arizona has done—should be allowed to define marriage differently, and not be required to accept the definition adopted by others. It is for this reason that I voted for the so-called Defense of Marriage Act when it was before the House a few weeks ago.

Now, however, there are some who have decided that their disagreement with this particular vote warrants their making public information about my private life—information they may have heard second- or third-hand about my sexual orientation.

That I am a gay person has never affected the way that I legislate. The fact that I am gay has never, nor will it ever, change my commitment to represent all the people of Arizona's 5th District. I am the same person, one who has spent many years struggling to relieve the tax burden for families, balance the budget for our children's future, and improve the quality of life we cherish in Southern Arizona. I intend to continue that mission if the voters of the 5th District, in their wisdom, decide that I should represent them in the 105th Congress.

Key People, Laws, and Terms

ACT UP A protest and activist group formed in 1987 in New York City, ACT UP's mission was to spark "direct action" on the AIDS epidemic. Formally named the AIDS Coalition To Unleash Power, but universally known by its acronym, the group was most active during the period 1987–1993 when it grew to over 100 autonomous branches throughout the United States and abroad. The group uses media-savvy and elaborate demonstrations to protest sluggish approval of AIDS drugs; discrimination against people with HIV; and inadequate funding for treatment, research, and prevention of AIDS, as well as other grievances. Some branches have remained active into the early 2000s.

Adoption LGBT people have been seeking the same adoption rights as heterosexuals, as well as "coparenting" arrangements in which partners of the same sex can both be recognized as the parents of a child. Coparenting arrangements are particularly significant in cases involving lesbian couples in which one partner becomes pregnant through alternative insemination (i.e., sperm donation).

The Advocate Founded in 1967, this Los Angeles magazine is the major national print publication regarding LGBT politics.

African Americans The LGBT movement has been modeled in large part on the African American civil rights movement and has included significant participation from and leadership by African Americans. In addition, a number of groups and organizations have been formed to concentrate on the unique concerns of those who are both African American and LGBT, including resisting racism in the LGBT community and homophobia in the African American community. Most recently, rising rates of HIV/AIDS in communities of color have mobilized African American organizations to address HIV prevention.

Age of consent laws   These laws establish the minimum age at which a person is deemed capable of consenting to a sexual act. In some U.S. states, ages are set higher for consent to same-sex than to opposite-sex activity.

AIDS epidemic   Since its emergence in the summer of 1981, the epidemic of acquired immunodeficiency syndrome (AIDS), caused by the human immunodeficiency virus (HIV), has most heavily impacted gay and bisexual men. Closely identified with gay men since its inception, AIDS has steadily moved into heterosexual and drug-using populations as well. AIDS has had an enormous impact on LGBT politics, on the one hand stoking fears of gay men and exacting a terrible toll on gay communities, on the other hand necessitating widespread recognition that homosexuality is common and that LGBT people are largely nonthreatening, particularly to those who know them personally. The ultimate impact of AIDS on LGBT politics, while undoubtedly enormous, remains yet to be fully assessed.

Amendment 2 (Colorado)   In 1992, Colorado voters passed a referendum approving an amendment to the state constitution nullifying all laws in the state designed to protect people from discrimination on the basis of sexual orientation. A political firestorm and national boycott ensued, but the amendment was never enacted because it was blocked by the court system. Ultimately, the U.S. Supreme Court in the case of *Romer v. Evans* ruled in 1996 that Amendment 2 violated the U.S. Constitution's Fourteenth Amendment guarantees of equal protection under the law.

Amendments to U.S. Constitution   Several Amendments to the U.S. Constitution have been extremely important to the development of the LGBT movement, including First Amendment guarantees of freedom of expression, Fourth Amendment protections of personal privacy (although these are limited by the case of *Bowers v. Hardwick*), and Fourteenth Amendment guarantees of equal protection under the law (upheld in the case of *Romer v. Evans*).

American Civil Liberties Union (ACLU)   The ACLU is a nationwide organization that uses litigation and other strategies to defend the freedom of expression, privacy rights, and other constitutional protections of Americans, including LGBT people.

American Psychiatric Association   A major development in the "normalization" of homosexuality in American society occurred when the American Psychiatric Association decided in 1973 to remove homosexuality from classification as a mental disorder in its *Diagnostic and Statistical Manual.*

Antidiscrimination laws   *See* Discrimination

Antisodomy laws   A number of U.S. states, the U.S. Universal Code of Military Justice, and many countries throughout the world maintain laws criminalizing sodomy. Although most commonly associated with anal intercourse between men, some antisodomy laws also prohibit oral sex between men and some still technically criminalize anal and oral sex between men and women. In the 1986 case of *Bowers v. Hardwick,* the U.S. Supreme Court upheld the constitutionality of the state of Georgia's law criminalizing sodomy (i.e., anal or oral sex). After decades of expanding Fourth Amendment personal privacy protections, the Court ruled that there was no constitutional privacy right to engage in consensual same-sex sexual relations.

Assimilationism versus liberationism   This refers to a debate in LGBT political discourse between individuals or ideologies that seek to assimilate into the wider society as it exists versus those who seek to change the wider society in the direction of personal liberation from traditional restrictions and mores. Assimiliationists often regard themselves as political pragmatists, while liberationists are likely to view them as willing to sell out for small concessions rather than seeking more comprehensive change.

Bashing   This is a catchall term used for physical violence directed against LGBT people on the basis of their sexual orientation.

Bias crimes   *See* Hate Crimes

Bisexuality   *See* Sexual Orientation

Bisexuality and policy/law   Bisexuality reflects an intermediate category in policy and law. Insofar as particular behaviors are addressed, those engaging in same-sex sexual relations are regarded the same whether their fundamental sexual orientation is homosexual, bisexual, or heterosexual. In terms of laws protecting (or in the case of the U.S. military, excluding) individuals on the basis of sexual orientation, bisexuality is generally recognized as a distinct and protected entity alongside homosexuality.

Bowers v. Hardwick   *See* Antisodomy laws

Briggs initiative   This was an initiative brought before the voters of California in 1978 to exclude LGBT people from eligibility to serve as teachers in public institutions. Its defeat was particularly significant because it headed off the passage of comparable legislation in other states.

Canada   The LGBT movement in Canada is closely linked to that of the United States in many ways. The largest cities, notably Toronto, Montreal, Vancouver, and to a certain extent the federal capital Ottawa, have large LGBT communities and organizations that often coordinate and cooperate with their counterparts in the United States, Europe, and elsewhere. However, LGBT people have a considerably more advanced state of formal protection under the Canadian federal Charter of Rights and Freedoms in such areas as the decriminalization of same-sex sexual activity, protection from discrimination, and recognition of same-sex couples.

Centers for Disease Control and Prevention   An agency within the U.S. Department of Health and Human Services, the Centers for Disease Control and Prevention (CDC) has since the emergence of the AIDS epidemic worked closely with LGBT communities to document, analyze, and prevent the further spread of the epidemic. The CDC has also been the target of protests at times by AIDS activists who feel that the agency has insufficiently focused on LGBT concerns.

Christian right   The "Christian right" is an umbrella term for a very socially conservative segment of the American population, composed primarily of evangelical and fundamentalist Protestants, who are a major power bloc in American politics in general and in the Republican Party in particular. Since the 1970s the Christian right, which traditionally shunned participation in politics, has increasingly resisted secularization in society, most notably by opposing abortion and the "gay agenda," as they term it. Most closely identified throughout the 1980s with the Moral Majority led by the Reverend Jerry Falwell and in the 1990s by the Christian Coalition led by the Reverend Pat Robertson, the Christian right remains the single most significant opponent of the recognition or expansion of LGBT rights in the United States.

Coming out of the closet Being "in the closet" or "closeted" is a term for those who fully or partially conceal their homosexuality. Revelation of one's sexual orientation is referred to as "coming out of the closet" or simply "coming out," which is seen by many as in part a political act because it often increases LGBT visibility and acceptance within society at large. Research has demonstrated that people who personally know someone who is out of the closet are considerably more likely to support LGBT rights.

Compulsory heterosexuality This is a theoretical term for policies, laws, or societal attitudes that make no provisions for homosexuality, thus requiring everyone to maintain at least the appearance of being heterosexual in their public lives.

Constructionism versus essentialism This refers to an academic debate that, with regards to sexual orientation, questions the degree to which homosexuality (or bisexuality or heterosexuality) is part of the innate nature, or "essence" of a person versus being more fluid and "socially constructed." Essentialists tend to view sexuality as fixed, unvarying, and largely genetically based; constructionists view most expressions of sexuality as shaped by particular societies and circumstances.

Counterculture This term, closely associated with the sociopolitical upheavals of the 1960s and 1970s, for social influences, including many LGBT ones, is viewed as being opposed to the general or dominant culture.

Cross-dressing Also known as "transvestism," cross-dressing refers to the full or partial adoption by an individual of clothing (and also possibly the demeanor, hair styles, etc.) of members of the other sex. Laws and policies sometimes limit or prohibit certain types of cross-dressing (particularly men in "female" dress) and social attitudes are also generally negative. Not all individuals who cross-dress are necessarily also LGBT.

Cruising Particularly common in societies that do not permit gay men to congregate openly, "cruising" occurs when gay men meet each other for anonymous sexual encounters in public areas, such as in certain parks, waterfront piers, or restrooms. Cruising locations are particularly susceptible to antigay violence and to police raids against "obscene behavior" or "solicitation" of sex.

Daughters of Bilitis *See* Homophile movement

Defense of Marriage Act (DOMA) This legislation was passed in the late 1990s at the federal level and in many states prohibiting recognition of same-sex marriages even if they are lawfully performed in a U.S. state. Critics argue that this violates the "full faith and credit" clause of the U.S. Constitution, which requires each state to recognize the legal actions of other states; supporters argue that there have always been public policy exceptions to the clause.

Democratic Party One of the two major political parties in the United States, the Democratic Party has traditionally been built upon a coalition of ethnic and racial minorities, city residents, organized labor, and more recently LGBT people. The Democratic Party is far more open to, and accepting and supportive of, LGBT individuals and concerns than its conservative rival, the Republican Party.

Demonstrations and direct actions   These are terms for particular forms of protest politics, often intended to attract media attention, in which a specific grievance is taken directly to its source, such as a city hall, a state capitol building, the White House, or the offices of a private organization. Demonstrations tend to include speeches, picket lines, and rallies; direct actions often include more confrontational tactics such as nonviolent civil disobedience, trespassing into restricted areas, and occasionally destruction of property, although rarely physical violence. LGBT groups have made wide use of the full spectrum of demonstration and direct action techniques.

Disabilities   Limitations in the ability of an individual to perform particular physical or mental tasks, often in the areas of mobility, vision, hearing, or intellect, are referred to as disabilities. Under U.S. law, accommodations for disabilities have increasingly been required under law, particularly the federal Americans with Disabilities Act. Homosexuality is not recognized as a disability, although people with HIV/AIDS may be recognized as disabled depending upon the degree to which their disease is symptomatic. In addition there is a distinct disability rights movement in the United States, which is modeled in part on the LGBT rights movement.

Discrimination   This refers to the exclusion of individuals from full participation in some aspect of social or political life on the basis of a particular personal characteristic such as race, ethnicity, sex, religion, age, or sexual orientation. Private discrimination is generally permitted under the law, but in the public sphere, discrimination is prohibited against particular categories recognized as being traditionally subject to discrimination in such areas as employment, housing, public accommodations, and voting. Sexual orientation is not a protected category at the U.S. federal level or in three-quarters of U.S. states, but it is in most of the nation's major cities. In addition, a significant number of private organizations have created voluntary antidiscrimination policies, and some that actively discriminate (notably the Boy Scouts of America) may receive some public disapproval.

Domestic partnership   With marriage closed to members of the same sex, an alternative category of "domestic partnership" for same-sex partners (and sometimes for unmarried opposite-sex partners) has been widely established, offering certain rights in such areas as insurance benefits, medical decision-making rights, and inheritance rights. Numerous U.S. cities and private organizations, as well as several western European countries, recognize domestic partnership to varying degrees. However, same-sex partners are not recognized at the U.S. federal level, and only the state of Vermont has a similar category, the "civil union."

Essentialism   *See* Constructionism versus essentialism

Europe   Relative to the United States, many countries on the continent of Europe have very progressive laws and policies regarding homosexuality. Consensual same-sex sexual activity has been decriminalized throughout the fifteen countries of the European Union and same-sex domestic partnerships (up to and including full marriage rights) have been recognized in most northern European countries, especially in Scandinavia and the Netherlands. The influence of the European Union, particularly its pro-LGBT social charter, has also led to considerable advances in LGBT legal protections among its member states in southern Europe and among aspiring members in eastern Europe.

Feminism The study of the significance of gender issues and of the traditional subjugation of women, feminism has been a powerful force within the LGBT movement. Many pioneering feminists, notably in the National Organization for Women, have been lesbians, prompting some to warn of a "lavender menace" that may discredit feminism in the eyes of homophobic individuals. Lesbian feminism remains a major, distinct school of thought within both LGBT and feminist communities, because of the unique perspective of lesbians and other "women-identified women."

Gay Activists Alliance and Gay Liberation Front *See* Gay liberation

Gay and Lesbian Alliance Against Defamation (GLAAD) Founded in 1985, GLAAD is a media-oriented activist organization working for "full, fair and accurate" representation of LGBT lives in film, television, print media, and other venues by opposing stereotyped or unbalanced representations.

Gay liberation Following the Stonewall Riots of 1969 and continuing through much of the 1970s, the LGBT movement was closely allied with various New Left causes in seeking to transform traditional society, notably through such groups as the Gay Liberation Front and the Gay Activists Alliance. The decline of left-wing liberationist movements and the rise of conservatism in society, as epitomized by the election of Ronald Reagan as president in 1980, coincided with the emergence of the AIDS epidemic. Thus in the 1980s, the attention of the LGBT movement was shifted away from liberation toward the protection of existing gains and even toward basic survival as a community.

Gay Men's Health Crisis (GMHC) The nation's first and largest AIDS service organization, GMHC was founded in 1981 in New York City and has played a leading role in combating HIV/AIDS, particularly in the gay male community.

Gender At the two extremes, gender is regarded as either a completely fixed, innate, unvarying biological characteristic with matching social characteristics or a fluid, changing socially constructed category only partially defined by anatomy. LGB people have been closely associated with challenging conventional gender norms and expectations, typified by "butch" lesbians or "effeminate" men, while transgender people actively transgress against gender norms.

Ghetto A term typically applied to city neighborhoods within which certain minorities are forced to live by law or economic realities. Post–World War II concentrations of gay men and lesbians in certain U.S. urban neighborhoods, notably Greenwich Village in New York and the Castro in San Francisco, are also sometimes called "gay ghettos" because gay men and lesbians chose and/or felt compelled by circumstances to live there.

Hate crimes Violent crimes deemed to be motivated in whole or part by the sex, religion, race, ethnicity, or sexual orientation of the victim are regarded by some as more dangerous and offensive than crimes with other motivations, such as robbery. Some advocate heavier legal penalties for perpetrators of hate crimes, because such actions can serve to terrorize an entire population; others believe that hate crimes essentially criminalize thoughts or beliefs and that the law should punish only actions, not intentions. The inclusion of anti-LGB hate crimes in the first federal Hate Crimes Statistics Act, signed into law by President George H. W. Bush in 1990 was one of the first recognitions of sexual orientation at the federal level.

Heterosexism   A more subtle form of anti-LGBT bias than homophobia (*see* below), heterosexism is an attitude or frame of mind in which heterosexuality is considered to be the norm and all people assumed to be heterosexual, with no provision or consideration for those who are not.

Holocaust   Among the first victims of Nazism in Germany were men identified as being gay, several thousand of whom were sent to concentration camps, where they were forced to wear pink triangles of identification. For this reason, gay men are sometimes included among the victims of the Holocaust, although antigay persecution for the most part occurred before the start of World War II and involved much smaller numbers than Jews, Roma (Gypsies), Slavs and other primary victims of the Nazis. Since the 1970s the pink triangle symbol has been reappropriated by LGB communities and used as a symbol of gay pride and identity.

Homophile movement   This is the name most commonly applied to the period of LGBT political activism before the Stonewall Riots of 1969, which ushered in the era of gay liberation. In contrast to the confrontational tactics of the post-Stonewall era, homophile organizations such as the Mattachine Society and ONE, Inc., for men, and the Daughters of Bilitis, for women, were relatively staid, even clandestine operations. The term "homophile," drawing on the Greek word *philia* (love) was considered less provocative than "homosexual." These groups created an early LGB network, the North American Conference of Homophile Organizations (NACHO).

Homophobia   The principal term used to describe anti-LGBT prejudice, homophobia literally refers to "fear" of homosexuality, but also relates to disgust with homosexuality and to feelings that homosexuals are sick, inferior, threatening, evil, or any number of other negative characteristics. Homophobia is often seen as a manifestation of xenophobia, or fear of the unknown, and as rooted largely in stereotypes and misconceptions about the nature of homosexuality. These misconceptions arise because homophobes are not aware that they are personally acquainted with homosexuals, often in their own families. Broadly speaking, homophobia remains pervasive in the United States, but indications are that both stereotypes and misconceptions have been declining since Stonewall more or less steadily (with some resurgence related to fear of AIDS in the 1980s.) Because homophobia is so pervasive, it is also commonly experienced by homosexuals themselves, in which case it is termed "internalized homophobia" and can be very damaging to self-esteem.

Homosexual panic   This is a legal defense, less and less commonly or successfully used in the United States but still common in some parts of the world, in which lesser punishments for assaults on gay men are given to perpetrators who claim that they were "panicked" by fear that someone perceived the perpetrator himself might be homosexual or approached him sexually.

Homosexuality *See* Sexual orientation

Human immunodeficiency virus (HIV) HIV causes acquired immunodeficiency syndrome or AIDS (*see* AIDS epidemic).

Human Rights Campaign (HRC) The HRC is the major LGBT organization at the national level, conducting extensive lobbying and issue advocacy at the national level.

Immigration At times, LGB people have been barred from entry to or immigration into the United States on the basis of their sexual orientation. HIV-positive status remains grounds for exclusion, and the same-sex partners of U.S. citizens are afforded few if any of the immigration advantages offered to married opposite-sex partners.

Lambda Legal Defense and Education Fund (LLDEF) Founded in 1972, the LLDEF is the premier U.S. organization providing legal advocacy for LGBT communities and individuals, serving as legal counsel in many important court cases.

"Lavender menace" *See* Feminism

Lavender vote This term is used to identify LGBT people as a distinct voting bloc, with a tendency to vote similarly and thus be targeted by politicians running for office.

Lesbian Avengers A direct action lesbian group active in the early 1990s, the Lesbian Avengers adopted confrontational tactics similar to those used by the AIDS protest group ACT UP.

Lesbian feminism *See* Feminism

Liberationism *See* Assimilationism versus liberationism

Log Cabin Republicans This is an LGB group within the Republican Party in the United States that views the party's traditional strain of libertarianism (i.e., the desire to keep government interference out of the lives of individuals) as beneficial to homosexuals. The ascendancy of social conservatives within the Republican Party since at least 1964, however, has often put the Log Cabin Republicans in confrontation both with their own party and with the predominantly left-leaning portions of the LGBT community.

March on Washington Large-scale marches on Washington for LGBT rights have been held four times: in 1979, when the movement was nascent; in 1987, with a focus on AIDS issues; in 1993 at the start of the Clinton administration; and in 2000 with an emphasis on the mainstreaming of LGBT issues. LGBT marches on Washington are but one of many types of sociopolitical protest marches on the nation's capital, such as those regarding civil rights, antiwar protest, or reproductive rights.

Marriage Access to the state-sanctioned, legal status of marriage remains one of the most significant areas of public life from which same-sex couples are officially excluded. Domestic partnership arrangements (*see* above) are increasingly widely recognized, but no U.S. state and no national-level governments other than a few in northern Europe extend marriage rights to same-sex partners on the same basis as opposite-sex partners (*see* Defense of Marriage Acts). Views on marriage within the LGB community vary along the fault line of assimilationism-liberationism (*see* above), with assimilationists seeking equal access to this social institution and liberationists seeking to redefine relationships or remove them entirely from government regulation.

Mattachine Society   *See* Homophile movement

Metropolitan Community Church (MCC)   A Christian religious denomination composed largely of LGB people, branches of the MCC are one of the major LGB institutions in some parts of the country, particularly outside the larger cities.

Military   Under America's Universal Code of Military Justice, all sexual activity between members of the same sex is prohibited and is grounds for discharge. Further, professed homosexual or bisexual orientation is regarded by the military as presumptively leading to homosexual behavior and as undermining the "unit cohesion" needed for effective military organization. At the outset of his administration, President Bill Clinton was unable to enact a campaign promise to end the ban on "gays in the military" due to strong congressional and public opposition. The ensuing "don't ask, don't tell, don't pursue" compromise policy, in which LGBT service members could remain in the armed forces as long as they hid their sexual orientation, has been widely regarded as a failure, with discharges actually increasing. Despite the formal ban on LGB people in the U.S. military, it is widely recognized that many do serve, often in an exemplary capacity, and that the integration of LGB people has been successfully carried out in the militaries of many NATO countries.

National Gay and Lesbian Task Force (NGLTF)   The NGLTF is one of two major national LGBT lobbying and political advocacy organizations, the other being the Human Rights Campaign. The NGLTF is regarded as the more left-leaning and grassroots of the two organizations.

North American Man-Boy Love Association (NAMBLA)   NAMBLA is perhaps the most controversial organization functioning on the fringes of the LGBT movement and seeking to benefit from the LGBT movement's growing credibility. As an organization promoting what it terms "intergenerational" relationships but what is commonly regarded as pedophilia or sex with minors, NAMBLA reinforces misconceptions about LGBT people as "child molesters" and is widely rejected from within the LGBT community itself.

Obscenity laws   Such laws are designed to outlaw forms of expression (e.g., some types of pornography) that are "obscene," and thus not constitutionally protected by the First Amendment. These laws have often been selectively applied to prohibit expressions of homosexual thoughts or conduct that would not be considered obscene if they related to analogous heterosexual themes.

ONE, Inc.   *See* Homophile movement

Out   This refers to the state of having "come out of the closet" (*see* above).

Outing   This is a term popularized in the early 1990s for the unwilling exposure of the homosexuality of public figures, often by more radical elements of the LGB community but also sometimes by the tabloid press. Targets of "outing" have frequently been political conservatives but also sometimes nonpolitical celebrities seen by critics as being hypocritical. Outing has been severely criticized as undermining the privacy rights that have been a major goal of the LGB movement, but proponents maintain that they are tearing down the power of the "closet."

Outrage!   This British direct action group is roughly analogous to Queer Nation (*see* below).

Passing   This term refers to the ability of a member of a disfavored group to appear to others as a member of a favored group, such as Jews who "pass" as Christians, blacks who "pass" as white, or LGB people who "pass" as heterosexuals. Because most LGB people are not readily identifiable as such to others, many functionally pass on a day-to-day basis while generally living their lives openly; others who remain fully or largely "in the closet" may make a lifelong pursuit out of passing.

Pink triangle   *See* Holocaust

Pride marches   Begun in New York City in 1970 to commemorate the first anniversary of the Stonewall Riots, pride marches are annual celebrations of LGBT identity held in locations throughout the world, usually during the month of June. Pride marches generally consist of a parade-like procession through the streets of a city past reviewers and spectators and on to a street festival and/or political rally at the end. Politically, pride marches provide an important venue for political activity and a source of visibility for groups that are often otherwise invisible.

Public opinion   The aggregate views of the American public about issues relating to homosexuality have changed considerably over the past several decades. Although large numbers retain serious reservations about the fundamental normality, morality, or acceptability of what some term the "homosexual lifestyle," younger generations express considerably more positive views. Similarly, support for equality under the law and for protection against discrimination has increased dramatically, constituting a majority for many issues (although not for same-sex marriage).

Queer   The word *queer* was historically one of the most offensive terms for LGBT people, particularly for gay men. Beginning in the late 1980s, however, LGBT activists reappropriated the word and began to use it as a term of empowerment, often with radical liberationist connotations. By some definitions, it includes all people who reject societal norms regarding sexuality (and thus may include certain heterosexual individuals).

Queer Nation   This is a radical direct action group most active in the early 1990s. The group is perhaps best known for developing the confrontational political slogan "We're Here! We're Queer! Get Used to It!"

Queer theory   This refers to an academic approach, closely related to gender studies, that uses postmodern techniques to deconstruct the homophobic and heterosexist biases and assumptions of the dominant culture.

Racism   Racism and homophobia share many of the same psychological and sociological roots, and the LGBT movement has adopted many of its tactics from those deployed in the battle against racism in the African American civil rights movement. In addition, for LGBT people of color, racism creates a double burden along with homophobia. African American and other LGBT people note that although LGBT people are oppressed, they are just as capable of racist attitudes and behaviors as members of the dominant culture.

Rainbow flag   This banner consisting of six horizontal bands of color representative of diversity emerged in the 1980s as perhaps the most important symbol of the LGBT community.

Religion   Many LGBT people find themselves in conflict with strict interpretations of the religions in which they were raised, particularly if they emphasize negative conceptions of homosexuality as sinful and heterosexual marriage as normative. Politically, conservative religions remain perhaps the single most significant opponents of the equality of LGBT people, and it is noteworthy that the northern European countries in which LGBT people have advanced the most are also the most secularized. Countries in which religion has a particularly strong influence are generally those also most likely to harshly punish homosexual behavior or attempts at developing LGBT communities.

Romer v. Evans   *See* Amendment 2 (Colorado)

Sadomasochism   Sadomasochism refers to sexual practices that involve the giving and receiving of sexual pleasure between consenting adults through the application of pain, although not generally actual bodily injury. Sadomasochism is practiced by people of all sexual orientations, but insofar as there is a sadomasochistic community (sometimes called a "leather" community because of their affinity for that material) it is often allied with LGBT communities in pursuit of sexual freedoms.

Safer sex   This term is used for steps taken to reduce the risk of transmission of HIV and other sexually transmitted diseases during sex, most notably the use of condoms. Pitched political battles have been fought over the degree to which government funds and institutions can be used to promote safer sex, particularly among children and teenagers, as well as safer drug-injecting practices, such as needle exchange.

Same-sex unions   *See* Domestic Partnership; Marriage

Separatism   This refers to a practical and/or ideological practice whereby individuals deliberately lead their lives outside some larger mainstream. The term is most closely associated with lesbians who seek to live women-centered lives with minimal contact with men and patriarchal institutions, although often less as a rejection of men than as an affirmation of women. To an extent, the existence of "gay ghettos" (*see* above) can also be construed as a form of separatism.

Sexual orientation   At its simplest, sexual orientation is determined by the gender of the individuals to whom an individual is sexually and emotionally attracted. Persons predominantly attracted to members of the same gender are homosexual (or "gay" for men and "lesbian" for women), those attracted to members of both genders are bisexual, and those attracted to those of the opposite sex are heterosexual (or "straight"). A fourth category, asexuality, for those who do not experience sexual attraction, is also sometimes added. Huge debates persist about the source and durability of sexual orientation, with some viewing it as innate at birth, others as fixed by the time of puberty, and others as variable over the life span. The question of the changeability or unchangeability of sexual orientation has figured prominently in public policy debates, with those viewing it as unchangeable generally more likely to support civil rights protections.

Stonewall Riots   On the nights of June 27–29, 1969, customers of the Stonewall Inn, a gay bar in New York City's Greenwich Village, spontaneously resisted a police raid, leading to three nights of violent confrontations. Although there had been previous instances of resistance to the police, the Stonewall Riots catalyzed a broad range of protest activity and organization building, thus launching the modern movement for LGBT rights.

Transgender   The term "transgender" refers not to sexual orientation but to gender identity. A transgender person may be heterosexual, homosexual, or bisexual. The key in this case is not the gender of those to whom the person is sexually attracted, but the individual's own gender. Those who are "transgender" have in some way "crossed over" from one sex by adopting the dress and demeanor of members of the opposite sex, or in some cases actually having sex reassignment surgery ("sex change operations"). In recent years, many gay and lesbian organizations have officially altered their names to include "transgender," in part due to a recognition that many LGB people express themselves in ways that are regarded as "gender atypical," or more like those of the opposite sex.

Resources

Selected National Groups

AIDS Action
1906 Sunderland Place NW
Washington, DC 20036
Phone: (202) 530-8030
Fax: (202) 530-8031
Website: http://www.aidsaction.org/

Founded in 1984, AIDS Action is solely dedicated to responsible federal policy for improved HIV/AIDS care and services, vigorous medical research and effective prevention.

American Civil Liberties Union (ACLU): Gay and Lesbian Rights Project
ACLU Lesbian and Gay Rights Project
125 Broad Street
New York, NY 10004
Phone: (212) 549-2627
Website: http://www.aclu.org/

The ACLU is a broad-based civil rights and liberties organization with special programs to address LGBT concerns.

Family Pride Coalition
P.O. Box 34337
San Diego, CA 92163
Phone: (619) 296-0199
Fax: (619) 296-0699
Email: pride@familypride.org
Website: http://www.familypride.org/

This organization works toward assisting lesbian, gay, bisexual, and trans-gendered parents and their families through mutual support, community collaboration, and public understanding.

Gay and Lesbian Advocates and Defenders (GLAD)
294 Washington Street
Suite 740
Boston, MA 02108
Phone: (617) 426-1350
Email: gladlaw@glad.org
Website: http://www.glad.org/

Formed in 1978, GLAD uses litigation to fight discrimination based on sexual orientation.

Gay and Lesbian Victory Fund (GLVF)
1705 DeSales Street NW
Suite 500
Washington, DC 20036
Phone: (202) 842-8679
Fax: (202) 289-3863
Website: http://www.victoryfund.org

Formed in 1991, GLVF recruits, trains, and provides qualified openly LGBT candidates with financial and technical support for campaigns.

Gay, Lesbian and Bisexual Veterans of America, Inc.
P.O. Box 29317
Chicago, IL 60629
Email: GLBVA@glbva.org
Website: http://www.glbva.org/

This is a national nonprofit organization for LGBT active duty, reserve, and veteran members of the U.S. armed forces, their families, friends, and supporters.

GenderPAC
1638 R Street NW
Suite 100
Washington, DC 20009-6446
Phone: (202) 462-6610
Fax: (202) 462-6744
Website: http://www.gpac.org/

Founded in 1995, GenderPAC is a nonprofit group focused on eliminating gender stereotypes and ending discrimination and violence on the basis of how individuals look, act, or dress in terms of gender or sexual orientation.

Human Rights Campaign (HRC)
919 18th Street NW
Suite 800
Washington, DC 20006
Phone: (202) 628-4160
Fax: (202) 347-5323
Website: http://www.hrc.org/

Formed in 1981 as the Human Rights Campaign Fund, the HRC is the largest gay and lesbian organization in the country. The HRC lobbies Congress, works with state and local groups, contributes money to campaigns for federal offices, and educates the public.

It's Time, America!
P.O. Box 65
Kensington, MD 20895
Website: http://www.tgender.net/ita/

Formed in 1994, It's Time America! is the first national civil rights group seeking to secure and safeguard the rights of all transgendered and gender-variant persons.

Lambda Legal Defense and Education Fund
120 Wall Street
Suite 1500
New York, NY 10005
Phone: (212) 809-8585
Fax: (212) 809-0055
Website: http://www.lambdalegal.org/cgi-bin/pages/

Formed in 1973, Lambda is the nation's oldest and largest legal organization working for the civil rights of lesbians, gay men, and people with HIV/AIDS.

Log Cabin Republicans (LCR)
1633 Q Street NW
Suite 210
Washington, DC 20009
Phone: (202) 347-5306
Fax (202) 347-5224
Email: info@lcr.org
Website: http://www.lcr.org/index.asp

The LCR is the nation's largest gay and lesbian Republican organization. Formed in 1993, the LCR lobbies Congress and contributes to congressional campaigns in support of Republican candidates.

National Center for Lesbian Rights
870 Market Street

Suite 570
San Francisco, CA 94102
Phone: (415) 392-6257
Website: http://www.nclrights.org

Formed in 1977, the NCLR is a national legal resource center that works toward advancing the rights and safety of lesbians and their families through litigation, public policy advocacy, free legal advice and counseling, and public education.

National Gay and Lesbian Task Force
1700 Kalorama Road NW
Washington, DC 20009-2624
Phone: (202) 332-6483
Fax: (202) 332-0207
TTY: (202) 332-6219
Email: ngltf@ngltf.org
Website: http://www.ngltf.org/

Formed in 1973, the NGLTF is the oldest continuously operating national LGBT group focused on eliminating prejudice, violence, and injustice against LGBT people at the local, state, and national level.

National Latina/o Lesbian, Gay, Bisexual and Transgender Organization
1420 K Street NW
Suite 200
Washington, DC 20006
Phone: (202) 408-5380
Fax: (202) 408-8478
Website: http://www.llego.org/main.html

Found in 1987, this group works for strengthening Latino/a communities at the local, national, and international levels.

National Stonewall Democrats
P.O. Box 77165
Washington, DC 20013-7165
Phone: (202) 783-8670
Website: http://www.stonewalldemocrats.org/main.html

The goals of this organization include making LGBT voters aware of the differences between the parties on LGBT issues and supporting Democratic candidates who support LGBT equal rights.

Parents, Families, and Friends of Lesbians and Gays (PFLAG)
1726 M Street NW
Suite 400
Washington, DC 20036

Phone: (202) 467-8180
Fax: (202) 467-8194
Website: http://www.pflag.org/

Formed in 1973 as a small group in New York City, PFLAG is now a national nonprofit organization with a membership of over 80,000 households and more than 450 affiliates worldwide that promote the health and well-being of LGBT persons, their families, and friends.

Partners Task Force for Gay and Lesbian Couples
P.O. Box 9685
Seattle, WA 98109-0685
Phone: (206) 935-1206
Website: http://www.eskimo.com/~demian/index.html

This is a national resource for same-sex couples, supporting the diverse community of committed gay and lesbian partners through a variety of media.

People for the American Way
2000 M Street NW
Washington, DC 20036
Phone: (202) 467-4999 or 1-800-326-PFAW
Fax: (202) 293-2672
Email: membership@pfaw.org
Website: http://www.pfaw.org/

This group "is committed to defending democracy and bringing the ideals of community, opportunity, diversity, equality and fairness together to form a strong, united voice."

Service Members Legal Defense Network (SLDN)
P.O. Box 65301
Washington, DC 20035
Phone: (202) 328.3244
Fax: (202) 797.1635
Email: sldn@sldn.org
Website: http://www.sldn.org/templates/index.html

Formed in 1993, the SLDN works toward ending discrimination and harassment of gay men and lesbian women in the military.

Treatment Action Group (TAG)
350 Seventh Avenue
Suite 1603
New York, NY 10001
Phone: (212) 971-9022
Fax: (212) 971-9019
Email: tagnyc@msn.com

Website: http://www.aidsinfonyc.org/tag/

Founded in January 1992, TAG is an AIDS organization dedicated to advocating for larger and more efficient research efforts toward finding a cure for AIDS and ensuring treatment for people with HIV/AIDS.

Selected State and Local Groups

Arkansas

Arkansas Equality Network
Phone: (501) 571-3157
Anne Shelley, executive director
Email: ARequality@aol.com

California

California Alliance for Pride and Equality
60 Granada Avenue
Long Beach, CA 90803
Phone: (562) 439-7304
Website: http://www.calcape.org/

This is California's main LGBT lobbying organization.

Lambda Letters Project
4577 Park Blvd #4
San Diego, CA 92116
E-mail: webmaster@lambdaletters.org
Website: http://www.lambdaletters.org

The Lambda Letters Project is a California-wide, nonprofit, nonpartisan organization dedicated to promoting gay, lesbian, bisexual, transgender, feminist, people of color, and HIV/AIDS advocacy.

San Francisco AIDS Foundation Home Page
995 Market St. #200
San Francisco, CA 94103
Phone: (800) 367-AIDS
E-mail: feedback@sfaf.org
Website: http://www.sfaf.org/

The San Francisco AIDS Foundation was founded in 1982 to assemble and disseminate critical information to gay men who were being diagnosed with a rare cancer.

Connecticut

Connecticut Coalition for LGBT Civil Rights
Phone: (860) 225-7445
Pura Gomez
Email: piwings@aol.com

Delaware

Delaware ACLU Lesbian and Gay Rights Project
Phone: (302) 654-3966
Peter Medwick
Email: medwick@pit.edu

District of Columbia

Gay and Lesbian Activists Alliance
Phone: (202) 667-5139
Email: equal@glaa.org
Website: http://www.glaa.org/

Florida

Equality Florida
1222 S Dale Mabry
Suite 652
Tampa, FL 33609
Phone: (813) 253-5962
Fax: (813) 447-9544
Email: eqfl@eqfl.org
Website: http://www.eqfl.org

Georgia

Georgia Equality Project
P.O. Box 78351
Atlanta, GA 30357-2351
Phone: (404) 872.3600
Fax: (404) 872-3602
Website: http://www.georgiaequality.org/

Hawaii

Marriage Project Hawaii
P.O. Box 11690
Honolulu, HI 96828

Phone: (808) 942-3737
Fax: (808) 947-4649
Email: MPH@hawaii.rr.com
Website: http://members.tripod.com/~mphawaii

Idaho

Your Family, Friends, and Neighbors, Inc.
P.O. Box 768
Boise, ID 83701
Phone: (208) 344-4295
Email: yffn@aol.com
Website: http://www.yffn.org/

Illinois

Equality Illinois
3712 N Broadway
Suite 125
Chicago, IL 60613
Phone: (773) 244-3371
Fax: (773) 477-6912
Email: info@equalityillinois.org
Website: http://www.ifhr.org

It's Time, Illinois!
P.O. Box 3932
Oak Park, IL, 60303-3932
Phone: (312) 409-5489
Email: ItsTimeIL@aol.com
Website: http://itstimeil.org

Indiana

Citizens For Civil Rights
P.O. Box 2461
West Lafayette, IN 47996
Phone: (765) 523-5767 (voice mail)
Email: ccr@nlci.com
Website: http://www.nlci.com/ccr/

Justice, Inc.
P.O. Box 2387
Indianapolis, IN 46206
Phone: (317) 634-9212
Fax: (812) 339-8109

Email: info@justiceinc.org
Website: http://www.justiceinc.org/

Iowa

Iowa Coalition for Human Rights
P.O. Box 1222
Iowa City, IA 52244-1222
Phone: (319) 339-1661
Fax: (319) 339-1661
Email: ichriowa@aol.com

Kansas

Freedom Coalition of Lawrence
P.O. Box 1991
Lawrence, KS 66044
Email: brownlcc@ukans.edu
Website: http://freedomcoalition.dhs.org/

Kentucky

Kentucky Fairness Alliance
P.O. Box 3912
Louisville, KY 40201
Phone: (502) 897-1973
Fax: (502) 896-0577
Email: kentuckyfairness@aol.com
Website: http://www.kentuckyfairness.org/

Louisiana

Louisiana Electorate of Gays and Lesbians
Phone: (504) 595-8586
Fax: (504) 595-8587
Email: legalinc@aol.com
Website: http://members.aol.com/legalinc/

Louisiana Lesbian and Gay Political Action Caucus
Phone: (504) 836-9086 (voice mail)
Fax: (504) 865-5784
Email: cdaigle@mailhost.tcs.tulane.edu
Website: http://www.lagpac.com

Maine

Maine Lesbian and Gay Political Alliance
P.O. Box 232
Hallowell, ME 04347
Phone: (800) 556-5472
Fax: (207) 761-8484
Email: heydave@aol.com
Website: http://www.firegirl.com/mlgpa/

Maryland

Free State Justice Campaign
8528 Bradford Road
Silver Spring, MD 20901
Phone: (301) 891-1111
Email: BlakeFreeState@aol.com
Website: http://www.freestatejustice.org/

Massachusetts

LGBT Political Alliance of Western Massachusetts
P.O. Box 1244
Northampton, MA 01060
Phone: (413) 549-5829
Fax: (413) 549-5829
Email: info@wmassalliance.org
Website: http://www.wmassalliance.org/

Michigan

Triangle Foundation
19641 West Seven Mile Road
Detroit, Michigan 48219-2721
Phone (313) 537-3323
Fax: (313) 537-3379
Email: Sean@tri.org
Website: http://www.tri.org

Minnesota

OutFront Minnesota
310 38th Street East
Suite 204
Minneapolis, MN 55409-1337

Phone: (800) 800-0350
Fax: (612) 822-8786
Email: outfront@outfront.org
Website: http://www.outfront.org/

Mississippi

Mississippi Gay Lobby
Phone: (601) 371-3019
Fax: (601) 371-3156
Email: GVV578A@prodigy.com
Website: http://www.missgaylobby.org/

Missouri

Privacy Rights and Education Project (PREP)
P.O. Box 24106
St. Louis, MO 63130
Phone: (314) 862-4900
Fax: (314) 862-8155
Email: prepstl@prepstl.org
Website: http://www.prepstl.org

Montana

PRIDE!
P.O. Box 775
Helena, MT 59624
Phone: (406) 442-9322
Fax: (406) 442-5589
Email: pride123@aol.com
Website: http://gaymontana.com/pride/

Nebraska

Citizens For Equal Protection
P.O. Box 55548
Omaha, NE 68155-0548
Phone: (402) 398-3027
Fax: (402) 445-6029
Email: cfep@geocities.com
Website: http://www.geocities.com/WestHollywood/Village/3805/

New Hampshire

Out and Equal—New Hampshire
P.O. Box 730
Concord, NH 03302-0730
Phone: 603-224-1686
Fax: 603-358-2145
Email: ONEofNH@aol.com
Website: http://members.aol.com/caglr/

New Jersey

New Jersey Lesbian and Gay Coalition
P.O. Box 11335
New Brunswick, NJ 08906-1335
Phone: (732) 828-6772
Fax: (732) 296-9787
Email: mail@njlgc.org
Website: http://www.njlgc.org/

New Mexico

Coalition for Equality in New Mexico
Phone: (505) 983-5758
Fax: (505) 995-0645
Email: Globall@cybermesa.com

Coalition for Gay and Lesbian Rights in New Mexico
Email: neuman@lanl.gov
Website: http://www.qrd.org/www/usa/new_mexico/coalition/

New York

Empire State Pride Agenda
New York City Office
647 Hudson Street
New York, NY 10014
Phone: (212) 627-0305
Fax: (212) 627-4136
Email: prideagenda@prideagenda.org
Website: http://www.prideagenda.org

New York Association for Gender Rights Advocacy
P.O. Box 524
Ithaca, NY 14851-0524

Phone: (212) 777-1215
Email: nyagra@nyagra.org
Website: http://www.nyagra.org

North Carolina

Equality North Carolina
P.O. Box 28768
Raleigh, NC 27611-8768
Phone: (919) 829-0343
Fax: (919) 828-3265
Email: project@equalitync.org
Website: http://www.equalitync.org

North Dakota

Equality North Dakota
P.O. Box 5222
Fargo, ND 58105-5222
Email: BUebel@webtv.net
Website: http://www.fmpflag.org/end.html

Ohio

Stonewall Columbus
1160 North High Street
P.O. Box 10814
Columbus, Ohio 43201
Phone: (614) 299-7764
Fax/TY: (614) 299-4408
Website: http://www.stonewall-columbus.org/

Oklahoma

Central Oklahoma Transgender Alliance
P.O. Box 60354
Oklahoma City, OK 73146
Website: http://www.ren.org/rafil/cota/c_o_t_a.htm

Oklahoma Gay and Lesbian Political Caucus
P.O. Box 61186
Oklahoma City, OK 73146
Phone: (405) 791-0202
Fax: (405) 528-0796
Email: gayoglpc@flash.net

Oregon

Basic Rights Oregon
P.O. Box 40625
Portland OR 97240
Phone: (503) 222-6151
Fax: (503) 236-6686
Email: BasicRO@aol.com
Website: http://www.teleport.com/~gerrit/oldBRO.html

It's Time, Oregon!
Phone: (503) 234-4704
Email: itstime@itstime.org
Website: http://www.itstime.org

Pennsylvania

League of Gay and Lesbian Voters (and Affiliated PAC)
5819-B Forward Avenue
Pittsburgh, PA 15217
Phone: (412) 421-4470
Fax: (412) 421-4470
Email: info@lglv.org
Website: http://www.lglv.org/

Philadelphia Lesbian and Gay Task Force
1616 Walnut Street
Suite 1005
Philadelphia, PA 19103-5313
Phone: (215) 772-2000
Fax: (215) 772-2004
Email: plgtf@op.net
Website: http://www.op.net/plgtf/

Statewide Pennsylvania Rights Coalition
P.O. Box 576
Howard, PA 16841
Phone: (717) 624-3339
Fax: (717) 624-8999
Email: sparc@sparc-pa.org
Website: http://www.sparc-pa.org

Western Pennsylvania Freedom to Marry Coalition
P.O. Box 81253
Pittsburgh, PA 15217-4253
Website: http://www.cs.cmu.edu/afs/cs/user/scotts/ftp/wpaf2mc/

Rhode Island

Rhode Island Alliance for Lesbian and Gay Civil Rights
P.O. Box 5758
Weybosset Hill Station
Providence, RI 02903-0758
Phone: (401) 521-GAYS
Fax: (401) 863-2045
Email: rialliance@aol.com
Website: http://members.aol.com/RIAlliance/

South Carolina

South Carolina G/L Pride Movement
P.O. Box 12648
Columbia, SC 29211
Phone: (803) 771-7713
Email: info@scglpm.org
Website: http://www.scglpm.org/

South Dakota

Free Americans Creating Equal Status (FACES of South Dakota, Inc.)
Email: onlc@sdsumus.sdstate.edu

Tennessee

Lesbian and Gay Coalition for Justice
P.O. Box 22901
Nashville, TN 37202-2901
Phone: (615) 298-5425
Fax: (615) 898-5881
Email: drturner@mindspring.com
Website: http://www.telalink.net/~lgcj/

Texas

Lesbian Gay Rights Lobby of Texas
P.O. Box 2340
Austin, TX 78768
Phone: (512) 474-5475
Fax: (512) 474-4511
Email: lgrltexas@aol.com
Website: http://www.lgrl.org

Utah

Gay and Lesbian Political Action Committee
Phone: 801-467-6204
Website: ghashang@netscape.net

Vermont

Vermont Freedom to Marry Task Force
P.O. Box 1312
Middlebury, VT 05753
Phone: (802) 388-2633
Website: http://www.vtfreetomarry.org/index.html

Virginia

Virginia Partisans Gay and Lesbian Democratic Club
P.O. Box 6243
Arlington, VA 22206-0243
Phone: (703) 658-5331
Email: info@vapartisans.org
Website: http://www.vapartisans.org/

Virginians for Justice
P.O. Box 342
Richmond, VA 23218-0342
Phone: (804) 643-4816
Fax: (804) 643-2050
Email: virginians4justice@juno.com
Website: http://www.visi.net/vj/

Washington

Legal Marriage Alliance of Washington
1122 East Pike
PAB 1190
Seattle, WA 98122-3934
Phone: (206) 464-3009
Email: lma@lmaw.org
Website: http://www.lmaw.org/

Log Cabin Republicans of Washington
P.O. Box 1802
Seattle, WA 98111-1802
Email: info@LogCabinWA.com
Website: http://www.LogCabinWA.com/

West Virginia

West Virginia Coalition for Lesbian and Gay Civil Rights
P.O. Box 11033
Charleston, WV 25339
Phone: (304) 343-7305
Email: wvlgc@aol.com
Website: http://members.aol.com/wvlgc/

Wisconsin

Action Wisconsin, Inc.: A Congress for Human Rights
P.O. Box 342
Madison, WI 53701-0342
Phone: (608) 283-3251
Email: info@actionwisconsin.org
Website: http://www.actionwisconsin.org

Wyoming

United Gays and Lesbians of Wyoming Fund for Social Change
P.O. Box 6837
Cheyenne, WY 82003-6837
Phone: (307) 778-7645
Email: info@uglw.org
Website: http://www.uglw.org

Selected Information, Media, and Resources

The Advocate
Website: http://www.advocate.com

Web version of the national LGBT magazine.

Gay and Lesbian Politics: WWW and Internet Resources
Website: http://www.indiana.edu/~glbtpol/

A selective guide to the best and most authoritative resources on politics, law, and policy related to LGBT people. Designed and maintained by Steve Sanders at Indiana University.

Data Lounge
Website: http://www.datalounge.com/datalounge

Provides a variety of services for and about LGBT people, including news.

The National Journal of Sexual Orientation Law
Website: http://sunsite.unc.edu/gaylaw/

The first online law journal in the country and the second devoted exclusively to legal issues affecting LGBT people.

ONE Institute/International Gay and Lesbian Archives (ONE/IGLA)
909 W. Adams Boulevard
Los Angeles, CA 90007
Phone: (213) 741-0094
Website: http://www.usc.edu/Library/oneigla/

Library and archive for LGBT history and heritage. Created in 1971 as the Western Gay Archives.

PlanetOut: NewsPlanet
Website: http://www.planetout.com/pno/

Provides a variety of services for and about LGBT people, including news.

Queer Resources Directory
Website: http://www.qrd.org/qrd/

One of the largest collections of LGBT material on the web.

The Source
Website: http://www.gaysource.com/index.html

A web-based gay community directory.

The Washington Blade
Website: http://www.washblade.com/

Web version of the national LGBT newspaper.

Chronology

Unless otherwise noted, information in this section was compiled by the authors from commonly reported newspaper stories, along with Barry D. Adam, *The Rise of a Gay and Lesbian Movement,* rev. ed. (New York: Twayne Publishers, 1995); Donald P. Haider-Markel, "From Bullhorns to PACs: Lesbian and Gay Politics, Interest Groups, and Policy." (Ph.D. diss. University of Wisconsin-Milwaukee, 1997); Mark Thompson, *The Long Road to Freedom* (New York: St. Martin's Press, 1994); and Alan S. Yang, *From Wrongs to Rights: Public Opinion on Gay and Lesbian Americans Moves Toward Equality* (Washington, DC: NGLTF, 1999).

1920   Congress first addresses homosexuality during a Senate investigation of "immoral conditions" of a homosexual nature at the naval training station in Newport, Rhode Island.

1924   The first gay rights group in the United States is established by a Chicago immigrant named Henry Gerber.

1945   The Veterans Benevolent Association becomes the first gay and lesbian membership-based organization in the United States.

1950   The U.S. Senate releases a report on the security threat homosexuals pose to the federal government. (The report is cited as U.S. Senate, 81st Congress, 2nd Session, Committee on Expenditures in Executive Departments, *Employment of Homosexuals and Other Sex Perverts in Government* (Washington, DC: 1950).)

1951   The Mattachine Society of Los Angeles is formed by a small group of communists.

1953   The security threat posed by homosexuals is raised within the context of communist infiltration of the government during the McCarthy hearings. Witnesses suggest that homosexual government employees could be blackmailed by communist spies.

First issue of *ONE,* a homosexual magazine, is published.

1954   Senator Wiley (R-WI) sends a letter to the U.S. postmaster general demanding that a gay magazine (*ONE*) be blocked from using the U.S. mail because of its devotion to the "advancement of sexual perversion." The postmaster general complies with the request until the decision is overruled by the Supreme Court in 1958.

1955 Daughters of Bilitis is formed in San Francisco by Del Martin and Phyllis Lyons.

1956 The first issue of the *Ladder,* a lesbian newspaper published by the Daughters of Bilitis, appears in print.

1958 The Daughters of Bilitis, New York chapter, is founded by Barbara Gittings.

1963 Four groups form the loose coalition East Coast Homophile Organizations (ECHO) at a January meeting in Philadelphia.

The early lobbying efforts of a homosexual group, the Mattachine Society, so enrage Representative John Dowdy that in May he initiates hearings on the issue and introduces a bill to revoke the Mattachine's permit to raise funds in Washington, D.C. During congressional hearings, Mattachine representatives try to frame homosexuality as a civil rights issue by discussing employment discrimination, but committee members use the venue to speak against the immorality of homosexuality and to question witnesses on deviant sexual behavior. The bill, HR 5990, overwhelmingly passes the House on August 11, 1964. The bill is watered down to the point of being largely symbolic and never reaches a vote in the Senate.

1964 Gay businessmen in San Francisco form the Society for Individual Rights (SIR). SIR engages in political work, social functions, and publishes its own newsletter, the *Vector.*

In December a group of ministers and homophile leaders form the Council on Religion and the Homosexual.

1965 The first gay protests at the White House and Pentagon (and at Independence Hall in Philadelphia) take place.

1966 The membership of the Society for Individual Rights reaches 1,000.

Homophile leaders and activists from fifteen groups hold a convention in Kansas City, Missouri.

In August homophile groups form a loose federation called the North American Conference of Homophile Organizations (NACHO). The groups combine resources to create a national legal fund to challenge antigay policies and actions. The organization also sponsors "days of protest" in cities around the country.

1967 In August the third national North American Conference of Homophile Organizations (NACHO) meets in Washington, D.C.

In September the first issue of *The Advocate,* a national gay magazine, appears in print, and the ACLU national board calls for decriminalizing consensual sex practices.

1968 Metropolitan Community Church, a gay congregation, is formed by Troy Perry in Los Angeles.

In June the Mattachine Society of New York successfully lobbies Mayor John Lindsay to issue an executive order forbidding city police from making arrests for "homosexual solicitation" without a signed citizen complaint.

In July gays engage in an antidiscrimination protest outside the San Francisco Federal Building.

In December the New Jersey Supreme Court rules that homosexuals have the right to gather in public, overturning the revocation of three New Jersey bars' licenses for "permitting apparent homosexuals to congregate."

1969 In June a police raid sets off the Stonewall Riots in New York City. In July the Gay Liberation Front is formed in New York City.

In August the fifth annual meeting of NACHO takes place, this time in Kansas City, Missouri.

In October the University of Minnesota recognizes a club for gays and sympathizers called FREE (Fight Repression of Erotic Expression).

In December the Gay Activists Alliance is formed in New York City as a less radical alternative to the Gay Liberation Front.

The California Supreme Court rules that the state cannot revoke a teacher's credentials over charges of homosexual conduct.

The Los Angeles chapter of the Gay Liberation Front is formed.

1970 Marches to commemorate the Stonewall Riots take place in June in New York City, Los Angeles, and Chicago.

The Daughters of Bilitis convenes in New York City and dissolves its national structure into a federation of autonomous chapters.

Black Panther leader Huey Newton call on blacks to view the Gay Liberation Front and the Women's Liberation Front as "friends and potential allies," and says that gays "might be the most oppressed people in our society."

After gay New York University students are not allowed to have a dance, 2,500 gays riot in New York.

The last annual NACHO meeting is broken up by radical gays.

Unidos, a Los Angeles organization for gay Chicanas/Chicanos, holds its first meeting.

Three demonstrations in October cap a week-long sit-in protest of New York University's antigay hiring policies.

The Reverend Troy Perry (founder of the Metropolitan Community Church) runs as a write-in candidate for California's lieutenant governor in the November elections.

1971 Gay pride marches take place in New York City, Los Angeles, Philadelphia, Detroit, San Francisco, and Washington, D.C.

New York City's Gay Liberation Front splinters into smaller groups. One is the Effeminists, a group of gay men who believe that gay men's oppression and women's oppression are caused by male supremacy and that both issues need to be addressed together.

In Minnesota the first same-sex marriage case in the United States, *Baker v. Nelson,* is decided. The plaintiffs argue that the state marriage statute, as interpreted to provide only for opposite-sex marriages, is unconstitutional on several bases. The court rules against the plaintiffs.

The First Gay Liberation National Conference is held in Austin, Texas.

In June the San Francisco Association for Mental Health issues a policy statement saying that "homosexuality can no longer be equated with sickness."

In July at city hall in Bridgeport, Connecticut, 200 gays protest police harassment. Meanwhile, 100 gays march in Dallas, Texas.

In October a mixed crowd of 500 gay and straight students attends a fund-raising dance for the Kansas Gay Liberation Front in Lawrence.

In November Indiana gay activist Charles Avery is named executive secretary of the newly formed People's Party.

1972   Gay delegates appear on the floor of the National Democratic Convention for the first time.

Los Angeles district attorney candidate Vincent Bugliosi campaigns at sixteen gay bars.

New York congresswoman Bella Abzug actively seeks the gay vote and campaigns in bathhouses.

The Gay Switchboard, an information and referral service, opens in New York City.

The February issue of the *New Republic* notes lesbian and gay organization and increasing political clout in an article entitled "The Gay Vote."

In March the California Democratic Council adopts a sweeping gay plank, endorsing the legalization of consensual gay sex; honorable discharges from the military; and a ban on discrimination based on sexual orientation.

In April William Johnson of the Church of Christ becomes the first open homosexual permitted for ordination in a major denomination.

In June an estimated 2,500 gays march in Philadelphia's first gay pride parade.

In San Jose, California, a lesbian wins custody of her children in what is believed to be the first such victory for an open lesbian.

In Chicago the Gay Community Counseling Center opens.

Gay teachers organize a caucus within the National Education Association.

In July Sacramento State University launches what is believed to be the nation's first college-affiliated gay studies program.

In August San Francisco's Gay Activists' Alliance disbands and is reformed as the Gay Voters' League, endorsing the reelection of Richard Nixon.

In September the Long Beach, California, gay bar owners association, FROGS (Friendly Relations of Gay Society), holds a two-week "Frog Festival," a public relations stunt attempting to win the approval of the straight community.

A New York City policy requiring known homosexual cab drivers to undergo regular psychiatric checks is scrapped after GAA demonstrations and sit-ins.

In October the lesbian magazine the *Ladder,* America's oldest existing gay publication, folds after sixteen years of publication.

1973   Jim Foster becomes treasurer of the California Democratic Committee.

Harvey Milk runs unsuccessfully for the Board of Supervisors in San Francisco.

Jim Owles runs for a New York City Council seat and loses.

Jones v. Hallahan, a Kentucky same-sex marriage case, results in a ruling against the plaintiffs, two females who sought to marry each other.

Jack Baker runs for a Minneapolis City Council seat but loses.

City Attorney Bert Pines, Mayor Tom Bradley, and Councilman Robert Stevenson, three Los Angeles candidates who courted the gay vote, are swept into office in an early show of gay voting power.

Connie "Mac" McConnohie runs for a Detroit City Council seat and loses.

Oregon wins its case permitting the firing of a teacher because she is a lesbian.

In February twelve gay and bisexual women form a gay group in Honolulu.

In April in Los Angeles, California, over 2,000 attend the West Coast Lesbian Conference.

The ACLU of Southern California forms a gay rights panel.

In May the All-Ohio Gay Conference in Columbus and march on the state capital takes place.

In June *Gay,* the nation's second-largest gay newspaper, folds in New York City after three years of publication.

The Lesbian Liberation Committee of New York's Gay Activist Alliance breaks away to form a separate organization, the Lesbian Feminist Liberation.

In August the American Bar Association adopts a resolution urging states to repeal all antigay sex laws.

Jo Daly of San Francisco becomes the first openly gay person appointed to a city position when she takes a post on the Cablevision Task Force.

In September the American Baptist Association, the American Lutheran Association, the United Presbyterians, the United Methodists, and the Society of Friends (Quakers) launch the National Task Force on Gay People in the Church to press for reforms in the National Council of Churches of Christ.

In October fifty gays and lesbians attend a conference in Champaign, Illinois, sponsored by the National Gay Mobilizing Committee.

The National Gay Task Force is formed in New York City to "focus on broad national issues" and bring "gay liberation into the mainstream of American civil rights."

The Lambda Legal Defense and Education Fund is incorporated in Albany, New York.

In December the American Psychiatric Association's board of trustees votes to remove homosexuality from its list of psychiatric disorders.

The U.S. Civil Service Commission proposes that new regulations keyed to job performance replace the ban on hiring or retaining homosexuals in federal agencies.

1974   The AT&T corporation enacts a nondiscrimination policy that includes sexual orientation.

A Washington state same-sex marriage case, *Singer v. Hara,* results in a loss for the plaintiffs, John F. Singer and Paul Barwick. The plaintiffs had argued that Washington marriage statutes did not prohibit same-sex marriages; therefore a license must be issued. The plaintiffs also argued for the first time that the state's Equal Rights Amendment (ERA) banned discrimination on the basis of sex, which they in turn argued had occurred in the denial of their marriage license.

The National Education Association votes to support gays' right to teach.

RFD, a publication for gay men in rural areas, begins publishing in Iowa.

In February gay fundamentalists leave the Metropolitan Community Church of Portland, Oregon, to establish a new evangelical church.

In April Kathy Kozachenko becomes the first openly gay person to be elected to a public office in the United States, taking a seat on the Ann Arbor, Michigan, City Council.

May sees the first introduction of gay rights legislation in Congress, sponsored by Bella Abzug and Edward Koch, both New York representatives.

A majority of 205 respondents to a poll by the *Advocate* magazine strongly back zaps, rallies, and other militant tactics for advancing gay rights.

A Philadelphia judge awards a lesbian couple custody of a transvestite teenage boy who is not biologically related to either of them.

In June, on its second birthday, the National Bisexual Liberation movement claims 1,600 members in five cities.

Hawaii holds its first gay pride parade.

The National Teachers Association votes to add the words "sexual orientation" to the antidiscrimination provisions of its membership policy.

Boston activists file incorporation papers for a Gay United Fund, the nation's first gay fund-raising and disbursement project.

In October more than $1 million in federal grants are awarded to the Gay and Lesbian Services Center of Los Angeles.

In November, Elaine Noble becomes the first open lesbian to be elected as a state representative in the United States in Boston, Massachusetts.

The Lesbian Mothers Defense Fund is formed in November in Seattle, Washington.

In December Minnesota State Senator Allan Spear reveals that he is homosexual.

1975   Two men from Phoenix are granted a marriage license by a county clerk. This license is later revoked.

On recommendation of the Boulder, Colorado, city district attorney, County Clerk Cela Rorex issues Dave Zamora and Ave McCord a marriage license. This causes a month-long rush on the clerk's office by same-sex couples seeking marriage licenses, until the state attorney general voids the D.A.'s recommendation. A court later revokes all of the licenses.

In January a national gay civil rights bill, HR 166, is introduced in the House of Representatives.

The University of Montana offers the state's first gay studies course.

The American Psychological Association and the American Association for the Advancement of Science agree that homosexuality is not an illness.

Rudi Cox of San Francisco becomes the first openly gay deputy sheriff in the nation.

In April in Iowa City 400 people attend the second annual Midwest Gay Pride Conference.

The Arizona Supreme Court holds gay marriage bans unconstitutional. The state legislature subsequently passes a bill defining marriage as possible only between a man and a woman.

In July the United States Civil Service Commission drops its ban on lesbians and gays in civilian federal jobs.

In August the Moscow, Idaho, City Council appoints openly gay Gilbert E. Preston to the city's Fair Housing Commission.

In October 400 lesbians and gay men in Washington, D.C., attend a GAA-sponsored three-day conference called "The Federal Government and Gays."

In November the Mississippi Gay Alliance holds the first gay and lesbian convention in the state.

In December in Philadelphia, sixty gay activists hold a sit-in at a city council meeting to protest alleged stalling on a gay rights bill.

Progay liberal George Moscone wins a run-off election to become San Francisco's mayor.

1976 In January Mayor Moscone of San Francisco appoints gay activist Harvey Milk to the Board of Permit Appeals.

The California Insurance Commission issues new regulations for insurance companies that forbid discrimination on the basis of sexual orientation.

In February candidate for president Jimmy Carter says he opposes discrimination on the basis of sexual orientation.

In April the Metropolitan Life Insurance Company accords gay couples married status for life insurance beneficiary rights purposes if they have lived together for at least a year.

In June after Jimmy Carter withdraws his support of a gay rights plank in the Democratic Party platform, the platform committee of the Democratic National Committee votes to remove it.

Courts force Rhode Island to allow gays to participate in the state's bicentennial parade.

The Democratic National Convention in New York City in July does not include any discussion of gay and lesbian concerns, and a subsequent protest attracts about 600 gays and lesbians.

In August the U.S. Immigration and Naturalization Service restricts its ban on known homosexuals to those who had been convicted of a same-sex crime.

In September President Gerald Ford, cornered by activists in Ann Arbor, Michigan, confesses that he was not aware that homosexuality was used as a basis for exclusion in immigration.

Controversial San Francisco gay activist Reverend Ray Broshears, who had advocated using guns for gay street patrol, is appointed to the Republican State Central Committee of California.

1977 A ballot initiative to repeal a gay rights law in Dade County, Florida, sets off a wave of similar initiatives around the country.

In the first official visit to the White House, fourteen gay and lesbian activists meet with Presidential Liaison to Minority Communities Midge Costanza.

Under congressional pressure, the federal Department of Housing and Urban Development repeals three-week-old regulations that would have allowed gay and lesbian couples to be considered for public housing.

The National Gay Leadership Conference, sponsored by Dignity International, the Gay Rights National Lobby, the National Gay Task Force, and the United Federation of Metropolitan Community Churches, meets in Denver. Over 400 representatives from various lesbian and gay groups determine that the movement must focus on education, legislation, and organization.

In September the Internal Revenue Service drops a rule that required gay educational and charitable groups to publicly state that homosexuality is a "sickness, disturbance, or diseased pathology" before they would be eligible for full tax-exempt status.

In October the International Association of Chiefs of Police votes to oppose the hiring of gay and lesbian police officers.

In November Harvey Milk becomes the first openly gay man to be elected to the San Francisco Board of Supervisors.

1978   The Log Cabin Clubs begin in California. Gay conservatives rally to oppose the Briggs initiative, which would have prevented gays from teaching in public schools. The Log Cabin Club is a reference to Abraham Lincoln and the heritage of the Republican Party.

After years of being denied recognition on campus, the University of Missouri's Gay People's Union receives official approval, gaining university funding.

In April nearly 1,000 demonstrators march in downtown Manhattan demanding passage of the city's gay rights bill, denied for seven years. The bill fails again.

A dinner sponsored by the Municipal Elections Committee of Los Angles, one of the first gay political action coalitions in the nation, raises $40,000 for southern California candidates supporting gay rights.

Openly gay student Dan Jones is elected student body president of the conservative Michigan State University.

In June the Triangle Gay Community Center, the first of its kind in New York City, is formally dedicated.

A record 240,000 people turn out for Gay Pride Day in San Francisco.

The U.S. Trademark Office refuses to trademark the title of *Gaysweek* magazine, calling it "immoral."

The American Nurses Association passes a resolution endorsing civil rights legislation banning discrimination on the basis of sexual orientation.

The Federal Communication Commission rules that gay people must be included in the "community ascertainment" efforts of radio stations.

The Pentagon gives gay veterans permission to upgrade their discharge status based on service records, which entitles them to a considerable increase in veterans' benefits.

In October the acclaimed gay documentary *Word Is Out* was aired on most PBS stations around the nation.

In November San Francisco Supervisor Harvey Milk and Mayor George Moscone are assassinated by political rival Dan White.

The Gay Activists Alliance of Washington, D.C., files a $10 million lawsuit against the Metropolitan Area Transit Authority for refusing to rent the group advertising space on buses. Two years later, the group wins in federal court.

1979 After two years of deliberation on a case involving the Pacific Telephone company, the California Supreme Court rules in May that privately owned utilities cannot discriminate against homosexuals.

The California Supreme Court also rules that, contrary to assumptions underlying much police harassment of gays, the state may not punish solicitation in public for a sexual act that is legal in private.

A Senate version of a civil rights bill for gays and lesbians is introduced by Senator Paul Tsongas (D-MA). The only national lobbyists for the gay community in Washington are Steve Endean (director and lobbyist for Gay Rights National Lobby) and Adam DeBaugh (field marshal for the Universal Fellowship of Metropolitan Community Churches). Cosponsors on the bill are Daniel Patrick Moynihan (D-NY), Lowell Weicker (R-CT), and Bob Packwood (R-OR).

In his January inaugural address, California Governor Jerry Brown calls for the inclusion of protections for gays in antidiscrimination laws.

More than 200 gay activists march on Sacramento to urge passage of AB-1, the California gay rights bill. A version of the bill does not become law for over a decade.

A task force appointed by Oregon Governor Bob Straub recommends specific policies for ending discrimination against lesbians and gays in housing, employment, criminal law, insurance, and government policies.

In January gay activist Harry Britt is appointed to Harvey Milk's seat on the San Francisco Board of Supervisors.

In February gay leaders from across the country attend a conference in Philadelphia to plan a national gay march on Washington.

In April gays in Houston protest police harassment.

In a May White House ceremony, President Carter names openly lesbian Jill Schropp from Seattle to the newly recognized National Advisory Council on Women.

Three thousand people riot at San Francisco City Hall over the verdict of manslaughter against Dan White for killing Harvey Milk and George Moscone (he received a sentence of seven years and eight months).

In August the American Presbyterian Church, representing more than 3 million members, adopts a policy opposing ordination of gay clergy, elders, and deacons.

U.S. Representative Larry McDonald (D-GA) introduces a measure that would put Congress on record opposing gay rights; it passes the House, but dies in Senate committee.

The Immigration and Naturalization Service announces that it will no longer ferret out homosexuals among visitors to the United States and will apply the ban on homosexual travelers only when sexuality becomes an issue. The State Department orders consular officials worldwide to continue to deny visas to gays.

In September an appointment to the Los Angeles Superior Court makes Stephen Lachs America's first openly gay judge.

Dignity, the Catholic gay organization, celebrates its tenth anniversary at an international convention in San Diego.

In October the first national March on Washington for Lesbian and Gay Rights draws more than 100,000 demonstrators.

During a tour of the United States, Pope John Paul II reaffirms the Catholic Church's position that homosexual activity is sinful.

The ACLU institutes a National Gay Rights Project.

New York City Mayor Ed Koch installs David Rothenberg, the openly gay founder of the Fortune Society, as a member of the city's Commission on Human Rights.

In December gay and lesbian Mormons hold their first national conference in Los Angeles.

Openly gay Harry Britt wins reelection to the San Francisco Board of Supervisors.

1980   The National Gay Task Force's annual budget reaches $260,000.

MELCA, Los Angeles's gay political action committee, raises $50,000 at a fund raiser.

At the Democratic National Convention there are seventy-seven lesbians and gays among the delegates.

"Gay Vote 1980" a nationwide drive to secure a gay rights plank in national party platforms results in about a dozen gay delegates in the Iowa caucuses.

The National Gay and Lesbian Archives are inaugurated in Los Angeles.

After more than 100 men are arrested at a gay bar in January, Chicago Mayor Jane Byrne publicly chastises police officers for campaigning against homosexual prostitution rather than "true crime."

Candidate for president Ronald Reagan says he will not condone homosexuality.

A formal statement from President Carter dashes hopes that his administration will issue an executive order banning antigay discrimination in the federal government or supporting a gay rights plank at the Democratic convention.

In April 500 people participate in the first gay pride celebration in St. Louis, Missouri.

In a reversal of policy, Federal Bureau of Prisons Director Norman Carlsen allows inmates to receive some gay publications.

Time magazine reveals that its best-selling issue for 1979 featured the cover story "How Gay is Gay?"

In May the American Jewish Congress adopts a resolution recommending abolishing antigay discrimination in employment, housing, and military service.

In June the Democratic Party adopts a plank insisting on protecting "all groups from discrimination," and opposing the ban on homosexual visitors and immigrants to the United States.

Two new lobbies target the gay rights movement, the American Family Institute and Americans Against HR 2074 (the federal gay civil rights bill).

In July the U.S. House of Representatives votes overwhelmingly to deny federal funding to legal groups that work for equal rights for homosexuals.

More than 200 members of the Committee of Black Gay Men from around the country attend a major planning conference in Chicago.

A statewide gay pride picnic in Bozeman, Montana, draws more than 200 participants.

More than 500 Christian fundamentalists demonstrate against the fifth annual Southeastern Conference of Lesbians and Gay Men, held in Memphis, Tennessee.

The Screen Actors Guild adds sexual orientation to its nondiscrimination clause for employment.

Gay leaders hail a Justice Department ruling that immigration officials may enforce antihomosexual provisions only if arriving foreigners voluntarily admit they are gay.

At their semiannual convention, American Bar Association members overwhelmingly defeat measures in support of gay civil rights.

Conservative Congressman Robert Bauman (R-MD) confesses to the afflictions of "alcoholism and homosexuality" after he is accused of soliciting a sixteen-year-old boy for sex. He loses his reelection bid in November.

The Human Rights Campaign Fund, a new political action committee to support progay candidates at the federal level, is established in Washington, D.C.

In December Gay Expo, featuring products from lubricants to designer fashions, attracts nearly 35,000 visitors to the Los Angeles Convention Center.

1981   This year marks the first appearances of what is sometimes called "gay cancer" in U.S. urban areas.

John Boswell's *Christianity, Social Tolerance, and Homosexuality* is published. Hailed as an epic, it opens a new era of gay and lesbian scholarship.

Education and fundraising for the illness later known as AIDS coalesces into the formation of the world's largest AIDS information and service organization in New York City, Gay Men's Health Crisis.

In January the Gay Press Association, comprising more than eighty publications from around the country, is founded at a New York conference.

In February Representative John Hinson (R-MS) is arrested in a Capitol Hill bathroom and charged with oral sodomy; he pleads no contest and is given a thirty-day suspended sentence.

In June in a first for her city, Chicago Mayor Jane Byrne officially proclaims June 28 "Gay Pride Parade Day."

In July eight Texas transsexuals successfully litigate against a Houston ordinance that forbids cross-dressing, forcing the city to repeal the law.

More than 250 people from six countries attend the Sixth Annual Conference of Gay and Lesbian Jews in Philadelphia.

In August leaders from seventeen local gay and lesbian groups form a town council in Lincoln, Nebraska, to work for gay legal concerns in their state.

In September, from his Manhattan apartment, author Larry Kramer spearheads mobilization of gay New Yorkers stricken by Kaposi's sarcoma, of which more than 100 cases have been reported.

Two hundred Christian fundamentalists marching to "bring San Francisco back to Jesus" are met by 2,000 gay demonstrators, including dozens of bearded men in nuns' habits.

The California Office of Post-Secondary Education grants Los Angeles's ONE Institute recognition as a Graduate School of Homophile Studies able to grant master's and doctoral degrees.

The tenth annual Miss Gay America Pageant takes place in Dallas despite the protests of religious groups and the Ku Klux Klan.

In October a gay rights bill is reintroduced in the U.S. Senate by Paul Tsongas (D-MA); cosponsors included Edward Kennedy (D-MA), Alan Cranston, Daniel Inouye (D-HI), Lowell Weicker (R-CT), and Robert Packwood (R-OR).

1982   All seven justices of the Florida Supreme Court agree that the Trask-Bush Amendment, aimed at forcing gay college groups off campus, is unconstitutional.

Minneapolis Police Chief Tony Bouza announces that officers using ethnic or antigay slurs will be disciplined.

The National Gay Task Force launches the Violence Project to combat the rise of homophobic violence in the United States.

The San Francisco Board of Supervisors unanimously orders the city's police department to recruit gays and lesbians.

In April the House Subcommittee on Health and the Environment, chaired by California Representative Henry Waxman, holds the first federal hearing on Kaposi's sarcoma and related opportunistic infections.

In May more than 500 gay men pack a New York University auditorium for a briefing on gay-related immunodeficiency (GRID).

More than 1,000 Texans rally in Dallas to protest poor treatment of gays by the police department.

In June the American Nazi Party holds an "antihomosexual" rally during Gay Pride Day in Chicago with over 2,000 people participating.

More than sixty-five lesbian and gay activists attend the Democratic Party's midterm convention in Philadelphia, pressuring for gay civil rights.

In August the Centers for Disease Control in Atlanta reports ten to twenty cases of Gay-Related Immune Deficiency (GRID) being discovered every week across the nation, with a total of 202 deaths attributed to the syndrome so far.

The first Gay Games are held in San Francisco with 1,300 athletes from ten nations.

In September former major league baseball player Glenn Burke comes out.

A groundbreaking report issued by a task force of the San Francisco Archdiocese of the Roman Catholic Church makes fifty-four progay recommendations, calling for an end to antigay violence and the recognition of the spiritual value of gay sexuality.

A YMCA in Phoenix is converted into a gay community services center.

In November the CDC reports 775 cases nationally, with 294 deaths, of the illness it is now calling Acquired Immune Deficiency Syndrome (AIDS). Scientists also begin to believe AIDS is caused by a virus.

In December it is discovered that AIDS can be transmitted by transfusion.

San Francisco gays start a "Dump Diane" campaign after Mayor Diane Feinstein vetoes a domestic partnership bill.

1983   United Press International (UPI) enacts a nondiscrimination policy that includes sexual orientation.

In January America's largest blood banks, the Red Cross, the American Association of Blood Banks, and the Council of Community Blood Centers, issue a joint rejection of proposals to ban blood donations from gay males.

Doctors in France isolate a virus (eventually known as HIV) they believe causes AIDS.

In February the Los Angeles Police Commission adopts recruitment policy reforms recommended by gay activists.

In March, in a first for that state, Ohio Governor Richard Celeste creates a blue ribbon commission on discrimination and sexual minorities.

Describing them as "prudent and temporary measures" the Department of Health and Human Services suggests that the government recommend voluntary screening of sexually active gay and bisexual men from blood donation programs.

In April Democratic presidential front-runner Gary Hart addresses MECLA, the major gay political fund-raising group in Los Angeles.

In May nearly 9,000 demonstrators in Manhattan and 10,000 in Los Angeles march to demand federal action on AIDS; similar marches take place in San Francisco, Chicago, and Houston.

San Francisco Mayor Diane Feinstein declares the first week of the month AIDS Awareness Week.

Mario Cuomo makes the first appearance ever by a New York governor before a gay group when he speaks at a dinner for the Fund for Human Dignity.

The International Ladies Garment Workers Union unanimously adopts a gay and lesbian rights resolution.

Angry over the New York City Council's repeated rejection of a gay rights bill, organizers reroute the Fourteenth Annual Gay Pride March in order to snarl traffic on Manhattan's West Side.

In June gay and lesbian activists organize a boycott against the *New York Times,* protesting the paper's meager coverage of the AIDS epidemic and of the gay movement.

In July Gerry Studds (D-MA), facing censure for his relationship with a seventeen-year-old congressional page, becomes the first member of Congress to come out as gay.

A nationwide toll-free AIDS hotline begins operation as a project of the U.S. Department of Health and Human Services.

In September at a fund-raising banquet for the Human Rights Campaign Fund (HRCF) in New York, the Reverend Jesse Jackson publicly invites gays to engage in "meaningful dialogue" with the civil rights movement.

Seattle's gay leaders, along with the ACLU, call on the city's police chief to investigate an AIDS patient list, called "AIDS Alert," that was circulated among local police officers; the chief apologizes and has the list destroyed.

The American Academy of Pediatrics approves a proposal that homosexuality be considered an "alternate choice of sexual expression."

A national AIDS vigil is held in Washington, D.C., following similar events across the country including a gathering of 10,000 in Los Angeles.

In November openly gay Richard Heyman is elected mayor in Key West, Florida.

Openly gay John Laird is elected mayor in Santa Cruz, California.

Openly gay David Scondras is elected to the Boston City Council.

In December the head of the Phoenix County Board of Supervisors proposes that medical experiments be performed on homosexuals instead of animals; he later says it had been a joke, but is forced to resign under public pressure a month later.

1984   Mayor Feinstein closes San Francisco bathhouses in an attempt to slow the spread of AIDS.

The director of the National Gay Task Force, Jeffrey Levi, testifies before the U.S. House Subcommittee on Criminal Justice in the first hearing on police harassment of gays.

A House report is released that lambastes federal handling of the AIDS crisis.

In January the U.S. Conference of Mayors passes a resolution calling for an end to antigay bias.

In March in *Board of Education v. National Gay Task Force,* a law prohibiting teachers from discussing homosexuality in the classroom is struck down by a federal appeals court; a year later, the U.S. Supreme Court, taking its first gay-related case in seventeen years, affirms the lower court's decision on First Amendment grounds.

Denver Mayor Federico Pena and U.S. Representative Pat Schroeder are among leaders boycotting Denver's annual St. Patrick's Day Parade after the parade's organizers decide to exclude gay marchers.

Presidential candidate Jesse Jackson attends a meeting at New York's Lesbian and Gay Community Services Center.

In April, two years after homosexual sodomy was legalized through litigation there, conservatives in Texas urge a ban on homosexual acts to prevent the spread of AIDS.

The United Methodist Church votes to ban the ordination of gay ministers.

In July 100,000 lesbians and gays march for gay rights in the streets outside the Democratic National Convention in San Francisco.

In August for the first time an organized gay presence is visible during the Republican National Convention.

Bobbi Campbell, the first person with AIDS to appear on the cover of *Newsweek* magazine, dies in San Francisco.

In September a federal government proposal for a list of Americans exposed to the AIDS virus draws fire from gay and civil rights leaders; the proposal is dropped.

In October the Federation of AIDS-Related Organizations hires a lobbyist in Washington, D.C.

The General Accounting Office reveals that the military's antigay exclusionary policy costs taxpayers millions of dollars annually—$23 million in 1983 alone.

In November the FBI releases more than 7,500 pages of material gathered on gay groups over a period of more than thirty years.

West Hollywood, California, residents vote for incorporation and elect a majority of openly gay city council members, making it America's first gay-controlled city. They also make Valerie Terrigno the first lesbian mayor in the country.

In November Massachusetts Democrat Gerry Studds, the first openly gay member of Congress, easily wins reelection after being forced out of the closet by a congressional investigation.

In December two flight attendants, placed on medical leave by United Airlines because they had AIDS, file a $10 million reinstatement lawsuit; three months later, they settle out of court for back pay and full benefits.

PBS announces the forthcoming broadcast of a show on its *NOVA* series titled "AIDS: Chapter One."

1985   In January the day after federal officials announced the availability of a blood test for HTLV-3, the virus suspected to lead to AIDS, sixteen gay organizations join the National Gay Task Force in urging gay men not to take the test on grounds of potential discrimination, unreliability, and questionable confidentiality.

In February the Reagan administration's proposed budget for 1986 reveals a $12 million cut in AIDS-related funding.

In March for the first time police recruits in Milwaukee are given sensitivity training on dealing with gays and lesbians.

The FDA licenses the ELISA test, the first procedure to detect the presence of HTLV-3.

In April 2,000 scientists and 30 nations are represented when the first International Conference on AIDS is held in Atlanta, Georgia.

Reflecting a nationwide trend, the Kirk and Nice Funeral Home of Philadelphia refuses to handle the corpse of a person who had died of AIDS.

In May under the threat of a lawsuit, the Big Brothers/Big Sisters organization of Sacramento, California, reverses its practice of excluding gay men and lesbians as volunteers.

In June Massachusetts Governor Dukakis earns the wrath of lesbian and gay activists when he orders the removal of two children from the care of gay foster parents.

The Harvey Milk High School, an education alternative for lesbian and gay youth, opens in New York City's Greenwich Village.

A meeting of fifty-three bathhouse owners from around the country unanimously agrees to promote "sexual responsibility" by distributing AIDS literature and condoms in their establishments.

In July a Minnesota judge denies custody of Sharon Kowalski, a paralyzed lesbian, to her lover; Kowalski's father is named conservator instead.

Entertainer Ann-Margret and Los Angeles Mayor Tom Bradley lead the city's first "AIDS Walk" to raise funds for the AIDS Project in Los Angeles.

In September the Defense Department announces that it will test all military recruits for exposure to HTLV-3 and bar those who test positive.

After an announcement by the New York City Board of Education that it would allow children with AIDS to attend school, nearly 10,000 parents in the city borough of Queens keep their children home in protest.

Elizabeth Taylor announces that she will chair the newly formed American Foundation for AIDS Research.

Actor Rock Hudson dies a year and a half after being diagnosed with AIDS. Hudson's death marks a turning point, increasing public support for AIDS funding and people with AIDS.

The AFL/CIO goes on record opposing HTLV-3 testing of workers by employers.

The U.S. House of Representatives passes an appropriations bill with an amendment providing that certain AIDS research funds "may be used by the Surgeon General for closing or quarantining any bathhouse or massage parlor which . . . can be determined to facilitate the transmission or spread of . . . AIDS."

The New York State Public Health Council, acting on Governor Cuomo's initiative, passes a sixty-day emergency measure giving local officials the power to shut down any establishment that makes facilities available for oral or anal sex.

Participants in San Francisco's annual memorial march for Harvey Milk plaster the side of the Federal Building with the names of those who have died of AIDS.

Warning that the AIDS epidemic is "more dangerous than nuclear war" right-wing extremist Lyndon LaRouche launches a campaign against gay civil rights, using the slogan "Spread Panic, Not AIDS."

Gay activists demonstrate against the *New York Post* for homophobic news stories, editorials, and headlines that refer to gay bars as "AIDS dens."

1986   The U.S. Supreme Court upholds Georgia's antisodomy law in *Bowers v. Hardwick.*

The ACLU's executive director and board of directors say their organization will seek to eliminate legal barriers preventing gays from marrying.

The Texas Board of Health gives tentative approval to adding AIDS to the list of the state's diseases requiring quarantine; the idea is eventually dropped.

Michigan lesbians hold the fourth in a series of blood drives to show their support for gay men.

The Reagan administration proposes to screen out immigrants who test positive for HIV antibodies.

The U.S. Justice Department announces a plan to scuttle its policy of asking prospective prosecutors whether they are gay.

In April gay leaders meet with Surgeon General C. Everett Koop for the first time in order to brief him on AIDS issues.

AIDS officially becomes the leading killer in New York City of men aged thirty to thirty-four and of women aged twenty-five to twenty-nine.

The mayor of Anchorage, Alaska, withdraws his support for legal employment protection for gays, saying that AIDS has turned gay rights into a health issue.

A California insurance firm that sought to identify applicants who might have AIDS is hit with an $11 million lawsuit filed by the National Gay Rights Advocates; the company later settles out of court.

Actress Elizabeth Taylor, testifying before a Senate appropriations subcommittee, calls for a "tenfold expansion" in AIDS funding.

The federal government announces awards of $100 million in a five-year program to evaluate promising AIDS drugs.

The police department of Atlanta, Georgia, decides to allow openly gay people to join the force.

Retired Redskins football player Jerry Smith discloses that he has AIDS. He dies in October.

In October Pope John Paul II issues a letter calling gay people "intrinsically disordered" and maintaining that homosexuality can never be reconciled with church doctrine.

Coretta Scott King publicly proclaims her "solidarity with the gay and lesbian community," and blasts the U.S. Supreme Court decision in *Bowers v. Hardwick*.

In November the *Wall Street Journal* begins using the word "gay" instead of "homosexual" in its headlines and articles.

In December, in the largest settlement in gay litigation history, the Pacific Bell Telephone Company establishes a $3 million fund to compensate individuals against whom the phone company had discriminated solely because of their sexual orientation.

1987   Randy Shilts publishes *And the Band Played On,* a book about the AIDS epidemic.

In January a conservative faction tries unsuccessfully to oust members of the Log Cabin Club, a gay Republican group, from the GOP.

In February a Brooklyn bishop's eviction of a chapter of Dignity, a national organization of gay Catholics, caps a series of purges of gay groups from church facilities around the United States following the pope's letter condemning homosexuality from the previous October.

In March the AIDS Coalition to Unleash Power (ACT UP) is formed in New York. Its main slogan is "Silence = Death." In its first major action, 250 activists block morning rush-hour traffic on Wall Street.

Surgeon General C. Everett Koop surprises Republicans by endorsing sex education among schoolchildren as part of the fight against AIDS.

As in other departments, Dallas police begin carrying gloves, masks, and insecticide for fear of contracting AIDS.

In April U.S. Navel Academy midshipman Joseph Steffan is discharged six weeks before graduation because of his homosexuality; he goes on to fight the decision in court.

In May President Reagan gives his first speech entirely devoted to the AIDS crisis.

Representative Barney Frank (D-MA) comes out of the closet, becoming the second openly gay member of Congress.

Representative Stewart McKinney (R-CT) becomes the first member of Congress to die of AIDS.

The *New York Times* agrees for the first time to use the word "gay."

In June sixty-four people are arrested at a Washington, D.C., protest of federal inaction on AIDS.

In July, allegedly under pressure from his wife, Ronald Reagan appoints an openly gay person, Dr. Frank Lilly, to the Presidential Commission on AIDS.

In August, while testifying at congressional hearings on AIDS, representatives of gay organizations—including the National Gay and Lesbian Task Force and the Human Rights Campaign Fund—conditionally endorse voluntary HIV testing and back away from their previous opposition to all testing.

In October the National March on Washington for Gay and Lesbian Rights takes place. More than 500,000 march in the largest gay gathering ever.

The AIDS quilt is displayed for the first time in Washington, D.C., garnering massive media coverage.

The U.S. House and Senate overwhelmingly pass the Helms Amendment, which forbids federal funding for AIDS education material that "promotes or encourages homosexuality."

Virginia ACT UP protesters disrupt Pat Robertson's announcement of his candidacy for president.

In October supporters of Lyndon LaRouche gather more than 100,000 signatures in California, qualifying for a ballot reprise of Proposition 64, the 1986 quarantine measure.

The chairman and vice chairman of the President's Commission on AIDS resign, citing lack of support for the commission from the White House.

In November Vincent Chalk, an Orange County, California, teacher who had been laid off because he had AIDS, wins reinstatement in a landmark ruling by a panel of three judges.

1988 New groups form across the United States in response to what they say is the ineffectiveness of traditional lobbying tactics. New groups form in Georgia, Kansas, Massachusetts, Maine, Minnesota, Missouri, New York, North Carolina, Tennessee, and Vermont, and are dedicated to direct political action. The week of April 29 more than thirty new and established gay and lesbian groups across the country stage a series of direct actions, including rallies and acts of civil disobedience. The protests are sponsored by a coalition called ACT NOW (AIDS Coalition to Network, Organize and Win). The week's actions culminate in a National Day of Protest on May 7.

In January the number of known U.S. AIDS cases passes 50,000, with nearly 400 cases reported each week.

Police arrest nineteen ACT UP activists protesting price gouging at the Burlingame, California, offices of Burroughs Wellcome, manufacturer of the anti-AIDS drug AZT.

In February 175 gay leaders gather in Virginia for a weekend "war conference" and raise the tactic of exposing closeted conservative politicians.

The nation's first lesbian sorority, Lambda Delta Lambda, forms at the University of California, Los Angeles.

A federal appeals court rules against the exclusion of homosexuals from the army; in a denied reenlistment case, an appeals court rejects the Pentagon ban as unconstitutional, but the ruling on the ban is later overturned.

In March a dozen gay activists are ejected from a Presidential Commission on AIDS hearing after disrupting the testimony of William Dannemeyer (R-CA), who told the panel that AIDS was God's punishment for homosexuality.

In May 8,000 protesters rally for California's March on Sacramento on May 7, the National Day of Protest, making it the largest march on the capital in the state's history.

Five hundred ACT UP members block rush-hour traffic in New York's financial district.

The *Boston Herald* reveals that the Massachusetts state police have infiltrated and spied on gay organizations.

In June ten ACT UP members are arrested for blocking a Philadelphia highway to protest the governor's slashing of the state AIDS budget.

The *Arizona Republic* reports that Phoenix police maintained files on people believed to be HIV-positive or to have AIDS.

Under pressure from gay activists, Circle K, a large firm that operates convenience stores, retracts a policy denying medical benefits to employees with AIDS.

The American Federation of Teachers and the National Education Association each approve gay rights resolutions at their conventions.

Activists in twenty-one cities rally on Free Sharon Kowalski Day, in support of the disabled woman and her lover, Karen Thompson, who is fighting to gain guardianship of her.

In a preconvention statement, presidential nominee George H. W. Bush endorses protection against AIDS-related discrimination.

In September gay Ohioans protesting state antisodomy laws hold "Kiss Across Ohio Day."

Fifty ACT UP members disrupt a speech by Senator Dan Quayle (R-IN), vice-presidential running mate for George Walker Bush.

More than 1,000 AIDS activists storm the Maryland offices of the Food and Drug Administration, closing the offices for the day.

Congress passes a major AIDS package that includes $800 million in research funding, but a filibuster threat by Senator Jesse Helms (R-NC) forces testing confidentiality measures to be dropped.

One hundred gay couples exchange symbolic marriage vows in San Francisco in a public appeal for legal recognition of their relationships.

Four hundred fifty Dallas lesbians and gay men buy a full-page ad in the *Dallas Morning News* to disclose their names in the first National Coming Out Day; the paper alters the ad and runs it late.

In December the U.S. Supreme Court rules that the National Security Agency acted within its rights when it fired a gay employee.

Three Alabama state judges ask HIV-positive defendants to make their pleas via telephone rather than in the courtroom.

1989 The U.S. Postal Service commemorates the origins of gay liberation with Keith Haring's donated logo for Stonewall under the objections of Jesse Helms.

In January the Gay and Lesbian Military Freedom Project (GLMFP), a loose coalition of civil rights groups, is formed.

In February a Texas judge says he gave a murderer a lighter sentence because his two victims were "queers."

In March 3,000 protesters stage the largest AIDS demonstration yet in New York City in an attempt to "take over" City Hall to draw attention to the collapse of the city's hospital system; 200 are arrested.

The Los Angeles County Sheriff's Department agrees to recruit gay men and lesbians.

In April GLMFP organizes a group of four women who testify at Defense Department hearings that the military's antigay policy has been used as a form of sexual harassment against all women.

In April hecklers taunting President Bush for his inaction on AIDS interrupt the president's nationally televised speech.

In May "bloody" hand prints of red paint appear on six Los Angeles county buildings, capping a year-long protest over the city's lack of a public AIDS clinic.

Seven thousand marchers converge in Madison, Wisconsin, to demonstrate for gay rights.

The only gay bar in the state of South Dakota closes after repeated vandalism and harassment.

In June Congressman William Dannemeyer (R-CA) submits to the *Congressional Record* a graphic account of what he says are the sex acts of the average gay man.

The Corcoran Gallery of Art in Washington, D.C., brings Robert Mapplethorpe into the headlines by canceling a traveling exhibit of his photographs, many of which are homoerotic.

In July, after being sued by a gay legal group, the TWA airline company agrees to reverse a three-year-old policy and let its frequent flier credits be used by companions who are not blood relatives or spouses of frequent fliers.

More than 90,000 employees of the IRS receive a new contract protecting them from on-the-job discrimination based on sexual orientation.

New York State's highest court rules that two gay people could constitute a family, granting the lover of a deceased man the lease to their rent-controlled apartment.

In September opening night of the San Francisco Opera season is disrupted by AIDS activists who blow whistles and throw leaflets from the balconies to demand increased attention to AIDS.

In October Secret Defense Personnel Security Research Center reports conclude that the gay ban is not supported by evidence and should be eliminated are leaked to Representative Gerry Studds's office and he makes them public.

In November David Dinkens publicly thanks his lesbian and gay supporters for their role in his election as mayor of New York City.

The Minneapolis Civil Rights Department rules that the local Roman
Catholic archdiocese discriminated against Dignity, a group of gay Catholics,
when it refused to renew the organization's lease for a religious facility on
the University of Minnesota campus.

Openly gay U.S. Representative Barney Frank (D-MA) easily wins reelection.

In December nearly 5,000 New York AIDS activists demonstrate outside St.
Patrick's Cathedral while several dozen disrupt services inside; 111 are arrested.

1990   CBS's commentator on its *60 Minutes* program, Andy Rooney,
comes under fire for antigay and antiblack remarks and is suspended for
three months without pay.

The phenomenon of the year becomes "outing." Started in August 1989
by the new gay and lesbian magazine *OutWeek,* the practice soon becomes
widely reported in the mainstream press. Many mainstream gay organizations take a stand against the practice.

Queer Nation is founded in New York City by four gay men to attack homophobia and heterosexism, especially hate crimes against gays. During the
year, chapters spring up around the country in cities such as Philadelphia,
Los Angeles, and Boston. Its founders are ACT UP members who wanted a
group that was not AIDS related. They are fighting for liberation, not assimilation.

New militant groups form around the country: in New York Art Positive
and GANG; in San Francisco Boys with Arms Akimbo; in Chicago Helms' Angels; and in Los Angeles Stiff Sheets.

Log Cabin Republicans moves to the national level when nine Log Cabin
clubs form a national federation. They play a critical role in electing gay-sup-
portive Republicans to high office, including Governor William Weld of Massachusetts and Governor Pete Wilson of California.

In January fourteen AIDS activists bring the Rose Parade in Pasadena, California, to a momentary halt with a banner reading "Emergency. Stop the parade. 70,000 dead of AIDS."

Activists targeting Georgia's antisodomy law set up a brass bed with in-
flatable same-sex dolls in provocative poses in front of the state capitol.

For the second consecutive year, the group Stop AIDS Now or Else backs
up nearly 14,000 cars during rush hour on the Golden Gate Bridge.

In a television first, the television series *Thirtysomething* shows two gay
men in bed together. After a Christian boycott, ABC scraps a rerun of the program.

In February the U.S. Senate approves a hate crimes bill that includes
crimes based on sexual orientation; President Bush later signs it into law.

At a service for a Staten Island victim of gay bashers, 300 supporters rally
against antigay violence.

Gay artist Keith Haring dies of AIDS-related illness.

In March protesters interrupt President Bush twice during a speech on AIDS; it is the first comment he has made on the epidemic since taking office.

More than 1,000 AIDS activists storm the National Institutes of Health in Bethesda, Maryland.

In June the Department of Justice drops a two-month refusal to accept calls about antigay crimes on its new hate crimes hotline.

In July, in a mostly symbolic action, the U.S. House votes to reprimand Representative Barney Frank for his relationship with a male prostitute.

Gay activists take to the streets, calling for a nationwide boycott of Miller beer and Marlboro cigarettes to protest campaign contributions made to North Carolina Senator Jesse Helms by the Philip Morris Corp. The boycott lasts nearly a year and is called off after the company agrees to establish a fund supporting gay and lesbian causes.

Hundreds of gay activists demonstrate outside a U.S. Marine barracks in Washington, D.C., to protest an earlier attack on three gays by Marines.

In July officials at Columbia University in New York grant subsidized married-student housing to a gay couple.

Queer Nation Philadelphia holds its first action, a kiss-in involving 100 people.

The National Endowment for the Arts (NEA) chairman bars grants totaling $23,000 to four performance artists dealing with gender politics.

Queer Nation Los Angeles holds its first action—a "queer-in" in a shopping mall that is met by eighty police in riot helmets. The action entailed nonviolent public displays of affection by Queer Nation members.

AIDS "breaks my heart," President Bush claims at a news conference, but he disagrees that allocating more federal money would alter the course of the disease.

On September 14 to protest high drug prices five ACT UP members unfurl a banner reading "SELL WELLCOME" and throw counterfeit $100 bills with the inscription "Fuck your profiteering, we're dying while you play business," sound foghorns, and chain themselves to the balcony as the opening bell sounds on the New York Stock Exchange floor (Wellcome was the main company selling the anti-AIDS drug AZT).

In October the Fund for Human Dignity, one of the nation's largest gay education groups, closes its doors after a bitter schism over the appointment of a heterosexual executive director.

Women from ACT UP-DC demonstrate at the Health and Human Services building.

In November President Bush vetoes a bill that would force pharmaceutical manufacturers to lower the price of AIDS drugs.

In December a federal district court judge in San Francisco orders the FBI to turn over any internal documents indicating whether the agency based denial of security clearances on sexual orientation.

Dr. Ellen Cooper, often criticized by AIDS activists, resigns from her post as head of the FDA's AIDS drug division.

Three same-sex couples, Ninia Baehr and Genora Dancel, Patrick Lagon and Joseph Melilio, and Tammi Rodrigues and Antoinette Pregil, file applications for marriage licenses with the Hawaii Department of Health, the state agency with jurisdiction over marriage. They are immediately denied.

1991 National Gay Rights Advocates, a public interest law firm, closes its doors.

The National Gay and Lesbian Task Force takes a public stand against the Gulf War, alienating some gays and lesbians.

Sherry Harris is elected to the Seattle City Council; she is believed to be the first openly lesbian elected official in Washington state and the first publicly elected African American lesbian in the United States.

Basketball star Magic Johnson announces he is HIV positive in a live press conference on ESPN and CNN. Days later, he retires from the Lakers and is appointed to the National Commission on AIDS by President Bush.

Controversy over outing reaches a new high after the *Advocate* magazine outs Pentagon Spokesman Pete Williams.

Researchers posit that gay men posses larger hypothalamus glands than straight men, which sharpens the debate over a biological root to homosexuality.

In January openly lesbian Gail Shibley is elected to the Oregon state house of representatives.

The CDC announces that AIDS is the second leading cause of death among men between the ages of twenty-five and forty-four.

On Valentine's Day, 275 gay and lesbian couples register their relationships at San Francisco City Hall as the city's domestic partnership law goes into effect.

The Cracker Barrel restaurant chain rescinds a policy that forbade employment of gays and lesbians, only to replace it with another that forbids employing people "whose sexual preferences fail to demonstrate normal heterosexual values."

In March two weeks of furious debate between the Irish Gay and Lesbian Organization and the organizers of New York City's annual St. Patrick's Day Parade, who wanted to ban the group from marching, culminates with New York City Mayor Dinkins giving up his honorary spot at the front of the parade and joining the gay and lesbian marchers in a show of solidarity.

President Bush calls ACT UP protests "an excess of free speech," and tells reporters that his administration has tried "to be very sensitive to the question of babies suffering from AIDS, innocent people that are hurt by the disease."

Austin gay activist Glen Maxey is elected to the Texas state house of representatives.

The Lambda Legal Defense and Education Fund's use of the controversial musical *Miss Saigon* as a benefit fund raiser causes a split within the organization and draws 300 lesbian and gay demonstrators to the Broadway performance to protest the play's racist stereotypes.

After more than two years of organizing, the National Lesbian Conference attracts 2,500 participants to Atlanta, but proceeds to collapse under the weight of its own "political correctness and lack of structure."

The first Black Lesbian and Gay Pride Day in Washington, D.C., draws hundreds of participants.

Los Angeles Superior Court Judge Sally Disco rules that the Boy Scouts of America may discriminate against gay men.

The National Institute of Health issues a statement opposing the Burroughs Wellcome Company's monopoly on AZT, the only federally approved anti-HIV drug.

On May 1 the case of *Baehr v. Lewin* (1993), now styled *Baehr v. Miike,* begins. Joe Melilio and Patrick Lagon join two lesbian couples in filing suit against the state of Hawaii to obtain marriage licenses. They say that the state's refusal to let them marry amounts to gender discrimination, violating the state constitution's Equal Rights Amendment.

The magazine *Outweek* folds after two years of publication.

In July at Dodger Stadium in Los Angeles, sixty-five Queer Nationals watching a ballgame see "WELCOME QUEER NATION" flash on the scoreboard, and take to the field to address allegations that Dodger team manager Tommy Lasorda's son was gay and had died of AIDS.

The first annual Colorado Outdoor Leather Dykes (COLD) festival attracts over 100 lesbians.

In August Marlon Rigg's graphic LGBT film *Tongues Untied* is aired on PBS stations.

In Boston 20 queer couples and 500 supporters celebrate a mass wedding outside the Catholic Holy Cross Cathedral.

When California Governor Wilson vetoes a gay employment rights bill it sets off a month-long explosion of protests beginning on the night of the August 29.

The following day protesters descend on city downtowns, damaging government buildings in both San Francisco and Los Angeles. About 7,000 protestors riot in San Francisco and 2,000 in Los Angeles. About 300 demonstrators disrupt Wilson's speech at Stanford University's centennial celebration, pelting the governor with eggs, papers, and oranges.

In September AIDS activists from Treatment Action Guerrillas (TAG), an ACT UP-NY spin-off, cover the Arlington, Virginia, home of Senator Jesse Helms with a giant condom dropped from a helicopter.

Hundreds of AIDS activists from around the nation came to Washington, D.C., for five days of protests and meetings about the future course of ACT UP.

In October Representative Gerry Studds (D-MA) exposes an official Pentagon internal study concluding that gay and lesbian civilian employees at the Department of Defense pose no special security risk.

Presidential candidate Bill Clinton declares that, if elected, he would drop the ban on gays in the military.

The Hawaii Court of appeals rules against the plaintiffs in the same-sex marriage case of *Baehr v. Lewin,* now styled *Baehr v. Miike;* they appeal.

In December Patricia Ireland, the married new president of NOW, says in an *Advocate* magazine interview that she has a female lover.

The San Francisco chapter of Queer Nation closes its doors, citing divisions over issues of race, gender, bisexuality, and religion.

1992   Gay, lesbian, and AIDS activists make this a pivotal year by mounting the most effective national political effort in the movement's history to help defeat a president; and the straight media and candidates take notice. Gay political fundraising achieves a historic milestone, raising at least $3.4 million in gay money toward the Democratic victory. Gay Republican organizing also peaks as Log Cabin Clubs are organized nationwide. The first openly gay delegates to the Republican convention win broad media attention. ACT UP's Presidential Project dogs candidates in the primary season on AIDS policy and gay issues.

Barry D. Adam (1995) says that by 1992 there are seventy-five gay and lesbian elected officials around the country, including eleven in statehouses.

Levi Strauss and Co., the world's largest clothing manufacturer, announces that it will offer spousal health benefits to gay and lesbian domestic partners.

Log Cabin Republican Clubs meet in Houston to denounce the antigay turn of the Republican National Convention.

A Texas state judge voids the Dallas Police Department's ban on employment of gay and lesbian officers as unconstitutional.

The school board in Coeur d'Alene, Idaho, votes to bar teachers from discussing contraceptives or homosexuality with students.

University of Colorado, Boulder, football coach Bill McCartney sparks controversy by lending public support to the antigay conservative group Colorado for Family Values.

At the Academy Awards ceremony, hundreds of Queer Nation demonstrators protest derogatory portrayals of lesbians and gays in the movies.

Retired professional tennis player Arthur Ashe discloses that he has AIDS.

President Bush names Anne-Imelda Radice, a conservative lesbian, to the post of acting chair of the embattled NEA.

Presidential candidate Ross Perot announces that he would not appoint a known homosexual to a cabinet position.

The General Accounting Office estimates that over the past decade the Pentagon has spent almost $500 million on purging the military of gays and lesbians.

The Democratic National Convention, held in New York City, witnesses an AIDS protest involving 20,000 demonstrators.

In August President Bush says on *Dateline NBC* that if he found out a grandchild was gay he would "love the child" but tell him that homosexuality is not normal and discourage him from working for gay rights.

In September John Schlafly, the eldest son of conservative activist Phyllis Schlafly, comes out as gay and the *Advocate* magazine outs conservative Louisiana Congressman Jim McCrery.

In October spanning over 15 acres and 22,000 panels, the Names Project AIDS Memorial Quilt is shown in its entirety on the Mall in Washington, D.C. Nearly 300,000 people view the exhibit.

In November lesbian and gay organizers across the country call for a boycott of Colorado and Colorado-based businesses in protest of the passage of Amendment 2, which would void gay civil rights laws statewide.

1993 The Log Cabin Republicans embark on an aggressive expansion effort. By fall, Log Cabin has opened a national lobbying and information office in Washington under the name Log Cabin Republicans, and increased club growth. Log Cabin claims a critical role in the GOP elective sweep, which sees the elections of LGBT-friendly Mayor Richard Riordan (R-Los Angeles), Mayor Rudolph Giuliani (R-New York City), and Governor Christine Todd Whitman (R-NJ).

In January a coalition of national groups forms the Campaign for Military Service in an effort to force the signing of an executive order by Clinton to end the ban on gays in the military.

On January 29 President Clinton announces that he has reached a compromise with Senator Nunn (D-GA) that the Department of Defense Military Task Force would take six months to study the impact of a repeal of the military's ban on gays.

On April 25 the Third National March on Washington draws an estimated 300,000 to 1 million people.

In May in *Baehr v. Lewin* (renamed *Baehr v. Miike*), the Hawaii Supreme Court holds that a statute denying marriage rights to same-sex couples may violate the state constitution's equal rights provision. It remands the case for trial to determine whether the state can demonstrate a compelling interest to justify the statute.

In September Congress rejects attempts to end the ban on gays in the military and enacts the "don't ask, don't tell" policy.

1994 Petition drives for statewide antigay ballot initiatives fail in Arizona, Florida, Maine, Michigan, Missouri, Nevada, Ohio, and Washington.

The Log Cabin Republicans dramatically increase their political activity, with members getting deeply involved in key races for the U.S. House, Senate, and state governorships, as well as hundreds of local and state office elections.

1995 In October in New Jersey group life and health insurers are allowed to screen policy applicants for HIV antibodies under regulations proposed by the state insurance department. Insurers are permitted to deny coverage to applicants who test positive or refuse to submit to tests.

In South Dakota organizers announce the creation of Free Americans Creating Equal Status (FACES), the state's first gay political group, in Rapid City.

In November Roberta Achtenberg loses her bid to become San Francisco's mayor.

Bill Crews is reelected mayor of Melbourne, Iowa, (population 669) after coming out.

Barbara Kavanaugh becomes the first lesbian elected to the Buffalo, New York, city council.

On December 8 Hawaii's Commission on Sexual Orientation votes five to two to recommend marriage rights for same-sex couples. This represents the first time that an official state body endorses marriage rights for gay couples.

1996   In response to the Hawaii same-sex marriage case of the previous year, thirty-seven states make efforts to outlaw same-sex marriages, and sixteen actually pass laws banning such marriages by the end of the year.

In an effort to help Democrats regain control of the California Assembly, the Human Rights Campaign creates the California Project—a coordinated effort that dumps over $200,000 into eleven key races. The effort succeeds with Democrats regaining control of the assembly by a margin of forty-two to thirty-eight.

Congress passes the so-called Defense of Marriage Act, which defines marriage as only between a man and a women for federal benefits purposes and allows states to refuse to recognize same-sex marriages performed in other states. President Clinton signs the bill in September.

During the 1996 election cycle, the Log Cabin Republicans contribute more than $76,000 to political candidates.

A Florida court rules that a convicted murderer is a better potential parent for his twelve-year-old daughter than her lesbian mother. The Florida First District Court of Appeals upholds a trial court ruling made in September 1995 that removed Cassie Ward from the home of her mother, Mary Ward, and her lesbian partner. That ruling placed the daughter in the home of her father and Ward's ex-husband, John Ward, who was convicted twenty-two years ago of murdering his first wife.

A host of conservative groups hold a rally that includes many Republican candidates for president to launch the National Campaign to Protect Marriage, an effort to forever deny gay couples the right to legal marriage. Presidential hopefuls Pat Buchanan, Alan Keyes, and Phil Gramm speak, while letters of support from Bob Dole and Steve Forbes are also read. (Only Richard Lugar fails to support the rally.) Also speaking are Don Wildmon of the American Family Association and Mike Gabbard of Stop Promoting Homosexuality Hawaii, among others.

In February GenderPAC (GPac) formalizes its articles of association. GPac lobbyists seek to represent all the marginalized groups that could be considered within their mission of fighting "gender-based oppression," including transgenders, bisexuals, the leather community, cross-dressers, the intersexed, and transexuals. Says a GPac spokesperson, "We're trying to cast as wide a net as possible in pursuing our motto of 'gender, affectional and racial equality.'"

On May 20 the U.S. Supreme Court upholds the Colorado Supreme Court's ruling and declares Amendment 2, the antigay ballot initiative, unconstitutional in *Romer v. Evans*. The high Court rules that the amendment violates homosexuals' equal protection rights. Colorado officials say taxpayers will shell out $950,000 to cover the plaintiffs' legal fees in the successful civil rights challenge to Amendment 2.

On June 17 the U.S. Supreme Court, by a six-to-three vote, orders the Sixth U.S. Circuit Court of Appeals to reconsider its ruling upholding a Cincinnati ordinance that denies protection against discrimination to homosexuals in light of the high Court's decision in *Romer v. Evans* involving a similar law. Chief Justice William H. Rehnquist and Justices Antonin Scalia and Clarence Thomas dissent. The amendment had passed by a percentage of sixty-two to thirty-eight. The case is *Equality Foundation v. Cincinnati.*

In July the Seventh Circuit Court of Appeals rules in favor of a young gay man who sued his former Wisconsin school for failing to protect him from constant, at times brutal, antigay assaults and harassment while he was a student. The appeal, *Nabozny v. Podlesny,* was brought by Lambda and is the first of its kind to challenge antigay violence in the nation's schools. The decision reverses a lower court's ruling throwing the case out and remands it to the federal district court in Madison, Wisconsin, for trial. Nabozny, from Ashland, Wisconsin, goes on to win over $1 million when the case is finally decided in his favor in December.

In August U.S. Representative Jim Kolbe (R-AZ) declares that he's gay before he can be outed by the *Advocate* magazine. The *Advocate* had planned on outing Kolbe for his antigay vote on the federal Defense of Marriage Act. Kolbe becomes the second Republican member of Congress to declare his homosexuality (Steve Gunderson [R-WI] was the first).

In September a state judge orders the state of Oregon to extend the same benefits to partners of homosexual workers as it does to spouses of heterosexual workers. Although the benefits exclusion also applies to heterosexual employees who are not married to their domestic partners, the judge rules that the policy discriminates against gays and lesbians because they cannot, under Oregon law, get married. The case is *Tanner v. Oregon Health Sciences University.* Oregon's attorney general appeals the ruling.

On November 5 in Hawaii a constitutional convention vote passes, meaning that the state constitution can now be changed to ban same-sex marriage. A constitutional convention is now scheduled for 1998. The convention is being pushed by the religious right as an alternative method to stop same-sex marriages by circumventing the legislature and the courts.

At least forty-four openly gay candidates for offices at all levels of government win their seats in the November elections.

California Assemblywoman Sheila Kuehl is chosen as the Assembly's speaker pro tem. This appears to be the highest position held by an open lesbian in state government.

Ed Flanagan, a Democrat, becomes the first openly gay person to hold a statewide office when he is elected auditor of accounts for Vermont.

Oregon voters reelect the only openly gay Republican state legislator, giving the state four gay legislators. This number ties with Maine for the most gay legislators.

Allan Spear, a state legislator from Minnesota, is reelected. Spear came out in 1974 and is now the longest-serving openly gay legislator.

Illinois elects its first openly gay legislator. Democrat Larry McKeon, who is also HIV-positive, wins 82 percent of the vote in his district.

Margo Frasier is elected sheriff of Travis County, Texas, becoming the first elected openly gay or lesbian sheriff in the country.

On November 14 activists in nearly twenty cities organize demonstrations at Chrysler dealerships to protest the company's refusal to include sexual orientation in its nondiscrimination policy.

By December, more than sixty foreigners have been granted political asylum in the United States because of political repression for their sexual orientation.

In the case of *Baehr v. Lewin* (1993) (now styled *Baehr v. Miike*), a court finds that the state has not demonstrated a compelling interest to justify its law that marriage is only between a man and a woman, and thus upholds the right of same-sex couples to be legally wed. The ruling makes Hawaii the first state to recognize that gay and lesbian couples are entitled to the same privileges as heterosexual married couples. The day after the ruling, the judge puts the decision on hold while the state appeals to Hawaii's Supreme Court. The stay will remain in effect until a ruling by that court.

1997   Nationwide there are now 120 LGBT elected officials who are open about their sexual orientation.

In January for the first time the Human Rights Campaign (HRC) and GenderPAC make a series of joint calls on Capitol Hill in Washington, D.C. The day's activities, organized by HRC's Senior Policy Advocate Nancy Buermeyer, are devoted to conducting basic education around bi/herm/trans issues, and discussing prospects for including transgendered in the Employment Non-Discrimination Act (ENDA) with the bill's sponsors. Lobbyists Dana Priesing (GPac), Deb Kolodny (BiNet USA/GPac), Nancy Buermeyer (HRC), Kris Pratt (HRC), and Riki Wilchins (GPac) call on a half dozen congressional offices. The advice of most legislative assistants is that trans-inclusion is probably not viable at this point, and might delay the bill's passage by five to ten years. The meetings also mark the first time a lobbyist specifically from a bisexual organization has been on the Hill representing the concerns of the bisexual community.

During the inauguration of President Clinton the first coordinated and official outreach targeting the gay and lesbian community takes place. Events include the first lesbian inaugural gala; a reception honoring the leadership of gay and lesbian Democratic clubs; the first performance by a gay chorus, the Gay Men's Chorus of Washington, at an official inaugural event; a performance by the Lesbian and Gay Bands of America, a San Francisco-based marching band, in the pre-parade festivities (a return engagement from 1993); and a procession by a local contingent carrying thirty panels from the NAMES Project AIDS Memorial Quilt. Unofficial events include a $100-a-plate breakfast tribute, sponsored by the Victory Fund, which nearly 200 people attend, and a black-tie gala called "Triangle Ball: The Gay and Lesbian Inaugural Celebration," sponsored by several of the largest national lesbian and gay organizations. That event alone draws 1,600 attendees.

In January *Time* magazine announces that it has chosen Dr. David Ho, pioneer of a new AIDS treatment, as its 'Man of the Year' for 1996.

The U.S. Postal Service issues regulations that prohibit discrimination for several categories, including sexual orientation. Right-wing groups protest the policy.

In February thirty-nine members of the U.S. House of Representatives send a joint letter to Secretary of Defense William Cohen urging him to "help stop the harassment and abusive investigations of gays and lesbians in the military."

A pipe bomb covered with nails explodes in a crowded Atlanta gay bar, injuring several people. President Clinton condemns the act.

Comedian Ellen DeGeneres makes history by coming out as a lesbian with the lead character on the ABC television show *Ellen*. Some local affiliates choose not to run the show.

In June New Hampshire becomes the eleventh state to pass a law banning discrimination on the basis of sexual orientation, although Maine repeals its law in a 1998 ballot challenge.

In July the Montana Supreme Court unanimously overturns the state's antisodomy law, which had made sexual activity between consenting adults of the same sex illegal.

The National Gay and Lesbian Task Force and thirty-two state groups launch the Federation of Statewide Lesbian, Gay, Bisexual, and Transgender Political Organizations.

In October Virginia M. Apuzzo is appointed by President Clinton to be the assistant to the president for management and administration, making her the highest ranking openly LGBT official in history.

In December New Jersey courts grant same-sex couples equal status with heterosexual couples for purposes of adopting children in state custody.

1998   In February Maine voters repeal their state's new gay civil rights law.

In March Washington becomes the twenty-sixth state to adopt a same-sex marriage ban.

In May, after offering to hold performances in high schools around the country, the openly lesbian band Indigo Girls faces several cancellations of their shows by fearful school administrators.

President Clinton signs an executive order prohibiting discrimination based on sexual orientation in the federal civilian workforce.

In July groups such as the Christian Coalition, Family Research Council, and Concerned Women of America run full-page ads in the *New York Times, Washington Post,* and *USA Today* claiming that "homosexuals can change." The move marks a new peak for the efforts of the "ex-gay" movement.

In October a national outcry erupts over the brutal murder of an openly gay college student, Matthew Shepard, in Wyoming.

In November openly LGBT candidates running for national office include Tammy Baldwin, Paul Barby, Grethe Cammermeyer, and Christine Kehoe. Baldwin wins her Wisconsin race for a U.S. House seat and makes history by becoming the first open lesbian elected to Congress, the first nonincumbent LGBT person elected to Congress, and the first woman elected to Congress from Wisconsin.

1999   This year is marked by the most significant efforts ever by national LGBT groups to mobilize and coordinate with state and local LGBT groups. Nevada passes a law banning discrimination based on sexual orientation in public employment.

In January the Arkansas Child Welfare Agency Review Board passes a resolution that would ban placing foster care children in the home of anyone who has engaged in same-sex sexual behavior or anyone sharing a household with someone who has engaged in same-sex sexual behavior.

In February, despite the mobilization over the murder of Matthew Shepard, the Wyoming legislature kills all bills that would have given the state a hate crime law.

The second annual National Freedom to Marry Day is celebrated with events around the country.

In March the murder of Billy Jack Gaither in Coosa County, Alabama, is decried by LGBT activists who renew efforts for a federal hate crime bill.

The Federation of Statewide Lesbian, Gay, Bisexual and Transgender Political Organizations sponsors its first coordinated week of actions focused on state government and statewide organizing called Equality Begins at Home. The campaign organizes 350 rallies, political and cultural events in all fifty state capitals plus the District of Columbia and Puerto Rico.

In April New Hampshire repeals its 1988 ban on adoption by homosexuals; the bill is signed by the governor.

In June the National Gay and Lesbian Task Force announces that it supports the inclusion of language protecting transgendered persons in the federal Employment Non-Discrimination Act (ENDA).

In July Missouri becomes the twenty-second state to enact a hate crimes law that includes sexual orientation.

For the first time the U.S. Senate passes the Hate Crimes Prevention Act, which would expand existing statutes to cover disability status, and gender and sexual orientation, and facilitate prosecution of such crimes. The act is approved as an amendment to SB 1217, the Commerce, Justice, State appropriations bill. However, the amendment does not make it through the House.

In August the New Jersey Supreme Court rules in *Dale v. Boy Scouts of America* that the Boy Scouts' ban on gay and bisexual leaders and members is illegal under New Jersey's antidiscrimination law.

In September Democratic presidential candidates Bill Bradley and Al Gore both state their opposition to California's ballot Proposition 22, which would ban the recognition of same-sex marriages.

In October a meeting of national LGBT groups, the National Policy Roundtable, calls for more people of color in leadership positions within the LGBT movement.

In November voters in Falmouth (Maine) and Spokane (Washington) block efforts to repeal local laws banning discrimination on the basis of sexual orientation, while voters in Greeley (Colorado) defeat an attempt to enact a similar law.

Over 1,500 LGBT people protest in front of the Oakland Police Department in response to a police officer's slur toward an African American transgendered person who was the victim of a hate crime.

New studies suggest that support for LGBT Americans has increased over the decade. The 1999 data indicate that 70 percent of Americans support the right of gays and lesbians to serve in the military, up from 55 percent in 1992. Also, by 1999 83 percent of adults support equal rights in employment, 75 percent support equal rights in housing, and 61 percent support the hiring of gay and lesbian high school teachers, up from 27 percent in 1977.

The Vermont Supreme Court rules that the state must provide the benefits of marriage to same-sex couples either by allowing same-sex couples to marry or by recognizing the relationship in some other manner.

2000   LGBT activists play important roles in the 2000 elections, with Republican presidential candidates meeting with LGBT representatives for the first time. Major party conventions are the most LGBT friendly ever.

Voters in California, Nebraska, and Nevada pass laws banning the recognition of same-sex marriages. Maine voters again nix a gay civil rights law, but Oregon voters block a proposal to ban LGBT school clubs or positive discussions of homosexuality.

In January a new study by the Policy Institute of the National Gay and Lesbian Task Force finds that more than 100 million Americans live in towns, cities, counties, or states with laws banning discrimination based on sexual orientation.

The National Gay and Lesbian Task Force says a record 466 LGBT-related bills are tracked in state legislatures, with 288 favorable to the LGBT community and 178 unfavorable.

In May Vermont passes historic legislation on same-sex civil unions. Effective in July, the law gives same-sex couples the right to form state-sanctioned civil unions and enjoy more than 300 benefits, rights, and responsibilities available to heterosexual married couples, including the right to make medical decisions in case of emergency, transfer property, inherit estates, oversee funerals, and file joint state income tax returns.

In June, after eleven years of attempts, the New York state senate passes a hate crimes bill that includes sexual orientation. Governor George Pataki later signs the bill.

The U.S. Supreme Court rules in *Dale v. Boy Scouts of America* that the Boy Scouts may ban homosexuals from their organization. The ruling leads organizations and cities to end official ties with the Boy Scouts.

In August the Chrysler Corporation, Ford Motor Company, and General Motors Corporation begin offering domestic partner benefits to employees' same-sex partners.

Republicans hold their national convention and pass an anti-LGBT platform. Openly gay Representative Jim Kolbe (R-AZ) addresses the convention, becoming the first openly gay elected official to do so.

LGBT activists hold protests in thirty-six communities as part of a National Day of Protest against the Boy Scouts of America's policy of discrimination against LGBT people.

Ronald Edward Gay opens fire in a Roanoke, Virginia, gay bar, killing one person and injuring six others. Gay later says his crime was motivated by harassment over his name.

In December by executive order governors in Delaware and Montana ban discrimination based on sexual orientation in public employment.

2001   U.S. Census 2000 figures begin to trickle out showing a considerable rise in the numbers of same-sex partner households, in some states by as much as 700 percent. The increase is attributed to knowledge of the census questions and more LGBT people coming out.

In April President Bush taps openly gay Scott H. Evertz to be director of the Office of National AIDS Policy, marking the first appointment of an openly LGBT person by a Republican president.

In May Hawaii becomes the twenty-sixth state to adopt a hate crimes law that includes sexual orientation.

As most state legislatures near the end of their annual sessions, the National Gay and Lesbian Task Force tracks 370 LGBT-related bills, of which 234 are favorable and 136 are unfavorable.

In May Texas adopts a hate crime law that specifically includes sexual orientation.

After ten years of lobbying by LGBT groups, Maryland enacts a gay civil rights law. Opponents fail to put the question to voters later in the year.

In July a Minnesota state judge overturns the state's antisodomy law. The decision follows an April ruling by an Arkansas circuit court judge against that state's ban on consensual sex between adult, same-sex couples, and Arizona's passage of legislation repealing that state's antisodomy law.

In July secret discussions between the Bush White House and the Salvation Army are uncovered that reportedly would arrange for the Salvation Army to lobby in support of Bush's plan to distribute federal funds to religious social service organizations. In exchange the Bush Administration would allow government-funded charitable organizations to discriminate on the basis of sexual orientation, even if local laws banned such discrimination.

Rhode Island joins Minnesota in banning discrimination against transgendered people.

In August LGBT lobbying leads Indiana Governor Frank O'Bannon to sign an executive order that prohibits discrimination based on sexual orientation in state employment.

In September President Bush issues a "stop-loss" order not to remove gays and lesbians from military service in the wake of the September 11 terrorist attacks and the beginning of Operation Enduring Freedom.

Following a the September 11 terrorist attacks, a national debate ensues over providing private and public assistance to the partners of LGBT persons killed in the attacks. By the end of the year the federal government says it will allow the states to decide who is eligible for benefits.

Michael Guest, an openly gay man, is sworn in as U.S. Ambassador to Romania. Guest was nominated by Republican President George W. Bush and was confirmed by the Senate. Guest's partner of six years, Alex Nevarez, attended the ceremony.

LGBT activists win five out of six LGBT-related ballot measures, three local measures in Michigan and two in Florida. Voters in Houston, Texas passed a measuring banning the city from providing domestic partner benefits.

Tempe, Arizona Mayor Neil Giuliano beats back a recall effort after a gay-related issue mobilized conservative activists.

In a runoff election openly lesbian Cathy Woolard is elected as the city council president in Atlanta, GA.

Almost 2,500 activists attended the National Gay and Lesbian Task Force's annual Creating Change conference in Milwaukee, Wisconsin.

In December President Bush signing a measure that finally allows the District of Columbia government to fund a program that provides health benefits to the domestic partners of city employees. The program had first passed in 1993, but Congress had blocked funding until 2001.

2002   Initial state legislative redistricting maps following the 2000 census leaves LGBT officials in Rhode Island and Texas with poor choices. After six terms in the state house, Rep. Glen Maxey (D-51) decides to retire rather than run against political allies.

Acting Republican Massachusetts Governor Jane Swift named openly gay Patrick C. Guerriero as her running mate for the 2002 election, marking the first such time an LGBT person has been named to run for Lt. Governor on a major party ticket.

For the first time the Minneapolis, Minnesota, city council has two openly LGBT members, Scott Benson and Robert Lilligren.

Vermont's Supreme Court rules against the last legal challenges to the state's civil union law, which allows same-sex couples the legal benefits of marriage.

Annotated Bibliography

Adam, Barry D. **The Rise of a Gay and Lesbian Movement.** Rev. ed. New York: Twayne Publishers, 1995.

Adam provides perhaps the best history and overview of the creation of a gay political movement in the major industrial democracies with descriptions of issues, groups, and government activity.

Bailey, Robert W. **Gay Politics, Urban Politics.** New York: Columbia University Press, 1998a.

Bailey argues that the LGB movement has been most influential in the country's largest cities, due chiefly to the emergence of clearly identifiable LGB communities, institutions, and voting constituencies. Findings include corroboration that self-identified LGB voters tend to be younger, better educated, considerably left of center on social issues, registered Democrats, and disproportionately white. The book also notes that LGB people in cities tend to be socially, but not necessarily economically, liberal and are most effective when functioning in broad-based electoral coalitions with non-LGB groups.

———. **Out and Voting: The Gay, Lesbian, and Bisexual Vote in Congressional House Elections, 1990–1996.** Washington, DC: National Gay and Lesbian Task Force Policy Institute, 1998b.

The single most rigorous analysis to date of the LGB vote in congressional elections, this publication establishes that the LGB vote can have an important impact, particularly in urban congressional districts; that LGB voters are an important part of the base of the Democratic Party; and that steadily increasing numbers of voters are self-identifying as LGB.

Bayer, Ronald. **Private Acts, Social Consequences: AIDS and the Politics of Public Health.** New Brunswick, NJ: Rutgers University Press, 1989.

A major work of synthesis, this book covers six major policy areas: bathhouse closure, blood supply screening, compulsory testing, quarantine, and prevention education. It provides a compelling explanation as to why the more coercive public health measures promoted early in the epidemic failed to materialize.

Bernstein, Mary, and Renate Reimann, eds. **Queer Families, Queer Politics: Challenging Culture and the State**. New York: Columbia University Press, 2001.

This is an edited collection of essays on LGBT politics written by activists and academics covering LGBT family issues, including adoption, domestic partnerships, and same-sex marriage.

Blasius, Mark. **Gay and Lesbian Politics: Sexuality and the Emergence of a New Ethic**. Philadelphia: Temple University Press, 1994.

Blasius presents a postmodern analysis tracking the development of a gay and lesbian political identity from its sources in individual sexual desire, and the ways in which such a political identity challenges dominant discourses.

Blasius, Mark, and Shane Phelan. **We are Everywhere: A Historical Sourcebook of Gay and Lesbian Politics**. New York: Routledge, 1997.

This collection of primary documents encompasses the prehistory and beginnings of a gay and lesbian movement, the period of gay liberation and lesbian feminism, the politics of AIDS, and contemporary LGBT politics.

Bull, Christopher, and John Gallagher. **Perfect Enemies: The Religious Right, the Gay Movement, and the Politics of the 1990s**. New York: Crown Publishers, 1996.

Journalists for the LGB newsmagazine *The Advocate,* Bull and Gallagher cover major antigay movements in the mid-1990s, including the Colorado Amendment 2 controversy, the early Clinton administration's gays-in-the-military debacle, the debate over same-sex marriage, and other issues. They demonstrate how the religious right and LGBT organizations demonized each other to help raise funds and mobilize supporters.

Button, James W., Barbara A. Rienzo, and Kenneth D. Wald. **Private Lives, Public Conflicts: Battles Over Gay Rights in American Communities**. Washington, DC: CQ Press, 1997.

A rigorous empirically driven examination of gay politics at the local level, this book's key focus is on how and why localities and school districts adopt antidiscrimination policies.

Cain, Patricia A. **Rainbow Rights: The Role of Lawyers and Courts in the Lesbian and Gay Civil Rights Movement**. Boulder, CO: Westview Press, 2000.

This is a history of the key role litigation has played in the LGBT movement with attention to landmark cases and important interest groups.

D'Emilio, John. **Sexual Politics, Sexual Communities: The Making of a Homosexual Minority in the United States, 1940–1970**. Chicago: University of Chicago Press, 1983.

This pioneering analysis traces the seeds of the contemporary LGBT community to the national mobilization for World War II, which enabled many LGBT people to relocate from their hometowns and create small communities in the nation's largest cities. The book traces the development of these communities through the postwar period up to the Stonewall era.

————. **Making Trouble: Essays on Gay History, Politics, and the University.** New York: Routledge, 1992.

This is D'Emilio's collection of his own essays on the rise of a gay movement. Although theoretically driven, the work is largely descriptive in nature.

Duberman, Martin. **Stonewall.** New York: Dutton, 1993.

Published near the twenty-fifth anniversary of the Stonewall uprising by an important participant in early 1970s LGBT politics in New York City, this history traces several key figures in the years leading up to and surrounding the Stonewall Riots, which sparked the modern mass movement for LGBT rights.

Epstein, Stephen. **Impure Science: AIDS, Activism and the Politics of Knowledge.** Berkeley, CA: University of California Press, 1996.

An analysis of how "knowledge" is constructed by researchers, activists, and policy makers, this book focuses on ACT UP activism and early controversies over whether HIV causes AIDS.

Haider-Markel, Donald P., Mark R. Joslyn, and Chad J. Kniss. **"Minority Group Interests and Political Representation: Gay Elected Officials in the Policy Process."** *The Journal of Politics* 62 (2): 568–577 (2000).

The authors analyze the influence of openly lesbian and gay officials on the local adoption of domestic partner policies. The findings suggest that the presence of openly lesbian and gay elected officials increases the likelihood that domestic partner policies will be adopted.

Hertzog, Mark. **The Lavender Vote: Lesbians, Gay Men, and Bisexuals in American Electoral Politics.** New York: New York University Press, 1996.

Testing for the existence of a "lavender vote" or consistencies in the electoral behavior of LGB people, Hertzog finds that LGBs are strongly liberal on domestic social issues; lesbians are disproportionately likely to be committed feminists; and LGB people are more mobilized in elections in which sexual orientation issues figure prominently. In addition, the LGB vote is already bigger than the Asian American vote, comparable to the Latino vote, and likely to grow over time, to perhaps the size of the Jewish vote. LGB voters are also not "captives" of the Democratic Party, but will tend to vote for the most pro-LGB candidate, regardless of party.

Jennings, M. Kent, and Ellen Ann Anderson. **"Support for Confrontational Tactics among AIDS Activists: A Study of Intra-Movement Divisions."** *American Journal of Political Science* 40 (2): 311–334 (1996).

The authors examine support for confrontational political tactics, such as protest. The study makes use of surveys of gays and straights that attended an AIDS quilt memorial. The findings suggest that a respondent's sexual orientation influences his or her support for disruptive political behavior.

Murray, Stephen O. **Social Theory, Homosexual Realities.** New York: Gai Saber Monograph No. 3, 1984.
This interdisciplinary analysis explores the major social science theories on homosexuality while critiquing those theories.

————. **American Gay.** Chicago: University of Chicago Press, 1996.
This book offers an examination of the historical development of homosexuality in North America with attention to the development and repression of gay communities, the definition of homosexual roles, and differences in homosexual identity across gender, race, and ethnicity.

Newton, David E. **Gay and Lesbian Rights: A Reference Handbook.** Santa Barbara, CA: ABC-CLIO, 1994.
An overall reference work to the gay and lesbian rights movement, this book features a brief history and overview of issues, a chronology, biographical sketches, primary documents, and a resource guide.

Phelan, Shane. **Identity Politics: Lesbian-Feminism and the Limits of Community.** Philadelphia: Temple University Press, 1989.
Phelan makes use of postmodern (queer) theory to explain and explore the social construction of lesbianism and lesbian identity.

————. **Getting Specific: Postmodern Lesbian Politics.** Minneapolis, MN: University of Minnesota Press, 1994.
Going beyond lesbian feminist theory, the book develops a "democratic identity politics" that deals with identity in terms of human experience and opportunities for political organizing.

Rayside, David Morton. **On the Fringe: Gays and Lesbians in Politics.** Ithaca, NY: Cornell University Press, 1998.
This is a comparative analysis of gay politics in the United States, Canada, and England, with detailed case studies of policies, interest groups, and LGBT elected officials in each country.

Riggle, D. B., and Barry L. Tadlock, eds. **Gays and Lesbians in the Democratic Process.** New York: Columbia University Press, 1999.
This edited collection of original empirical research on LGBT politics directs special attention to public opinion and policy.

Rimmerman, Craig, Kenneth Wald, and Clyde Wilcox, eds. **The Politics of Gay Rights.** Chicago: University of Chicago Press, 2000.
This edited collection of original empirical research on LGBT politics is divided into sections on local, state, and national policies and politics.

Sherrill, Kenneth. **"The Political Power of Lesbians, Gays, and Bisexuals."** *Political Science and Politics* (September 1996): 469–473.

This short article succinctly identifies the five key reasons that LGBT people should be regarded, in the words of the author, as politically "powerless": (1) the relatively small number of LGBT people relative to heterosexuals; (2) societal hostility to LGBT people; (3) the lack of personal safety of many LGBT people; (4) the relatively weak job security and prospects for advancement of some LGBT people, with resulting economic problems; and (5) problems with creating cohesion among a population "born into diaspora," that is, distributed more or less randomly throughout the population.

Shilts, Randy. **And the Band Played On: Politics, People, and the AIDS Epidemic.** New York: St. Martin's Press, 1987.

A landmark work both for its own content and for the impact it had on politics and policies. It focuses on gay communities (especially in San Francisco and New York); Washington, D.C., policy makers; and health authorities at the Centers for Disease Control and other major agencies. Sometimes criticized as inaccurate and incomplete, the work remains the single most important account of AIDS politics up to 1985.

Teal, Donn. **The Gay Militants: How Gay Liberation Began in America, 1969–1971.** New York: St. Martin's Press, 1971.

A contemporaneous history of the early "gay liberation" period, this work begins on the nights of the Stonewall Riots of 1969 and works forward through subsequent protests, emerging militant groups, and the overall burst of organizing and activity that decisively launched the LGBT rights movement.

Thompson, Mark, ed. **The Long Road to Freedom: The Advocate History of the Gay and Lesbian Movement.** New York: St. Martin's Press, 1994.

This book presents highlights from twenty-five years of the oldest and most prominent national LGBT news publication in the United States.

Vaid, Urvashi. **Virtual Equality: The Mainstreaming of Gay and Lesbian Liberation.** New York: Anchor Books, 1995.

This is an excellent source book on the history of gay and lesbian politics and the successes and failures of the movement written by an activist.

Wilchins, Riki Anne. **Read My Lips: Sexual Subversion and the End of Gender.** Ithaca, New York: Firebrand Books, 1997.

A brief manifesto by a founder of GenderPAC, which deals with transgender and other gender-related issues, this work combines the authors's personal experiences with theoretical and pragmatic political considerations. Strongly arguing for a liberationist (rather than an assimilationist) approach to politics, the author urges a broad-based coalition encompassing homophobia and "transphobia" as well as sexism, racism, and class inequality.

Witt, Stephanie L., and Suzanne McCorkle. **Anti-Gay Right: Assessing Voter Initiatives.** Westport, CT: Praeger, 1997.

This is an edited collection of essays on state and local ballot initiatives concerning gay civil rights.

Index

About the Authors

Raymond A. Smith is adjunct assistant professor at Hunter College, City University of New York. He is the editor of the award-winning *Encyclopedia of AIDS*.

Donald P. Haider-Markel is assistant professor of political science and director of the Survey Research Center of the Policy Research Institute at the University of Kansas in Lawrence.